Crafting the Third World
Theorizing Underdevelopment
in Rumania and Brazil

ID0879324

To Betsy,
with affection — Joe

Crafting the Third World

*Theorizing Underdevelopment
in Rumania and Brazil*

Joseph L. Love

STANFORD UNIVERSITY PRESS
Stanford, California 1996

Comparative Studies in History, Institutions, and Public Policy
John D. Wirth, Editor

Stanford University Press
Stanford, California
© 1996 by the Board of Trustees of the
Leland Stanford Junior University
Printed in the United States of America

CIP data appear at the end of the book

Stanford University Press publications are distributed exclusively by
Stanford University Press within the United States, Canada, Mexico,
and Central America; they are distributed exclusively by Cambridge
University Press throughout the rest of the world.

For Katy and David

Preface

This book has a longer history than I was aware of when I thought I was commencing it in 1980. As an economics major in college a quarter-century earlier, I had been interested in development issues and had encountered the structuralism—though not yet called such—of Raúl Prebisch, probably best known for his thesis of unequal exchange in the world market between an agricultural Periphery and an industrial Center. I wrote an undergraduate thesis on a topic in Brazilian economic development in the late 1950s, when the Brazilian economy was outstripping those of all its Latin American counterparts. Under President Juscelino Kubitschek, economic policy was largely guided by the structuralist theses of Prebisch, Celso Furtado, and others who believed in a vigorous interventionist role for the state.

The Brazil of the late 1950s and early 1960s was a fascinating place. Not only was its economic growth outstanding during the 1950s, but the new salience of multinational firms was driving a heady nationalist and populist politics. That economic development was a sine qua non of nationalist aspirations was clear from the studies of the Instituto Superior de Estudos Brasileiros, formed in 1955, the year Kubitschek was elected. The period was one of political mobilization, crisis, and conflict, especially after the recession of the early 1960s and the abrupt resignation of President Jânio Quadros in August 1961. The late 1950s and early 1960s were moreover a period of political and cultural experimentation. These were the years of Francisco Julião's Peasant Leagues; the birth of a radical theology and a new social engagement of the church, especially evident in the Juventude Universitária Católica; the urban literacy movements that led Paulo Freire to write *Pedagogy of the Oppressed* a few years later; the publication of João Guimarães Rosa's *Devil to Pay in the Backlands* (*Grande Sertão: Veredas*), for many critics the most distinguished Brazilian novel of the century; Marcel Camus's film *Black Orpheus*; and the bossa nova musical style that brought Brazil onto the world stage.

Brazil was a little-studied and poorly understood country in the United States at the time. As a graduate student of Brazilian history, I did further work in economic development, but my main research interests converged on the problem of regionalism as a set of economic and political issues. In writing a book about São Paulo, the agricultural and industrial dynamo of the Brazilian economy, I became increasingly conscious of the degree to which a Center-Periphery framework was useful in describing São Paulo's relations with Brazil's other states and regions. The economists Hans Singer and Celso Furtado had used the Center-Periphery framework to model a process of internal colonialism in Brazil. To understand São Paulo's place in the nation, I read widely in Brazilian economic history, including the theory that informed the work of such economic historians as Furtado. Because structuralism and then dependency had major impacts on the thinking of the Third World, I began to consider a project on the history of Latin American ideas on economic development or even something on the Third World in general.

While studying São Paulo's relations with the rest of the country, I had learned that in the 1930s a Rumanian economist, Mihail Manoilescu, had provided Paulista industrialists with what seemed to be a scientific rationale for industrialization in a preeminently agricultural country. In reading Manoilescu, I became curious about the intellectual and cultural milieu in which he wrote *The Theory of Protectionism* and soon discovered a rich and unsuspected tradition of Rumanian economic thought, much of it a protest literature against the economic orthodoxy of neoclassical economics and its attendant ideology of liberalism. As I began to study the Rumanian language, I realized a project was born: I would examine how the problem of backwardness was theorized in two nations in different world-regional contexts, one in East Central Europe, which, between the world wars, gave rise to many of the propositions in postwar development theory, and one in Latin America, the locus of structuralism and dependency analysis in the postwar period.

Although this is a study of ideas in two nations in different world regions, it may be obvious to Rumanianists that I know Brazil better. I have nonetheless tried not only to master the relevant primary and secondary sources on Rumania but further to appreciate something of the differences in national mentalities, unstated assumptions, and political styles in the two countries, before, during, and after my stay in Rumania in 1981–82. The reader may judge how successful that effort was.

I offer my thanks to the following organizations for financial support at different moments in the gestation of this work: the National Endowment for the Humanities; the International Research and Exchanges Board (IREX); the Fulbright Program; the J. Simon Guggenheim Foundation; and the Research Board, the Center for Latin American and Caribbean Studies, the Russian and East European Center, and International Programs and Studies, all at the University of Illinois. Thanks as well are owed to the personnel of the institutions in other locations where I worked for extended periods—the Academie de Studii Economice and the Academie Română in Bucharest; St. Antony's College, Oxford; and the Instituto de Estudos Avançados at the Universidade de São Paulo.

Whatever competence I have achieved as a Rumanianist I owe in great measure to my colleague Keith Hitchins, who unsparingly offered me historiographical and bibliographical assistance over more than a dozen years. Among several kindnesses he extended to me was the unrestricted use of his enormous personal library on Rumania, complementing the considerable collection of the University of Illinois, which also has excellent holdings on Brazil. I wish to thank John D. Wirth, who read the manuscript in its entirety, offering a penetrating critique couched in wry humor. My thanks as well to William Maloney, who read several chapters from an economist's perspective. The errors in fact and theory that remain, of course, are my own responsibility.

I further acknowledge the assistance of other people who helped make this project a book: Curtis Blaylock, Daniel Chirot, Valeriu Dinu, Boris Fausto, Nicholas Georgescu-Roegan, Dinu Giurescu, Adolfo Gurrieri, Michael Hall, Nils Jacobsen, Carlos Guilherme Mota, Ignacy Sachs, and Paul Simionescu, as well as two former teachers, Albert Hirschman and Juan Linz, who offered counsel early in the project. Others who helped me are no longer living: Roman Cresin, Nicolae Marcu, Henri H. Stahl, and Paul Sterian. Furthermore, I am manifestly indebted to those whom I interviewed and others who corresponded with me; the names of those whom I cited—some deceased—are included in the Reference Matter. I am grateful as well to Cambridge University Press for permission to reprint passages from "Economic Ideas and Ideologies in Latin America since 1930."

Thanks finally to Laurie, my wife, who accompanied me to Rumania and Brazil.

J.L.L.

Contents

(Photographs follow page 118)

Explanatory Note

Though I have considered economic, political, and intellectual contexts, this book is a history of ideas, not an exercise in the sociology of knowledge. In such a history, attribution of authorship and priority of "discovery" are important elements in the story. The following conventions were adopted to order the material: *Editions*. I have sought to follow five principles: First, to use the original edition as a general rule. Second, when the first was not available to me, to ascertain that the edition used was not different from the first on the substantive points analyzed. In Portuguese, Rumanian, and Spanish, the words *edição, ediție,* and *edición* usually mean "printings" and are not different from the original edition, unless revision is specifically indicated. Third, I used later editions, in addition to the first, if I was specifically interested in the changes in, and impact of, revised editions. Fourth, in the few cases where they exist, I have preferred the "definitive" annotated editions. Fifth, I have used the English edition in certain UN publications when both Spanish and English versions appeared the same year. In a few cases, I have used the only edition available to me. In the notes I have indicated the date of publication of the work in question and, if the first edition was not used, the date and language of the first edition in brackets. *Foreign language titles*. On the assumption that readers of Portuguese and those of Rumanian would not necessarily read the other language, in the text I have put in English the titles of works cited, with the original language title in a footnote. *Orthography*. Spelling and accent reforms occurred in both Portuguese and Rumanian during the period under study. I have observed original spellings in the notes and bibliography and modern spelling in the text. Though changes were minimal in other languages cited, it will be observed in the English bibliography that "Rumania" is spelled three different ways—Rumania, Roumania, and Romania. I have adopted the first of these in the text, a common one for the period studied. *Definitions*. Terms will be defined when introduced in the text, but here I should state that throughout this book "liberal" and "liberalism" refer to classical or "nineteenth-century" liberalism, an ideology that advocated the unrestrained action of markets to set prices and allocate resources, rather than the peculiar American sense of "liberalism," a relatively egalitarian ideology in which the state actively intervenes in economic and social processes.

Crafting the Third World

*Theorizing Underdevelopment
in Rumania and Brazil*

1

Introduction

Development economics—the subdiscipline dealing with the special problems of underdeveloped countries—is now a half century old, and the decade of the 1980s saw the publication of historical sketches, memoirs, and even a book-length history of the subject by H. W. Arndt.[1] The creators of the field and those who followed quickly in the steps of the first generation were men whose training in economics was much influenced by the Keynesian revolution but who held a wide variety of views on the applicability of (standard) neoclassical theory to the intractable problems of those countries which, together, came to be known as the Third World in the 1950s and 1960s.

This study takes a different approach. The central subject is not the analyses and prescriptions of Western economists but what economists (*lato sensu*) in Rumania and Brazil, two underdeveloped countries in East Central Europe and Latin America, respectively, wrote about the problem of backwardness in changing national and international environments. The "indigenous" efforts examined will focus on attempts to theorize the problem of underdevelopment along structuralist lines, omitting a survey of the rather sizable "orthodox" or neoclassical efforts to address those same problems. This choice is justified by the considerations that several histories of economic thought already exist for both countries at issue and that structuralist thought is palpably more original. Furthermore, structuralism lends itself to a more coherent comparative treatment than "full" catalogs of all economic ideas in the two locations. Reference to neoclassical and other schools will be introduced, however, to illuminate and critique the structuralist array of theses and arguments.

"Structuralism" means a variety of things in economics, as in other disciplines, and my definition is broad and simple. Structuralism refers to theoretical efforts to specify, analyze, and correct economic structures that impede or block the "normal," implicitly unproblematic, development and functioning allegedly characteristic of Western economies.[2] Because of these impediments and blockages, standard classical or neoclassical prescriptions were rejected by structuralists as inappropriate, inapplicable.[3] Some structuralist theory, in fact, was designed to move the economy to the point at which neoclassical economics *would* be applicable.

"Economic backwardness,"[4] the standard term used before 1945, lost out in the postwar era to "underdevelopment," though such major postwar scholars as Alexander Gerschenkron and Paul Baran still favored the former term. Another, Hla Myint, thought the term "backward" accurately described the peoples of underdeveloped areas and that "underdeveloped" should be reserved for natural resources.[5] "Underdeveloped" as a term to characterize the economies and societies of Asia, Africa, and Latin America later yielded to more euphemistic substitutes—"traditional," "less developed," and "developing"—the last-named of which would seem to imply that the problem is self-solving.[6] In this work "backwardness" and "underdevelopment" are used synonymously, and they connote a yawning gulf between the advanced capitalist nations of the developed West and those with low per capita incomes and archaic social structures whose theorists characterized them *with reference to* the West. From this perspective, these economies were not just located in less advanced positions along the same trajectory but seemed to face major "barriers to entry" into the comity of modern nations. In short, because of both internal and external factors, these economies did not "work" in the Western, neoclassical sense. The problem was to discover whether, how, and why they could be made to so work. Finally, "development" was understood not only as a state of high per capita income or the process of achieving it, but it also connoted a diversification of structures of production and consumption, as well as a greater degree of equity for a given population than existed before development occurred. Industrialization was viewed as a necessary part of the process for agrarian states.

The issues posed by structuralist theorists (or more simply, writers) included many problems that remain major stumbling blocks for the Third World today and may be grouped in three categories:

First: Problems of markets, and labor markets in particular.

1. Highly skewed factor endowments—in particular, an excess supply of unskilled labor and a relative shortage of capital. Consequent upon these conditions were, in the view of the writers in question, disguised unemployment, underemployment, and high productivity differentials between manufacturing industry and traditional agriculture.

2. Factor immobility, creating dualism in labor markets, in which the links between capitalist and precapitalist activities (especially traditional agriculture) are poorly developed.

3. More generally, market failure as a generalized proposition. Markets may be highly inefficient, owing, for example, to factor immobility, monopolies, or imperfect information available to producers or consumers. Capital markets, moreover, may be poorly organized or virtually nonexistent.

4. The perverse operation of certain markets, in which prices send the "wrong" signals. In peasant agriculture, for example, more labor or commodities may be offered for sale as prices fall.

5. The (alleged) inability of neoclassical economics to offer an adequate explanation of peasant economic behavior. Because peasants may respond to price signals in labor or commodity markets in a different way from capitalist farmers, a different economic calculus needs to be invented. As the Soviet theorist Alexander V. Chayanov noted, peasants may rationally treat their own and their families' labor inputs in a manner quite different from a capitalist farmer who, when facing shrinking profits, dismisses hired workers.

Second: Problems of trade and the international economic system.

6. A persistent disequilibrium in the foreign trade balance because of the structure of internal demand and, ultimately, because of the distribution of income. Upper social strata, it was held, place immense pressure on the import bill because of their desire to consume products made with advanced technologies.

7. The allegedly perverse role of traditional international trade patterns in economic development. Ricardian prescriptions for trade based on mutual advantages for agricultural and industrial exporters were rejected as disadvantageous to the agricultural country, which faced a purported process of "unequal exchange," in the short or longer runs, to be described in later chapters. Some writers further transmogrified class analysis into the notion of "plutocratic" and "proletarian" nations. Similarly, it was argued that the analysis of unequal exchange could be applied to *domestic* patterns of trade, where "internal colonialism" occurred.

8. Related to item 6, a generalized dependency of "local," or "peripheral," underdeveloped national economies on "global" or "central" economies of the developed West, organized in a single system. In part, this matter was seen as a reflection of backward, low-efficiency agriculture's trading with modern, high-efficiency industry. Moreover, conjunctural and technological change emanated from the Center, whose cycles of expansion called the tune to which the world economy marched. In short, critical, if not altogether determining, variables in the peripheral economy were beyond the control of local statesmen, merchants, and producers. Peripheral countries whose economies were focused on a few exports were highly vulnerable to volatile prices in primary commodity markets.

9. Consequently, the historicity of the international development process: no repetition of the development patterns already achieved by the leading industrialized countries was possible, thought some, while others believed that stages of economic development might bear some likeness to those of the first industrialized countries but would occur in more complex ways.

Third: Growth as a solution, growth as a problem, and the role of the state in fomenting and balancing growth.

10. The special character of manufacturing industry, which was linked with a

generalized notion of modernity. Manufacturing was associated by its champions with rising per capita incomes and with a power to absorb economically redundant rural populations. Furthermore, as manufacturing rose in importance relative to agriculture in the national economy, it would lessen dependence on the vicissitudes of international trade, exacerbated by the violent oscillations of primary commodity prices. In addition, a strong industrial economy offered a strategic capacity to defend the nation-state externally. Most writers believed that manufacturing's special character had to do with its unique association with economies of scale and economies external to the firm. As a result, its development, involving a certain "lumpiness," required concerted action on a variety of fronts, that is, a "big push," and therefore state intervention.

11. The differential effects of growth on social classes as well as regions. Economic growth along capitalist lines tended to produce a concentration of income with respect to social class and geographic area, it was held, contrary to the "spread effects" predicted by neoclassical theory.

12. Structurally induced inflation. Inflation has its root causes not in monetary policy but in "underlying" imbalances especially inherent in the nonmodern sector of the economy.

13. The different role of the entrepreneur in these circumstances from that of his West European exemplar. Here a wide variety of views existed. Could a "conquering bourgeoisie" be created? Could another class take its place? Could the state itself provide the leadership, a kind of *Ersatzklasse*? Was any elite solution to the problem of underdevelopment possible, or did the masses have to enter the picture as the driving force toward development?

14. The perceived monopoly-monopsony character of the economy of the Center, and the consequent need for state intervention in the Periphery, internally and externally. For some, the increasingly noncompetitive nature of the world industrial economy after 1880, or more obviously after 1920, required not only the countervailing power of the state in foreign markets but corporate organization of noncompeting groups within the national economy.

In addition to the structuralist discourse that tried to address the alleged failures of neoclassical analysis and prescriptions in neoclassical terms, or at least in an eclectic fashion, was Marxist structuralism.[7] Here historicity was implicit by definition, in historical materialism. Marxism in the Periphery, like other schools, had as its major tasks the explanation of, and exit from, backwardness. It encompassed a variety of inventive efforts before World War I to theorize the interaction of capitalist and precapitalist modes of production. Furthermore, Marxists disagreed among themselves on assigning priority in the transformation of the Periphery to relations of exchange (the market) or to relations of production.[8] But such efforts at theorizing were only the most global Marxist response to the problem of underdevelopment. A variety of less totalizing problems were addressed, such as immiserizing growth, the result of malign structural change owing to capitalist penetration of the local economy, and transnational class alliances that prevented the development of a local bourgeoisie along the lines predicted by Marx.

There was no single Marxist view. Some writers adopted a reformist perspective, whereby, in a kind of alleged orthodoxy, they proclaimed support for an embryonic national bourgeoisie to develop capitalism. Marx was right, but his call for social revolution would become relevant only at an unspecified future date. "Legal" Marxism, in the tradition of Peter Struve in Russia, supported an unfolding process of bourgeois-directed capitalist development.[9]

This book is a comparative historical study, which will show how the timing of the absorption of institutions and ideas and the response to economic conjunctures led to the rediscovery or reinvention of similar ideas (theories, propositions, explicit and implicit assumptions, policy prescriptions), as well as the discovery of novel ideas. The book looks at two "indigenous" efforts to define, specify, and analyze the problem of underdevelopment. East Central Europe, including the Balkans, and Latin America were the earliest world regions whose intellectuals extensively theorized the problem of backwardness, if we except Russia, whose socialist revolution posed such a radically different set of options after 1917 that it became part of the basic context in which backwardness would be defined, interpreted, and addressed. The role of the state, which already loomed large in nineteenth-century Russian development, now became the supreme arena for decision making, and state ownership defined a new pole on the continuum of paths out of backwardness.

One writer considers East Central Europe and South America the "first large scale laboratories of underdevelopment" and notes that their coercive labor systems in the early modern period have often been compared in their relation to an expanding commercial capitalism of the West.[10] At least four Polish economic historians have sought to compare the socioeconomic structures of the two regions.[11] In the current century, the financial problems the two world regions shared in their relations with the West were illustrated by the fact that they were sometimes advised by the same men—Sir Otto Niemeyer and Edward Kemmerer in the 1920s and 1930s and Jeffrey Sachs in the 1980s.[12]

There is, furthermore, a certain comparability between Latin America and East Central Europe if one considers these areas—unlike the Middle East, Asia, and Africa—as "quasi-Europes" or "epigonal Europes" in their formal cultures (Robert Redfield's Great Tradition)—their legal codes, "high" art forms, and dominant religious traditions. Their elites' aspirations, sometimes their self-deluding perceptions of local societies, certainly their desire to impress foreigners, all tended to focus on the degree of Westernization. This is not to deny the vigorous search for authentic local roots in some circles, much less the frequently felt ambivalences or even societal self-deprecation. But for leaders and intellectuals in these world regions, with the exception of those who saw the

Soviet Union as the Second World alternative, progress was a road, rough but not impassable, leading to Europe, the First World.

One of the two case studies below is set in a Balkan country. East Central Europe, where an array of newly independent or redefined countries after World War I faced the multiple tasks of nation- and state-building, economic development, and strategic defense, was a precursor of the Third World proper, a kind of proto–Third World.[13] Some of the ideas that would enter the textbooks on development economics in the postwar era appeared there first *in nuce*, or more fully elaborated.[14] Second, East Central Europe, the belt of new or enlarged countries from the Baltic to the Aegean,[15] formed the original empirical focus of men who took the first steps to create the subdiscipline of economic development in the 1940s.[16] Though contemporary and especially later statements by the first two students of the problem—Kurt Mandelbaum and Paul Rosenstein-Rodan—emphasize the chance element, relative availability of data, or potential generalizability in this choice of world region for initial study,[17] it is clear enough that in the mid-1940s the region was seen as one of historical turbulence and of strategic importance for the Great Powers. One need only note that Sarajevo and Danzig, flashpoints in 1914 and 1939, lay within its perimeter. Furthermore, most of the original development theorists had been born in Central or eastern Europe and had received their early schooling or even took university degrees there—Paul Rosenstein-Rodan, Ragnar Nurkse, Nicholas Kaldor, Thomas Balogh, Hans Singer, Alexander Gerschenkron, Kurt Martin (*né* Kurt Mandelbaum), Peter T. Bauer, Gottfried Haberler, Paul Baran, and Michal Kalecki.[18]

The Austro-Hungarian Empire of the Belle Epoque had been characterized by enormous differences in economic development between industrialized Vienna and the rural eastern and southern extremes of the most culturally and economically heterogeneous state of prewar Europe. An economist who knew both modern Vienna and backward Bucovina, incorporated into Rumania in 1918, was the renowned Austrian theorist Joseph Schumpeter, whose first teaching post (1909–11) was at the University in Czernowitz (Rumanian, Cernăuţi), the capital of Bucovina. In *The Theory of Economic Development*,[19] published in German in 1912, Schumpeter was the first economist of the century to give serious attention to the problems under consideration here. In this work the young Austrian scholar expounded his subsequently celebrated thesis of entrepreneurship as the engine of growth and development. In an age when economic equilibrium was the cynosure of neoclassical theorists,[20] Schumpeter's study constituted a new departure and was rediscovered by development specialists after World War II. Whether or not Schumpeter's experience in backward Bucovina had a specific effect on his thought, one may speculate that the sharp contrasts in levels of economic development—the dualism of the Dual Monarchy—may have prompted the fundamental question, How does economic development begin?[21] This question would be taken up by three later students at Vienna, Rosenstein-

Rodan, Gerschenkron, and Nurkse,[22] and by the other economists named above whose early studies and formative experiences had occurred in Central and East Central Europe.

The themes of planning and industrialization dominated in the early postwar years, and in the view of an unsympathetic observer, the trade theorist Harry G. Johnson, such emphases derived from the experience of the new Balkan nations in the interwar period. "While [the early theorists of development were] fundamentally concerned with policies for developing the Balkan states on the German model, the central concepts were presented as universals and later proved equally congenial to the psychological attitudes of the new nations." The economists responsible for these developments, in Johnson's view, were Mandelbaum, Kaldor, Rosenstein-Rodan, and Balogh.[23]

The inclusion of a Latin American case study of theorizing underdevelopment presumably requires less justification. The earliest region to attain formal independence in the Third World, Latin America was also the first region in which a native school of development theory arose—that associated with the UN Economic Commission for Latin America, or ECLA. Latin American structuralism and the dependency school that largely developed from it[24] are arguably the most influential Third World contributions to development theory.

The two case studies focus on countries rather than regions, and the rationale for this choice is that the largest unit in which a coherent policy could be formulated was the territorial state.[25] This was partly because the state was conceived of as the most powerful instrument for accelerating or even inducing economic development; its geographic limits also coincided with boundaries for data collection and the unimpeded flow of trade. The territorial state is not the exclusive concern of this study, however, and one of the principal themes is the interaction (or at least the similarity) of ideas at the world-region level, partly transmitted through international institutions.

Within East Central Europe and Latin America, why Rumania and Brazil? Though the relevant national studies have yet to be undertaken, interwar Poland, the largest of the "succession states" to the Austro-Hungarian, Russian, and German empires, might turn out to be the most important contributor to postwar development theory. But the problems and proposed solutions of East Central Europe were a common currency, and Rumania was among the most important contributors. Brazil, on the Latin American side, was the largest country in the region in population and area. It was, furthermore, the Latin American nation where structuralist theorizing was arguably most extensively developed in the postwar era and had the greatest impact on state policy; only Chile would be a strong rival in this respect. Furthermore, the connection between Rumanian structuralism and the Brazilian variety was stronger than in other Latin American countries.[26]

To undertake a comparative study involving two countries so different in size, climate, and historical development as Brazil and Rumania requires some defense. Both were societies with Latin-derived languages and cultures, and both shared values and assumptions derived from Roman law—even before Rumania's independence from the Ottoman Empire.[27] Semislavery existed in the Rumanian provinces of the Turkish Empire in the sixteenth century, and increasing corvée requirements arose by the eighteenth century. Rumania thus experienced the "second serfdom," in Friedrich Engels's phrase, but not the first.[28] Brazilian labor relations were characterized by chattel slavery from the sixteenth century. Thus systems of coerced labor characterized both from the same era, and coercion in both continued into the nineteenth century.

During the same century Rumania, like Brazil, obtained its political independence from a patrimonial empire in decay. Neither the Ottoman nor the Portuguese Empire experienced real absolutism.[29] Both Brazil and Rumania organized their new states as constitutional or quasi-constitutional monarchies, heavily dependent on the Great Powers in the achievement of their formal sovereignty. The two nations were also dependent on Western technology, capital inputs, and export markets as they became more fully integrated into the expanding international economy after 1875. In the global division of labor implicit in the reigning liberal ideology, both Rumania and Brazil were repeatedly characterized in the nineteenth and early twentieth centuries by their nationals as "essentially agricultural": the same phrase was used, or sometimes in Rumania, "eminently agricultural."[30] During the last century Brazil's one-life titled nobility—which did not have any special legal status as a group—bore some similarities to Rumania's *boier* (boyar or noble) stratum,[31] and landed elites in both countries presided over an export agriculture anchored in latifundia and labor systems based on compulsion—chattel slavery in Brazil before 1888 and corvée requirements in much of Rumania between 1864 and 1921.[32]

In the period after the Napoleonic Wars, both Rumania and Brazil looked to western Europe for intellectual and cultural leadership, and to France in particular. But because—like most of the world—Rumania and Brazil did not undergo bourgeois revolutions, their modernization and Westernization tended to be superficial, especially before the interwar period. "Progress" often took the form of writing French-inspired legal codes, adopting Parisian fashions in dress and the arts, raising obelisks in the capital cities, and a hundred other forms that could be characterized as superstructural. Elites in both nations admitted to themselves the superficiality of many of the reforms undertaken. For the Brazilians, the expression for the "Potemkin village" phenomenon was *para inglês ver* (for the Englishman to see);[33] for the Rumanians, it was expressed in more philosophical terms—*formă fără fond* (form without substance).[34] The Brazilian phrase—"inglês" applying to all non-Portuguese foreign merchants in Brazil—also implied the eagerness of Brazilian elites to impress foreigners with their nation's progress, and a similar yearning for European approval characterized Rumanian elites.[35]

The reforms were initiated by Westernizing elites who wanted modernization without social mobilization. For such groups, especially in the nineteenth century, liberalism was readily embraced for its emphasis on rationalization, secularization, and material progress. Economic liberalism, associated with the abolition of colonial monopolies in Brazil and the end of Turkish capitulations in Rumania, was seen in the nineteenth century as part of a broader civilizing and Westernizing movement, even though there were conflicts with the West over French and British prodding to secure rights for Jews and even Gypsies in Rumania and for black slaves in Brazil.

The clash of liberal ideals and realities of coerced labor produced laughably hypocritical legal efforts to reconcile social fact and legal theory. Under Brazil's draft constitution of 1823, which broke with the colonial regime's monopolies and provided for broad economic liberties, the government was enjoined to enforce "contracts" between masters and slaves.[36] Likewise in Rumania, following a law in 1866 permitting the use of military force to ensure that peasants fulfilled their labor "contracts," a statute six years later extending the landlord's power was titled the "Law for the Protection of Labor." Even at the outset of the current century, ancient feudal dues in kind, associated with serfdom, were written into peasants' contracts with landlords.[37] One writer considered below, Constantin Dobrogeanu-Gherea, expatiated at length on the "monstrous" nature of Rumania's legal and economic regime, which combined capitalist and allegedly feudal elements in grisly fashion.

Like Brazil, independent Rumania emerged from a patrimonial (if non-Western) empire attempting to institute administrative reform. Rumania's parliamentary government was controlled by an oligarchy. But like Brazil's political system after 1930, that of Rumania underwent a crisis and partial transformation[38] owing to military and political consequences of World War I—above all, a significant if incomplete land reform. By the postwar Treaty of Trianon, Rumania's leaders managed to double the national territory and population as a reward for timely declarations of war. Thus, as one of the succession states to the Austrian and Russian empires, "Greater Rumania" was even more obviously the locus for a debate about economic development than had been the "Old Kingdom" without Transylvania and Bessarabia.

In both countries, observed economic vulnerability owing to wide swings in commodity prices eventually produced a reaction among intellectuals who demanded industrial economies, though largely in different periods. If Germany and Russia were "late industrializers" in Alexander Gerschenkron's phrase, Brazil and Rumania were "late, late industrializers" in Albert Hirschman's words. Yet both achieved significant degrees of industrialization in advance of the Third World at large. In the twentieth century, Rumania first, and then Brazil, moved toward industrialization as a solution to backwardness. Both countries made some industrial progress before World War I, but the first effort at a "big push" in

Rumania would come in the 1930s and in Brazil in the 1950s. In each case the role of the state loomed large.

Yet the character of the state itself was a problem. If Rumania and Brazil did not approach the "kleptocratic" regimes of the worst-governed Third World states today, their political leaders nonetheless tended to view their respective states as "patrimonial" rather than "bureaucratic," in Weberian terms, with negative consequences for rational development. If *şmecherie* (peculation from public coffers with verve) and *bacşiş* (baksheesh) perhaps indicated a more cynical civic culture in Rumania than in Brazil, the latter's *trem da alegria* (joy ride at public expense) and the persistence of clientelism show the issue is a matter of degree. One dimension of the problem was a sustained pressure to expand the public payrolls. For would-be elites without land, and more generally for young men of modest means in both countries, employment in the state apparatus, rather than in commerce or industry, tended to be the preferred occupation.[39]

This study compares Rumania in the years circa 1880 to 1945 with Brazil, 1930 to circa 1980. Thus Rumanian thought is examined from the long depression in the international capitalist economy (1873 to 1896) to the end of World War II, and Brazilian ideas are considered from the Great Depression of our own century to the "lost decade" for Latin American economic growth, beginning in 1980. More tidily, perhaps, but with a procrustean precision, one could date the study from the consequences of the depression of 1873 to those of the recession of 1973. The period treated in each country study begins with an international economic crisis—the 1880s for Rumania, the 1930s for Brazil. It ends in Brazil with a world recession especially sharp in Latin America, while the Rumanian case terminates with a foreign occupation, followed by an externally imposed social revolution after World War II that changed the terms of economic discourse.

The history of the capitalist Center's domination of an expanding but imperfectly transformed Periphery might be studied from the late Middle Ages, the sixteenth century, or E. J. Hobsbawm's "dual revolution" of the late eighteenth century. I choose to introduce the Rumanian case in the last quarter of the nineteenth century, with some necessary glances backward at earlier eras. The period at issue coincides with the "Second Industrial Revolution," characterized by greatly increased productivities of new and existing industries in the West, partly owing to the application of science to production;[40] with the Great Depression of 1873–96 and the consequent rise of new tariff walls, as the continental states attempted to defend their agricultural establishments; with the Age of Monopoly Capital, in which trusts and cartels came to dominate markets in banking and capital-intensive industries; with the Age of Imperialism, in which the capitalist powers greatly expanded their capital exports and extended their rule over almost all of Africa and much of Asia; and with the rise of Germany to political and economic preeminence in Europe.

In this era Russian Marxists and populists were engaged in a "controversy over capitalism,"[41] and a basic issue was, To what degree was mimesis of the developed West possible? To what extent desirable? In Germany Karl Kautsky and Eduard David were trying to explain why Marx's laws of the concentration and centralization of capital did not seem to hold for agriculture; meanwhile, conservative German social theorists were anxious about the decline of the *Mittelstand* of artisans, shopkeepers, and wealthy peasants. All these debates would have repercussions in Rumania, where the Russian and German literatures would be adapted inventively to local circumstances.

With a brief look at earlier developments, I pick up the Brazilian debate in the 1930s, when the crisis in the international trading system stimulated a search for theoretical justifications for industrialization, to replace ad hoc antiliberal arguments. The Brazilian story continues until circa 1980, when both Chayanovian neopopulism and a Marxist analysis of modes of production challenged the adequacy of dependency analysis.

Why a "skewed" or overlapping periodization, when most comparative studies focus on contemporaneous subjects? The more important reason is that the phasing of similar elements and processes (e.g., the rejection of liberalism) in the two case studies came at similar though different moments of perceived crisis and led to some similar results—the "discovery" or "rediscovery" of certain perspectives and propositions, though sometimes in different combinations and with different emphases. Another consideration is that, beyond first-approximation similarities between the nations of East Central Europe and South America sketched above, there was a "genetic" connection in one major area of structuralist thought, that dealing with the trading process. The bridge was the economic and political writings of Mihail Manoilescu, whose works achieved considerable attention in Iberia and Latin America in the 1930s and 1940s. Both his economic and political writings had a particularly strong impact in Brazil, where his major works circulated among industrialists and statesmen, including Roberto Simonsen, Brazil's most influential spokesman for industry, and possibly Getúlio Vargas, the president and dictator of Brazil from 1930 to 1945.

Beyond Manoilescu's theses about the international trading process and his justification of industrialization, he was important for supplying a well-articulated ideology of corporatism, in which economy and polity would be organized into formal corporations supervised by the state, to a Brazilian political elite increasingly committed to a nonmobilizing modernization of the national economy. Manoilescu was not the only European corporatist whose ideas were discussed in Brazil, and other economists whose works might be considered structuralist also wrote on corporatism, notably François Perroux and Werner Sombart; but only the former of the two had a direct impact in Brazil. Moreover, a broadly diffused "ideology of productivity,"[42] associated with corporatism in European industrial circles after World War I, had repercussions in Brazil. The state, argued the corporatists, would encourage the organization of producers' groups and act as a balance wheel in an era when the free market had been largely replaced by cartels, oligopolies, powerful trade unions, and administered prices.

The relationship between corporatism and Latin American structuralism* is not a simple one, but there is a family resemblance, at least for some varieties of structuralism. In the case of Manoilescu's corporatism, it seems that his voguish and persuasive political essay *The Century of Corporatism* (1934), written five years after his economic treatise *The Theory of Protectionism*, reinforced the influence of the latter in Brazil. Both were carried along by the author's unabashed elitism in politics and statist orientation in economics. In both Brazil and Rumania, furthermore, a political mentality prevailed that was amenable to state intervention in economy and society; the tempo of such intervention increased after World War I but had existed before the war as well. The most striking example was valorization, the Brazilian effort to control international coffee prices between 1906 and 1929.[43]

Differences as well as likenesses are instructive in a comparative study, and the differences between the two national contexts were manifestly important. Most obvious, the geographic extent of Brazil, almost half the South American continent, contrasts with that of Rumania, a middling state on a small continent. This commonplace should be qualified, however, with the observation that interwar ("Greater") Rumania was a relatively large country in East Central Europe, smaller only than Poland and Yugoslavia, and struggling to incorporate territories as large as the Old Kingdom of 1914. On the fringes of Europe—as it was perceived by its intellectual leaders—Rumania was a nation with a 2,000-year history of foreign conquest and exploitation. The country's Latin heritage dated from the conquest of Dacia by the Roman Emperor Trajan in 101–6 A.D. Formal independence from Turkish rule was achieved only in 1877. Rumania was a densely populated nation of peasants, overwhelmingly landless before World War I.

Brazil, with a huge demographic and economic frontier, by contrast, was viewed by most of its intellectuals as a "new" country, dating from the sixteenth century, and a "fragment" society of western Europe.[44] Its formal independence had been achieved 50 years earlier than Rumania's. Brazil too had a peasant population, but it received much less attention from social scientists than Rumania's until the 1970s. In any case, Brazil had no "kulak" class of wealthy peasants comparable to Rumania's *chiaburime*—such was the gap between the Brazilian middle classes and increasingly urbanized elite, on the one hand, and peasants, on the other. Because Brazil never had a land reform, and localized rural over–

---

*Latin American structuralism, associated with the pioneering work of the Argentinian Raúl Prebisch, emphasized structural unemployment, owing to the inability of traditional export industries to grow and therefore to absorb excess rural population; external disequilibrium, because of higher propensities to import industrial goods than to export traditional agricultural commodities; and deteriorating terms of trade—all of which a properly implemented policy of industrialization could help eliminate. Prebisch's early work is treated in Chapter 8.

population was often thought to be resolvable by migration—a process as old as the Portuguese colony itself—the intellectual traditions associated with rural populism and neopopulism appeared very late. The presence of an economic frontier in Brazil, through which virgin lands were brought into national markets, separated the two countries less radically than it might seem, however; this because the Brazilian latifundium was a dynamic phenomenon—as Caio Prado noted in the 1930s—and one systematically depriving peasants of land after they had cleared it, as other social theorists were to specify in the 1970s.

Another difference between the two countries concerned their responses to international conjunctures, a fact which helps to justify the lagged treatment. Rumania, as a relatively inefficient producer in the international grain market, began to lose ground to "overseas," that is, non-European, competitors in the Great Depression after 1873, whereas Brazil faced no such problem in its relatively efficient coffee industry; the problem was not perceived in Brazil until the next Great Depression 50 years later. In each country it was argued that the developed countries had violated the rules of their own game.

A further difference was the contrasting role that international institutions played in the development of economic ideas and policy in the two nations. The League of Nations, established by the victorious Allies in 1919, evinced little interest in the special problems of "backward" countries, even those of the "new" or enlarged succession states. The League, guided by British and French statesmen, had even less interest in the Latin American nations, a fact which contributed to Brazil's withdrawal from the organization in 1926, and least of all in the colonial world, which before 1945 had begun to disintegrate only on the eastern fringes of the Mediterranean. Moreover, the League served as a financial policeman for both the defeated Central Powers and succession states, performing the same function as the International Monetary Fund after World War II: the loans it approved were certificates of good financial conduct. After the war, the United Nations, by contrast, was sufficiently decentralized that a more autochthonous discourse on the problems of economic development could be elaborated in the organization's regional office, the Economic Commission for Latin America, established in Santiago, Chile, in 1948.[45] The history of ideas is notoriously international, and this is a fortiori true of Brazilian economic thought after the creation of ECLA. The comings and goings of Brazilians to Santiago and Spanish Americans to Brazil, as well as their publications in both Portuguese and Spanish editions, are part of a complex story.[46]

Another relevant contrast between Rumania and Brazil concerns the interaction of institutional and intellectual life. Whereas postwar Brazilians enjoyed the advantage of the continual exchange of ideas with Spanish Americans and others in ECLA and elsewhere, prewar Rumanians had access to a much broader range of economic discourse than did their Brazilian contemporaries. The former were much closer to continental currents of thought which opposed the dominant liberalism of neoclassical economics regnant in Britain, the United States, and France. I refer particularly to Marxism, the German Historical School in its various phases, classical (or Russian) populism, and the "neopopulism" of Alexander Chayanov. In addition, Rumanian economists before 1945 probably had a firmer grasp of neoclassical economics than their Brazilian contemporaries because of their familiarity with Austrian marginalism. Part of this prewar intellectual sophistication is explicable because of Rumanian proximity to European centers of learning, traditional and expanding patterns of trade with Central Europe, and the proximity of a different constellation of Great Powers. But beyond these obvious facts, Rumanian universities had become accustomed in the latter nineteenth century to expect European doctorates from their professors, whose published theses became the basis for a research tradition.

By contrast, in Brazil there were almost no holders of doctoral (research) degrees, which could be obtained only abroad. The modern university, with a faculty of arts and sciences—as opposed to isolated professional schools—was a product of the interwar years, and the Universidade de São Paulo and its newly contracted European professors set the standard in 1934. In addition, Brazil suffered from a relative dearth of social research institutions until after 1945. There was nothing comparable to Dimitrie Gusti's Rumanian Institute of Social Sciences, organized at the end of World War I; in particular, Brazil had no interwar counterparts to Rumania's Economics Institute and Business Cycles Institute.[47] Admittedly, the contrast between the intellectual milieux of Brazil and Rumania should not be exaggerated, and some of the leading figures in the Rumanian debate, including Manoilescu himself, did not hold doctorates. Yet the fact that such figures debated with men who did implied a certain level of professional discourse.

As conjunctural crisis began two generations earlier in Rumania than in Brazil, so the importation and adaptation of nonliberal "European" responses came earlier as well, and perceived crisis and ideological currents combined in different ways. In Rumania the early reception of Hegel paved the way for serious debates about and within the Marxist tradition by the 1880s. In Brazil, and in Latin America in general, Marxism would by and large have to await the formation of the Third International in 1919; and non-Comintern Marxism was largely a post-1945 phenomenon. For contrasting examples, consider that Marxism entered Rumania before a dependency analysis was elaborated by Dobrogeanu-Gherea on heterodox Marxist foundations prior to 1914, whereas in Brazil, more than two generations later, dependency in its initial form preceded its Marxist incarnation. German-language social thought in general had little impact in Brazil until after World War II, and, though classical populism would have no reverberations at all in Brazil, neopopulism would find expression there a half-century later than in Rumania.

Still other relevant contrasts could be mentioned that affected the economic debates. In Rumania, especially after the country doubled its territory following World War I, the integration of non-Rumanian-speaking minorities was a leading political issue, and the country's notorious anti-Semitism was based in part on the view that Jews constituted a nationality and therefore were not Rumanian. Brazil had the good fortune to possess one of the Third World's relatively homogeneous cultures, in which the overwhelming majority spoke a single tongue and, formally at least, professed a single religion, Catholicism. The "foreign nationality" issue rose only briefly in the 1930s and early 1940s, when the Vargas dictatorship sought to force the acculturation of relatively small German and Japanese minorities. Another difference also sprang from the territories Rumania annexed from neighboring states: the much greater importance in the Balkan country of the strategic argument for industrialization.

So far our comparisons have been qualitative. Yet in comparing national, and by extension, world-regional, patterns of thought about economic backwardness, some brief but explicit quantitative comparisons are useful in specifying concrete likenesses and differences. Unfortunately, both the range of statistics and the quality of data are limited for the periods in question, but the available sources make possible some rough comparisons. I divide the material into five categories, which will be used to compare Rumania and Brazil contemporaneously and diachronically, because in some respects the latter country began to accelerate its drive toward development two decades after Rumania.

1. *Standard of Living.* One comparative measure is readily available for the interwar years—Colin Clark's estimate of real annual national product per person employed, measured in dollar-denominated "international units."[48] This standard has two drawbacks: it ignores nonmarketed goods and services as elements in the national product—especially important in underdeveloped countries—and omits nonmonetized measures of welfare. Another standard is Morris D. Morris's Physical Quality of Life Index (PQLI), a composite measure of nonmonetary indicators of well-being. It has the advantage of avoiding the biases of monetary measures and can be approximated for Brazil and Rumania from historical data.[49] It has the disadvantages of potential bias in its equal weighting of variables and the possible exclusion of relevant indicators.

Using Clark's standard, we learn that Rumania had 393 international units per person at work in 1913, a figure that fell to 318 in 1929, only one-sixth that of the United States.[50] The decline apparently owed to the extensive destruction of property during World War I, falling wheat prices and loss of international market share, and a chaotic land reform.[51] For Brazil, the real annual product per person at work in Clark's international units in 1928 was 163; in 1940, 200; and by 1946, 297—a figure still below Rumania's in 1929. Thus, by this standard, Rumania was more "developed" or "advanced" than Brazil circa 1930–45 and continued to be so into the 1980s, though by a much narrower margin, according to available figures for Gross Domestic Product (GDP) per capita.[52] Since measurements must be taken as approximations, however, such conclusions must be regarded as tenuous.

Morris's Physical Quality of Life Index has been widely used in the last two decades to compare tangible living conditions in developed and underdeveloped countries. The index is a combined measure of infant mortality, life expectancy, and literacy, equally weighted. Consider the figures for the 1930s in the table on page 17.

Taken together, these data, like per capita income, show Rumania to be the more "advanced" country in the interwar years, but far behind a developed country of the period, the United States.[53] (Once again, measurements are gross, and the differences between Brazil and Rumania may not be significant.)

2. *Economically Active Population and Rural-Urban Population Distribution.* The sectoral composition of the labor force (economically active population) and the degree of urbanization tell a somewhat different story for the relative positions of Brazil and Rumania. Before 1945 Brazil may have been more industrialized, using the criterion of the distribution of its labor force: a smaller share of its work force was in agriculture; it had a larger service sector; and its population was more urbanized—all possible indications of a more modern economy than Rumania's.[54] Counting manufacturing, mining, handicrafts, and construction as "industry," in 1920 Brazil had a larger proportion of its labor force in industrial activities than did Rumania in 1930—13 and 9 percent, respectively—but the Brazilian figure is probably exaggerated because the more reliable census of 1940 shows only 10 percent in industrial pursuits. By 1956 Rumania's industry accounted for 17 percent of the labor force, a share not attained in Brazil until the 1960s.[55]

There was an impressive shift in Brazil's economically active population out of farming between 1920 and 1960; the share of agriculture fell from 67 to 54 percent (and to 45 percent by 1970). The proportion of workers in farming and related pursuits in Rumania declined from 80 percent in 1913 to 70 percent in 1956. Thus in the latter year, agriculture accounted for a higher percentage of employment than that in Brazil in 1920. This contrast accounts in significant measure for the greater concern with the problem of the peasantry among theorists in Rumania. Although the share of workers in industrial pursuits was slightly higher in Rumania than in Brazil during the early postwar period, the service sector's relative share of employment in the Balkan nation was only 14 percent in 1930 and a like share in 1956. By contrast, services accounted for 25 percent of the labor force in Brazil in 1920 and 27 percent in 1940.

The urbanization of twentieth-century Brazil was likewise much more rapid than that of the European nation. There was no Brazilian census in 1930, but by 1940 31 percent of the Brazilian population was considered urban, as against 20 percent in Rumania in 1930. By the late 1960s, a majority of the Brazilian people were classified as urban. Granted, the urban-rural comparison is only approxi-

The Physical Quality of Life Index for the 1930s

Country	Infant mortality per 1,000 births	Life expectancy (yrs.)	Literacy (%)	Physical quality of life index
Rumania	178.0	42.0	57.0	30
Brazil	158.3	42.7	31.4	25
United States	69.0	59.7	95.7	74

S O U R C E : Ludwig, *Brazil: A Handbook of Historical Statistics* (1985), p. 132; Brazil: IBGE, *Estatísticas históricas do Brasil*, 2d ed. (1990), p. 52; Hauner, "Human Resources," in Kaser and Radice, *Economic History of Eastern Europe, 1919–1975* (1985), 1: 76–77; Trebici, *Romania's Population and Demographic Trends* (1976), p. 80; U.S. Bureau of the Census, *Historical Statistics of the United States*, Part I (1975), pp. 55, 60, 382; Morris, *Measuring*, p. 45.

N O T E : Infant mortality and literacy rates for Rumania are for 1930; infant mortality for Brazil is an average of 1930–40. The Brazilian literacy rate is an average of figures for the census years 1920 and 1940. Literacy in Rumania was collected for the population aged ten and older, while in Brazil it was for five and older, biasing the Rumanian data upward. In compensation, the Brazilian data for infant mortality are biased slightly downward (i.e., favorably) by the fact that only a single number for the decade is provided in the source. Life expectancy for both is measured at birth, rather than at age one—the standard for the PQLI in the postwar period and the age used for the U.S. figures above. Thus both the Rumanian and Brazilian data for life expectancy are biased downward, though the Brazilian number is an average for 1930–40 and that for Rumania is for 1932. U.S. data are biased downward in that all data are for 1930. The upper and lower bounds used for the calculation of the PQLI correspond to the postwar period (1950s and later), thereby biasing all three calculations downward absolutely, but the relative outcome is not significantly affected because we are comparing countries in the same prewar period.

mate because of different national definitions of "urban" population, but the greater apparent urbanization in Brazil may also imply the existence of more vigorous markets in the service sector, even before the capitalist economy was abandoned in Rumania in the late 1940s.[56]

3. Composition of, and Change in, the National Product.[57] If "industry" is again defined to include manufacturing, construction, handicrafts, and mining (including petroleum extraction), Rumanian industry accounts for 23 percent of GDP in 1926, a share that rises to 30 percent in 1937.[58] Brazil approximated the first figure in 1939 and the later one in the early 1960s.[59] Likewise, in Rumania, industry's output as a share of the value of total national product was approaching that of agriculture during the late 1930s and accounted for 50 percent of output by 1950, as against 28 percent for agriculture. In Brazil the output of agriculture would sometimes exceed that of industry in the years 1947–52, after which period industry took a definitive and widening lead.[60]

In Rumania, agriculture accounted for more than a third of GDP in the interwar period (34 percent in 1938), but in Brazil primary production provided only 26 percent in 1939. The difference was accounted for by services. The "tertiary" or services sector (including government) in Rumania provided 37 percent of GDP in 1938, while in Brazil services of all sorts—everything that was not "agriculture" or "industry"—accounted for 52 percent of national income in 1939.[61]

4. Characteristics of Manufacturing Industry. Both Rumania and Brazil conducted economic censuses in 1919 and 1939, permitting direct comparisons of the manufacturing component of the industrial sector in each nation. For 1919, unfortunately, the Rumanian census surveyed only "large industry," defined as firms with more than 20 workers and/or those with motors of more than 5 horsepower. Yet these firms in all likelihood provided the overwhelming bulk of production because "small-scale" industry in the 1901–2 census supplied less than 5 percent of Rumania's total industrial output by value.[62] In any event, a comparison of firms by size and labor concentration by size of firm cannot be made. All the same, an indicator of a relatively more "modern" industry in Brazil is the share of energy supplied by sources other than steam power. For 1919, only 36 percent of the total horsepower in Brazil was generated by steam power among all firms surveyed, whereas the corresponding share among (large) firms in Rumania was 45 percent. Therefore, 64 percent of Brazil's energy was supplied by hydroelectric power, gasoline, or other "modern" sources—a share 9 percent greater than that of Rumania's "large" industrial firms. In the subsectors of metallurgy and textiles—the first a "modern" capital goods industry and the second a traditional consumer goods enterprise—the Brazilian data show steam power provided only 28 and 25 percent, respectively, of the energy used, contrasting to 60 and 50 percent, respectively, in the Rumanian figures.[63] The proportion of "small" enterprises—defined in Rumania as those having fewer than 20 workers and in Brazil those having fewer than 25 workers[64]—was 98 percent in Rumania and 88 percent in Brazil in 1939, possibly revealing greater economies of scale in the latter country. Moreover, at that time the concentration of labor in "large" establishments reached 73 percent in Brazil and only 55 percent in Rumania.

Other manufacturing data, however, indicate that Rumania was the more advanced country. Using the criterion of total employees in a given industry, we find that in 1939 the largest industries in Brazil, in rank order, were textiles, foodstuffs (including beverages), wood products, metallurgy, and construction. In Rumania the most important industries as measured by personnel employed were, in descending order, textiles, metallurgy, foodstuffs, wood products, and chemical products.[65] But as measured by total employment, metallurgy in Rumania was almost as large as foodstuffs, and two capital goods industries, metallurgy and chemical products, together approached the combined size of the two "classic" or pioneer industries, textiles and foodstuffs. In Brazil the two leading capital goods industries, metallurgy and construction, accounted for less than a third of employment in the two "classic" branches of production.

To reiterate, Brazilian manufacturing in the interwar period was more "advanced" in the respects of having a higher degree of concentration of labor in "large" firms and in the use of relatively modern forms of energy. Yet the results are mixed in that, as indicated by the relative size of the work force in modern and traditional industries, Rumania may have had a more modern industrial structure. Further, industry accounted for a larger share of GDP in the Balkan country, though the share of the active population in industry may have been larger in Brazil during the interwar years. In addition, Rumania had advanced further in import-substitution industrialization than Brazil by the late 1930s: 79 percent of the industrial goods by value consumed in Rumania were produced there at that time, a figure Brazil achieved in 1949.[66]

5. *The Composition and Concentration of Foreign Trade.* One indicator of the diversification of a national economy and its dependency on others is the degree of concentration of its exports and imports, both with respect to the array of products exchanged and the number of trading partners. The ten leading export goods in Brazil accounted for 95 percent of the total value of exports in 1910, 82 percent in 1930, and 63 percent in 1940. Coffee alone accounted for 41 percent in 1910, 63 percent in 1930, and 32 percent in 1940.[67] For Rumania, mineral resources (essentially oil) and vegetable products (basically cereals and wood derivatives) accounted for 95 percent of the value of Rumanian exports in 1919 and 89 percent in 1938.[68] Comparing the latter figure with that for Brazil in 1940, one may infer that Rumania had a higher degree of concentration of exports, that is, Brazil had experienced a greater degree of export diversification by the outset of World War II.

Furthermore, Rumania had become increasingly dependent during the interwar years on a single trade partner, Germany. The latter bought only 8 percent of the Balkan country's exports in 1906–10, by value, a share smaller than those of Belgium, Austria-Hungary, and England; but by 1929 Germany was the leading recipient of Rumanian exports, with 28 percent of the total, a figure that rose to 43 percent by 1939. In a similar but more pronounced trend, Rumania bought about a third of its imports from Germany in 1910, already the largest supplier, a figure that fell to 24 percent in 1929 and then rose dramatically to 56 percent in 1939. Brazil likewise experienced trade concentration in a single partner: it sold 36 percent of its exports (by value) to the United States in 1910 and the same share in 1939. By 1950 the South American nation shipped an enormous 55 percent of its foreign sales to the United States, a figure that dropped to 39 percent a decade later. Brazil's imports in 1910 were less concentrated. The country then received 29 percent of its foreign goods from Britain, but by 1939 the United States had replaced Britain as the largest supplier, with 33 percent, a share that rose to 35 percent in 1950.[69] By these measures, then, foreign dependency in both Rumania and Brazil was large. Such dependency would strongly affect the character of the development debate, having its greatest impact in Rumania during the 1930s and in Brazil during the 1960s and 1970s.

To summarize, in both Rumania and Brazil trading dependency was combined with other typical features of economic underdevelopment, called "backwardness" before 1945. Though the data examined do not all point in the same direction, Rumania seems to have been the more advanced of the two by the economic indicators examined, as well as by institutional features treated earlier.

Such findings, plus the influence of the Rumanian economist Manoilescu in Brazil, as well as the "reinvention" (independent rediscovery) of ideas there, support the overlapping but lagged periodization of this study.

It bears repeating that the direct link between ideas in Rumania and Brazil is the less important reason for undertaking a comparative study. Three processes were at work: the borrowing of ideas having their origins elsewhere, the adaptation and transformation of these ideas, and the independent creation or recreation of propositions appearing at other times, in other places. In the ethereal ambient of intellectual history, there will frequently be disputes about whether borrowing applies in a given instance; but in general, it is the rediscovery process that has been neglected. In the history of economics, there is the famous example of the more or less simultaneous and independent "discovery" of marginal utility, the foundation of neoclassical economics, by Léon Walras in Switzerland, Karl Menger in Austria, and Stanley Jevons in England.

Even if we reject Robert Merton's contention that multiple discoveries of scientific and quasi-scientific propositions are the rule and unique discoveries the exception, the reinvention of similar ideas under similar circumstances remains the chief justification for the comparative study at hand.[70] In this study, ideas and the creativity of their authors will not be emphasized at the expense of contexts and the social process of intellectual creation.[71] Further, I am interested in the diffusion of ideas, their reception or rejection, as part of the context to be examined; I am especially concerned with two groups of "consumers"—industrialists and their associations, as well as the state apparatus, that is, incumbent political leaders and high bureaucrats. The attitudes of industrialists, the most forward-looking sector of the "national bourgeoisie," and those of state officials were especially important in gauging the impact of structuralist ideas. Finally, I consider the perceived failure of certain ideas, theories, and practices as part of the dialectic between sets of ideas and the ideologies they implicitly or explicitly represented.[72]

These several considerations dictate the structure of the book: I attempt to follow the dialectic of the ideas—including their discovery, borrowing, adaptation, transformation, and frequent reemergence or reinvention—rather than the continuous careers of the men and women who produced the ideas. I have avoided the temptation to set the problem in the framework of Thomas Kuhn's "paradigms" or Imre Lakatos's "scientific research programs" because the disputes over the usefulness of the Kuhn and Lakatos models for the history of economic ideas would seem to make such an effort gratuitously problematic and polemical.[73] These reflections should make clear that the story I wish to tell is anything but neat and simple. There was a continual interaction between "mainstream" neoclassical economics and its Keynesian extension, on the one hand, and "peripheral" or "indigenous"—sometimes heretical, underground—economic thought, on the other. A similar process occurred with "mainstream" European Marxism and local varieties. Furthermore, the contact between mainstream and indigenous ways of thinking had its institutional bases not only in international organizations like the League of Nations and the United Nations but also in universities and foundations in developed countries. The international dimension is so important that I found it impossible to tell the story without including a formal section on developments outside Rumania and Brazil. Consequently, the following narrative is divided into three parts. The first concerns economic ideas in Rumania, circa 1880–1945; the second, international currents of heterodox and orthodox economic ideas, especially in western Europe and Latin America, circa 1920–50; and the third, ideas in Brazil, 1930–circa 1980.

Part I

RUMANIA

2

From Liberalism to the Marxist–Populist Debate

From the perspective of what would later be called the Third World, Rumanian intellectual history before 1945 offers a precocious and rich Marxist critique of an economy and society in which liberalism was the dominant ideology, though one extensively adapted to local circumstances and interests. The Marxist critique was made richer by its encounter with populism and was kept vital by a subsequent debate among writers holding sharply differing positions within a Marxist discourse. A brief sketch of the economic aspects of Rumanian liberalism will introduce the radical critiques that followed. Simply put, economic liberalism was that corpus of ideology, theory, and policy prescription that sought to free economic activity from all constraints on the market and to promote the international division of labor through the alleged complementarity of parts of the world economy. Its reception and application in the Balkans largely had to await the independence of the states emerging from the Ottoman Empire in Europe, which, in the Rumanian case, was achieved in greater degrees of formal autonomy between 1859 and 1877.

As the nineteenth century unfolded, *boieri* (boyars or nobles) and their families increasingly sought Western goods, which had to be purchased in European currencies. But there could be no free export of grain to pay for such imports until the Turkish monopoly of sea routes leading to the mouth of the Danube had been broken. This was effected when Russia defeated Turkey in a war in 1828–29, securing for itself control of the river's mouth and adjacent shores of the Black Sea. By the Treaty of Adrianople of 1829, ending the conflict, the Sublime Porte lost the right to requisition grain from the principalities of Wallachia—modern Muntenia and Oltenia—and Moldavia;[1] further, Count Pavel Kisseleff, in effect the Russian overlord of the two quasi-states still under Turkish suzerainty, permitted the increased flow of trade between them. But Western powers had also played a role in the Adrianople accord, and both the Dardanelles and the Danube were opened to international commerce. Thus, as European shipping became more and more important on the Danube and the Black Sea after 1829, landlords shifted their wheat surpluses from the Ottoman Empire to Western markets.

As trade and other contacts beyond the Ottoman lands developed, it was clearly not Russia but the West whose cultural and economic achievements Rumanian elites sought to emulate. Liberalism as a combination of social values, theory, and economic policy prescription was viewed in nineteenth-century Rumania as part of a broader process of "civilization," or Westernization.[2] The *boier* elite began to abandon the caftan and increasingly adopted French fashions and tastes in the decades following the Napoleonic Wars; it chose the French language as its vehicle of communication, in a manner similar to the Russian nobility's earlier Francophonia. As the century advanced, the use of French became mandatory for all those laying claim to general education. Westernization, civilization, and economic progress tended to be viewed as closely related processes, at least until the 1860s, when members of the conservative and nationalist Junimea ("Youth") school first expressed skepticism about the effectiveness of importing Western institutions, whole cloth. They were reacting in part to the liberal economics taught in the new universities at Bucharest and Iaşi (Jassy), founded in the early 1860s.

As in Brazil a half-century earlier, economic liberalism had the enormous appeal of breaking through the limitations on national growth and development imposed by foreign rule. In the judgment of the historian Nicolae Iorga, Rumania for over a millennium had labored under a succession of nomadic "predatory" states.[3] The Ottoman Empire followed, subjugating Wallachia and Moldavia during the fifteenth to seventeenth centuries. At times, the empire forced sales of Rumania's agricultural products at such low prices the Marxist economist and historian Lucreţiu Pătrăşcanu referred to the practice as "the trade of plunder."[4] By the nineteenth century, in the words of another student, "economic liberties were in harmony with the movement of national rebirth, of passing to a European style of life, of breaking the chains of the regime of Turkish capitulations." Liberal economics was seen not only as a necessary guide for development and a counterpart to liberal political institutions but was insistently pressed on the Rumanians by Britain and France, which helped guarantee Rumanian independence from Turkey.[5]

Yet the *boieri* were much more eager to introduce freedom of commerce than a free labor market. Serfdom had been theoretically abolished in Wallachia and Moldavia in the middle of the eighteenth century by the Phanariot[6] prince Constantin Mavrocordat, but *boieri* found ways to evade the law through the extension of corvée labor. Following a Western model of modernization, in 1863 the first ruler of a united Rumania, Prince Alexander Cuza, secularized monastic estates, accounting for about 20 percent of the national territory.[7] The following year, with Turkish suzerainty in advanced decline, *boieri* became absolute owners of their estates.[8] Simultaneously, peasants obtained their full legal freedom, including the formal abolition of corvée, as well as plots of land, though lords retained a larger share of the country's agricultural property.[9] The Napoleonic Code was introduced, ushering in formal contract law, but it had the effect of camouflaging the fact that rural labor contracts were really part of a continuing system of lord-serf relations. Such fact became more obvious after the reformist Cuza was forced to abdicate in 1866, and practices akin to serfdom extended into the twentieth century. By 1905 a quarter of the peasantry had no land, and another quarter had less than two hectares.[10]

Among the several early writers supporting the adoption of liberal economics was the aristocrat Alexandru Moruzi (1815–78), who defended free trade and saw tariff walls as barriers to Westernization as well.[11] Another was Prince Nicolas Suțu [Soutzo] (1798–1871), one of the most important political figures of the mid-nineteenth century. Son of the Domnitor of Moldavia and Țara Româ-nească (Wallachia), he helped Kisseleff elaborate the Organic Regulation, a decree that standardized feudal dues owed by villagers to their lords, lengthening the effective time of corvée service per year.[12] Despite this notoriously antiliberal action, Suțu helped popularize the works of Adam Smith, David Ricardo, Jean-Baptiste Say, and Michel Chevalier among the Rumanian elite. Writing in French about his native Moldavia in 1840, Suțu believed that the principality was "essentially agricultural," a judgment he repeated in 1866.[13] This assessment was in all likelihood influenced by the alleged beneficent effect of the international division of labor suggested by Smith and Ricardo, whose thesis of "comparative advantage" was probably familiar to Suțu.[14] Still another aristocrat, Ion Ghica (1816–97), the most influential free-trade economist of the nineteenth century, believed in his country's agricultural vocation and generally opposed "artificial" industries, that is, economic activities in which the country lacked a relative advantage in its factor endowments. Ghica favored the development of large properties and the advance of capitalism over precapitalist systems in agriculture.[15]

The reception of liberalism in Rumania was similar to that in Brazil, as noted in Chapter 1, in the regard that its defenders were not bourgeois opponents of an absolutist state exercising mercantilist policies but, as often as not, were latifundists (or sons of estate owners) controlling a dependent labor force by extraeconomic means. Furthermore, there was no tradition of industrial protectionism of a mercantilist sort under the Old Regime in either colony, Rumania or Brazil. Rumanian liberalism for some, such as the Marxist Constantin Dobrogeanu-Gherea, was a slavish copy of Western liberalism which failed to put into effect the bourgeois reforms implemented in the West.[16]

A feature that distinguished Rumanian liberalism from its Brazilian counterpart was the relative importance of French rather than British theorists, for the reason that the Rumanians who introduced the doctrine in their country in the nineteenth century were largely French-educated and often were sons of *boieri*.[17] Liberalism in its broadest sense, with its values of secularism, materialism, and

rationalism, held a strong appeal for reformist members of the Rumanian generation of 1848. Thus the relative salience of Adam Smith and the English school
may have been smaller than in Brazil.[18] In any event, liberalism and in particular
its prescription for the international division of labor met the needs of Rumania's
boier class, who used it to gain absolute ownership of their estates, to expand their
sales of grain abroad (to satisfy their increasing appetites for Western imports),
and to extract rising amounts of de facto corvée labor from their peasants, under
the guise of state-enforced labor contracts.

Liberalism in its purest form of (relative) laissez-faire had a short life in Rumania. It could be fully implemented only after the country had obtained its
formal independence in 1877, when Rumanians took up arms alongside Russia
against Turkey in the Near East Crisis. But, largely as a consequence of the Great
Depression that had begun in 1873, the high tide of liberalism in Europe was to
end six years later, when Germany introduced a steep grain tariff. Other continental powers followed suit. In 1885 Rumania denounced its commercial convention with Austria-Hungary because of Imperial restrictions on Rumania's
agricultural exports. In the following year a customs war broke out between the
two countries that lasted until 1893. With the customs tariff of May 1886, Rumania ended its brief experience with "classic" liberalism, raising tariff walls
against the manufactures of Austria-Hungary, its main supplier of industrial
goods at the time. This was the beginning of a period of a "statist liberalism,"[19] in
which liberalism was increasingly adapted to, and associated with, nationalist
aspirations, even xenophobia. The latter phenomenon took the form of anti-
Semitism in Moldavia because of the relatively large Jewish population, overwhelmingly urban, and the Jews' perceived leading economic position in Moldavian towns and as leaseholders of large estates.

More significant for ideological and economic history, the Rumanian Liberal
Party fastened onto industrial development "as a means of reducing . . . non-
Rumanian influence and the dependence on Habsburg imports at the same
time."[20] In one classic interpretation—Ştefan Zeletin's—the Liberal-dominated
state became the most important element in the capitalist development of Rumania.[21] At any rate, by the time Rumanians established an independent state,
Friedrich List's notion of protectionism based on the "infant industry" argument
had already entered the national political discourse.[22]

The industrial protection policies apparently had a beneficial effect, at least in
the medium term. In the years preceding World War I and perhaps as early as the
1880s, Rumania's Old Kingdom (Wallachia and Moldavia) achieved rates of
industrial growth of 6 to 8 percent a year in real terms, well above the continental
average.[23] Rumania's overall economic growth rate, too, was more than respectable for the last three decades before World War I, as the country began to export
petroleum and its international wheat trade revived.[24] The value of foreign sales
rose from $9 million in 1850 to $136 million in 1914. Between 1880 and 1910,

Rumania's annual rate of export growth, at 3.3 percent, was higher than that of the "periphery" of European states as a whole (2.8 percent). And per capita income, by one estimate at $307 in 1910, was higher than that of Portugal and the other Balkan states, excepting Greece. But there was a price to pay: 80 percent of all industrial shares were in foreign hands, as was 75 percent of the capital in banking at the time of the war.[25] In addition, there is abundant evidence that the income differential between the peasantry and other sectors of society was widening.

Toward the end of the nineteenth century, two schools of thought would offer critiques of the society in which a dominant statist liberalism, championed by a protectionist, industrializing Liberal Party but resisted by an agrarian and more free-trade-oriented Conservative Party, tended to hide an ugly social reality. These schools, which in neighboring Russia were locked in conflict for control of the national Left, were populism and Marxism.

Rumania's traditions of populism[26]—especially but not exclusively derived from the Russian discourse—and Marxism interacted, mixed, and resulted in fruitful and sophisticated debates in the two decades before World War I; as a consequence of the war, both populism and Marxism were transformed. At an intellectual level Leninism and the Third International (from 1919) redefined Marxism, while the theories of Chayanov and the "peasantism" of the Green International—an association of peasant-based parties in East Central Europe— played a similar role in the transformation of populism. Most important politically was the extension of the franchise to the peasant masses. In fact, the presence of populism in Rumania and its absence, in the eastern European sense, in Brazil[27] figures significantly in the divergent intellectual traditions of the two countries. It figures also, as I shall try to establish, in the greater sophistication of Rumanian social thought before World War II.

In Rumania, populism and Marxism were both interpreted as ideologies appropriate to latecomers to the world of the industrial revolution. Exponents of the two schools agreed on most of the calamities and some of the benefits of the rise of capitalism in Rumania. In particular, both addressed the exploitation of the peasantry: they associated the action of the direct oppressors, the traditional landed class (the *boieri*), with Rumania's being pulled into the "vortex" of international capitalism as an agricultural supplier to the industrialized West.[28] Both schools decried the twin evils of latifundism and absenteeism of landlords, who leased their estates to rapacious tenant farmers organized into trusts.[29] They further denounced the rising rents peasants had to pay landlords and mounting corvée requirements.[30] Populists (*poporaniști*) and Marxists, passionately and articulately defending their respective positions, engaged one another's arguments in their journals and produced a sophisticated discourse on development before the war of 1914.

Populism, like the corporatism whose development it influenced in Rumania, is notoriously difficult to define. One may begin by saying it is an ideology of those who see their society as backward, even archaic, relative to the capitalist West. Industrial capitalism, a powerful force emanating from abroad, is viewed as transforming local agriculture-based societies in undesirable ways: it ruins, then proletarianizes, the peasant and artisan classes, partly through a process of unequal exchange both between town and hinterland and between industrial and agricultural societies at the international level. In its mature phase, the exponents of populism sought forms of noncapitalist modernization, making it akin to socialism. In any case, its supporters sought to defend small producers against the massifying and depersonalizing forces of industrial civilization.[31] The roots of populism can be traced to England, France, and Germany, where economists and other social theorists began to contest the analysis of the classical economists ("the English school") early in the nineteenth century. Populism's concern for the classes threatened by industrialization found an echo in the concerns of conservative intellectuals in Germany and Austria who sought to save the *Mittelstand*—shopkeepers, prosperous artisans, and peasant farmers—from destruction by a triumphant industrial capitalism in Wilhelmine Germany.[32]

In eastern Europe populism appeared in a variety of forms, all of whose adherents viewed manifestations of capitalism in those societies as destructive. Moreover, capitalism at the local level was seen as degenerate and essentially doomed to failure against the superior competition of the West. The best-known and most important variety was no doubt the Narodnik movement in Russia. Its origins can be traced to the writings and political activity of Alexander Herzen, the exiled aristocrat who was the first writer (from 1849) to associate Russia's tradition of the peasant commune (the *obshchina* and its council, the *mir*), not with a vision of the past, as it was for the Slavophiles, but with a vision of the socialist future. He foresaw the possibility of avoiding the evils of capitalism by moving directly to a socialist economic organization, based on the living tradition of the *mir*. Herzen thus was the first to theorize the possibility of "skipping stages" in moving from "feudalism" to socialism.[33]

In Russia Herzen could build on, and transform, the conservative school of Slavophilism, a native reaction to Hegelianism which lacked a counterpart both in Rumania[34] and in Latin America. By the 1860s, Russian populism, in its violent form, insisted that action was urgent because the transition to socialism had to be begun *before* capitalism had triumphed in the countryside, immiserizing the peasantry and destroying the *obshchina*, the base on which a socialist society could be constructed. The People's Will, viewing the state as the driving force behind Russia's efforts to catch up with the West, assassinated Alexander II in 1881, but tsarist reaction under Alexander III triumphed easily, a lesson not lost on the Bolsheviks a generation later.

In Russia, populism and Marxism were movements with strong Hegelian foundations, both dating from the middle years of the nineteenth century. Alexander Gerschenkron holds that there could have been no Russian Marxism without the populist tradition, while Andrzej Walicki argues that Russian populism would be inconceivable without Marxism as a predecessor.[35] Both are right in that they refer to different moments in the two movements as they developed and interacted in the latter years of the nineteenth century. Populism and Marxism both viewed the penetration of capitalism into Russia and its consequences as *the* social problem, and advocates of the two schools engaged in a modes-of-production debate as it applied to their country. While the populists strived to overcome it, to pass beyond it, the Marxists viewed the development of capitalism in Russia as a grim necessity—or an accomplished fact, as Lenin argued in *The Development of Capitalism in Russia* (1899).

It is hardly surprising that in Rumania, a country cheek-to-jowl with Russia, this ideological exchange had major repercussions. Not only was the Russian state the leading foreign intervenor in Rumania in the nineteenth century, but the outstanding exponents of both populism and Marxism in that nation had spent their formative years in Russia, absorbing the radical ideologies prevailing there. In Rumania the two traditions of populism and Marxism would find expression, respectively, in the works of Constantin Stere, who spent his youth in (Russian) Bessarabia—now the Republic of Moldova[36]—and in those of Constantin Dobrogeanu-Gherea, who spent his early years in the Ukraine. Their debates, and those of their ideological allies in Rumanian journals from 1890 to 1920, asked basic questions about the path to capitalist development, including the issue of whether the existing economy of Rumania could be defined as capitalist, precapitalist, or some fusion of the two.

Rumanian populists, despite the impact of Russian ideas on their work, did not develop a revolutionary or putschist tradition; rather, their voices were reformist, as those of the Marxists tended to be as well.[37] The Rumanian populists also differed from their Russian exemplars in lacking the communal traditions of the *obshchina*,[38] at least to the same extent. Constantin Stere, their most prominent spokesman, was born in 1865.[39] Stere was the scion of a *boier* family that held property in Russian Bessarabia, and for his political activism as a youth he was exiled to Siberia. Stere subsequently immigrated to Rumania and there became a theorist of populism (from 1893), law professor, and sometime rector of Rumania's first university at Iaşi. He attached himself to the Liberal Party, though he never concealed his populist convictions. His journal, *Viaţa Românească* (Rumanian life), founded in 1906, was not only a vehicle for populism but a cultural and political forum.[40] Viewing tsardom as a greater evil than the German Empire, he espoused the German cause during World War I. Despite the damage done to his position in politics by the German occupation of Rumania and the subsequent Allied victory, Stere managed to enter Rumania's postwar parliament as a representative from Bessarabia, now part of Greater Rumania. He played an important role in writing the Peasant Party's program in 1921. Stere's magnetic personality contributed to his role as one of the outstanding political figures of his generation.[41]

Stere outlined his political position as early as 1893–94, and it appealed to small property owners in city and countryside.[42] A decade later he eloquently denounced the evils of latifundism, now combined with capitalist production for international markets, which together, he argued, resulted in the poverty of the masses. In 1906 latifundists owned over four million hectares, according to government statistics, while peasants held three million; the former averaged 4,000 hectares per estate and the latter, only 3.25 hectares per plot.[43] Stere disclosed that in Upper Moldavia, one foreign trust of lessees (*arendaşi*), the Fischer Association, controlled 242,000 hectares.[44] In the three counties concerned, which Stere called "Fischerland," 140,000 peasants did not even own a cow, and almost half of all children died before reaching age five.[45] Writing in the wake of the peasant revolt that swept the country in 1907, Stere believed it was no accident that in Dobrogea, on Rumania's southern border, where peasants owned 71 percent of the private property, there was no revolt.[46] Elsewhere peasants suffered from decreasing food consumption (and an overdependence on maize); as a result, the rural population suffered from pellagra as well as tuberculosis. Between 1876 and 1901–5, cereal exports had increased from 60,000 to 250,000 wagonloads, but the number of cattle in Rumania had decreased, and the consumption of maize had fallen from 230 kilos per person in 1876 to 130 in 1901–5. Meanwhile, the share of the crop that the peasant had to remit to the landowner or lessee at harvest time had greatly risen.[47] Stere even held that the net income of the landless peasantry at that time was negative, anticipating one of the concerns of Chayanov and the neopopulists.[48]

Like the Marxist Dobrogeanu-Gherea, Stere rejected the idea that Rumania's development simply lagged behind that of the West. In *Viaţa Românească*'s manifesto in its first number in 1906, Stere had proclaimed, "Our situation is not only backward, which would be bad enough; it is abnormal, which is much worse." Stere and his group saw the problem as a cultural one as well: the development of the peasantry was "the *means* of attaining a truly national culture."[49] They campaigned for agrarian and parliamentary reform, including an extension of the suffrage to peasants.

Stere's major work, a polemic against the Rumanian socialist movement and a critique of the agrarian structure, appeared in *Viaţa Românească* in 1907–8, a period encompassing the great peasant revolt. Entitling his study "Social Democracy or Populism?," Stere met his opponents, of whom Constantin Dobrogeanu-Gherea and Cristian Racovski were the most prominent, on their own ground, citing propositions and empirical findings by Marxist authors to build his case for populism. The work offered an analysis of, and solution to, the peasant problem. In his study Stere sought to establish the relevance of peasant-based populism and the irrelevance of Marxist socialism for the Rumania of his day. He estimated that peasant tillers numbered 3.5 million, while workers in industrial enterprises totaled only 40,000.[50] Thus peasants were 87 to 88 times more numerous than factory workers in Rumania, and the latter were considerably fewer than artisans.[51] Under such conditions, social democracy—the Marxist analysis and program of the Second International—was irrelevant, Stere believed: it did not address the problems of the vast majority of the people, and because the formal proletariat was so small, Marxists had no chance of taking power to implement their program.[52]

Industrialization, a process the government had attempted to stimulate with concessions to new enterprises in 1886 and 1906, Stere contended, with some exaggeration, had palpably failed.[53] Thirty years of protectionism had resulted only in the exploitation of the consumer, who had to import at artificially high prices or buy local goods at similar expense.[54] In truth, Stere believed, the basic conditions for industrialization in Rumania were lacking. Rumania could never hope to become an industrial state because large-scale industry (*industria mare*) required large markets. There was no such market within the country, even for textiles. Further, Stere believed, large-scale industry required foreign markets because modern labor-saving technology reduced the level of employment and therefore consumption at home. Within the industrialized countries, as Marx had shown, an "industrial reserve army" was required to keep wages at a minimum level. Consequently, a struggle for markets and colonies was occurring among the industrial powers.[55] Marx and Kautsky both had made the point that capitalism requires an export trade, Stere noted.

To obtain large markets such as the Great Powers enjoyed, Rumania would have to acquire colonies or protectorates by force or win markets abroad through the superiority of its wares. Could the nation compete in foreign markets under these conditions? The answer was obvious: Rumania could not outvie the Western powers militarily or industrially, in part because of the vast technological lead of the West. Moreover, Rumania's level of civilization—today we might say "human capital"—put the nation *hors de concours*, because 80 percent of its people were illiterate.[56] In fact, the existence of the industrial giants meant that other countries were forced to become their agricultural suppliers, as India had become for England.[57] For these several reasons, "only [economic] interest, ignorance, or the *idée fixe* of a maniac [could] explain the chimera of Rumanian industrialization."[58] Despite these firmly held views, Stere agreed with the Socialists that capitalism had begun to transform Rumania, especially in the regions where entrepreneurial leaseholders were attempting to maximize profits on the estates of absentee *boieri*.[59]

Capitalism's progress within Rumania, Stere held, was different from that in the West. Capitalist profits quickly flowed out of the country. He implied that this situation derived in large part from the importance of Jewish-owned banks in Rumania and the fact that a large share of the entrepreneurial classes were Jewish or otherwise non-Rumanian. Thus for Stere capitalism in Rumania was a "vaga-bond capitalism."[60] At the international level, capitalism was also a baneful force because the international economy was divided into exploiting and exploited states, an idea shared by Gherea and Racovski and later developed by Mihail Manoilescu.[61]

Yet agriculture, continued Stere, despite its partial transformation by capitalist forces, was not subject to Marx's laws of the concentration and centralization of capital. On this point Stere cited the authority of Karl Kautsky, the most re-spected Marxist theorist at the turn of the century, as well as that of the economic historian Werner Sombart.[62] Furthermore, in a nation overwhelmingly com-posed of peasants, cottage industry was necessary to employ peasants during the long winter months. Cooperatives would also be useful adjuncts to agriculture, as would some industrial enterprises to employ surplus labor; yet there was no substitute for a free landowning peasantry. Insofar as large-scale industry had a role (and it was beginning to, in oil extraction) state monopoly was advisable.[63] Stere was of the opinion that whatever role Marxist analysis had in charting the course of industrial society, it was of little value for the agricultural society of Rumania. There was no single path to development, as the divergent histories of England, France, and Germany illustrated.[64] Rumania should follow the exam-ples of successful agricultural modernizers, such as Denmark, where the coopera-tive movement had made the country prosperous.[65] Implicitly Stere and other populists interpreted peasant agriculture as an autonomous mode of production, noncapitalist and anticapitalist. They artificially separated peasant farming from the rest of the economy, and Stere and others denied that the peasantry was internally differentiated. In this manner Rumanian populists denied the ten-dency, which Lenin had noted in Russia, toward the creation of kulak minorities and rural proletarian majorities.[66]

The socialist reaction to Stere's study came fast, in the works of Cristian Racovski and Constantin Dobrogeanu-Gherea. Like Stere, both were born out-side Rumania. We shall consider the former first, and the latter at greater length, because of his pivotal role in defining the terms of Marxist discourse in Rumania. Yet Racovski was to play the more important role on the world stage. A Ruma-nian citizen until the Bolshevik revolution, Racovski had intimate contacts with socialist leaders in many European countries; after 1917 he would play a major role in the politics, administration, and diplomacy of the USSR. Though born in Kotel, Bulgaria, in 1873, Racovski spent his youth in Rumania, where his family owned an estate in Dobrogea, bordering Bulgaria on the Black Sea. Studying medicine in Switzerland, France, and Germany, he became an activist in the Second International, representing the Rumanian socialists at many European meetings. Racovski was forced into exile for supporting the peasant uprising of 1907 and was expelled from Rumania and other countries on several later occa-sions for his political activities. As the Rumanian delegate at the Zimmerwald conference in 1915, he sided with Lenin against the majority in signing the antiwar and pro-revolution manifesto. After the February Revolution in 1917, Racovski went to Russia from Rumania. Subsequently becoming a Soviet citizen, Racovski held major party and administrative positions in the Ukraine until 1923 and then served as the USSR's ambassador to England. In 1925–27 he was the Soviet ambassador to France. He was then recalled to the USSR and later expelled from the Communist Party by Josef Stalin, whose policies Racovski opposed. In the last Moscow show trial (1938), he was condemned for espionage and died in a Siberian labor camp, probably in 1941.[67]

To Stere's "Social Democracy or Populism?," Racovski replied directly in "Populism, Socialism, and Reality," published in 1908.[68] Should there be any doubt about it, Racovski first argued that socialists (i.e., the Marxists) were not only concerned with the urban proletariat but with a new rural proletariat as well.[69] Rumania's lack of a large industrial establishment did not mean capitalism did not prevail in the country.[70] Capitalist production now existed in Rumania, held Racovski, as the rapid rise in foreign trade over the course of the nineteenth century had proven, and the country was being linked ever more securely to the world market. By 1905, cereal production had risen five times above its level in 1866, the year the contract labor system came into existence.[71] Racovski went on to argue that the rural masses, contrary to Stere's assertions, were increasingly proletarianized by this process.[72] Rumania, it may be inferred, with its overwhelming peasant mass, was becoming a nation of proletarians. Immiseration of the peasantry was intensifying because Rumania had to compete on the world market with more efficient "overseas" producers such as Argentina.[73] Citing Werner Sombart, on whose scholarly authority Stere had relied extensively in his essay, Racovski observed that as small as Rumania's industrial proletariat currently was—about 3 percent of the total population—it nonetheless amounted to a slightly larger share than did the Prussian working class in 1848, relative to Prussia's total population, when Marx and Engels had published *The Communist Manifesto*. If, at that time, the Prussian proletariat had been significant for its potential growth, would not the same be true of its Rumanian counterpart in the early twentieth century?[74]

Just as Rumania had borrowed foreign institutions, in a like manner it could accelerate its process of capitalist growth by borrowing technology. Therefore, Racovski implied, although "skipping" capitalism as a mode of production was out of the question, the transition to socialism could be accelerated by assisting capitalism's advance. Progress in industrial development was highly desirable because the productivity of industrial workers was seven times greater than that of agricultural workers in the country.[75] Furthermore, Stere was wrong, argued Racovski, when he implied that Rumania could not develop a large internal market, because new wants would stimulate new production as capitalism developed.[76] Finally, a populism that foresaw the Rumania of the future modeled on the village economy was an infelicitous and mechanical copy of Russian *narod-nichestvo*, Racovski held, because the Balkan country had no communitarian socialist tradition like the *mir*.[77]

Thus liberalism, populism, and Marxian socialism were foreign doctrines that penetrated Rumania in the nineteenth century, and all had their roots in the industrial West. To resonate in Rumania, each ideology had to be adapted to its Balkan setting.[78] Though liberalism became the "organic" ideology of the state and dominant social elements, its ideals were mocked by social realities. Populism and socialism, tailored to local realities, provided damning critiques of what Stere and Racovski considered a grotesque pasquinade of liberal society. In this ongoing enterprise, both schools would evolve in continual dialogue with each other and with foreign theorists. But perhaps the fiercest critic of Rumanian reality was the man who adapted Marxism most extensively—Constantin Dobrogeanu-Gherea.

3

Marxism in Backwardness: Gherea and His Critics

Cristian Racovski had established that Marxism was relevant to the analysis of backwardness, defined in relation to modern capitalist economic and social configurations. And yet Marx had developed his system to critique the structures and movement of capitalism in the developed West so Racovski only began to answer the question, How much did Marxist social science need to be adapted to fit the circumstances of underdevelopment? The issue was being faced in Russia, but Russia could claim the advantages of a backward yet resource-rich and rapidly industrializing Great Power.

The questions were these: What is the nature of the local economic system—capitalist or precapitalist? Do unique "social formations" exist that combine features of capitalism and precapitalist modes of production? How do these social formations relate to the laws of motion of capitalism at the international level? If the national economy in question is by some definition precapitalist or semi-capitalist, can the local bourgeoisie develop a viable capitalist economy at home? Or if not, can the state do so? And in class terms, can state officials act as an *Ersatzklasse*, in the absence of a "conquering bourgeoisie"? Further, if capitalist economies pass through historical stages, how are these stages to be identified, and do they pertain to states or to larger entities? If stages, can some be skipped? Should the working class and progressive intellectuals support the development of capitalism? Marxists supplied inventive answers to these questions, and it is hardly surprising that the analyses of creative thinkers, all claiming Marxism as their method, were often not compatible.

Racovski was not alone in asserting the relevance of Marxism, and therefore adapting it, to conditions in prewar Rumania. Constantin Dobrogeanu-Gherea (like Racovski and Stere, a foreigner by birth) moved the debate on peasant society to the level of the mode of production. For better or worse, the only mode that Marx and Engels described with precision was capitalism itself, leaving room for inventive speculation about other modes and providing a legacy of controversy about the ill-defined Asiatic mode. Gherea was one of the first theorists to argue, in 1910, that traditional modes of production in backward countries interacted with capitalism to form a unique amalgam—in fact, a new mode, and in the event, a monstrous one. His novel proposition can be contrasted with the fact that eleven years earlier Lenin had characterized Russia's economy as one in which capitalism, even in agriculture, was inexorably eliminating the precapitalist regime.[1] The significance of Gherea's achievement is shown by the fact that nearly 70 years after his book appeared, Europeans, Latin Americans, and Africans were still "discovering" modes of production in which capitalism subordinated precapitalist modes in unique patterns.

It is a felicitous irony that in a country known for its nationalism, social conservatism, and anti-Semitism, and one in which formal education was a source of prestige, among Rumania's most celebrated and honored social and literary critics was an immigrant Jew, autodidact, and Marxist. Dobrogeanu-Gherea knew Engels and carried on a correspondence with leading Marxists of his generation—Karl Kautsky, Rosa Luxemburg, Victor Adler, August Bebel, Georgy Plekhanov, and Vera Zasulich. He was an active participant in the Second International and received a message of fraternal greetings from the congress of the International at Copenhagen, signed by Lenin, Luxemburg, and Plekhanov, among others.[2]

Born Solomon Katz in the Ukrainian district of Ekaterinoslav in 1855, Constantin Dobrogeanu-Gherea embraced Russian populism, the Narodnik movement, while still a minor, and quickly fell afoul of the authorities. His brief experience at the University of Kharkov reinforced his radicalism, and he became a follower of Mikhail Bakunin. He participated in the "To the People" movement in the summer of 1874, on which occasion thousands or even tens of thousands of radical Russian youths began to test the strength of their social commitment by living among, learning from, and politicizing peasants and workers. A step ahead of the police, Gherea moved from Kharkov to Odessa, then to Chişinău, in Bessarabia (today's Moldova); in March 1875, he crossed the Rumanian border and stopped in Iaşi (Jassy), the capital of Rumanian Moldavia. He was not yet twenty years old. Like many other youths of the Russian Empire who had participated in the "To the People" movement, Gherea had acquired the rudiments of a trade, or two. He initially supported himself as a stonecutter in Iaşi and also worked in a smithy.[3] Three years later, his life took another dramatic turn when he was kidnapped by the notorious Okrana, the tsar's secret police, in Galaţi, at the confluence of the Danube and the Siret rivers. (Russian troops were in Rumania at the time because of war with Turkey, at the end of which conflict Rumania would secure its formal independence.) Gherea was subsequently imprisoned in St. Petersburg but was soon exiled to a village on the White Sea. He escaped on a fishing boat to Norway and thence made his way across Europe to Vienna and finally in 1879 to Rumania, where he settled in Ploieşti.[4]

Coming out of a Narodnik tradition—he was still reading Flerovsky (pseud. for Vasily Bervi) and Nikolai Chernyshevsky in the 1870s and 1880s—Gherea apparently converted to Marxism gradually. He was studying Marx in 1875, the year of his arrival in Rumania. Contacts with Russian exiles in western Europe seem to have played a role in his embrace of Marxism.[5] The transition was not complete by the time of his study and defense of Marx's work (1884), as is clear from his pamphlet *What the Rumanian Socialists Want* in 1886.[6] Evident in this early work, however, are elements of his attempts to adapt Marxism to the seemingly inhospitable terrain of a backward, peasant-based economy. Gherea argued in this essay that Rumania's socialist revolution depended on the prior attainment of socialism in the industrialized West, where Marx had foreseen the overthrow of capitalism. Rumania, he contended, had already adopted Western social usages, and would not—because of the coming revolution in the West— pass through all the stages that had occurred in the development of European capitalism.[7] He argued, conventionally, that liberalism, the dominant economic ideology of the West, had been the product of changes in the economic and social structure. Gherea then departed from convention in asserting that Rumania had adopted Europe's superstructural forms—ideology, political institutions, social fashions—without having undergone changes in its economic base or infrastructure.[8]

In the West the transformations had occurred under the leadership of a dynamic and powerful bourgeoisie. In Rumania, by contrast, Gherea believed the bourgeoisie was weak and corrupt.[9] Despite protective tariffs, government support was insufficient for the establishment of heavy industry in Rumania, a condition he associated with a dynamic bourgeoisie. In 1886 Gherea's views were still influenced by Russian populism, as shown by his contention that Rumania could not industrialize: foreign markets were dominated by powerful Western competitors, and the domestic market was too small to permit large industrial firms without ruining the artisan class, thus reducing the potential size of the market. In these circumstances, Rumania should concentrate on agriculture (as the Narodniki had indicated for Russia), but farming should be organized along socialist lines.[10]

In "Role of the *Pătură Cultă* [cultured stratum] in Social Transformations," published in 1892, Gherea further developed the thesis that changes in the advanced capitalist countries directly affect backward or underdeveloped countries (*țările înapoiate*). Because changes in European stock markets or in the size of American grain harvests affect the whole world, how, he asked, could the great social transformations associated with these economic phenomena not affect underdeveloped countries?[11] Just as the class controlling the means of production rules the other classes within a state and imposes its social form on the others, "in a like manner do countries whose means of production are strongly developed . . . hold in economic subjugation [*robie*] underdeveloped countries, and even impose on the latter the former's social forms."[12] Exploitation could be avoided only by emulating the West, as Engels had noted in the case of Russia, whose leaders had pursued a modernization policy after that country's defeat by England and France in the Crimean War.[13] As proof of the transmission of social and cultural superstructures from the West, Gherea cited Rumania's transformation from a feudal into a (superficially) bourgeois society through the agency of a social group he called the *pătură cultă*, not a local bourgeoisie. This group was not bourgeois at all, but rather consisted of the enlightened sons of the old *boier* class, formally but not in fact denied control of their serfs by reforms of the 1860s. Emancipation, indeed, was a prime example of the formal rather than substantive reform that was taking place in Rumania.

In 1908, almost two decades after writing "Role of the *Pătură Cultă*," Dobrogeanu-Gherea returned to the same themes. Reacting to Constantin Stere's charges that Rumania was overwhelmingly an agrarian nation and that Marxist socialism as a program for the nation was an absurdity, Gherea held that Rumania was already a "semicapitalist" country and that the process of capitalist penetration was too far advanced to skip capitalism on the route from feudalism to socialism. Though contending that Marxist laws of development were valid for a backward agricultural country like Rumania, Gherea conceded that such laws manifested themselves in a much more complex and confused fashion than in the West.[14]

In the same year, 1908, he wrote that Rumania had a legal structure appropriate for a capitalist society but neither a capitalist class nor a proletariat. Backward countries such as Rumania were becoming satellized as the capitalist world economy expanded. Gherea now borrowed and reinterpreted the notion of *formă fără fond* (form without substance) from the Junimea school, whose leaders had been trained in Germany and steeped in Hegelianism. In Gherea's Marxist terms, superstructure (form) had preceded the base in that Rumania had adopted Western institutions without the social and economic conditions requisite for their effective functioning.* Commenting on the gap between the formal and the real country, Gherea noted that the situation contrasted sharply with that in absolutist Russia, where the "real" state of development was ahead of that of the legal

---

*Dobrogeanu-Gherea, "Post-scriptum" (1977 [1908]) pp. 478–82. The Junimea was a cultural and political society founded at Iași in 1863 by Titu Maiorescu and others who had studied abroad, principally in Germany. (Maiorescu, who had studied at Berlin, Paris, and Giessen, held a doctorate from the University of Vienna.) Junimists argued that Rumania had not attained a state of development corresponding to the adoption of institutions associated with the economically advanced West and that the (failed) revolution of 1848 against the Ottoman Empire had not been the result of real aspirations of the country. Maiorescu was deeply influenced by Hegel on the evolution of culture and believed that institutions, such as the state, could not change the organic "base," i.e., society; rather, change had to flow from the latter. See "Junimea" (1964), pp. 935–36; and "Maiorescu, Titu" (1972), 1: 353–96. Alexandru Xenopol, a younger Junimist, had adapted the "form without substance" notion to serve a materialist argument for development, though not a Marxist one, before Gherea. See Chapter 5.

system. Under the circumstances, Rumanian socialists should strive for the development of an authentic capitalism, which would bring in its train an enforceable modern legal system, instead of the sham the country then knew.[15]

In *Socialism in Underdeveloped Countries*, written in 1912, Gherea elaborated on the theme of the differences between the evolution of the central capitalist countries and their backward dependencies. In the latter, evolution was much faster, and of a different character, because changes in the form or superstructure preceded those in the base. This situation resulted from the fact that the advanced capitalist countries determined the evolution of the whole system.[16] Gherea proceeded to formulate a "law of backward societies," those on the Periphery of the capitalist Center: "In advanced capitalist countries, social forms follow the social [and economic] base; in underdeveloped countries, the social base comes after the social forms."[17] Therefore, Gherea believed, the transition to socialism would be easier in backward areas because such nations would adopt socialism as a result of its triumph in the West. The majority of the population in Rumania was already undergoing proletarianization, Gherea averred, and this would hasten the transition when the right time came.[18]

Gherea did not provide answers for two problems immediately consequent on these theses. Why did he not conclude, as the Marxist Li Ta-chao did for China in 1920,[19] that the proletarianization of peasants in his country made it ripe for revolution? Apparently Gherea thought the process was in its early stages and was partially blocked by a fusion of precapitalist and capitalist institutions. Nor did Gherea deal with the problem of the potential superficiality of the socialist transformation emanating from the West: he did predict that socialism as a form would precede that of the socioeconomic base in Rumania.[20] Yet, given his compelling arguments for the superficiality of bourgeois modernization by the *pătură cultă*, why, one might ask, at least in the short and middle terms, should the adoption of socialist forms in backward countries after the revolution in the West affect the local base more than the transformations capitalism had wrought? Gherea did not say. Yet part of his achievement was to envision and analyze underdevelopment as a *syndrome*, not simply the starting point from which backward countries would follow the trajectory already traced out by the developed countries. His Marxist model was contemporaneous with Julius H. Boeke's earliest work on economic dualism, attempting to explain why the price mechanism did not constitute a sufficient incentive to development in Eastern societies.[21]

Gherea believed that backward countries in the capitalist orbit suffered both from capitalism (*boier* exploitation of peasants to maximize profits in the international market) and the insufficient development of capitalism (its incapacity locally to destroy feudal relations of production).[22] In this regard, Gherea again noted that the Rumanian bourgeoisie had utterly failed to transform the national economy, as its exemplar had done in advanced capitalist countries. The bourgeoisie of western Europe had betrayed its defense of the Rights of Man after

1789, but the bourgeoisie of Rumania had nothing to betray. Although the Western bourgeoisie had to fight for the creation of liberal institutions, they were subsequently imported into Rumania in a process in which the local bourgeoisie "played the smallest possible role."[23] Rather, it was the *boieri*, who, under Western influence, created the liberal state in Rumania. The local bourgeoisie, such as it was, took the place of the *boieri* as a new "semifeudal class," keeping intact many feudal social relations.[24]

Yet, beyond the matter of the ruling class, a Marxist in a country overwhelmingly populated by peasants would have to address the agrarian issue, even without Stere's powerful challenge. Dobrogeanu-Gherea had raised the question at the Zurich congress of the Second International in 1893, and it became an absorbing concern for him in the following decade.[25] Gherea's magnum opus appeared in 1910 and was the capstone of a literature addressing the central problem of Rumanian society in the era: peasant unrest. Three years earlier, following years of increasing labor dues and falling peasant incomes, a rebellion had swept the country. Originating in Moldavia, the movement quickly spread to Wallachia as well. Partly because of fears of foreign intervention if it did not act decisively, the Rumanian government brutally suppressed the uprising. When the army completed its task, 10,000 peasants had been shot.

The laconic title of Gherea's study, *Neoserfdom (neoiobăgia)*, epitomized the proposition that a new and monstrous mode of production had reared its head in Rumania.[26] Put briefly, the mode was a fusion of precapitalist social and economic relations in the countryside and the economic relations and superstructure of an advancing capitalism at the national and international levels. In the traditional form of *iobăgie*, there had been three basic features: the peasant was fixed to the lord's land; he was forced to provide corvée labor for his master; and he had to pay tribute in kind as well as other forms of feudal dues.[27] *Neoiobăgia* was a hybrid form having the following defining characteristics: its relations of production were largely "serf-based, feudal"; at the ideological and legal level, it was overlaid with a liberal-bourgeois legal system that had the effect of leaving the peasant at the mercy of the landlord;[28] it further included a tutelary legislation that declared the inalienability of peasant land and regulated relations between the lord and the workers; at the economic level, the system did not provide the small peasant farmer enough land for subsistence, forcing him to become a vassal of the owner of the land he farmed as laborer and sharecropper.[29]

The international market in Gherea's model played a decisive role in initiating the process. A medieval system of social relations, Gherea thought, had still characterized the Rumanian countryside at the beginning of the nineteenth century. Peasants had been largely self-sufficient, and the economy largely had been a "natural" one. The ruling *boier* class had received dues in kind and in corvée labor. Towns at the time had only begun to introduce a money economy. Subsequent events, however, especially the signing of the Treaty of Adrianople

(1829), which opened Rumania's Black Sea ports for commerce with the West, set in train an intensification of the exploitation of peasants by landlords, thought Gherea.[30] This process resulted because *boieri* saw opportunities to obtain hard currencies and thereby to secure a flow of Western goods; such wares were deemed especially desirable after the Westernization of the *boier* class had begun with the Napoleonic Wars. As a result, Rumania had entered the "great world division of labor" and now "sends food to the West and receives from it industrial and cultural goods." Concomitant with Rumania's growth of trade came a monetized economy, a development that had required centuries to consolidate in the West.[31]

Thus for Gherea, as for many others, Western markets partially revolutionized the national Rumanian economy. With the appearance of a money economy, Gherea held, the exploitation of the peasantry no longer had any limits because grain had become an international commodity. Craft industries, many of which were focused in peasant households, began to disappear as well because of the stream of Western goods entering the national market paid for by agricultural exports.[32]

Gherea now returned to his early theme that Western culture lacked a material base in his country, where bourgeois institutions had arrived first. Rumania's nineteenth-century liberals, Gherea wrote, had believed institutions would "produce civilization, and not vice versa." But the Western countries that supplied the models Rumanians copied (principally France, Belgium, and England) had followed their own agendas. They had wished to "civilize" backward countries like Rumania so as to make local inhabitants produce goods the West demanded and to consume goods the West offered in exchange. Gherea's view of this matter, however, was ambivalent because he believed the institutions copied from the West and the backing of France and England were necessary—both for the achievement of national independence against Turkey and for the construction of a national state. Liberal institutions and the Western powers, he conceded, had also supported Rumania against absorption by Austria and Russia.[33]

The author proceeded to develop his thesis on the contradiction between the political and legal institutions of his nation and its economic and social institutions. This contradiction was responsible for the monster that resulted. It began with the land reform (*împroprietărirea*) of 1864, which process gave the peasants roughly a quarter of the country's arable land; the rest remained with the *boieri* and the state. Of the half million peasants who had received land, only 72,000, Gherea estimated, had obtained viable plots.[34]

For the first time, peasants and landlords received absolute property rights to their holdings, a process that had occurred during the Age of Absolutism in western Europe. The Rumanian landlords benefited from this measure by no longer having to provide the peasants rights of usufruct.[35] But the majority of peasants lacked sufficient land to support themselves, and the lords lacked labor to farm their estates. The state sided with the traditional nobility, so the result was foregone: forms of *iobăgie* reappeared instead of a wage regime. This development had its inexorable logic because the *boieri*, in addition to their traditional mentality, lacked both capital (including draft animals and agricultural equipment, largely held by the peasants) and a knowledge of farming.[36] Bad harvests in 1865 and 1866 intensified the recrudescence of *iobăgie*.

Rumania's Generation of 1848, who looked to the West for inspiration, had come to power with Prince Alexander Cuza, the first ruler of the united Danubian Principalities. Cuza began to organize an independent state in 1861, and he and his allies in the Generation of 1848 introduced a constitution based on that of Belgium, with ample provision for civil liberties. But in 1866, when the *boieri* forced Cuza's abdication, the state began to side more completely and consistently with the landlord class. Ironically, the first measure associated with the resurgence of feudal social relations was a law establishing the inalienability of peasant property, which in theory was to be parceled out in tiny plots. Yet the same tutelary legislation prohibited the peasant from leaving his village, thus requiring him to face a labor monopsonist, his former master. Holding a plot too small to support his family, the countryman again turned to the landlord, who was in a position to draw up a formal contract to secure access to peasant labor. To enforce it, the lord, who now for the first time represented the state at the local level, could call in the rural police (*dorobanți*) to "urge" the peasants to comply with the contract. The same statute of 1866 said no higher level of state authority could interfere in the enforcement of labor contracts so the peasant had no right of appeal. Dues of the old regime continued or reappeared in new guises—dues in kind, corvée, and others. A law of 1872 made more explicit the use of military means to enforce peasant contracts.[37] Although this measure was revoked a decade later, the practice continued informally. Meanwhile, as the decades wore on, more and more corvée days per year were demanded of the peasant, and his rents rose. In Rumania, therefore, extraeconomic compulsion of the labor force and contract were combined to exploit the peasant: Rumania had "a double agrarian regime . . . both capitalist and serf-based . . . absurd, hateful . . . a monstrous regime."[38]

"Neoserfdom," as Gherea styled Rumania's system, had the advantage for the *boieri* of freeing them of all traditional obligations to the peasantry; they could now exploit labor without any hindrance from the state. Further, they did not have to deal with free workers, who, in a capitalist regime, at least had legal equality with property owners and could refuse or abandon poorly remunerated employment.[39] The system tended to proletarianize the peasantry. The peasants' inalienable properties were subdivided into smaller and smaller strips as the population grew. But proletarianization did not mean the peasant received a salary for his labor; rather, he had to work the lord's property in *dijmă* or metayage, offering half his produce while providing his own tools and animals.[40] Thus the system concentrated real property in the hands of the landlord class, while still subjecting peasants to an ever-lengthening number of days of effective, if not formal, corvée labor.[41] In *neoiobăgia*, a social system unknown in the West or in Rumania in previous centuries, the peasantry got the worst of both modern and "feudal" worlds. Because of the problem of landlord absenteeism and widespread farming by lessees (*arendaşi*), agriculture, moreover, had become a predatory activity in which leaseholders tried to maximize short-term profits at the expense of the soil and forests. Peasants likewise had no incentive to conserve the soil on land they did not own and had no guarantee of farming it in subsequent years. The process was producing tragic results. The economic system, Gherea concluded, combined the capitalist prerogative to use and abuse the land with the lords' prerogative under serfdom to use and abuse the peasant.[42] Moreover, intensified latifundization was a result, rather than a cause, of the new regime: extensive rather than intensive agriculture, semiservile labor, and the fact that landowners did not have to furnish tools and draft animals (thus freeing capital for investment) all favored the expansion of the latifundium system.[43]

Yet *neoiobăgia* had another dimension that grew out of the grafting of the modern onto the medieval. This was the rise of bureaucracy, ostensibly established to pursue a course of national modernization but necessary for the consolidation of the *neoiobag* regime. Bureaucracy (implicitly including the army) became more powerful as the peasantry became more rebellious, because of its role in repression. Though the state had been the creature of the *boier* class, the bureaucracy had its own interests to pursue, and it exploited the peasantry through lawless acts, even torture, just as the lords extracted surplus directly from peasant labor. Although the *boieri* denounced the corruption of state employees, the bureaucracy grew more powerful after the rebellion of 1907. It was challenging the ruling class as state budgets and the public employment roles grew, thought Gherea. He even asserted that the bureaucracy was tending to become "the true dominant class."[44]

Throughout the period of neoserfdom, Gherea argued, the state had made laws that were effectively applied only when they were in the interest of the landowning class—such as the registration of peasants in the year of the revolt, 1907, and the funding of a 6,000-man rural gendarmerie.[45] All in all, Gherea estimated that the state controlled 25 percent of Rumania's national product, or about twice the percentage that the French government accounted for in the French product.[46] In Rumania's "parasitic, bureaucratic state" incumbent political groups transformed themselves into an oligarchy.[47] Gherea then examined a populist-inspired solution to these problems—the Casă Rurală, a state-run rural mortgage program. But he found that its only effect was to differentiate the peasantry and to help the rich peasants exploit the poor ones, who could not pay the installments on their loans.[48] His solutions for these problems, grave as he depicted them, were reformist. He prescribed the division of large estates and the introduction of true capitalist relations of production in agriculture, including the abolition of the (tutelary) inalienability of peasant land. He also championed universal suffrage, seen by many social progressives in Europe as the key to power for the toiling masses, and the industrialization of the country, in part to permit a more intensive and efficient agriculture.[49]

In his later years Gherea remained faithful to a socialist vision of Rumania's future, calling for the triumph of socialist power through legal or—in principle, at least—revolutionary means.[50] Loyal also to the idea of international proletarian solidarity, Gherea went into exile in Switzerland from 1916, the year Rumania entered the war, until 1919. Upon his return, he shared the conviction of many of his comrades that the socialist movement would triumph in western Europe; yet he believed, consistent with his earlier thesis, that Rumania would receive socialism from the outside. The country lacked the objective and subjective conditions for revolution.[51] Dobrogeanu-Gherea never gave his full support to the Russian Revolution, still clinging to his social democratic convictions, among which the goals of terminating precapitalist labor relations and bringing the masses to power through universal suffrage loomed large as remedies for his country's social and political distress.[52] He died in 1920, one year before the socialist movement in Rumania was split by the organization of the Rumanian Communist Party.[53]

Gherea's last published writings concerned the "oligarchy," a theme he had taken up in *Neoserfdom*. He held that this ruling group had its origins in the state bureaucracy, created under a highly restricted suffrage in the previous century. The oligarchy's wealth, whether in land, commerce, banking, or industry, had its inception in its members' association with the state, which was used as a source of enrichment. "The greatest industry," Gherea declared, was "the political industry."[54] Presumably Gherea had in mind not only sinecures, patronage, and peculation but monopoly concessions, special knowledge of impending state actions, and state-let contracts.[55] But the "oligarchy" remained poorly defined in class terms and a nebulous analytical concept. Further, if it had such an intimate symbiosis with the state, it seems unrealistic to have pinned reformist hopes on that state, as Gherea's social democratic successors did. Dobrogeanu-Gherea's great contributions lay in his earlier writings, notably his adaptation of Marxism to describe the realities of backward countries and his conception of neoserfdom, the fusion of "feudal" and capitalist modes of production.

Five years after Dobrogeanu-Gherea's death, his analysis of Rumania's development was challenged within a Marxist discourse. Rejecting Gherea's notion of the "oligarchy" as an aberration, Ştefan Motaş (1882–1934)—better known to his countrymen by his pen name, Ştefan Zeletin—used Marxism to define and defend the role of the national bourgeoisie. Like Gherea, Racovski, and Stere, Zeletin was active in politics, serving in the senate as a member of General Averescu's People's Party. Yet on the whole, he opted for the *vita contemplativa*:

Zeletin, a Moldavian, began his schooling as an Orthodox seminarian but then pursued secular studies at the University of Iaşi, where he took his first degree in 1906. Three years later, he began his scholarly peregrinations, studying at Berlin, Leipzig, Oxford, and Paris and taking his doctorate in philosophy at the University of Erlangen (Germany) in 1912.

Zeletin published his most important essay, *The Rumanian Bourgeoisie: Its Origin and Historical Role*,[56] in 1925 and was named to the chair of philosophy at the University of Iaşi two years later. This work earned him an important, if controversial, place in the debate on Rumanian development because it constituted an impressive effort to "tame" Marxism, to achieve its *embourgeoisement*; Zeletin occupies a position in the history of Rumanian Marxism akin to that of Peter Struve in Russia.

Zeletin, indeed, was a Rumanian *Kathedersozialist*, who recruited Karl Marx and Rudolf Hilferding, along with a former Marxist, Werner Sombart, as authorities to justify building a Rumanian capitalism and nurturing a still-embryonic national bourgeoisie. More than anyone else, Zeletin made Marxism respectable. At the same time, he was an unalloyed example of Antonio Gramsci's "organic intellectual," providing an elaborate rationalization of the existing distribution of wealth and power. In particular, his work tended to justify the historic role of the National Liberal Party, which had made extensive use of the state for its financial and industrial projects.[57] He made the work of Gherea, of whom he was a fierce critic, his point of departure for a defense of the national bourgeoisie. Zeletin agreed with Gherea that the triumph of socialism was inevitable, but capitalism had to be developed first. Thus despite the sharp differences in their analyses, the positions of Gherea and Zeletin can be seen in large measure as differences of emphasis: whereas Gherea stressed the ultimate victory of socialism in Rumania, Zeletin stressed the immediate task of building capitalism in the country, a necessary development if socialism were to follow.

In Zeletin's best-known work, *The Rumanian Bourgeoisie*, he described how such a class had come into being in the preceding century. Zeletin framed the study within a Marxist periodization of world capitalism, relying especially on Hilferding's *Finance Capital* (1910). According to this scheme, capitalism had passed through three stages, in which different elements of the system were dominant—commercial, industrial, and finally finance capital, the latter rising to preeminence circa 1880. To these stages corresponded three ideologies—mercantilism, liberalism, and imperialism.[58] But inspired by Hilferding, Zeletin held that late-arriving bourgeoisies, following the path blazed by those of America and Germany, would skip the liberal phase and move from mercantilism directly to imperialism.[59]

For Zeletin, the Rumanian bourgeoisie, initially so dependent on the importation of foreign goods and capital, would eventually achieve economic independence, as its Western exemplars had done.[60] Rumania's transition to capitalism, bringing in its train the beginnings of a bourgeoisie, had commenced with the Treaty of Adrianople in 1829, by which Britain and France forced Turkey to open the Bosphorus to international commerce. As Gherea had noted, this event had quickened the interest of Rumania's upper classes to acquire Western goods, as well as opening a lucrative new market for Rumanian grain.[61] Liberal ideology could have been of use in creating a bourgeoisie only after the economic transformation had been set in motion in 1829. True, liberal ideology had started to penetrate Rumania before the economic revolution; but before that time it had simply been a tool for the lesser *boieri* to demand the privileges of the greater ones.[62] In Zeletin's view, the customs union between Ottoman-ruled Moldavia and Wallachia in 1847 stimulated the emergence of both the bourgeoisie and the Rumanian state—and the latter's development was greatly advanced by the formal union of Wallachia and Moldavia in 1859. These events had depended in part on the expansion of Western capitalism into the two principalities.[63]

Following the analysis of Sombart of earlier nations' capitalist development, Zeletin held that Rumania, contrary to the analysis of Dobrogeanu-Gherea, had followed a typical rather than an exceptional, much less a "monstrous," course. Western economic and cultural penetration of Rumania rose rapidly after 1829, but its full impact occurred only after the Anglo-French victory over Russia in the Crimean War in 1856.[64] In the early nineteenth century there had been no unified ruling class, thought Zeletin. Jewish capital, originating in Poland, had tended to weaken the power of the traditional *boieri*, who consumed Western goods lavishly.[65] But in the years following the triumph of the *boieri* over Prince Alexander Cuza in 1866, Western capitalism had ushered in a social and political revolution. Zeletin agreed with Gherea that after 1866, Rumania had been ruled by an oligarchy. That oligarchy had played a role similar to that of absolutist monarchs under the regime of commercial capitalism in the West. There still existed no single powerful ruling class as in Western absolutism, and the process of circulation overshadowed the process of production, breaking down internal barriers to trade.[66] The *boier*-derived oligarchy, beginning with the Brătianu family's foundation of the Bancă Națională in 1880, had become a financial oligarchy. Therefore, there had been no need for a bourgeois revolution.[67]

Owing to the wave of agricultural protectionism in Europe following the introduction of American grain in the late 1870s and early 1880s, Rumania had been thrown onto its own resources, but its industrialization had begun only after implementation of the tariff of 1886.[68] Having completed the mercantilist phase of capitalism, the country was now passing directly to the imperialist phase, just as had already occurred in the United States and Germany. The founding of the Bancă Națională by the Brătianus and their collaborators in the Liberal Party in 1880 and the establishment of the state-associated Bancă Românească (also Liberal dominated) in 1910 tended to nationalize capital in Rumania. Thus, "with [the rise of] finance capitalism, our society jumped directly from mercantilism to imperialism, from the development of forces of national production to their organization under the supremacy of high finance." No longer was there a struggle between industrial and financial capital; instead, the finance oligarchy, as in other countries in the age of imperialism, was organizing production. In Rumania's development, mercantilism and imperialism, that is, the development and organization of production, had become one process, as had happened with the "late bourgeoisies" of Germany and the United States.[69] Industrialists were slowly becoming the salaried agents of bankers, and the class of great landlords had disappeared. The peasants got both land and the franchise as a result of the Great War, but they were not a united class; only the industrial proletariat could oppose the bourgeoisie's power, and the proletariat was still minuscule.[70] In the meantime, the land reform of 1918–21 had pushed the bourgeois revolution nearly to completion.[71]

Rumania's many social problems were necessarily associated with the transitional phase to finance capitalism, Zeletin asserted. In the nineteenth century, rural crises were a natural consequence of initial phases of capitalism because the new mode of production made peasants free, but it could not change their mentality or yet provide industrial employment. Peasant rebellions were "a general phenomenon" in the transition from the old [feudal] regime to the bourgeois regime, Zeletin asserted, and their character was reactionary. Eventually, industry would absorb the surplus agricultural population as finance (monopoly) capitalism developed.[72]

Zeletin proceeded to critique Gherea's Marxist socialism. Like the Junimea, Gherea had conceived of modern Rumanian society developing from the "form" to the "base" and therefore could not see the development of national society as a natural process.[73] In Zeletin's view, the basic problem was the contrary of what Gherea had suggested: the root cause of social ills lay not in Rumania's material base, where capitalism was developing more or less normally, but in the ideological superstructure, where a "medieval" spirit still prevailed.[74] Universal suffrage had opened unparalleled opportunities for a peasant-based reaction, and it would be folly to set the working class against the bourgeoisie.[75] In *Neoliberalism*, a collection of essays that appeared two years later, Zeletin pursued these themes, again asserting that the Rumanian bourgeoisie's development had been "normal."[76] "Neoliberalism" for Zeletin was the ideology and set of policies that correspond to the imperialist phase of capitalist development.[77] In the postwar era of *Planwirtschaft* and *économie dirigée*, neoliberalism, thought Zeletin, corresponded to the need for organization inherent in the current phase of capitalism. Thus government intervention was necessary, and the state could limit the rights of individuals for the general welfare.[78]

The development of national independence, national culture, and the state depended on the development of the bourgeoisie. But the latter in turn required state assistance.[79] Rumania's "plutocracy" had a positive role to play in the nation's current state of development because it was a necessary element in off-setting the power of foreign capital. Its historical task was to industrialize Rumania.[80] Zeletin went so far as to justify embezzlement from the national treasury and the general amorality of Rumanian capitalism—again asserting that Rumania was simply repeating the experience of early capitalism elsewhere. Yet the plundering of public monies had reached its limits, he intoned, and the adventurers responsible for such matters must now seek to develop national capital, having completed this local version of "primitive accumulation."[81] Since the bulk of the capital in the country was still in the hands of foreigners, Zeletin contended, the national bourgeoisie had the historic role and duty to "reconquer today's Rumania for Rumanians."[82] Despite these overtly apologist considerations on the financial and industrial bourgeoisies, Zeletin maintained that Marx's analysis regarding the victory of the proletariat was right in the long run.[83]

The socialists did not leave Zeletin's views on development unanswered. A year after the appearance of Zeletin's *Rumanian Bourgeoisie*, two Social Democrats attempted to refute Zeletin, defending the position of Gherea, who had died in 1920. One of these, Şerban Voinea (1893–1972), whose real name was Gaston Boeuve,[84] had recently outlined Gherea's position for German-speaking Marxists in Otto Bauer's theoretical journal in Vienna, *Der Kampf*.[85] In this essay Voinea had defended Gherea's position that the laws of motion for peripheral societies are different from those in the industrial West in that changes within the ideological superstructure precede those in the material base. Voinea had argued that the socialists had to struggle against *neoiobăgia* by allying themselves with the bourgeoisie and on this point implicitly agreed with Zeletin. Like Gherea, Voinea contended that the transition to socialism in Rumania would be determined by events in the West.[86] But he went further, addressing an issue about which Gherea had said little, to argue that the sudden introduction of socialist institutions in his country (and implicitly in other backward countries) would have an effect analogous to the introduction of capitalist superstructural institutions a century earlier: a "neocapitalism" would replace "neoserfdom."[87]

Voinea was eager to distinguish his position from Zeletin's, even if both supported the rise of a national bourgeoisie. *Oligarchic Marxism*,[88] the title of Voinea's response to Zeletin's *Rumanian Bourgeoisie*, pointed up the theoretical and empirical insufficiencies in the latter's argument. Accusing Zeletin of twisting Marxist analysis, in effect Voinea argued that his opponent, in modern parlance, was a "circulationist": he had misused Marxist method by interpreting international market relations as the determining forces in the rise of Rumanian capitalism, thus making the mode of exchange or circulation decisive in economic development, rather than the mode of production.[89] Furthermore, asserted Voinea, Zeletin's facts were wrong: Rumania had known a money economy, commercial capital, and usury long before the Treaty of Adrianople.[90]

Whereas Zeletin had accused Gherea of borrowing ideas from the Russian debate about the development of capitalism in backward countries, Voinea replied that Gherea's argument was original because the liberal institutions on which he based his case existed only in Rumania, while Russia had labored under an autocracy.[91] Voinea accused Zeletin of theoretical incoherence by pointing out that the latter had borrowed his idea on the "contradiction" between feudal (agricultural) production and capitalist circulation not from Marx but from Nikolai Danielson, a theoretician of the Narodniki;[92] in this way Voinea threw the charge of populist inspiration back at Zeletin.

In the same year, 1926, another Social Democrat, Lothar Rădăceanu, attacked Zeletin for his analysis of the ever-nebulous Rumanian oligarchy.[93] Rădăceanu argued that the oligarchy had penetrated the national economy through its control of politics, as Gherea had established. Gherea was wrong, however, in believing that *neoiobăgia* was unique to Rumania; other students had verified the existence of similar phenomena in other parts of Eastern Europe.[94] The Rumanian state was created for international capital, Rădăceanu continued, and did not need to be bourgeois except in appearances, as Gherea had pointed out.[95] An antagonism existed between a rising bourgeoisie and the oligarchy in the contemporary period, contrary to Zeletin's views, because the oligarchy maintained elements of *neoiobăgia* and favored state-connected industries.[96] Nonetheless, the bourgeoisie had become reactionary and now sided with the oligarchy, owing to its fear of a Communist revolution.[97]

But the Communist writer Lucreţiu Pătrăşcanu pointed out that Rădăceanu's clinging to Gherea's chimerical oligarchy ensnared him in an ideological trap, which resulted in moral bankruptcy: Social Democratic leaders supported the dictatorship of Carol II in 1938, apparently as a progressive force against the "oligarchy."[98] Rădăceanu had still another turn to make, and he joined the communist-controlled government of Petru Groza after the war.[99]

Pătrăşcanu, who associated the Socialists' moral failure with what he considered to be Gherea's theoretical error, was the leading theoretician of the Rumanian Communist Party in the 1930s and 1940s. He played a major role in overthrowing the Nazi-allied regime of General Ion Antonescu in August 1944 and helped set up the coalition government that progressively led to a Communist monopoly of power in Rumania. Pătrăşcanu served as minister of justice in the postwar Groza government, but his influence dwindled in the late 1940s, when Moscow-trained politicians took over the Rumanian Communist Party. He was purged in 1948 (as too independent of Moscow) and executed in 1954 for right-wing deviationism, following a show trial.[100]

Pătrăşcanu, the son of a professor and himself a lawyer and economist, had studied in Germany. Born in 1900, he took his Ph.D. in 1925 in economics at Leipzig, where he wrote a dissertation on the recently completed Rumanian agrarian reform.[101] Pătrăşcanu's scholarly contributions were various, but his chief contribution to Marxist thought in Rumania was his effort to establish the "normality" of Rumania's capitalist development—yet normality in a sense different from Zeletin's. Like the Marxist writers before him, Pătrăşcanu's analysis of contemporary Rumanian society was conditioned by his understanding of national history, interpreted in the light of historical materialism. His main study in this regard was *A Century of Social Unrest, 1821–1907*. Written between 1933 and 1943, when the author's efforts were interrupted by periods of imprisonment and clandestinity, Pătrăşcanu's work is nonetheless cogent and informed by many of the best monographic works of Rumanian social science.

In this essay and in his postwar course notes, Pătrăşcanu held that Rumania had experienced feudalism from the beginning of the two principalities in the fourteenth century through the mid-eighteenth century. He believed that an exchange economy had developed in Rumania by the latter date, and at this time *iobăgia* had arisen as well. Pătrăşcanu contended that from 1749, when serfdom was formally abolished in Moldavia,[102] but former serfs remained landless and were still required to render corvée labor, to 1864, when feudal obligations were formally terminated, Rumania had not experienced a feudal, but a *iobag* regime, identifiable with the "second serfdom" in eastern Europe.[103] Therefore, it was a different mode of production than the one Gherea had identified, though Pătrăşcanu did not use the term. Under the earlier feudal regime, Pătrăşcanu wrote, the peasant controlled the means of production and paid the lord in kind. He served only three days of corvée labor (*clacă*) per year. But the chief characteristic of the *iobag* regime, after Prince Constantin Mavrocordat's reforms of 1742 and 1744, was "rent [paid] in labor." By the late eighteenth century, clacă was as much as 30 days per year.[104]

Money was already circulating in the seventeenth century, Pătrăşcanu held,[105] contrary to Zeletin. As the use of money in the national economy increased during the eighteenth century, it permitted the transformation of goods into commodities and ultimately allowed *boieri* to seek accumulation without limits. Therefore, the transformation of products of the soil into commodities was the "determining factor" in the change of relations between *boier* and peasant and the transition from feudalism to *iobăgie*.[106] Commercial and usury capital were responsible for the exchange of commodities and the circulation of money and prepared the way for industrial capital, with its generalized phenomenon of wage labor. This process had begun as early as the sixteenth century in the West but was still occurring during the mid-nineteenth century in eastern Europe.[107] Rumanian capitalism, however, faced a major impediment that had not existed in the West. Under Ottoman rule, which saw its greatest abuses under the Greek Phanariot princes in the years 1711–1821, there was little primitive accumulation because of the Turkish policy of forcing the sale of goods to the Porte at "ridiculous prices," which Pătrăşcanu termed "the trade of plunder."[108]

In observing that Dobrogeanu-Gherea had judged that the new regime reached its culmination with the reforms of 1864, Pătrăşcanu asked why there had been no peasant revolt immediately or in 1872, when a law was introduced that forced peasants to accept labor contracts *manu militari*, of which Gherea had made so much. Significantly, there had been no peasant revolt until 1888, and the most important rebellion came almost two decades later, in 1907.[109] The explanation of this anomaly for Pătrăşcanu was not *neoiobăgia*, Dobrogeanu-Gherea's hybrid and monstrous system, but the penetration of capitalism into the countryside,[110] the pace of which increased rapidly after 1880, and especially with the new century.[111] Yet extensive leasing as well as the spread of wage labor showed that capitalism had already begun to affect Rumanian agriculture in the nineteenth century.[112] Capitalism retained strong traces of the *iobag* regime, and the articulation, or, in Pătrăşcanu's phrase, the "weaving together of new and old forms of exploitation, of different relations of production," deepened social conflict and ultimately gave it a more violent form.[113] This was different from Gherea's *neoiobăgia* because the latter was not the product of an all-conquering capitalism but a uniquely articulated mode of production.

Pătrăşcanu adduced statistical evidence showing that industrial production in Rumania's large factories had accelerated in the 1880s and then again in the prewar years of the current century. The number of manufacturing firms organized as joint stock concerns also grew rapidly from 1903 to 1913.[114] The growth of large industry and large banking also increased the differences in income between city and village, at the expense of the latter.[115] Even in agriculture, despite Şerban Voinea's denial, capitalist labor relations had made great strides, asserted Pătrăşcanu.[116] Not only had wage labor made extensive gains in Moldavia in particular by the early twentieth century, but another important source of evidence of the advance of capitalism in the countryside, tenancy based on cash rents, was widely replacing the *dijmă* (sharecropping). Some 62 percent of the agricultural properties in Moldavia (circa 1907?) were leased to tenant farmers or corporations.[117]

For Pătrăşcanu, the complex of causes associated with the rise of modern capitalism in the late nineteenth and early twentieth centuries offered the central explanation of the peasant uprisings of 1888 and 1907. Nor was Rumania's history unique. The Russian rural movements of 1905–7 had similar causes, as did rural dimensions of the October Revolution; both experiences were related to the growth of Russian industry.[118] Zeletin was wrong in his judgment that the peasant uprisings were reactionary. Rather, said Pătrăşcanu, they were progressive because, by the period in question, the only two progressive classes were workers and peasants. Although the beginning of the 1907 rebellion in Moldavia had anti-Semitic elements, peasants, argued Pătrăşcanu, principally rose up against the latifundium and labor contracts, as well as demanding the right of suffrage.[119] Yet peasants could never seize the initiative in the political process, Pătrăşcanu held,[120] and they required working-class and socialist leadership for success. But workers and their socialist allies had not responded adequately to the challenge in

1907: Dobrogeanu-Gherea and Racovski had even opposed the peasant uprising, and peasants' demand for land and the vote were supported only by worker organizations during the summer of 1907—after the revolt had been crushed.[121]

The Rumanian bourgeoisie was far from being a progressive class by the twentieth century, Pătrăşcanu judged. This was the case for three reasons. First, if the peasantry had been turned into consumers of industrial goods, the Rumanian bourgeoisie would not greatly have benefited because the latter class was able to meet only a small share of the domestic demand for industrial products.[122] Second, the Rumanian bourgeoisie itself now contained a large number of rural property owners. After 1881 the Liberal Party had alienated public lands, often to bourgeois purchasers. Finally, the national bourgeoisie was ideologically constrained in opposing large estates because of its belief in the "sacred rights of property" and the related struggle against the Socialists.[123] Consequently, the . development of capitalism in Rumania from 1864 to 1907 had strengthened the national bourgeoisie to the point that it had achieved political preponderance, but that class was no longer a progressive force: such a role had ended in 1848.[124]

Pătrăşcanu struck an intermediate position between those of Gherea and Zeletin on the degree to which Marxism had to be adapted to explain the peculiar features of Rumanian development. Gherea had adapted Marxism the most, while Zeletin had argued for a rather mechanical reproduction of Marxist stages of development of backward countries like Rumania.[125] His stages referred not to the capitalist system but to individual countries. Unlike Zeletin, Pătrăşcanu, as a militant in the Rumanian Communist Party in a time of war and upheaval, did not foresee a long period of bourgeois domination. Rather, by the middle of World War II he was calling for a "bourgeois-democratic" revolution, which required further land reform, including the expropriation of properties over 50 hectares,[126] nationalization of Rumanian banks, an effectively enforced eight-hour day for workers (long championed by the International Labor Office), and, in foreign policy, a close association with the USSR.[127]

Pătrăşcanu's other most important work was *Basic Problems of Rumania*, written when he was under house arrest in 1942–43 without access to Marxist works[128] and published the following year. His access to other sources was limited by his incarceration, and Pătrăşcanu chiefly relied for his data, though not his interpretations, on the leading economic history of the twentieth century, Virgil Madgearu's *Evolution of the Rumanian Economy After the World War* (1940).[129] Did Rumania at the time have a capitalist economic system? For Pătrăşcanu, capitalism was defined not by profits or rent but, as Marx had stated, by a wage-labor regime, in which the majority of the working population, separated from the means of production, sold their labor power as a commodity on the market.[130]

If this was the standard, Pătrăşcanu had to confront the fact that the majority of the labor force in the Rumania of the early 1940s was still rural. Pătrăşcanu argued that the agrarian reform of 1918–21, whose purpose had been to further the advance of capitalism,[131] had been severely limited. The 1930 census revealed that large properties (over 50 hectares) still constituted 32 percent of the private rural property and 18 percent of the arable land.[132] Moreover, using a monograph of the Gusti school (for Dîmbovnicul), Pătrăşcanu asserted that *iobăgie* still existed in Rumania in the 1940s, in the form of corvée labor.[133] Nonetheless, using the calculations of Roman Cresin, a leading young agricultural economist, Pătrăşcanu estimated that 40 percent of the labor in Rumanian agriculture was paid wages of some sort. Going beyond the evidence, Pătrăşcanu held that virtually all medium and large properties used wage labor.[134] The author also argued that monographic village studies showed that, contrary to Sombart's generalization,[135] and consistent with Marx's predictions, there existed a tendency toward the concentration of agricultural property in Rumania into fewer hands. Cresin's researches had established that the number of propertyless peasants had increased during the Depression from 464,000 in 1930 to 740,000 in 1936.[136] Almost half the peasants with one to three hectares had no oxen to work their lands and therefore should be considered proletarians, Pătrăşcanu argued.[137] Over half the peasants with property had fewer than three hectares. This amount of land was too small for subsistence, and another 20 percent had only three to five hectares, which, in Pătrăşcanu's opinion, did not free them from the need for "supplementary income." Therefore, he reasoned, some three-fourths of the peasants had to seek incomes outside their family plots by selling their labor power.[138] The noncapitalist sector of agriculture formed a reserve of labor power for the capitalist sector.[139] Thus Pătrăşcanu disputed the views of Madgearu and other Peasantists,[140] who had argued that the typical form of agricultural organization in Rumania was the noncapitalist family plot. Pătrăşcanu conceded that Rumanian agriculture as a whole was a mix of capitalist and precapitalist relations of production. Their coexistence still distinguished the Rumanian economy from those of Western capitalist nations.[141]

As a Marxist-Leninist, Pătrăşcanu rejected the assumption that concerned so many social scientists of his time and later—the notion of absolute rural overpopulation. A relative overpopulation, he held, was caused by the incompleteness of the 1918–21 agrarian reform; the mixture of capitalist and precapitalist forms of labor exploitation; and the extensive use of female and child labor in agriculture, which had created a degree of unemployment among the adult male population.[142] For the sorry state of agriculture, Pătrăşcanu also blamed the behavior of the relatively monopolized industrial sector, pointing out that industrial prices from 1916 to the early 1940s had risen twice as fast as agricultural prices. Thus peasant farmers could not afford to modernize their capital equipment.[143]

Agricultural credit, the very existence of which was a sign of capitalist development, was increasingly dominated by the commercial banks (rather than state-sponsored credit institutions): 43 percent of peasant debts in 1934 were owed to private banks. Such credit, in the present stage of capitalism directed by finance capital, had become a means of expropriating the peasantry.[144] Even so-called state aid to agriculture in the 1930s, which had taken the form of supporting grain prices, had helped the large farmer rather than the small peasant, who usually did not produce commercial grain.[145] Pătrăşcanu saw the rural population as increasingly divided into a mass of wage laborers and small groups of kulak farmers—the *chiaburime*—whose existence he believed gave the lie to the article of faith of the Peasantists that the peasantry constituted a single class. The political movement *Ţărănismul* (Peasantism), believed Pătrăşcanu, represented the non-financial sectors of the bourgeoisie—the financial element being associated with the Liberal Party from the nineteenth century—and in particular the bourgeoisie of the villages, the *chiaburime*.[146]

Pătrăşcanu also offered an explanation of the development and current situation of the urban bourgeoisie, a group he argued had developed out of commercial and usury capital. The bourgeoisie's efforts to form a state in 1821 and 1848 had not been strong enough to overthrow the old regime, and the state that arose in the third quarter of the century represented a compromise between the bourgeoisie and "large property." Furthermore, even in the twentieth century the bourgeoisie had a large (and presumably growing) agrarian component in the *chiaburime*.[147] Pătrăşcanu believed that although Rumanian capitalism and its attendant bourgeoisie had many special characteristics, by and large the two phenomena fitted into the evolution of European capitalism in the imperialist (and monopolist) phase, as analyzed by Hilferding and Lenin.[148]

To Dobrogeanu-Gherea and Lothar Rădăceanu, who argued that Rumania had been dominated by a state-associated "oligarchy," Pătrăşcanu replied that Rădăceanu had offered no consistent definition of oligarchy. The mistake of Gherea, on whom Rădăceanu had depended, derived from his faulty analysis in *Neoiobăgia*: if capitalism as such did not exist in Rumania, it was logical to deny the existence of a bourgeoisie. Therefore, wrote Pătrăşcanu, an "oligarchy" had to be invented—an entity that did not exist in the modern history of any European country. Gherea, the Communist theorist asserted, had confused the ruling class with its political apparatus. The latter need not be—and in contemporary history usually was not—composed of owners of large capital; rather, it was composed of "specialists"—lawyers, economists, journalists, and other professionals.[149]

In the age of liberalism, the international bourgeoisie had been liberal and relatively progressive. But in the monopolist and imperialist age of capitalism, that class had become reactionary and currently supported fascism, stated Pătrăşcanu. The Rumanian bourgeoisie had followed the same trends, especially after World War I. Gherea's incorrect interpretation had led later Social Democrats to the wrong practical conclusions—namely, reformist tactics and collaborationism with King Carol's dictatorship (established in February 1938) as an anti-oligarchic force.[150] In Rumanian capitalism, by the 1930s the driving force in the industrialization effort had been the state, Pătrăşcanu reasoned.[151] The tariff level of 1938 under the newly installed dictatorship was eight and a half times greater than the level of the National Peasants' tariff schedule of 1929. The state was deliberately creating monopolies, and after 1933 it had become not only the chief purchaser of industrial goods but the leading financier of industry as well.[152]

State intervention, asserted Pătrăşcanu, was a "natural phenomenon" in the monopolist phase of capitalist development.[153] Using Madgearu's data, Pătrăşcanu demonstrated that in the 1930s there had been a rising degree of concentration and centralization of capital in the larger industrial firms, as well as a diminution of wages from 1929 to 1942, on the order of 30 percent. A similar tendency toward concentration had occurred in banking; the number of banks had fallen from 1,000 in 1929 to fewer than 500 in 1939, a trend that had continued into the 1940s.[154] Manufacturing had grown rapidly in the Depression decade, especially in state-assisted heavy industry. Steel production, for example, had more than doubled between 1929 and 1939, reaching 266,000 tons in the latter year, and had doubled again in 1942–43.[155] Yet the purchasing power of the masses had fallen during the 1930s, and manufactured imports had declined from 34 percent of the total value consumed to 8 percent in 1938.[156] The size of the industrial proletariat per se had been about 0.8 million in 1930, or nearly 8 percent of the 10.5 million population; it had risen to 10 or 11 percent by the early 1940s, Pătrăşcanu estimated.[157]

The association of state, finance capital, and heavy industry was the economic foundation of the dictatorial regime of Carol II after 1938, Pătrăşcanu believed. In *Under Three Dictatorships* he wrote that the Brătianu family, which had dominated the Liberal Party and the Bancă Românească, had not been able to control the metallurgical industry—in particular, the Uzinele Malaxa, which depended on the state-associated Bancă Naţională,[158] no longer under Liberal control after 1929. The heavy industry group was behind Carol's coup in 1938, Pătrăşcanu thought, inaugurating a royal and corporatist dictatorship.[159] The metallurgical industry, inefficient compared to foreign competitors, required state support to be profitable, and the state consumed 70 percent of its output, chiefly for armaments, in 1937–38.[160] Thus the dictatorship was related to a division within the bourgeoisie because the privately owned firms that depended on metallurgical inputs did not want to pay the high prices of the domestic suppliers.[161] Meanwhile, the armaments industry had achieved fantastic rates of profit, up to 910 percent per annum![162] King Carol himself had a large personal investment in metallurgy, owning 30 to 35 percent of the stock of Malaxa.[163] Large rural property owners also supported the dictatorship, thought Pătrăşcanu, because of its grain subsidies, but they were less powerful than the subsidized industrialists.[164]

To explain Rumania's territorial expansion into the USSR consequent on the German invasion of June 1941, Pătrăşcanu argued that economically driven imperialist tendencies had characterized Rumanian capitalist development by 1940 and had not been peculiar to the Great Powers.[165] Among other things, by the

4

Dualism and Neopopulism

The idea of a dual economy—a modern urban, industrial sector connected with overseas commerce and finance, and a largely passive peasant sector, failing to adapt to changing international conditions—was by no means a concern of Marxists alone. It was seen as *the* problem of Rumanian development in the 1930s by social scientists of all persuasions. The "scissors" that had opened between agricultural and industrial prices in the 1920s yawned wider in the 1930s, and the peasant tumbled further, and even hopelessly, into debt. In 1932, according to official statistics, 64 percent of peasant cultivators were debtors.[1] That year the Rumanian parliament tried to relieve peasants' distress by writing off 50 percent of their debts and converting the other 50 percent into 30-year bonds at 4 percent interest, to replace usurers' rates up to ten times higher. But urban debtors soon demanded similar treatment, and credit dried up immediately. Banks turned to the Bancă Naţională, which was unable to compensate commercial banks for their losses.[2]

The plight of the peasantry had been noted by Gherea's generation, and land reform following World War I had not solved its economic problems. The Rumanians' discovery of economic dualism was part of a much broader concern of social scientists with the coexistence and interpenetration of modern capitalism and a variety of precapitalist economic elements and systems. To locate the Rumanian debate, we must first consider the problem of dualism in the context of economic theory.

After World War II the notion of economic and sociological dualism became a major tenet of development economics, but its first important theorist had done most of his work earlier. This was Julius H. Boeke, the Dutch economist whose work on dualism in the Dutch East Indies began with his dissertation of 1910, the same year that Dobrogeanu-Gherea published *Neoserfdom*. But Boeke's most influential works (in English, rather than Dutch) appeared between 1942 and 1953. His conclusions were supported empirically by the work of J. S.

Furnivall, who expanded Boeke's notion of dualism in a sociological direction, using the term "plural society," which sociologists now sometimes call "segmentation."[3] Boeke held that neoclassical economics was culture-bound, and its putative laws did not hold in non-Western settings. In particular, colonial peasants would not respond to the stimulus of the price mechanism, which was the foundation of the capitalist system. For various cultural reasons, non-Western peasants preferred leisure to economic gain, at least above a certain level of income. In neoclassical language, employers faced a rigidly inelastic labor supply, intelligible as a situation of backward-sloping labor supply curves. Above a given wage level, precapitalist laborers would simply choose to maximize leisure rather than income.[4] Boeke's version of dualism has found little favor in recent decades—it has been challenged at theoretical and empirical levels[5]—and a much more widely accepted view is associated with the work of W. Arthur Lewis, who theorized in 1954 an "infinitely elastic supply of labor" that would pass from the traditional agricultural sector to the modern sector, industrial or otherwise, at a given wage. The problem was to create sufficient employment in areas with higher productivities to drain traditional agriculture of its redundant labor until wages there approximated those of the modern sector(s).[6]

The intuitive notion of dualism in technology, lifestyles, and standards of living was already a commonplace in underdeveloped countries before World War II, and some writers saw strong links between the traditional and modern economies, while others did not. If strong links were hypothesized, they were sometimes seen as exploitative, as in Gherea's *neoiobag* regime.[7] In Rumania, the relationship between leading and lagging sectors was interpreted in a variety of ways, but Rumanian writers tended to view the connection as feeble, absent, or exploitative. Even Mihail Manoilescu, who advocated strengthening ties between city and village by siphoning off surplus agricultural labor to manufacturing industry, believed trading agricultural for industrial goods exploited agricultural producers, until such time as wages rose in peasant agriculture.

A dualist view of Rumanian society could already be found in the works of nineteenth-century writers, as the nation's capital, Bucharest—"the Paris of the Balkans"—underwent rapid growth and Westernization.[8] We have seen that an explanation of dualism at a philosophical level, pointing up the superficiality of the modern sector, had been developed by Titu Maiorescu and the Junimea school from 1863. Dobrogeanu-Gherea had adapted the Junimean view to hypothesize a Marxian law, whereby dualism was explained by the tendency of backward countries to modernize the superstructure before the base, combined with a grisly interaction between feudal and capitalist social relations at the material level—the worst of both worlds for the peasant. Subsequently, Zeletin, in noting the huge gap between traditional and modern Rumania, held that the relationship, however exploitative, was part of the normal, rather than an abnormal, passage from backwardness to capitalist modernity.

The spread between the incomes in the agrarian and urban economies diminished with the Rumanian land reform of 1918–21 but then intensified with the price-scissors issue in the 1930s, when the dual economy issue again came to the fore. Looking back on the Depression decade, Gheorghe Ionescu-Şişteşi, who had directed the Institute of Agronomic Research and had served as minister of agriculture in several governments during the 1930s, noted how sharply the domestic terms of trade had turned against agriculture from the eve of the First World War to the Second: in 1940 it took 2.3 times as many kilos of corn to buy the same bundle of 26 manufactured goods as in 1913 and 2.6 times the amount of wheat.[9] A British observer, Hugh Seton-Watson, noted in the same year that "great indignation is caused by the glaring contrast between the wealth of the large cities, particularly Bucharest, and of the upper section of the ruling class, and the misery of the majority of the people. Bucharest is not so wealthy as a Western capital, but Western capitals are not surrounded by villages whose inhabitants eat only *mămăligă* [corn mush] and are inadequately clad."[10]

Throughout the decade of the Great Depression social scientists tried to analyze the problem. In 1934 the economist Constantin Ianculescu had seen an alarming prospect in the combination of agricultural minifundization and a population growth rate of 1.5 percent a year. The consequences, he believed, would be evident within a generation. "A permanently unemployed agrarian proletariat will be created, giving birth to the gravest social questions," wrote Ianculescu, foreseeing huge numbers of unemployed peasants drifting toward the cities. His solution was industrialization.[11] The demographer Sabin Manuilă agreed with the solution but believed that peasants should not be rushed to the cities unprepared. Idle rural groups should be sent first to "semiurban" centers, where agricultural products could be industrialized.[12]

Mihai Popa-Vereş in 1938 thought that the country's economic dualism, in which the village was subordinated to the city, had begun with the penetration of Western capitalism after the Treaty of Adrianople (1829)—a commonly held, if erroneous, view.[13] For Popa-Vereş, dualism had become "blatant" after the tariff law of 1886, ushering in a period of industrial protectionism. The lack of an organic relationship between city and village (countryside) had allowed foreign companies to take over the grain trade, he implied. The city remained hegemonic with a per capita income four times higher than in the rural zone.[14] The basic problem was the antagonism between the capitalist "spirit" (apparently in Werner Sombart's sense),[15] based on a quest for profit, and that of a primitive, self-sufficient, and fossilized peasant culture. But this "economic dualism"—a phrase Popa-Vereş specifically employed—required the transformation of the village:[16] the solution was to make the whole economy a modern capitalist system.

Mihail Manoilescu, whose consideration of the problem of dualism is treated at greater length in Chapter 6, was as pessimistic as any about the course of economic events for the villages during the decade of the Depression. As a result of the prolonged crisis, he saw emerging a new city-to-city system of exchange in Rumania that virtually excluded the village economy. In this matter Manoilescu seemed to approach a Boekean view.[17] He later wrote, following Ernst Wagemann's *New Balkans*, that in the classic progression for an economy's focus on subsistence to domestic market to foreign market, Rumania had skipped the middle stage and therefore had not experienced an intensive exchange between city and rural areas (villages) historically, nor did such an organic relation exist at the time of publication (1944).[18]

The school that dealt most directly with the gulf between town and city and made rural development its central concern was a new version of populism. The transformation of populism into a more modern doctrine in the face of an advancing capitalism in Rumania occurred after a number of structural changes had shaken the country. Most important of these was the land reform at the end of the world war. Despite its incompleteness, peasants as a whole benefited significantly from the division of the great estates, and if grain exports declined, it was partly because peasant food consumption rose.[19] Though land reform figures vary significantly in the literature, one leading authority estimated that in the postwar reform through 1927, the government, driven in part by fear of the Soviet example, took or legalized the seizure of six million hectares from landlords, offering near-nominal compensation. Peasant holdings of arable land, including minifundia, rose from 60 to 90 percent of the total.[20]

The enfranchisement of peasants, before 1919 limited to indirect elections, linked various forms of populism to mass politics; in 1926 the Peasant Party of the Old Kingdom merged with the Rumanian National Party of Transylvania to form the National Peasant Party. The new organization soon replaced the National Liberal Party as the most important party for the remainder of the interwar period. Indeed, "peasantism" throughout East Central Europe became the politics of the masses.[21] There was in addition a "Green International" of peasant-based parties in the region, though it had little effect on domestic politics in Rumania.[22]

At the level of economic analysis, in Europe at large, the behavior of the peasant in a traditional economy increasingly transformed by capitalism had been a problem for both Marxist and neoclassical economists at the turn of the century. Why did the peasant not respond "correctly" to price signals, as a profit maximizer and loss minimizer? Despite advancing proletarianization in the countryside, why did the peasant farm not cease to exist, according to Marx's laws of the concentration and centralization of capital, which seemed confirmed by the behavior of the industrial sector of the advanced capitalist countries after 1880?

In *The Agrarian Question* Karl Kautsky, the Marxist authority whom Stere had cited triumphantly to buttress his case for populism, had conceded to Sombart that small farms were not disappearing and large estates were not expand-

ing in the German countryside.[23] But otherwise Kautsky remained an orthodox Marxist and demonstrated how capitalism had revolutionized agriculture,
though in less straightforward ways than industry. This fact owed, in part, to the
phenomenon of differential (Ricardian) rent, Kautsky held, making some farms
inherently more productive than others, and thus the tendency toward an equalization of the profit rate present in industry did not apply to agriculture.[24] Further, argued Kautsky, the peasant was willing to engage in superexploitation of
his own and his family's labor and to decrease his consumption below a level a
hired laborer would accept. The peasant cultivator, unlike the capitalist, did not
consider labor expended on production for personal consumption a cost.[25] The
expansion of large holdings was limited by estate owners' need for small holdings
to obtain and reproduce labor power. The number of large and small farms
tended toward stability precisely because large farms were labor-intensive, and
their size was limited by the availability of rural labor.[26] Kautsky believed that if
employment opportunities were limited to the self-employed peasant sector,
peasants would limit the size of their families. But if opportunities existed to
work outside the farm, they would not, and larger numbers would stimulate the
process of proletarianization.[27] Publishing in 1899, the same year as Lenin's *Development of Capitalism in Russia* appeared, Kautsky believed the vast majority
of German peasants were already proletarians or semiproletarians selling labor
power.[28]

The study of the peasant economy was most significantly advanced in the
1920s by the Russian theorist Alexander V. Chayanov, whose works in German
were probably more influential in Rumania than his Russian writings.[29] Chayanov's guiding hypothesis in analyzing the peasant family's economic behavior was
the effort to balance consumption (the satisfaction of family needs) against the
"drudgery" of farm labor.[30] In other words, the peasant tried to achieve a psychological balance between a maximization of income and a maximization of leisure
(or a minimization of drudgery), a notion analogous to Boeke's, emphasizing
peasant efforts to maintain traditional or "normal" standards of living. Like Kautsky, Chayanov believed peasants did not consider labor an implicit cost and
would sometimes engage in a degree of superexploitation of self and family to
maintain a given level of income. In years of a bad harvest, they might also seek
other employment. "As a result," wrote Chayanov, "we have the situation—
normal for Russia but paradoxical from a Western viewpoint—in which periods
of high grain prices are, at the same time, periods of low wages."[31] Chayanov was
especially interested in explaining demographic cycles of the peasant family.
Based on empirical research in Russia, he believed that economic activity and the
amount of labor expended depended less on profitability (the key to capitalist
production) than on family size and the above-mentioned balance between satis-
fying consumption demands and "the drudgery of labor."[32] He further argued
that economic differentiation among peasants was due more to the moment in

the family demographic cycle than to petty capitalist accumulation by "kulaks," the thesis then prevalent in the USSR.[33]

Chayanov's investigations and theories, often called "neopopulism," became important in postwar development economics after an anthology of his writings was published in English in 1966;[34] but his work had important reverberations in interwar East Central Europe, where economists were studying the low productivity, overpopulation, and underemployment in the countryside.[35] Local economists were carrying out similar studies, some of them writing before the publication of Chayanov's major works, or apparently unaware of the Russian economist's contributions. In Poland, as early as 1917 Leon Biegeleisen showed that across a variety of countries small farms had higher net revenues per hectare than larger farms.[36] The Polish National Institute of Rural Economy in the 1920s found a negative profit level for small farms, consistent with Chayanov's explanation. Some Polish researchers tried to model the behavior of the peasant farmers independently of Chayanov's work. The Polish school, like Chayanov, "stressed the elasticity and adaptability of peasant farms." The Poles, however, focused on overpopulation (as opposed to the demographic cycle) more than Chayanov had because of the greater man-land ratio in Poland than in the Soviet Union. Further, several Polish economists tried to establish how many peasants could leave farming without a decrease in total output.[37] Similar researches on the peasant economy were being conducted throughout East Central Europe.[38] Even in relatively backward Bulgaria, detailed empirical studies of peasant behavior were conducted in the interwar period, and Chayanov's work was used. Bulgarian agronomists and economists also tried to estimate the economically nugatory agricultural labor force, which amounted to 37 percent in 1926 and 46 percent in 1935, according to one study.[39]

In Rumania, the interwar period was rich in studies of peasant culture and economy—a project at the core of a rapidly developing social science tradition.[40] Most impressive of the approaches to peasant issues was Dimitrie Gusti's "monographic" school, which in the 1920s and 1930s sent multidisciplinary teams of researchers to live in representative villages to study all aspects of peasant life, including household budgets and other aspects of peasant economy.[41] Gusti had trained with Wilhelm Wundt, Karl Bücher, and Gustav von Schmoller in Germany, where he took his Ph.D. at Leipzig, and had also studied with Emile Durkheim in Paris.[42] Gusti founded Rumania's leading intellectual journal of the period, *Studies in [Social] Science and Social Reform*[43] in 1919 and in the 1930s was able to obtain King Carol's patronage for his group's researches. Using methods devised by Ernst Engel, Frédéric Le Play, Ernst Laur, and Chayanov, Gusti and his students tried to determine to what extent the local peasant economy in a given region was capitalist, "natural" (subsistence-oriented), or mixed, studying both money budgets and those in kind, for whole villages.[44] Among the many impressive publications of the Gusti group, especially for its breadth, was the five-volume *60 Rumanian Villages*, directed by Anton Golopenția and D. C. Georgescu.[45]

Like Poland, Rumania had an official Agronomic Research Institute which undertook economic studies. A member of the institute, Nicolae Cornăţeanu, defended peasant holdings in 1935 with the results of a survey that showed the superior productivity of small plots. He conceded, however, that if labor had been accounted for in capitalist terms, peasant income would be negative in much of the country.[46] In fact, the method Cornăţeanu had used excluded any imputed cost of (unpaid) labor by the peasant and his family.[47]

Most studies were more pessimistic. Even before the Great Depression, a Ministry of Agriculture researcher, Constant Niţescu, published detailed budget studies of peasant households for 1925 in Vlaşca (a county near Bucharest); he concluded that if imputed costs and consumption of the goods produced were taken into account, most peasant families had negative incomes.[48] A work based on peasant budgets for 1934–35 pointed out that the farmers in question sought nonfarm employment because their minifundia were incapable of sustaining their families anywhere near the level of income of domestic servants in Bucharest.[49] And the broadly based collection *60 Rumanian Villages* was likewise pessimistic that poor peasants could sustain their modest level of consumption on the produce of their holdings. In that work, P. Stănculescu and C. Ştefănescu concluded that of the poorest landowning peasant families (defined as those who held 3 or fewer hectares), 86 percent consumed more than they produced on their minifundia; of families with 3.1 to 5 hectares, 70 percent consumed more, and even of those with 10.1 to 20 hectares, 41 percent lived beyond what they could produce on their farms.[50] Thus many supplemented, or received the bulk of their income as agricultural laborers or craftsmen.

As in Bulgaria, Poland, and elsewhere in East Central Europe, in Rumania there was much concern with labor redundancy in agriculture—a concept which in the development literature after World War II would be known as "disguised unemployment." This term entered Western economics in 1936, when the Cambridge economist Joan Robinson defined disguised unemployment as "the adoption of inferior occupations [in terms of productivity] by dismissed [industrial] workers." She gave several examples, such as "selling match-boxes," "cutting brushwood," and "digging potatoes."[51] When the term was used in the postwar development literature, the same types of jobs were mentioned, and the idea was attributed to Robinson, but the men and women who took such jobs were by no means moving from higher to lower productivities. Therefore, the concept of disguised unemployment in the economic development literature was related to Robinson's but was a distinct idea. Furthermore, although the British economist coined the phrase that later took on a new meaning, she did not originate the concept in the postwar sense.

In fact, the notion of disguised unemployment in East Central Europe goes back to the late 1920s.[52] A similar notion, "organic unemployment," was also present in the colonial economics of India and Indonesia at the time.[53] The first use of the term "disguised unemployment" in English in the postwar sense was probably that of Michal Kalecki, in a review of the German edition of Mihail Manoilescu's *Theory of Protectionism* in 1938. The Polish economist wrote that "in an agricultural country there is some unemployment, manifest or disguised."[54] In any event, not only the idea but the attempt to operationalize the concept is clearly present in the Rumanian literature in the 1930s.

At least for one author in the Depression years, the concern with disguised unemployment was a reaction to the crisis of unemployment of the West, whose travail was well publicized in international press reports. In 1933 the engineer Grigore Manoilescu, brother of the economist Mihail, argued that the notion of unemployment in Rumania had to be defined differently from that in the West, where it was based on rigidities induced by formal labor contracts.[55] Grigore Manoilescu alleged that there existed "hidden unemployment" in the state bureaucracy and even commerce and industry, but above all in Rumanian agriculture. He reasoned that there were eight million men and women in rural areas between 15 and 60 years of age to work 13.6 million hectares of arable land. If one agricultural worker could work four hectares a year (the prewar and premechanization estimate for Germany), only 3.4 million people were required, and 4.6 million were therefore nugatory—58 percent![56] Though Rumania did not have the overt unemployment of the Western countries, its true situation was just as grave because unemployment was "chronic and structural. . . . It is hidden in millions of people who are inadequately nourished, badly clothed, and who live in miserable dwellings," wrote Manoilescu.[57] Nor was Grigore Manoilescu alone in his dismal assessment of rural employment. In 1935 Aurel Frunzănescu estimated that only 44 percent of the manpower in Rumanian agriculture was used efficiently and that, even if all auxiliary activities were considered, less than 55 percent of the annual work days in agriculture were spent productively.[58]

The economist who exercised the greatest influence at the policy level regarding these issues was also the man who had introduced Chayanov into the Rumanian debate on the peasantry. Virgil Madgearu discussed the Russian's theories in 1925 in his journal *Independenţa Economică* (Economic independence).[59] Madgearu, the son of a merchant at the grain port of Galaţi, took his doctorate at Leipzig with Bücher in 1911. A professor at the Academy of Commercial [later Economic] Sciences, Madgearu was from 1919 to 1929 the secretary-general of the Institutul Social Romîn (Rumanian Institute of Social Science), with which Dimitrie Gusti and other leading social scientists were associated. Madgearu also became the secretary-general and theoretician of the National Peasant Party. He was a ranking Rumanian politician in the 1920s and 1930s, during with time he repeatedly held ministerial posts. In his policies as well as his theories Madgearu was an eclectic, unlike the doctrinaire if inconsistent Mihail Manoilescu.[60] Madgearu is best remembered by scholars today for his now-classic work, *The Evolution of the Rumanian Economy After the World War*.[61] In this scholarly study, Madgearu offered evidence in support for his Peasantist view of economic policy, pointing out that in a decade of rapid industrialization, 1928–38, industry had absorbed only one-twelfth of the annual surplus of peasant laborers.[62]

In 1930 Virgil Madgearu was instrumental in organizing the Agrarian Bloc, a coalition of East Central European countries that attempted to form a "counter-monopoly" against Western industrial exporters, to induce the latter, through the League of Nations and other means, to grant preferential prices and quotas against "overseas" (and lower-cost) suppliers. In September of that year Madgearu made the Bloc's case at Geneva for a preferential regime, and a permanent secretariat was established at Bucharest in October. At its peak in the early 1930s, the Bloc consisted of ten countries, but its efforts ultimately failed, as did those of the major overseas producers to control grain output and prices during the Depression years.[63] The Agrarian Bloc was a forerunner of Third World attempts in the postwar period to organize markets, and the League of Nations was perforce the independent agrarian states' best, though inadequate, surrogate for a series of UN agencies and commodity cartels that would be more responsive to Third World voices.[64]

At the level of production, the nature of the peasantry as a social class presented a thorny issue for Marxist and non-Marxist alike—not only in Rumania but universally—a fact to which Teodor Shanin alludes in the title of his Chayanov-influenced study, *The Awkward Class*.[65] According to *A Dictionary of Marxist Thought*, a peasantry by definition has access to the means of production (implements and land) and is thus distinct from an agricultural proletariat (composed of wage laborers) and also distinct from serfs, who are subject to extraeconomic coercion. A peasantry by this definition, however, "must pay a rent or a tribute to maintain its possession of the land," in labor, kind, or money.[66] A farmer who was proprietor of his land in this scheme would be a petit bourgeois, not a peasant. But the owner of a minifundium, so common in Rumania, was often worse off than the rural proletarian and was certainly not a bourgeois. Furthermore, Marx himself—for instance in his notorious comments on the peasantry in *The Eighteenth Brumaire of Louis Napoleon*—explicitly included small landholders in his harsh judgments.[67] At all events, owners of minifundia and small plots are considered peasants in this discussion.

For Virgil Madgearu and the Rumanian Peasantists, the peasant economy based on petty commodity production organized by family units did not involve an internal differentiation of the peasantry because, as Chayanov argued, the family demographic cycle tended to keep differences in wealth from becoming extreme—a view sharply at odds with Lenin's *Development of Capitalism in Russia* (see chap. 3 above). As a Rumanian Marxist scholar later put it, the Marxist view—more precisely, the Leninist view—held that the peasantry was a "conglomeration" of classes with contradictory interests.[68] But Madgearu and his National Peasantists followed Chayanov in arguing that the demographic cycle would keep the peasantry relatively undifferentiated over time; they denied, at least partly for political reasons, that the post-land reform peasantry was becoming stratified into a kulak class (*chiaburime*) and a far larger rural proletarian mass. That is, the National Peasantists defined the peasantry as a single class.

Peasantism in Rumania as a doctrine was associated not only with Chayanovian neopopulism but also with a form of corporatism. For the more extreme enthusiasts in Madgearu's National Peasant Party, *ţărănismul* (Peasantism) in a programmatic sense meant that a society in which the vast majority of the population were peasants who (allegedly) worked their land as a family should have a "Peasant State." This state would intervene in agricultural markets to provide stable and high prices for their goods, as well as cheap credit to peasants. Interestingly, at least two Peasantist writers claimed not to oppose the development of industry but only to seek a more just relationship between industrial and agricultural prices.[69] Like the prewar agricultural oligarchy, an artificial industrial class (growing out of one sector of the rural oligarchy) was now exploiting the peasants, alleged Ion Scutaru for the Peasantists, through high industrial prices.[70] In the Peasant State, cooperativism and solidarism (presumably in Léon Bourgeois's sense) would free the peasant from the capitalist exploitation inherent in the "individualist" bourgeois state.[71] For Scutaru, group interests in the Peasant State would prevail over those of the individual, and class collaboration would replace class conflict. As in Mihail Manoilescu's vision of corporatism, the Peasant State would pursue a policy of Rumanianization of industrial property, which, among other things, had anti-Semitic implications.[72]

Lucreţiu Pătrăşcanu, the leading Communist authority of the period, noted that such projections for the sweeping beneficent effects of a new political regime were not unique; Hitler had made similar claims about the Nazi state, and Pătrăşcanu argued sensibly enough that Fascist Italy and Nazi Germany did not have new states because they did not represent new relations among social classes. In a like manner, he inferred, class relations under a Peasant State would not change either.[73]

Rumanian Peasantism in its several forms did not contribute significantly to theoretical explanations, at least in economics, and was probably more derivative than studies in Poland. It is interesting that the concept of a peasant mode of production—implicit in Chayanov's work and a tenable implication of the view that the peasantry was a unified class—was not pursued. But important and high-quality empirical studies were undertaken in Rumania; furthermore, the idea of disguised unemployment in agriculture was developed in such a way that it clearly anticipates the postwar usage in the Third World proper, with the implication that idle peasant labor should be transferred to industrial or other high-productivity activities.

On the concept of disguised un- or underemployment, one of the founders of modern development theory, Paul Rosenstein-Rodan, has written, "Since the 1940's, [the thesis of underemployment in agriculture] has been made one of the cornerstones of the theory of development of underdeveloped countries."[74] Yet the proposition has generated great controversy in the postwar era, and Doreen Warriner, a British economist who emphasized the importance of disguised unemployment in the agriculture of East Central Europe between the wars, subsequently modified her views. In the introduction to the second edition of *The Economics of Peasant Farming* (1964), she states that the studies of the interwar years (including her own), focusing on man-days of labor per year, considerably overestimated labor redundancy in peasant agriculture by failing adequately to take into account the seasonality of farm work. Thus, in an extreme case, if 230 man-days are needed per year, but must be worked in three months, three men, not one, will be needed. Warriner did not try to reestimate redundancy, and this caveat on her earlier work implicitly assumes little labor mobility in agriculture. In retrospect, the author believed that her calculations incorrectly focused on disguised unemployment and ignored the more important long-term fall in output per head in agriculture. This led to an exclusive emphasis on industrialization, as opposed to focusing on the productivity issue—raising output per farmer.[75]

At a theoretical level, Gunnar Myrdal has argued that the idea of agricultural underemployment rests on several unrealistic assumptions: that all idleness is involuntary, that "the labor input of those who remain in agriculture instantaneously rises sufficiently to fill the gap" left by those who move out of farming, and that fixed labor requirements exist in agriculture. Myrdal believes that the concept of "disguised unemployment" has meaning in advanced capitalist economies, for which Robinson coined the term, but not in underdeveloped countries, where the allegedly "disguised unemployed" are part of the permanent labor force, not temporarily displaced workers.[76]

In its strongest form, the thesis of disguised unemployment in agriculture implies no rise in output beyond some point (assuming constant technology), as more and more workers are added to a unit of land. On the contrary, the Chicago economist Theodore W. Schultz, like Lewis and Myrdal a Nobel Laureate, argues that there is no such thing as measurable zero marginal productivity in agriculture. For him, there are no empirical data to sustain the contention that full employment throughout the year is possible in peasant agriculture.[77] Yet Schultz's test case, which showed a decline in agricultural production after the influenza epidemic of 1918–19 in a heavily populated area of rural India, has been challenged in turn. The concept of disguised unemployment has been refined and defended in recent years, assuming a selective transfer of labor from agriculture to industrial or other nonagricultural activities and a reorganization of the remaining labor force in farming.[78]

5

Manoilescu I: Unequal Exchange

The Peasantists were not the only group interested in the exchange ratios of agricultural and industrial goods. Another cluster of writers, if not a school, wanted to restructure the Rumanian economy to end reliance on "unequal exchange" in the international market by promoting industrialization, leaving aside the problems of agriculture. In the process, "surplus" population in peasant farming would be absorbed in a rapidly expanding nonagricultural labor force, an objective these writers shared with the various currents in Marxism and postwar neoclassical theorists such as W. Arthur Lewis. The leading exponent and the only formal theorist in the trade-oriented tradition was Mihail Manoilescu, a political as well as an economic theorist and an extraordinary figure in the increasingly polarized Rumanian politics of the 1930s. Yet behind Manoilescu, whose theory of industrial protectionism was published in 1929, stood a tradition.

There were several proponents of industrialization—opponents of reliance on agricultural exports—during the nineteenth century, but their voices grew especially audible during the period when government action to that end became more feasible after the creation of a fully independent state in 1877. Before independence, the Ottoman regime, under pressure from Western governments, had kept customs duties in Moldavia and Wallachia to a minimum, thereby precluding any protectionist policy.[1] In the 1850s and 1860s Dionisie Marțian had called for a policy of industrialization. The torch was subsequently taken up by Petre Aurelian, Bogdan Petriceicu Hașdeu, Mihail Kogălniceanu, Ioan Roman,[2] and Alexandru Xenopol, most of whose works on the subject, however, appeared after 1877.[3] In part, Rumania's pro-industrialization writers were reacting to the growing agricultural protectionism of the states of central Europe, particularly that of Austria, in the wake of the Great Depression after 1873. They were also reacting to the fall in prices of Rumania's agricultural exports.[4]

For our purposes, the most important of these writers was Alexandru D.

Xenopol because of his probable, though unacknowledged, influence on Mihail
Manoilescu in the years between the two world wars.[5] Like so many other
Rumanian professors, Xenopol, a Moldavian, received his higher education in
Germany, where he was sent to study with financial assistance from the Junimea
group.[6] Xenopol lived in Berlin from 1867 to 1871, when he received his doctorate, and could hardly have failed to be impressed by the importance of the
economic foundations of Bismarck's new German Empire.[7] Before becoming a
professor of Rumanian history at Iaşi, he served as a magistrate and grew interested in economic issues in part because of his legal and judicial experience.[8]
During the 1880s he became an important intellectual figure in the Liberal Party,
the exponent of an industrialized Rumania.

Xenopol was a passionate defender of the thesis that Rumania was the victim
of a process of unequal exchange between the exporters of industrial goods and
those of agricultural products.[9] Nor was this view altogether unique in East
Central Europe: the Forty-eighter Party in neighboring Hungary under the Dual
Monarchy also favored industrialization by 1875, partly because of the view that
free trade produced unequal exchange.[10] Unlike earlier members of the Junimea,
Xenopol was a materialist, and he believed that cultural development was based
on material progress, of which industrialization was a major aspect in modern
times.[11] As an advocate of protectionism, Xenopol reversed the position of Alexandru Moruzi (1815–78), who associated the unimpeded flow of goods across
national borders with the advance of (Western) civilization.[12] For Xenopol, too,
civilization, nation-building, and economic development were simultaneous
processes, but he associated with economic development the division of labor
within a given society. In a country dominated by traditional agricultural techniques, there was little economic specialization.[13] Xenopol would have approved
of Durkheim's concept of "organic solidarity," by which the division of labor in a
national society creates bonds difficult to destroy.

Xenopol's most radical views on industrialization were expressed in *Economic
Studies*, a collection of articles he first published in 1879 and revised and expanded
in 1882. Heavily influenced by the protectionist views of Friedrich List and
Henry Carey, Xenopol went far beyond his German and American inspirers to
assert that the exchange of manufactured for agricultural goods on the international market constituted exploitation. Following the classical economists,
Xenopol accepted the labor theory of value, which had now been abandoned by
the rising marginalist school associated with Jevons, Menger, and Walras. Xenopol focused on the different productivities of labor embodied, in his view, in
agricultural and industrial production. He associated farming, at least the traditional kind known in Rumania, with *muncă brută*—raw, unskilled, or brute
labor—and industry with *muncă inteligentă*—intelligent or skilled labor. Rumania
was exporting agricultural goods embodying much more labor than was embodied in the industrial goods it imported.[14] In foreign trade, he calculated that a ton

of imports, which he equated with industrial goods, was worth 828 lei (presumably in 1872), while a ton of exports, equated with agricultural goods, was only worth 158 lei; thus the difference in value was more than five to one.[15] Elsewhere he even calculated that the difference was ten to one—a figure frequently later cited by Manoilescu, and in Ion Veverca's estimation, not by coincidence.[16]

Like Manoilescu a half-century later, and in tones just as polemical, Xenopol held that the international division of labor was a swindle. Western (or as he put it, British and French) economic theory was ideology at the service of particular national interests, a theme echoed in the 1930s by Manoilescu and by some Third World economists after World War II.[17] In fact, argued Xenopol, even England and France, as well as Germany and the United States, had built their industrial preeminence on protectionist policies. Only medieval Venice and Flanders had established their industries primarily on unassisted private initiative. England, beginning with Edward IV—later followed by Cromwell—and France, beginning with Colbert, had successfully pursued state-induced policies of industrialization.[18] Tedentious though his interpretation of the two nations' development was, it served Xenopol's purpose of showing the need for state intervention in his own country.

Despite its sponsorship of his foreign study, Xenopol rejected the Junimea school's doctrine of modern Rumanian history as *formă fără fond* (form without substance). Perhaps adapting Hegel's idealism to make the state the demiurge of history in a materialist world and adapting the "upside-down" notion of Rumania's development by the Junimists, Xenopol saw his country's development ("civilization") as *fatally* one of *sus în jos*—from above to below—and argued that the state would have to induce development, and industrialization in particular. The state would provide "external" protection with tariff barriers, but "internal" protection for industry was also required, in the form of tax concessions, subsidies, guaranteed purchases, and export premia.[19]

Further, *sus în jos* implied that highly capitalized industries with large numbers of workers per firm would have to precede small ones with modest capital investments and few workers per unit, and the state needed to concentrate its efforts in the former group.[20] Rumania's economic development was "upside down," and necessarily so, if it were to catch up with the West in an era of international cartels.[21] As a result, what would have been an abnormal form of development in the West was a "normal" one for a backward country like Rumania.[22] Consequently, the country had railroads before highways, a banking and insurance system before industry, political independence before economic independence, and a written constitution before constitutional practice.[23]

There were many dangers inherent in the economic position of a country that remained purely agricultural, thought Xenopol. One was a dependency on the industrial countries, which set both the prices of their own goods on the world market and the agricultural prices of their nonindustrialized trading partners.[24]

Xenopol was apparently unaware of the economic "law" of the German statistician Ernst Engel, viz., that as income rises, the percentage of income spent on agricultural goods tends to fall. In any event, Xenopol held that there were limits to the gains Rumania could obtain from the export of foodstuffs.[25] Further, the stratification of agricultural and industrial countries in the world market was a dynamic process, and Xenopol seemed to imply that the poor would get poorer if Rumania and other agrarian countries persisted in their agricultural specialization. The (alleged) losses in foreign trade over time also had an opportunity cost because Rumania sacrificed capital that might have been invested.[26] Xenopol had no doubt that Western countries could and did impede the industrialization of backward agrarian countries by their use of the doctrine of free trade.[27] For these reasons, the international division of labor had to be rejected. The peoples of backward areas of the Continent, including Rumania, along with those of Asia, Africa, and Latin America, were "slaves whose labor built the civilized fortress of [Western] Europe." The West exploited the rest of the world through the exchange of goods produced by skilled labor for those produced by brute labor.[28]

Petre S. Aurelian, Xenopol's contemporary, was equally ardent in his defense of manufacturing industry and adduced more considerations against agricultural exports and in favor of industrialization. Trained in agronomy in France, Aurelian traveled widely in Europe, observing economic conditions. Like Xenopol, he was associated with the National Liberal Party. A publicist, professor, and man of affairs, Aurelian played an active role in politics, serving several times as minister and heading the Rumanian government at the close of the nineteenth century. Among his many works, *Our Economic Future*[29] was a polemical statement sponsored by the National Liberal Club in 1890, defending the industrialization policy implemented by the Liberals in the tariff of 1886. Publishing late in the Great Depression of the nineteenth century, Aurelian believed that his country faced grave and hitherto unknown difficulties in the international grain market because of rising "overseas" producers. He had in mind the United States, the Dominions, and most recently Argentina, whose cereal production, Aurelian wrote, had quadrupled between 1878 and 1890.[30] Rumania, he suggested somewhat prematurely, could no longer compete successfully in international agricultural markets. For Aurelian, furthermore, the fact that the United States had the highest per capita income and the highest per capita tariff charges (of nine wealthy countries he compared) exposed the fallacy of free trade arguments—and by implication the fallacy of the thesis of comparative advantage.[31] Finally, there was another consideration. Like Xenopol, Aurelian was impressed by the rapid rise of German industrial power in the last quarter of the nineteenth century, but for him this phenomenon was simply the most advanced case of a general European trend. Russia, Hungary, and even Bulgaria and Serbia were industrializing. In asking how Rumania could fail to fall in step with her neighbors, Aurelian not only referred to the danger of becoming an economic "tributary"—an allusion perhaps to the country's unenviable status under the recently ousted Ottoman regime—but also insinuated that the danger was strategic as well as economic.[32]

In the twentieth century, the exploitation-through-trade thesis, linked with pro-industrialization arguments, was carried forward by Ion N. Angelescu, a professor of finance in Bucharest with a doctorate in economics from Munich. Angelescu was to become finance minister at the end of World War I.[33] He was impressed by the economic dependence of Rumania on the belligerent powers in 1915 and advocated the creation of new non-agriculture-related industries. To this end, he recommended state intervention in the economy to organize production through a "central economic commission."[34] In 1915, writing in the same journal published by the National Liberal Party, Angelescu had provided a detailed estimate of Rumania's total national wealth (not annual product), showing that, of an economy worth 26 billion (milliard) lei in 1913, two-thirds was accounted for by agricultural land and forests and 5 billion by industry and commerce. Of the latter amount, "large industry"[35] in 1908 accounted for only 0.5 billion in fixed and circulating capital—less than 2 percent of national wealth.[36]

After the war, Angelescu argued that industrialization was even more feasible in Greater Rumania, which had rich sources of energy and enhanced supplies of raw materials. Agriculture depended on foreign markets, and its products needed to be valorized. The modernization of the country's backward agriculture relied on industry to raise agricultural productivity. The nation's exports, Angelescu noted, and therefore its labor, were reckoned as two or three times less valuable than English goods and English labor (per unit of time worked). Angelescu further urged the reduction of industrial imports to improve the nation's trade balance, in effect recommending import-substitution industrialization. Beyond this, Rumania must offer more valuable goods—manufactures—on the world market, he asserted.[37] Angelescu believed, as Xenopol had, that western Europe exploited backward countries through trade and lending practices,[38] but he had no theory to explain how and why this occurred. That task was assumed by Mihail Manoilescu, whose theses are considered in the remainder of this chapter and the one that follows.

A man of many parts, Mihail Manoilescu had an international reputation as a theorist of corporatism as well as an economist. Yet it also seems that he wanted to succeed at politics more than at anything else—he was "furiously ambitious," in the words of the British ambassador in 1940,[39] and was a stereotypical Balkan politician in his opportunism. Born in 1891, Manoilescu came from a modest though educated family in Tecuci, the same Moldavian county where Ştefan Zeletin had been born nine years earlier. Both the younger man's parents were later secondary school teachers at Iaşi, capital of the former principality of Moldavia; his father was a militant in the Rumanian Socialist Party of Gherea and Racovski. On his mother's side, he had political connections in the Conservative Party.[40] Manoilescu studied engineering at the School of Bridge and Highway

Construction (later renamed the Polytechnic) at Bucharest and led his class every
year. There he also became a friend of the future king, Carol II. Manoilescu
received his engineering degree in 1915, and during World War I worked in the
National Munitions Office to develop better ordnance. His energy, cleverness,
and ability to form useful connections enabled him to become director-general
of Industry in 1920 and to organize the first industrial exhibition of Greater
Rumania in 1921.[41] This was the beginning of his campaign to stimulate Rumanian industrial development.

A rising star in the government of General Alexandru Averescu[42] from 1926,
Manoilescu gained a reputation for both efficiency and articulateness, virtually
running the country's ministry of finance as undersecretary. In the late 1920s he
also played a major role in the accession of Carol to the throne, after Carol had
been judged unfit by the Rumanian parliament, which was under the sway of
Prime Minister Ion I. C. Brătianu. For conspiring to crown Carol, Manoilescu
was tried by a military court but was acquitted. The trial gave him a certain
notoriety, and the acquittal was also viewed as an endorsement of Carol, whose
coronation took place in 1930.[43] In the same year Manoilescu was named minister of public works, then minister of industry and commerce, and in May 1931 he
was appointed governor of the National Bank. Yet in July 1931, his meteoric rise
in politics came to an abrupt halt when he refused to authorize National Bank
credits for a major commercial bank belonging to one of the king's cronies and
the bank failed.[44] His refusal antagonized the king, and Manoilescu's services in
high government circles were not sought again until the crisis of 1940, when
Germany followed the USSR in seeking to shrink the Greater Rumania that had
emerged in 1919.

Manoilescu also was prominent in private organizations and served, at various
times, as president of the national civil servants' society, of the national engineers'
association, of the congress of the national industrialists' association (UGIR), and
of the Rumanian Chamber of Commerce. Under Rumania's quasi-corporatist
constitution of 1923, he represented the Chamber of Commerce in the Rumanian senate. He also participated in various meetings of the International Chamber of Commerce, as well as attending other pan-European conferences, lectur-
ing in different parts of Europe, and, in 1930, representing Rumania at the
League of Nations in Geneva. As a politician, he founded a corporatist party in
1933. In the preceding year, he had launched a journal to propagate his political
views, *Lumea Nouă* (The new world or New people) and attended the Fascist-
sponsored Corporatist Congress at Ferrara. Of the various right-wing intellectuals present at Ferrara, only Manoilescu and Werner Sombart were invited to
Rome to report personally to Mussolini on the event.[45] The Rumanian theorist
was proud of his acquaintance with the Italian dictator, whom—according to
Manoilescu—he had convinced to recognize the legitimacy of Rumania's claim
to Bessarabia against the Soviet government in 1927.[46] Manoilescu was also on

good terms with some of the intellectual and pseudo-intellectual figures in Nazi Germany, notably Werner Sombart and Alfred Rosenberg. His work as a political theorist also impressed António Salazar, the dictator of Portugal, and the Portuguese law professor Marcelo Caetano, Salazar's future successor, during the Rumanian's visit to Lisbon in 1936.[47]

As a personality, Manoilescu had certain gifts: he was deemed handsome and personally charming, so much so that one unsympathetic commentator quipped that had Manoilescu chosen to become a screen actor, cinema would have profited, and politics would have lost nothing.[48] The same writer accused Manoilescu of political corruption, and foreign observers agreed.[49] If true, however, this trait would hardly have distinguished him in the Rumania of the 1930s, in which milieu *şmecherie* (imaginative peculation or embezzlement) was widely admired. As his memoirs reveal, Manoilescu had a high opinion of himself, and he resented the reputation of the economist Virgil Madgearu, also a rival in politics.[50]

Manoilescu's opportunism in politics is well documented, and he changed political orientations and parties several times.[51] During the 1930s, his support for Mussolini was sometimes histrionic.[52] In 1937 he won a seat in the Rumanian Senate on the ticket of the Iron Guard, then called "All for the Country."[53] Yet his backing for the only local fascist party to achieve power by its own action outside Germany and Italy was probably based on opportunism rather than conviction, as was his timely anti-Semitism.[54] In 1940, following the fall of France and the Soviet seizure of Bessarabia in June, King Carol II again called on Manoilescu, this time to direct Rumania's foreign affairs. The British ambassador at the time considered the new appointee strongly anti-Semitic and a German tool as well: Sir Reginald Hoare wrote London "that such a creature should be made Minister for Foreign Affairs . . . is even more deplorable than it is comic."[55] In any case, events proved Manoilescu more clever than wise. His activity as foreign minister brought opprobrium on him in August 1940, with a new national disaster. Rumania had acquired Transylvania from Austria-Hungary at the end of World War I, and the postwar Hungarian state had pressed an irredentist claim. Working under the pressure of Hitler's war timetable, the Nazi and fascist foreign ministers, Joachim von Ribbentrop and Galeazzo Ciano, met their Hungarian and Rumanian counterparts at Vienna and decided to resolve the border dispute by fiat. The settlement became notorious in Rumania as the "Vienna *Diktat*." Ciano's laconic diary catches the drama of the moment: "Ceremony of the signature at the Belvedere [Palace]. The Hungarians can't contain their joy when they see the map. Then we hear a loud thud. It was Manoilescu, who fainted on the table. Doctors, massage, camphorated oil. Finally he comes to, but shows the shock very much."[56] Manoilescu acquiesced in Rumania's cession of half of Transylvania to Hungary. Within a week of the Diktat, his political career had ended in disgrace, and King Carol had lost his throne.[57]

Despite this debacle, Manoilescu remained loyal to the Axis cause, and his politics affected his economic views in the late 1930s and early 1940s. He turned away from his long and passionate defense of allegedly scientific protectionism in favor of Nazi policy, which emphasized Rumania's agricultural complementarity with Germany. Rumania was to be part of the agricultural hinterland of the *Grossraumwirtschaft* (Greater German Economic Space). The Manoilescu of the war years argued that within the German system Rumania would receive higher prices for her exports than she would on the international market.[58] He offered no evidence for this contention, and in fact, Germany exploited the resources of Rumania ruthlessly.[59]

Bucharest was liberated in August 1944; Rumania immediately joined the Allies; and Manoilescu was jailed in October. He remained in prison until December 1945, awaiting trial for his role in the loss of Transylvania. The ex-foreign minister was cleared of charges five months later, partly, perhaps, because Rumania had regained its pre-1940 frontiers with Hungary. Manoilescu then proceeded to write his memoirs. But in December 1948, he was again incarcerated by the newly consolidated Communist regime. The politician-theorist died two years later as a result of prison-induced ailments and was condemned posthumously for pro-Axis press articles written during the war.[60] Because of his Axis sympathies, Manoilescu's works were banned by the postwar regime; but a generation later his economic works, which anticipated many Third World claims, aspirations, and indictments, were mentioned in official publications as an important Rumanian contribution to the analysis of underdevelopment.

Manoilescu was a man of considerable learning, writing fluently in French and later delivering speeches by memory in German and Italian as well.[61] He had a gift for polemical prose, though his treatises in economics and political theory have a didactic tone, sometimes featuring whole paragraphs in italics. In economics Manoilescu was self-taught, having an engineering background, like such other social theorists as Georges Sorel, Vilfredo Pareto, and Herbert Spencer. He became interested in economic theory as a result of his work in the secretariat of finance, reorganizing the Rumanian tariff structure in 1927 to favor industrial protection.[62]

Manoilescu's *Theory of Protectionism and International Exchange* (1929),[63] translated from French into five other languages, including Spanish and Portuguese, already had repercussions in his own day in Brazil and in other countries where Iberian languages were spoken, and he was well aware of the currency of his economic ideas in Latin America.[64] His *Century of Corporatism* (1934)[65] was equally well-known. The impact of his ideas outside Rumania will be described and evaluated in later chapters, as will the alleged connection between his economic writings and the structuralist school associated with the United Nations Economic Commission for Latin America.

———

Manoilescu's ideas appeared in a period of much greater receptivity to heterodoxy than was the prewar era. The concept of economic planning, which was widely discussed in East Central Europe in the interwar years, had grown less out of the Russian Revolution than the *Kriegswirtschaft* of Germany and the other belligerent powers in the later years of World War I.[66] A growing penchant for planning meshed with a rising tide of economic nationalism in the region, focusing on industrialization and exacerbated by capital flight, as foreign investors disinvested in the 1930s.[67] Furthermore, in the 1920s and 1930s, corporatist industrialists shared an "ideology of productivity." In Italy, for instance, "Technocratic accents . . . became the rhetoric of the industrial leadership as it pushed for lower labor costs [including lower wages] in the name of productivity and rationalization."[68] A contemporary watchword among Latin American industrialists as well, rationalization was often equated with cartelization, to terminate "ruinous" competition.

Yet a rising rate of monopolistic combination did not necessarily halt the spread of industrialization beyond western Europe and the United States—on the contrary. Manoilescu was not unique in his day in perceiving that the Depression, by inducing protectionist reactions among the Great Powers, was stimulating the diffusion of manufacturing beyond the highly industrialized states.[69] But industrialization was a long-run proposition, and in the shorter run, Rumania, along with other agriculture-exporting countries, had already begun to experience the "price-scissors" problem—a widening gap between industrial and agricultural prices—in the late 1920s. The scissors opened farther and cut deeper in the 1930s.

The decline of prices for agricultural commodities relative to those for manufactured goods had two principal medium-term causes, both growing out of the war. One was the effort by the major industrial countries of continental Europe to achieve self-sufficiency in wheat production in the 1920s, hedging against another international conflict; the other was technological advance, notably the diffusion of the tractor, in the high-productivity agriculture-exporting nations, a process stimulated by the vital need for grain during the Great War. The issue remained, however, why industrial prices did not fall as well, given the greatly expanded manufacturing potential in the belligerent powers and the tendency for industrialization to spread to new countries. During the Great Depression many economists noticed that industrial prices tended to be downwardly rigid, and the causes of the latter phenomenon were identified as early as 1927 by the Swedish economist Gustav Cassel in a report for the League of Nations. Cassel pointed to monopolistic tendencies in the labor and manufactures markets of the industrial West.[70] "From 1913, a very serious dislocation of relative prices has taken place in the exchange of goods between Europe and the colonial world" owing to these monopolies, he wrote in 1927.[71] These causes of high and downwardly rigid industrial prices were to be cited by later writers in the interwar years, including Manoilescu himself.[72] They were reiterated in an Economic Committee report of the League in 1935. That document further pointed out that agricultural producers could not control supply as readily as their industrial counterparts, and individual farmers sometimes increased quantities of goods offered for sale to make up for falling unit prices, thereby exacerbating the problem. Thus individual interest conflicted with group interest. All these considerations would be put forth again after World War II in the analysis of the United Nations economist Raúl Prebisch.[73]

Manoilescu's ideas were widely discussed in Rumania and elsewhere in East Central Europe in part because of the salience of the peasant issue. In Rumania, the peasant had been the recent beneficiary of a major land reform, and such reforms had occurred, with greater or lesser intensity, in most of the region. But the newly enfranchised peasant was also now a political force to contend with in East Central Europe and especially in Bulgaria and Yugoslavia. As "overpopulation" was widely diagnosed in the region,[74] how to make the peasantry more productive was an issue for which Manoilescu, among others, offered a solution.

Manoilescu agreed with the French journalist Francis Delaisi that the Continent's economy after the war was still sharply divided into "two Europes," the title of Delaisi's book, published the same year as Manoilescu's *Theory of Protectionism* (1929).[75] In Delaisi's dualist scheme, "Europe A" was industrial Europe, the "Center" in Werner Sombart's terminology,[76] and was a compact area bounded by a line passing through Stockholm, Danzig, Cracow, Budapest, Florence, Barcelona, Bilbao, Glasgow, and Bergen. "Europe B," the "Periphery," as Sombart and Latin American structuralists would style it, was agrarian—highly diverse, much poorer, and much less well integrated.[77] Beyond these two components lay "overseas Europe," or, in a later phrase, "lands of recent settlement," mostly populated by migrants from B but supplied with abundant capital from A.

Although overseas Europe was largely agricultural, it enjoyed modern equipment, wrote Delaisi. Because of the high productivity in overseas Europe's agriculture, the economic symbiosis between Europe A and overseas Europe was much stronger than that between the former and Europe B. This was because overseas Europe took more of A's exports than B or any other region of the world and more than twice the per capita value of exports that A sent to B. Therefore, agrarian Europe had become increasingly irrelevant to the interests of the developed West. However, wrote Delaisi, as a result of the postwar land reforms across eastern Europe, 100 million peasants (counting those in Russia) had now received land—creating a potentially vast market. Europe B, with capital and agricultural machinery supplied by A, could eventually become the latter's main trading partner because overseas Europe's markets were closing (presumably because of industrial protection policies).[78]

Why would Manoilescu, who published a book defending the industrialization of agrarian countries the same year Delaisi's essay appeared, be attracted to the latter's arguments for a preferential tariff protection scheme that would have Rumania remain an agricultural exporter? Owing to his political ambitions and commitments, Manoilescu found himself alternately supporting two different economic policies with contrasting theoretical foundations during the years

1929–44. Such policies had to do with how to confront the low prices Rumania received for its agricultural exports. One tack was to seek, by bilateral or multi-lateral agreements, an upward adjustment of the relative prices at which Rumania's grain was exchanged for industrial goods on the international market. The other, which his *Theory of Protectionism* explicitly called for, was to abandon traditional agricultural specialization on the world market and to pursue import-substitution industrialization.

Having published the original French edition of his treatise in 1929, Man-oilescu the politician found himself at the Geneva headquarters of the League in the following year, arguing for the "closing" of the price scissors by international agreement. As minister of industry and commerce in the government of George Mironescu (1930–31), Manoilescu demanded a preferential tariff regime for East Central Europe. He nonetheless used elements of his trade theory to underscore the importance of the plausible assertion that goods embodying western Europe's labor exchanged for those involving a multiple of labor units expended in East Central Europe; consequently, he alleged, western Europe had more to lose by a contraction of trade, under a growing international tendency toward autarky.[79] Furthermore, a diminution of intra-European trade stimulated industrialization in the eastern portion of the continent, contrary to the West's interest. In this matter, Manoilescu was adding his own arguments in presenting the case of the newly formed Agrarian Bloc.[80]

The Bloc proved ineffective, however, and Manoilescu presented a more radical (and politically unrealistic) view at the Vienna meeting of the International Chamber of Commerce in 1933. He recognized, as Cassel had before him and Prebisch would later, that in times of depression industrial prices were "sticky" because of the power of organized labor, compared to its unorganized counterpart in farming in the agriculture-exporting countries. Nevertheless, the "imperative of the [world] crisis," he proclaimed, was for the industrial countries, whose terms of trade had improved dramatically since 1913, to adjust their export prices downward relative to those of their agricultural trading partners, by low-ering wages and profits; meanwhile, manufacturing in agricultural countries should be protected by "exaggerated" tariffs—presumably as a reprisal.[81]

As economist—as opposed to politician—Manoilescu was chiefly concerned with the relationship between the purchasing power of a unit of labor expended in producing a good traded on the world market in terms of the labor of other workers abroad—a concept later developed as the "double factorial terms of trade." Manoilescu held that labor productivity in industry (manufacturing and mining) was superior to that in agriculture, by a ratio of four or more to one, in empirical studies. This superiority owed to "specific capital," that is, the capital per worker, which was much higher in industry than in agriculture. Specific capital also indicated the "degree of mechanization" in a given industry (or economic activity).[82]

Using data for 1937 in the final edition of his treatise on production and trade (published in Rumanian), Manoilescu calculated that average industrial wages in Rumania were 4.6 times greater in industry than in agriculture; capital per worker ("specific capital") was 4.1 times greater; and labor productivity was 4.6 times greater. Yet the average rate of profit was only 1.8 percent greater in industry than in agriculture.[83] Employing data from the Ministry of National Economy to measure productivity and profitability for specific industries, Manoilescu found that there was no correlation between general profitability and productivity; rather, capital per worker "determined" (i.e., was highly correlated with) productivity. For Manoilescu, these findings and the small spread between profit rates in industry and agriculture noted above showed that the individual interest in profit could and did in fact diverge from the "national" interest in productivity.[84] Manoilescu apparently did not know the work of A. C. Pigou, who had demonstrated in *Wealth and Welfare* (1912) and *The Economics of Welfare* (1920) that differences owing to indivisibilities in capital-intensive forms of production could arise in social and private marginal net product.[85] Later Paul Rosenstein-Rodan would use such indivisibilities and the external economies to which they give rise to argue for a state-led "big push" to overcome structural deficiencies in the economies of underdeveloped countries.[86]

Manoilescu, like Marx, Ricardo, and other classical economists, believed in the labor theory of value, although the Rumanian thought there were "qualitative" differences between labor inputs, which were explained by the amount of capital per worker, and that these differences were stable over time. They could therefore be used to establish a hierarchy of economic activities (i.e., branches of production).[87] Manoilescu further developed a "coefficient of quality," showing which industries could produce a given value of output with minimal inputs of labor and capital. Such a coefficient could be used by state planners to rank industries, and the concept could be modified to measure agricultural productivities as well.[88]

Because labor productivity was so much greater in industry than in agriculture, "the passing of backward agricultural states from agricultural occupations to those of industry offers a greater advantage [to them] than to industrial countries."[89] As labor moved from agriculture to industry, in the longer run, however, Manoilescu believed a tendency toward the convergence of agricultural and industrial productivities would occur, and those of the United States already revealed this tendency.[90] Until such convergence occurred, low-productivity labor in agriculture should be moved to high-productivity manufacturing; or, in its precise formulation, stated in neoclassical terms, when the marginal productivity of labor in agriculture is below that in other sectors, surplus labor should be moved to manufacturing or other, higher-productivity activities. The Rumanian theorist was remembered in postwar development theory primarily for this, the "Manoilescu argument," which remained a hotly debated subject. Viewed from the perspective of costs of production, the argument could be put differently: the large gap between (traditional) agricultural and industrial wages, reflecting a large productivity differential, was an impediment to industrialization that could be offset by a compensatory tariff on, or subsidies for, industrial goods. This argument was later developed by Kurt Mandelbaum, Raúl Prebisch, and the Nobel Laureate W. Arthur Lewis.[91]

Manoilescu adapted his formulae to measure productivity of land as a factor of production, and therefore yield per hectare,[92] but he made no effort to measure the productivity of services; thus he could only measure the value of physical product. He apparently believed that commerce (the major component of services) did not produce wealth, but only redistributed it, although he allowed that commerce produced "relative utility" as opposed to the "absolute utility" of production.[93]

In the matter of international trade, the issue for Manoilescu was not comparative advantage, as for Ricardo, because this theory "prescribed" a division of world labor into industrial and agricultural specialists; rather, the issue was whether a given economic endeavor within a country had a labor productivity higher than the national average. If it did, its development should be encouraged.[94] Specialization in traditional agricultural pursuits required four to ten hours of Rumanian labor to purchase the product of a single hour of English labor. Thus international trade was a swindle. Protection for industry was justifiable, not just in terms of Friedrich List's "infant industry" argument, by which an enterprise would take advantage of economies of scale and external economies over the intermediate run to bring costs down to internationally competitive levels; rather, protection was justified because a sheltered industry that had a labor productivity higher than the national average of economic activities was a boon from its first day of operation.[95] Further, for Manoilescu protection was a valid policy for the longer as well as the short term, if differentials in productivities across different economic activities persisted.[96] The more the productivity of a given good exceeded the average national productivity, the more the domestic price of that good could justifiably exceed the foreign price.[97]

To engage in agricultural exports, Manoilescu argued, a country's comparative advantage in domestic agriculture over its foreign counterpart must be greater than the "intrinsic superiority" in labor productivity of industry over agriculture within the country.[98] Such cases were rare, Manoilescu thought, because agriculture in Rumania and other underdeveloped countries with dense populations was primitive in technique and consequently was labor-intensive. If the comparative advantage in domestic agriculture over that of a foreign country (or "all other countries") was zero, and if labor productivity in domestic industry was four times greater than that in agriculture, then the inferiority of domestic labor productivity over its foreign counterpart could be 75 percent "without the solution of industrial production ceasing to be advantageous."[99] Further, if the price of a good produced in an agricultural country were three times that of its foreign counterpart, and its labor productivity were greater than the highest labor productivity of any other national product, then a tariff of 200 percent (to bring the goods to the same price level in the local market, assuming labor productivity determines price) "would be justified in practice and in theory" because of the growth in national income that the production of the new good would effect.[100] In the long run, the productivity gains for agricultural countries, whose incomes would rise, would benefit the industrial countries, with which the former would now trade more extensively.[101] Thus the industrialization of backward countries "has nothing in common with autarky,"[102] although it was at odds with the "free trade" doctrines of the League of Nations.[103]

Manoilescu distinguished between profitability and productivity: the former criterion guides the actions of individual entrepreneurs, while the latter should be the cynosure of nations, as directed by the state. In (high-productivity) industry, workers receive high incomes, creditors to industrial enterprises receive high rates of interest, the state receives large tax revenues, and entrepreneurs obtain high profits. In (low-productivity) agriculture, even when the product can compete at the world price and the capitalist farmer receives a large income, "the benefit to the nation (that is, the sum of individual benefits to workers, creditors, the state, and entrepreneurs) is small in comparison with the national benefit obtained in industry."[104] The assumption of the "liberal school" that there was a coincidence between profitability and productivity was false.[105]

In a variety of forums Manoilescu emphasized the exploitation inherent in international trade. In a brash moment he wrote, "It is scientifically absurd to speak of growing rich by one's own work only. [It is] only by organizing and exploiting others' labor that anybody can become rich." The same held true for nations as well as for individuals, he inferred.[106] Because the exchange of industrial goods for agricultural products and raw materials on the world market was a cheat—*un marché de dupes,* he called it[107]—Manoilescu demanded the replacement of an allegedly outmoded "socialism of classes" by a "socialism of nations," the Rumanian's way of expressing the notion that the modern world was divided into "proletarian" and "plutocratic" nations.[108] He thus anticipated demands by Third World governments in the 1970s for a New International Economic Order, and the Rumanian's path toward the new order was basically the same as theirs: if the First World did not agree to a major shift in the international relative prices of industrial and agricultural goods, the backward agrarian countries should industrialize through protectionist policies.[109]

To what degree did Manoilescu convince Rumanian industrialists of the validity of his argument? More broadly, to what degree were the "practical men" who directed Rumania's manufacturing industries affected by the economic theories circulating in the 1920s and 1930s? The organ of the national industrialists' association offers some answers. The General Union of Rumanian Industrialists (UGIR) was founded in 1903 as a reaction to the financial crisis of 1900–1902 and was extended from the Old Kingdom to Greater Rumania in 1922.[110] In the early 1920s, the organization's concerns tended to be practical and its position somewhat contradictory on government interference in the labor market. The first issue of UGIR's *Bulletin*, in 1922, espoused a doctrine of social harmony between capital and labor, denying, as some corporatists would have it, that workers and factory owners formed separate social classes.[111] UGIR opposed the creation of a corporatist labor chamber one year later, a project designed to diminish class conflict, because the industrialists' association feared an "army" of bureaucrats in the new labor courts.[112] In the interwar years UGIR objected frequently to government efforts to legislate and enforce the eight-hour day, the objective of the Geneva-based International Labor Office.[113] Yet on the matter of suppressing "communist discord" spread by "foreign" workers, UGIR expected "the full support of the government."[114]

In the 1920s the posture of the association was generally defensive on the position of industry in the national economy. UGIR spokesmen in 1926 argued that Rumanian manufacturers could legitimately use imported inputs, but they retreated to a defensive position one year later to meet the charge that their enterprises were "artificial"; in response, they pointed to the cotton-cloth industries in Switzerland, France, and Germany, which lacked local supplies of raw cotton. For the director of UGIR, the ultimate argument for the protection of industry was a social one: its employment of national laborers, whose loss of work would produce grave social conflict.[115]

Industrialists also employed an obvious pro-manufacturing argument in a country surrounded by neighboring states from which it had gained territory after the war, namely, that industry had a strategic role to play in maintaining the integrity of Greater Rumania.[116] More apologetic was the contention in 1928 that the country should industrialize, precisely because former trading partners, Germany, Czechoslovakia, Italy, and Austria, were agrarianizing—presumably a reference to renewed efforts to raise wheat production in Central Europe. As late as 1930, the president of UGIR stated, "We have always recognized that the principal branch of production in the country is agriculture" and admitted that it deserved special attention.[117]

In the 1930s UGIR spokesmen, like their counterparts in Brazil, became more aggressive in supporting the cause of manufacturing, and they cited both Manoilescu's political activity on their behalf and his theory of protectionism. As early as 1927 UGIR had praised the high tariff that the Rumanian engineer had authored in that year, and four years later a spokesman for the organization approvingly cited *Theory of Protectionism* on the assertion that manufacturing was the most productive branch of economic activity.[118] The very fact that Manoilescu held high posts in UGIR and the national Chamber of Commerce offers indirect evidence of the acceptance of his ideas by Rumanian businessmen. In

1931, the National Economic Plan would be executed by a government in which Manoilescu was minister of industry, and a UGIR leader expressed confidence in him. According to the plan, when the interests of industry and agriculture came into conflict, the state—the same UGIR official noted with approval—was to decide in favor of the solution that represented the largest increase in national income—a clear allusion to Manoilescu's productivity thesis.[119]

UGIR became more assertive about industry's role in the economy in the 1930s, when the share of manufacturing rose in the national product. A leader of the organization alleged in 1936 that industry, directly or indirectly, now paid half the country's taxes.[120] UGIR repeatedly expressed the view that manufacturing was a boon to Rumanian labor and adopted the position defended by Manoilescu (although others took a similar stance) that manufacturing could absorb surplus labor from agriculture. In this way, the interests of industry and agriculture were complementary, UGIR spokesmen believed.[121] Therefore the "Manoilescu argument" for moving unproductive labor from agriculture to industry was adopted by the industrialists to support their own interests, though their concern with, and appreciation of, economic theory was slight.

Meanwhile, the Rumanian government moved decisively in the direction of state-led industrialization, so long sought by Manoilescu, after King Carol's coup d'état in 1938.[122] In April of that year the Ministry of Industry and Commerce was transformed into the Ministry of the National Economy, which was to stimulate and control virtually all aspects of economic life.[123] At the ideological level, the Higher Economic Council, a government advisory body led by the intriguing but always influential Constantin Argetoianu, had been charged with producing a general economic plan in 1938. It declared firmly for state-induced industrial development in 1939: industrialization would secure national economic independence, raise the general level of income, and move the "surplus population" out of agriculture into industrial enterprises.[124]

6

Manoilescu II: Internal Colonialism and Corporatism

While Manoilescu courted Rumanian industrialists, by 1940 he had also extended his foreign trade thesis to encompass economic relations within national boundaries. The same kind of "unequal exchange"—a phrase he specifically employed[1]—that occurred between agriculture and industry in international trade also occurred within backward countries, he alleged. Ultimately, however, surplus labor in agriculture would be drawn into the cities, potentially raising wages in agriculture to the same level as those in industry. Thus industrialists who employed former peasants were furthering development.

From his trade theory, in 1940 Manoilescu derived a model of internal colonialism *avant la lettre*, possibly the first in the world that attempted to measure the process.* His scheme had four elements—the city or "primate region" with an urban, industrial node; the agricultural hinterland; the foreign trade sector; and the state. In the Rumania of the Depression era, the contrast between the wealth of the cities and the poverty of the countryside was stark, as noted in Chapter 4.

---

*M. Manoilesco [sic], "Triangle" (1940). Manoilescu did not use the phrase "internal colonialism," which gained broad currency only in the 1960s. For a history of the idea of internal colonialism and a survey of its different traditions and contemporary uses, see Love, "Modeling" (1989).

By my definition, internal colonialism is a process of unequal exchange, occurring within a given state, characteristic of industrial or industrializing economies, capitalist or socialist. As the economy becomes more differentiated with regard to region, factors and income flow from one or more geographically definable area to another, based primarily on price mechanisms, and secondarily (or not at all) on fiscal transfers; the state may nonetheless play a decisive role in setting price ratios, and differential regional effects of foreign trade are relevant. At the minimum, the process involves a structural relationship between leading and lagging regions (or city and hinterland) of a territorial state, based on monopolized or oligopolized markets, in which growth is progressively "inequalizing" between populations of these constituent geographic elements, rather than "equalizing." Internal colonialism is distinct from colonialism per se, in which an alien state enforces monopsony in labor markets, or even prescribes wage levels and labor drafts, such as the *repartimiento* of the Spanish American empire or the *corvée* of French colonial Africa. This definition can be applied to Manoilescu's model and one developed by Hans Singer and Celso Furtado in Brazil after World War II (see Chapter 10). The definition by itself does not, of course, establish that the phenomenon exists.

Other Rumanian scholars were attempting to analyze and suggest remedies for the deteriorating commodity terms of trade of agricultural goods against those of manufactures.[2] But Manoilescu went on to model the problem, deriving his analysis largely from his theory of international trade. He purported to demonstrate how urban, industrial areas exploited rural, agricultural hinterlands within national boundaries. Using Rumania as a case study, he discerned exploitation in three processes, two of them commercial and a third fiscal. The first was international trade. Having data on the value and nature of the commodities exported, Manoilescu was easily able to demonstrate that the greater part of Rumania's exports (by value) originated in agriculture, though this share was decreasing as the century advanced and petroleum exports rose. It was more difficult to measure the destination of imports, but again, by their nature, Manoilescu was able to dichotomize imports between those destined for the cities and those for the countryside.[3] By this reasoning, in 1913 Rumania's villages exported goods worth 530 million gold (French) francs and received 120 million in return; the cities and the mineral sector (i.e., the oil industry) exported 141 million and received 551 million in return. Thus a gain of 410 million francs to the cities was the same net loss to the villages.[4] In 1937 the villages exported 18,300 million lei (Rumanian currency) and received 2,400 million from abroad; the cities and mineral producers exported 13,266 million and received 29,166 million, resulting in a net transfer of 15,900 from the villages to the cities.[5] The towns were great beneficiaries in this exchange and the villages and countryside great losers, according to Manoilescu: the bulk of exports originated in the countryside and villages, but the cities received most of the imports. Manoilescu summed up his argument with the judgment, "The economic triangle formed by the village, the city and the export market play the special role of transforming the commodity surplus produced by the village into consumer goods, to the advantage of the city."[6]

Part of the problem was that great landlords, whom Manoilescu considered "rural" *qua* producers, were "urban" *qua* consumers and spent much of their foreign proceeds in the cities. Before the nineteenth century, when industry got its start, the situation had been even worse, Manoilescu surmised, because the cities under Phanariot rule and Turkish suzerainty (i.e., unalloyed colonialism) were almost wholly centers of consumption; agricultural exports were used to purchase luxury manufactures abroad. Incipient industrialization, he thought, had indirectly diminished the exploitation of the countryside by reducing dependence on international trade.[7] In accordance with his international trade theory, Manoilescu also perceived a greater transfer of income from the countryside when foreign trade was greater.[8] Manoilescu believed that as workers were transferred to industry in ever-larger numbers, in the long run rural wages would rise, thus reducing the exploitation of rural labor and bringing about the possibility of an equalization of wages and productivity between city and hinterland.[9]

For such reasons backward countries should industrialize, he held. As noted in

Chapter 5, Manoilescu is remembered in modern development theory for the "Manoilescu argument,"[10] and nowhere does he sum up this proposition better than in his little-known study "The Economic Triangle": "Marginal workers, whose labor in agriculture is needed less and less, and whose personal consumption may even surpass the value of their production, form an unproductive category from the economic point of view, and a destitute group from the social point of view. They form a class of underemployed [*demi-chomeurs*]." He adds that such persons should migrate to urban areas to seek industrial employment.[11]

For Manoilescu a second process of exploitation occurred in direct trade between the city and the countryside. The latter, he held, typically has a positive commercial balance with the city, just as the agricultural-exporting country typically has such a balance with its industrial trading partner. Both typically have a negative balance of payments, however.[12] (Here Manoilescu is referring to capital flows; the balance of payments—current, capital and cash accounts—could not be negative over the long run.) One source of income transfer occurred through the mechanism of debt repayment, Manoilescu observed. The land reform in Rumania had diminished the exploitation of the peasantry, but usury had done much to restore it. The countryside was greatly indebted to urban creditors, and usurers received 14 percent annual interest on their loans, according to Manoilescu, in a period of falling agricultural prices.[13] Villagers also paid indirectly for interest on state bonds, assets almost entirely held by landlords and urban dwellers.[14] Payments on foreign-held debt were also covered by exports, the bulk of them from the countryside.[15]

Manoilescu was not able to determine directly what percentage of agricultural income was spent on products of the cities; but by relying on scientific studies of village life by Dimitrie Gusti's Institutul Social Român, including peasant budget data, he was able to make an estimate. Using the same materials, he also established a lower bound for consumption of agricultural goods in the cities.[16] Having estimates for both urban and rural dwellers' expenditures on each other's goods, he concluded that there was a net flow of goods (or payments) to the urban areas.[17]

These two forms of exploitation, urban-rural and international (both involving the subordination of agricultural producers to urban-industrial groups), were, Manoilescu believed, characteristic processes of modern capitalism, according to the models examined here and in the previous chapter. A third form was also present in Rumania but was circumstantial rather than necessary. This was fiscal exploitation, a problem Manoilescu had investigated firsthand as undersecretary of finance in 1926. Though urban inhabitants in Rumania paid the treasury four times more per capita than their rural counterparts in 1925, they received six times as much in state expenditures.[18] Manoilescu calculated that in 1925, 68 percent of state outlays went to the cities, while only 12 percent went to the countryside; the remainder was sent abroad for debt servicing.[19]

The Great Depression increased the differentiation between the country's constituent sectors, owing to the widening "price scissors" between agricultural and industrial goods in Rumania. Because the income gap between urban and rural inhabitants was growing in the 1930s, thought Manoilescu, urban areas depended on each other more than ever for their markets, since the peasantry was destitute.[20] In general, Manoilescu argued, the gap in income and wealth between city and countryside was greater in underdeveloped countries than in modern industrial nations.[21] Because all trade between industrial and agricultural producers involved exploitation, Manoilescu held, the state, at least in theory, could address the problem of internal colonialism to limit exploitation in a way it could not in international commerce.[22]

Although exploitation of ethnically subordinate groups did not form part of Manoilescu's analysis, as it did in some later treatments of internal colonialism,[23] ethnic differentiation of exploiter and exploited did not escape him, but it occurred in a manner contrary to that observed in the 1960s by Pablo González Casanova in Mexico, where the Indian communities formed an oppressed minority. Manoilescu noted that ethnic minorities in interwar Rumania—a country that had doubled its national territory after World War I—were overwhelmingly urban dwellers, while ethnic Rumanians formed almost the whole of the peasantry. Thus the townsmen, and by implication the exploiters, were not only the ethnically Rumanian landlords who spent their wealth in the cities but also Jews, Germans, and Hungarians, who composed a disproportionately large share of the urban population and tended to control industry, banking, and commerce.[24] Despite the withering criticisms from contemporary critics of Manoilescu's theory on trade and productivity (see following section), one might still argue that Manoilescu's model of internal colonialism survived to the extent that it described a process of income flows accurately, even if the author's explanation of the underlying causes was incorrect. In particular, the exploitation of town by countryside had more to do with social configurations (landlord-peasant relations) than with trade as such.

Manoilescu's economic program today would be described as state-directed import-substitution industrialization. Presumably, if the agrarian country succeeded in transforming itself into an industrial nation, it could—and would be advised to—follow the practice of presently industrialized countries and ultimately export manufactures.[25] But Manoilescu does not seem to have made such a strategy explicit;[26] he preferred to emphasize the long-run gains from expanded trade to be reaped by the currently industrialized countries[27] and did not consider the implications for those countries even further behind in the race toward high productivities than the ones that would adopt his policies. If he had, the political appeal of his argument might have been strengthened because the later a country jumped on the bandwagon, the fewer countries would remain to exploit through unequal exchange.

Although Manoilescu's *Theory of Protectionism* was published in six languages by the late 1930s and was well-received in some journals,[28] as a whole the economics profession in the 1930s greeted Manoilescu's theses with hostility.[29] The Swedish economist Bertil Ohlin, perhaps the leading neoclassical trade theorist of the 1930s,[30] criticized Manoilescu's assumptions: Why should the average productivity of all national industries be considered representative of that of the export industries? What justified the assumption that the price level of factors is everywhere equal, when it was known that money wages in the United States were more than ten times higher than in Rumania? Why did Manoilescu consider only labor productivity in his calculations and ignore capital and land?[31] (Manoilescu did consider these two factors in theory and gave formulas for their measurement but attempted to obtain cross-country empirical data only for labor productivity.) "It goes without saying," Ohlin remarked, "that the output per worker does not provide any test as to productivity, as the quantity of other productive factors used per worker is widely different in different industries." Wages, Ohlin argued, were a better measure of labor productivity across industries.[32] In addition, Ohlin observed, Manoilescu's assumption of constant costs and fixed prices on the world market, in the face of changing trade relations, led to the absurd conclusion that "it would pay to produce only manufactured goods and import agricultural products" in his "agricultural country."[33] Ohlin's "fundamental criticism," however, was that, as Manoilescu assumed that factors of production can move from activities with low productivities to those with high productivities, the benefits from protection arise from the allegation that protection causes the transfer. But why, Ohlin asked, did this transfer not occur *without* protection inasmuch as price signals should favor the industries with higher productivities?[34]

Jacob Viner, the leading trade theorist in the United States in the 1930s, agreed with Ohlin's critique but thought he had conceded "too much" to Manoilescu. If domestic prices or wages were higher in one economic activity than in another, one had to consider the *reason* for it, which might well be artificial wage rates through trade union monopoly. Viner agreed that protection of manufactures could raise the real income of a country if it had a comparative labor advantage in manufacturing and if trade union monopoly kept wages so high in industry that imports could underprice domestic manufactures. But he pointed out that free trade could achieve the same end by forcing a reduction in industrial wages and revealing true comparative advantages in market prices. Viner dismissed Manoilescu's book with the judgment, "The task of finding an intellectually satisfactory economic defense of protection still awaits achievement, and has not been carried forward by this attempt."[35]

In 1937, five years after writing his review of *The Theory of Protectionism*, Viner published a major theoretical volume, defending and extending the neoclassical theory of international trade. Among his contributions was the "liberation" of the doctrine of comparative costs from the labor theory of value, accepted by Ricardo and some non-Marxist economists into the 1930s, including, of course, Manoilescu.[36] In his *Studies in the Theory of International Trade*, Viner pointed out that "the association of the comparative cost doctrine with the labor-cost theory of value" was a "historical accident." Most classical economists other than Ricardo expressed real costs as ultimately subjective phenomena—what were later called "disutilities" (e.g., the postponement of consumption or the irksomeness of labor)—though "they generally assumed that disutilities were proportional to quantities of the services of the factors [of production]." Nevertheless, a later commentator, Nicholas Georgescu-Roegen, was skeptical that Viner had had the last word.[37]

Not only was Manoilescu attacked in western Europe and the United States; in Rumanian academic circles his theses were probably contested more than they were accepted in the 1930s. A sharp critic of both *Theory of Protectionism* and *Century of Corporatism* was George Taşcă, rector of the Academy of Commercial and Industrial Studies in Bucharest and a former minister of commerce and industry.[38] Taşcă, a liberal antifascist with doctorates in both law and economics from the Sorbonne, reiterated several of Ohlin's arguments. A striking point of his own, aimed more at Manoilescu's nationalist credentials than his economic analysis, began with the concession that his opponent might be right that a Rumanian peasant gave ten days' labor for one day's labor embodied in a manufactured product purchased abroad. But because Manoilescu allowed that national manufacturing industry was only one-fourth as productive as foreign competing industries, the same Rumanian peasant under a closed economy would have to exchange forty days' labor instead of ten, to acquire the same industrial product. Writing in 1937, when Rumanian imports from Germany were rising rapidly (to exceed half the total by 1939), Taşcă twisted the knife by adding that in the first case, the peasant would be exploited by a German industrialist; in the second, because of the underrepresentation of ethnic Rumanians in manufacturing enterprises, he would be exploited by an industrialist of Rumania's German minority community.[39]

A critical but more favorable review of the expanded German edition of Manoilescu's *Theory of Protectionism*, published in 1937, was that of Michal Kalecki. The Polish economist, then working in England, was regarded in the postwar period as one of the leading macroeconomists of his generation and an authority on economic development. Though noting with interest Manoilescu's assertion that capital per worker rather than the quantity of labor expended determines prices, as per Ricardo, Kalecki criticized Manoilescu for not using neoclassical criteria for economic optima, based on the marginal productivities of labor and capital. He further noted that if Manoilescu's "specific capital" was the key to high levels of productivity, new capital investments had to be obtained at the expense of some other economic activity, and he asked if capital-starved agriculture would provide it. Nonetheless, Kalecki agreed with Manoilescu's policy prescription of protection for new industries as a means of engendering capital formation and employment in underdeveloped countries.[40]

Nor did Manoilescu find wide acceptance of his theses in Hitler's Germany, whose economists, as well as political leaders, he was courting, beginning with Werner Sombart.[41] Carl Brinkmann, reviewing the German edition of Manoilescu's treatise on trade in 1938, criticized the Rumanian's approach to trade theory as outdated and static, based as it was on the classical's treatment of comparative costs, the labor theory of value, and average costs, whereas modern theory was based on comparative prices, modern (neoclassical) value theory, and marginal costs.[42] Otto Fröhlich gave Manoilescu's theses equally bad marks in the same journal, *Weltwirtschaftliches Archiv*.[43]

In 1939, however, Ernst Wagemann, head of the Institut für Konjunktur-forschung (Business Cycles Research Institute) in Berlin, gave Manoilescu qualified support—with an *arrière pensée*. A leading apologist for the *Grossraum-wirtschaft*, Wagemann wrote that he feared Manoilescu's analysis of international trade was "too good" and that unequal exchange occurred universally between agriculture and industry. He added that the industrialization of agrarian countries required foreign physical capital, which could be obtained only by export credits earned through the sales of traditional agricultural products.[44] He contended that because Germany now took more than half the Balkan countries' exports (as opposed to one-sixth in 1931), the *Grossraumwirtschaft* offered the best hope for Balkan progress. Development of the export market would ultimately lead to development of the domestic market, Wagemann asserted, but Germany could still profit from this eventuality by supplying the Balkan countries with capital goods.[45] Elsewhere Wagemann was more critical of Manoilescu.[46]

Other strictures could be made about Manoilescu's supply-side economics, which assumes, for instance, that the new income created would necessarily be used to purchase "higher-productivity" goods. Furthermore, as services at the end of the twentieth century loom ever larger both in national product and international trade, the Rumanian economist's omission of the tertiary sector appears as an increasingly serious weakness in his theory.[47] Another problem is inconsistency in his voluminous writings, and it is sometimes difficult to separate Manoilescu's economic policy flipflops (e.g., for or against commodity price agreements in international trade as the prime objective, for or against autarky) from sudden turns in his theoretical analysis; the latter type of volte-face sometimes appeared in academic journals as well as in the shriller polemics of his corporatist review, *Lumea Nouă*. Asserting that the advantage of industrial countries in international trade falls secularly and "continuously,"[48] Manoilescu ignored the fact that the sharp and sustained depression of agricultural prices from 1925 to 1935 was not "predicted" by his theory. Further, the allegation that international trade was the *basis* for the wealth of Western countries[49] implicitly conflicted with his observation that rich countries trade less with poor countries than with each other.[50] In the latter case, who was exploiting whom?

Manoilescu nonetheless had an important insight about the development process that was expanded and rigorously formulated by the American economist Everett Hagen in 1958. After considering longitudinal and cross-country data showing that wages (a measure of productivity) were consistently higher in manufacturing than in agriculture, Hagen demonstrated theoretically that "protectionism raises real income, relative to free trade, if the increase under protection in the aggregate cost of the industrial product to its buyers is less than the increase in income to the factors which shift from agriculture to industry." At the empirical level, citing the cases of the United States, Japan, the Soviet Union, and—perhaps less convincingly—Brazil, Colombia, and Mexico, Hagen wrote, "The broad historical record suggests that protectionism may have accelerated economic development."[51] Hagen traced the origins of his thesis to insights by Gottfried Haberler and Jacob Viner but not to Manoilescu, whom he also mentions.[52]

On the matter of the evolution of the world economy, it is clear that the Rumanian trade theorist—or as Ronald Findlay prefers to call him, the Rumanian "writer"[53]—failed to take into account the dynamism of modern industrial capitalism. Manoilescu's assumption of static costs and prices implied a static technology, and had he lived into the 1960s he would have seen that developed countries' control of technological innovation made irrelevant much of the diffusion of industrial production to the Third World. Productivities in the dynamic sectors of manufacturing were still *relatively* low in Third World countries, and the income gap between developed and underdeveloped countries was not obviously closing.

Beyond his shortcomings as a theorist, Manoilescu's political activity and inconsistency in his advocacy of economic policies probably diminished the currency of his writings as an economist after the war. It seems probable that given his reception in parts of both agrarian Europe (including Iberia) and Latin America, Manoilescu would have attracted more attention as a precursor of development economics had it not been for his politics. In 1937, he was elected on the Iron Guard's ticket to the Rumanian senate, and in 1938, he saw political opportunity in an association with Nazi Germany. Up to that time, as a professor of economics at the Polytechnic in Bucharest and in many venues abroad, mostly of an academic nature, Manoilescu defended the thesis of the closed economy. He now began to support Hitler's *Grossraumwirtschaft*, and, though he was subsequently anything but consistent, Manoilescu renounced his thesis on international trade.[54] To take the public position that Rumania should become a supplier of agricultural goods and raw materials for Greater Germany seems to stand in the sharpest contradiction to Manoilescu's professed theoretical convictions. In 1939 he asserted that Germany would pay prices well above those of the world market;[55] this action would implicitly eliminate or mitigate the degree of exploitation of the agricultural exporter by its industrial trading partner. In his academic writings in the 1940s, Manoilescu oscillated but usually defended some degree of industrialization for Rumania and other agrarian countries.

Finally, to understand Manoilescu's influence, we must give some attention to the economic aspects of his political thought. In his own day, Manoilescu was as well-known for his theory of corporatism as for his economic theses, although—and perhaps significantly—after the defeat of fascism he judged *The Theory of Protectionism* to have been his most important work.[56] His contemporaries considered *The Century of Corporatism* equally influential, if one may judge by its reception in Iberia and Latin America. Our interest concerns the relation between his political and economic views and the ways in which his political propositions contributed to the diffusion of his economic theses. There was such a relation, as is implicit in the judgment of the Brazilian demographer Josué de Castro that Manoilescu was a "Neo-St.-Simonian," emphasizing the pro-planning, pro-industrialization, elitist, and organicist elements in Henri St.-Simon's thought.[57]

Corporatism was an ideology that had its roots in the organicist social theory of medieval Europe, but its more immediate precursor was the "solidarism" of Léon Bourgeois (1851–1925), who sought to avert or minimize class struggle.[58] Frédéric LePlay (1806–82) was among the early theorists who called for collaboration between workers and capitalists. Corporatism had articulate defenders in Germany and Italy as well as in France before Italy became a corporate state during the course of the 1920s and 1930s. In Rumania, corporatist elements had already appeared in the constitution of 1923, allowing for a limited representation of corporations in the senate, along with directly elected members. Manoilescu himself represented the Chamber of Commerce in the Rumanian senate from 1932 to 1937.

In the interwar years corporatism was defended as the *tierce solution, der dritte Weg*, to the problems of the modern economy, a path different from those laid out by communism and free-market capitalism. For a variety of corporatist theorists, prices would be set to achieve a just division of the social product, based on costs of production.[59] Although Manoilescu's *Century of Corporatism* appeared in 1934, near the high tide of the vogue of that doctrine, his views on the subject had developed alongside his economic thought from the early 1920s. In 1923, the same year the new Rumanian constitution was approved, he had written a pamphlet titled *Neoliberalism*,[60] in which the author argued that postwar liberalism was fundamentally different from its nineteenth-century forebear. For Manoilescu, neoliberalism accepted the need for the representation of social classes rather than of individuals and sought to effect an "equilibrium" of such groups. Unlike the old gendarme state, its neoliberal successor would be a permanent interventor in the social process. The nation, rather than the individual, was now the "elementary organic unit" of society. Instead of the freedom and equality of individuals, neoliberalism would seek to secure the freedom and equality of nations. In Rumania, a neoliberal party could not be based on a single class, for the reason that it must have authority over selfish class interests.[61]

In 1932, after his association with several political parties and currently out of favor with the king, Manoilescu pronounced himself a full-fledged corporatist. He launched *Lumea Nouă*, a monthly political review, in April; in September, he outlined his theory of corporatism in his maiden speech in the Rumanian senate.[62] Manoilescu proceeded to organize a corporatist party in 1933.[63] The following year he published *The Century of Corporatism: Doctrine of Integral and Pure Corporatism*.[64] The century in question was our own. Just as the last century had been that of liberalism, so this one would be that of corporatism, whose historical necessity Manoilescu now proclaimed. All [European?] societies had been corporately organized until the French Revolution, but the industrial revolution had required the liberal state and the destruction of mercantilist policies to maximize capitalism's economic potential.[65] In the new corporatist society, the guiding principle of organization would be substituted for that of profit.[66] Among the competing versions of corporatism, Manoilescu distinguished his own with the assertion that true corporatism had two basic characteristics: it was "integral" because it included not only economic corporations but also noneconomic corporate bodies such as the army and the church. It was "pure," he intoned, because corporations formed "the only legitimate basis" for the exercise of political power and could not be subordinated to the state. Thus the Fascist system in Italy failed the test because corporations in Italy were manifestly controlled by the state.[67]

For Manoilescu the "dominant," but not the sole, reason for the rise of corporatism in the current century was the West's loss of its industrial monopoly, resulting in the Great Depression, as European countries failed to place goods in their agricultural dependencies.[68] Thus, as traditional markets disappeared, the West faced an economic crisis that could be properly confronted only by implementing the new principle of organization.[69] There was a widespread tendency toward autarky, and this trend could stimulate national economic integration ("solidarity").[70] The corporatist state would not be neutral, as the nineteenth-century liberal state sought to be, but must be "the bearer of ideals." In this respect, Fascist Italy offered the "prototype" of the new state—apparently not withstanding the fact that Italian corporations were controlled by the regime.[71]

In the past century, liberty was the (social) ideal; under corporatism, the ideal would be organization, which Manoilescu termed the fourth factor of production.[72] The four "imperatives" to be achieved by the corporate state were organization, national solidarity, peace and international collaboration, and "decapitalization," that is, decreasing the rate of profit, when necessary, for the public interest. Manoilescu repeated his earlier thesis that there was a clash between the benefit to the individual entrepreneur and the benefit to the collectivity, a notion he preferred to call "productivity," apparently in the sense of the average value (or a weighted average) of output per worker. This conflict in fact was the "great antithesis" between corporatism and liberalism in economics.[73] Production and foreign trade must be directed toward goods that permit the acquisition of a maximum of the product of foreign labor with the minimum expenditure of labor of one's own nation. This was "organized production and organized trade."[74] Thus, in a backward agrarian country, the implementation of the corporatist regime was a means for achieving the author's economic program.

At the level of economic theory, of course, the previous criticisms of his arguments apply to the short and rhetorical version embedded in *Century*. It may also be asked why, if the social weal in the form of labor productivity rather than entrepreneurial profit was the value to be maximized, Manoilescu did not pursue the notion of price formation as a function of accords among corporations and trade unions in an age of highly organized labor and capital markets.[75] Othmar Spann, the Austrian corporatist, believed, however naively, that the relationship between functional corporations should determine prices and that collective bargaining would force employers into cartels, thereby promoting corporatism.[76] During the 1930s other corporatists such as François Perroux also concerned themselves with price formation under oligopolistic conditions, as did leading noncorporatist economists such as Edward Chamberlin and Joan Robinson.[77]

Manoilescu wrote that in its social dimension, the corporation was a "vertical" form of social solidarity, as social classes were a "horizontal" form. Furthermore, in "integral and pure corporatism," the state was both a corporation and a "supercorporation" to coordinate and equilibrate corporate bodies.[78] It would replace political parties in balancing reactionary and revolutionary tendencies and also in integrating social classes, a function sometimes attributed to parties. Parties were outmoded, but the corporate regime would not forcibly end them, Manoilescu announced in *Century of Corporatism*.[79] Yet only two years after writing *Century*, he reversed himself in a work called *The Single Party*,[80] declaring Europe's authoritarian regimes to be a necessity during the period of transition from liberalism to corporatism.

Given the controversial and inconsistent figure that Mihail Manoilescu cut, it is hardly surprising that his political ideas were vigorously attacked in Rumania, including those that were closely associated with his trade theory. George Taşcă, the professor who had sharply criticized Manoilescu's economics, took on the latter's corporatism in the same essay: Manoilescu caricatured liberalism by presenting a laissez-faire straw man, wrote Taşcă, when in 1923 Manoilescu had in fact presented a modern, interventionist version of the doctrine in his essay *Neoliberalism*. Manoilescu wanted autonomous corporations, unlike those existing in present-day corporatist regimes, but in reality a choice had to be made between strong corporations and a strong state, thought Taşcă.[81] He also continued his critique of Manoilescu's trade theory, leading the latter to reply that the link between his economic and social thought was "conditioned and limited."[82]

Was there any consistency in Manoilescu's political writings, as opposed to his political activities? One finds a consistent defense of elite leadership, which Manoilescu himself pointed out.[83] Philippe Schmitter, who has most fully placed Manoilescu's political thought into the context of the development of corporatism—and who provides a discussion of his economic theses as well—does not take into account the Rumanian's opportunism in his shift from supporting industrialization to the *Grossraumwirtschaft*, even though he sees a certain logic in the shift from a defense of the corporatism of autonomous corporations to that of the single party. The latter was the instrument for achieving corporatism, although there was a contradiction here, Schmitter notes, for in *Century of Corporatism* two years before *Single Party* Manoilescu had predicted the end of political parties.[84] Schmitter did not follow Manoilescu's political career closely, and he missed the latter's attempt to position himself for a major political role in Rumania under Nazi aegis.

Indeed, had the Rumanian's political associations in the late 1930s and the war years been less closely linked with Rumanian fascism and the aspirations of the Third Reich, his emphasis on the double factorial terms of trade, the "Manoilescu argument" that disguised unemployment in agriculture should be remedied by moving idle labor to industrial activities, his attempt to theorize about unequal exchange, and his model of internal colonialism all might have been more influential in Third World nations in the postwar era.

Part II

TRANSIT

7

The International Context

The transit of theorizing about unequal exchange, dependency, disguised unemployment, and other issues of underdevelopment from East Central Europe to Latin America was by no means a simple one. The sources of a structuralist analysis to explain Latin America's underdevelopment were various, and the complex story involves Manoilescu and other corporatists; Keynesian economists originally from East Central Europe; trade theorists working in a neoclassical tradition; and the changing international environment, as evidenced by neoclassical economists at the League of Nations working on more practical problems.

We shall begin with three corporatist economists, Manoilescu, Werner Sombart, and François Perroux. Manoilescu's thesis on international trade has some strong similarities with the original structuralist thesis of Raúl Prebisch in the early postwar period, associated with the United Nations' Economic Commission for Latin America. Prebisch's analysis laid the foundation, built on by the ECLA-associated Celso Furtado, for the Brazilian structuralist tradition. A connection between the ideas of Manoilescu and Raúl Prebisch (and by implication those of Hans Singer) has been inferred by Jacob Viner, the celebrated trade theorist; Juan Noyola Vázquez, the Mexican economist who pioneered the structuralist thesis on inflation; Costin Murgescu, a major figure in the economics profession of postwar Rumania; Ivanciu Nicolae-Văleanu, a historian of economic thought in that country; and Philippe Schmitter, a prominent student of European and Latin American corporatism.[1]

Given the intellectual exchange of the regionwide structuralist school and its Brazilian members from the late 1940s onward, it is relevant to look at the publication of Manoilescu's work across Spanish- and Portuguese-language areas, and not just publications in Brazil alone, because of the possible "feedback" to the Brazilian milieu, as well as the direct impact there of Manoilescu's ideas. Consequently, I will briefly survey the diffusion of Manoilescu's ideas in the Iberian and Ibero-American world. Publication of Manoilescu's work in Spanish and Portuguese and citations of his work are indications of his projection in the Hispanic world, which, directly or indirectly, through Latin American structuralism, may have affected Brazilian economic thought.

The Rumanian's two most important works, *Theory of Protectionism* and *Century of Corporatism* (both composed in French) were published in Portuguese and Spanish; his *Single Party* also appeared in the latter language.[2] Manoilescu, moreover, was proud of his reputation as an economist in South America.[3] Thus I will seek to answer the question, To what extent and in what ways did Manoilescu prepare the way for the postwar propositions of Raúl Prebisch and the Latin American structuralist school? According to Prebisch, at the international level, unequal exchange derived from differential productivities and different demand patterns between an industrial Center and an agricultural Periphery in the world trading system, combined with different institutional arrangements in capital and labor markets in the two elements. Industrialization would provide an exit from the increasingly lagging position of the Periphery. I will begin to evaluate Manoilescu's influence on Prebisch by looking at the spread of the Rumanian's ideas. Judging by publications in translation and citations, the Rumanian writer had his greatest impact in four countries of the Iberian world: Spain, Portugal, Chile, and Brazil. I shall consider the first three instances, reserving Brazil for later treatment, and try to account for his lack of popularity in Argentina, where Prebisch was developing his ideas in the 1930s and 1940s.

Although he was frequently invited by the São Paulo industrialists' association to visit Brazil,[4] Manoilescu never made the journey, but he did visit Iberia. In 1936, four months before the outbreak of the Spanish civil war, the Rumanian lectured in both Spain and Portugal. In the latter country, interest in Manoilescu's work focused on *The Century of Corporatism* rather than his arguments for protection. The Portuguese dictator António Salazar had come to power in a political and financial crisis in 1927 but established a formal corporatist regime only in 1933. Manoilescu met with Salazar and his future successor, Marcelo Caetano, and his praise for the corporatist dictatorship was recalled a half-century later by one of Portugal's leading novelists, José Saramago.[5] According to the Rumanian, Salazar had read *Century* and discussed its contents at their meeting.[6] Caetano, then a law professor, demonstrated his knowledge and approval of the work in his tract *The Corporative System*.[7] None of Manoilescu's major works was published in Portugal, perhaps because the people who mattered could read *Century of Corporatism* in the French original[8] and because *Century* and *Theory of Protectionism* both found publishers in Brazil in the 1930s.

Caetano apparently had no objection to the brief economic analysis found in *Century of Corporatism*;[9] however, the Rumanian economist's theses on trade and industrialization found little resonance in official Portugal during the 1930s, partly, one may assume, because of the ideological predominance of agrarian interests, as represented in the "neophysiocratic" ideas of Quirino de Jesús and

Ezequiel de Campos.[10] Portuguese support for industrialization at the official level was dominated by engineering criteria rather than any formal economic analysis (involving optimization, opportunity cost, and the like) until late in the Salazar regime.[11] In addition, it is possible that Manoilescu's anti-imperialism, though it clearly focused on Britain and France, lessened the appeal of his economic message in official Portugal, where the metropolis was heavily committed in the 1930s to the defense and expansion of trade with its colonial empire.[12]

In Spain, by contrast with Portugal, the Rumanian's economic writings had more impact than those on corporatism, though the latter was already influential by the mid-1930s in a tract published by a former Spanish labor minister.[13] Manoilescu's argument for state-induced industrialization elicited the interest of economists who tended to view Spain, like Rumania, as a backward agrarian country. The first article discussing Manoilescu's thesis on trade and industrialization appeared in 1936, following his visit to Spain and Portugal, and his economics was discussed more frequently in the 1940s. By that time, industrialization in Spain was beginning to receive more attention as a solution to backwardness. Manoilescu's popularity as an economist in the new authoritarian regime may have also received a boost from the fact that during the civil war, the Rumanian enthusiastically backed General Francisco Franco's cause and authorized the publication of his *Single Party* in Spanish on Nationalist-held territory.[14]

The contrasting reception accorded the Rumanian's economic ideas in Spain and Portugal, of course, had partly to do with the differing domestic and international political circumstances in which the two peninsular nations found themselves during the 1930s and 1940s. Portugal, because of its pro-Ally neutrality in World War II, did not face the commercial constraints Spain did after the Axis began to crumble. Spain's pro-Axis neutrality during the war resulted in the country's increasing political and economic isolation from 1943 onward. As a consequence, in the 1940s Spanish economists high in the regime used *Theory of Protectionism* as an argument for industrialization, self-sufficiency, and—facing the hostility of the victorious Allies—even autarky, *faute de mieux*.[15]

In Spain, Manoilescu's attack on comparative advantage was first discussed in a lead article of the country's most important economics journal by Luis Olariaga, a chairholder at the University of Madrid, shortly after the Rumanian's lectures in the Spanish capital in March 1936. Olariaga discussed Manoilescu's thesis and the objections to it by Ohlin, Viner, and the French economist Firmin Oulès. Although accepting these criticisms to the extent of finding Manoilescu's analysis overly simplified, Olariaga nonetheless believed that "at bottom there is doubtless a correct intuition [in Manoilescu's thesis], and the problem he poses responds, within certain limits, to a real situation."[16]

From 1940 to 1945, Manoilescu's views were discussed by at least four Spanish economists—Pedro Gual Villalbí, José Ros Jimeno, Higinio Paris Eguilaz, and Manuel Fuentes Irurozqui—in contrast to the relative lack of interest in his economic studies in Portugal.[17] Not only that, but after appearing in serial form in Spanish, *Theory of Protectionism* was published in book format by the Ministry of Industry and Commerce, with an introduction by Fuentes Irurozqui, the inspector-general of trade and tariff policy.[18]

During World War II Manoilescu's ideas on industrialization were used to support autarkic views, given the country's lack of foreign exchange at the end of the civil war in March 1939, the scarcity of foreign inputs and investments when the general European conflict broke out six months later, and the rising isolation of the Spanish government as a pariah regime when the Axis began to lose the war. In his *Theory*, the work Spaniards cited on this issue, however, Manoilescu was not a defender of autarky, although he had briefly supported autarky in a Rumanian-language study following the collapse of the World Monetary Conference in 1933.[19] In the judgment of the leading student of Spanish autarky, Manoilescu's study, along with a work of a Spanish engineer, Antonio Robert, mark the transition from autarky to industrialization for its own sake.[20]

Juan Antonio Suanzes, the organizer and first director of Spain's industrial development corporation, the Instituto Nacional de Industria (INI), accepted Manoilescu's thesis that industry's productivity was much greater than agriculture's and was an enthusiast of Manoilescu's industrialization *à outrance*.[21] And yet, though INI was founded in 1941,[22] autarky as a desideratum during the war years was also manipulated by agrarian interests. Industrialization as the Spanish regime's foremost policy goal remained a bizarre idea in the early 1940s. In Spain at the time there still existed an "agrarian fatalism";[23] therefore, policy differences with Portugal were a matter of degree.

As in Portugal, engineers like Suanzes and Robert rather than economists tended to determine Spain's industrial policy, and they failed to take into account opportunity costs, that is, allocation of scarce resources; they pursued an engineering optimum rather than an economic optimum.[24] Consequently, in Spain, as in Portugal, *productivismo* ("productivism") and *ingenierismo* ("engineering-ism")—attitudes more than theories—prevailed in the early years of the Franco era.[25] Because autarky did not have a defensible rationale as an economic policy in the postwar world—bringing losses in export opportunities, technological diffusion, and efficiency in selecting proper proportions of capital and labor—it was largely defended with cultural values of nationalism and nationality during Spain's protracted political and economic isolation.[26] Nevertheless, during the years 1945–48 "industrialization" came to replace "autarky" as the watchword of the regime.[27]

For a variety of reasons having to do with civil war losses and postwar exhaustion, as well as a drastic curtailment of foreign trade, economic stagnation tended to characterize the Spain of the 1940s, and major growth in manufacturing came in the 1950s, when government policy tipped decisively toward industry; only in the latter decade did industrial output surpass that of agriculture.[28] The state's support for most dynamic industrial sectors, beginning in the 1940s, was a policy of which Manoilescu would have approved. Yet those same industries were most technologically dependent on foreign sources, which constrained growth when foreign exchange was scarce.[29]

In Latin America, Manoilescu's ideas received favorable attention in Chile, which, along with Argentina and Brazil, was one of the three most industrialized countries in the region in the 1930s and 1940s. At the time, Chilean statesmen, industrialists, and publicists were discussing European ideas on corporatism and economic "rationalization" (principally cartelization) as a form of countermonopoly against the industrialized countries. Some of them argued that industrialization was a necessary condition for economic independence and high living standards.[30] There was another reason for believing the Rumanian's theses would be well received in Chile: Friedrich List had probably been more celebrated there than in any other Latin American country. List, the originator of the "infant industry" argument, held that under certain conditions a local industry could become as efficient as its foreign competitors, given a time factor that would permit a reduction in unit costs of production, through economies of scale and economies external to the firm. List found his Chilean paladin in Malaquías Concha, who would popularize the German economist's views between the 1880s and World War I.[31] Though List was known elsewhere in Latin America, including Argentina and Brazil, he was probably better received in Chile, where, according to one economist's research, industrialization as a sustained process may have begun earlier than in any other Latin American country.[32]

It was in comparison to List's ideas that Manoilescu's trade theory probably first came to the attention of Chilean economists shortly after World War II, though it is notable that *Century of Corporatism* had already found a publisher in Chile in 1941.[33] In 1945 Edgar Mahn Hecker published an article in *Economía*, the economics journal of the University of Chile, titled "On the Protectionist Arguments of List and Manoilescu."[34] The writer followed Manoilescu's own reasoning on this matter, and by concentrating on the productivity gains from transferring labor from agriculture to industry within a given national economy, Mahn followed the Rumanian's interpretation on the differences between himself and List. Whereas List defended long-run gains from industrialization (as against short-run losses), Manoilescu contended that the advantage to the national economy at issue was immediate, assuming that the new industrial undertaking had a labor productivity higher than the national average of economic activities.[35]

Two years later Mahn published a translation of Manoilescu's "Labor Productivity and Foreign Trade" in *Economía*. This was a succinct presentation of the Rumanian's central theses, a statement originally appearing in *Weltwirtschaftliches Archiv* in 1935.[36] Here Manoilescu summarized the arguments of his *Theory*, showing empirically that labor productivity was much higher in industry than in traditional agriculture and asserting that for poor countries to specialize in agriculture in international trade produced a situation of unequal exchange; thus industrial protection was justified. It is noteworthy that Manoilescu may have been known through this medium to future principals of ECLA because one of the organization's leading economists, Aníbal Pinto, became the editor of *Economía* a few years later. In retrospect, however, Pinto, who was studying in London when Manoilescu's article appeared, attaches less influence to the Rumanian than to other economists.[37]

Another medium through which Manoilescu's theories may have found a South American audience is the publications and teaching of Ernst Wagemann. The German economist, who had discussed the Rumanian's ideas in *The New Balkans* (1939),[38] had been born in Chile, where he received his early education before studying in Germany. In 1925 he became director of the Institut für Konjunkturforschung in Berlin, and he remained one of the most important economists in Germany through World War II. Wagemann knew Manoilescu personally and with some reservations had ventured a favorable assessment of the Rumanian's trade theory, at least *in abstracto*. He said so not only in *The New Balkans* (1939) but also in *Population and the Fate of Nations* (1948).[39] After Germany's defeat and the collapse of the *Grossraumwirtschaft*, which Wagemann and Manoilescu had both defended,[40] the German economist returned to the country of his birth. He arrived in Santiago in 1949 to direct the National University's Instituto de Economía and to edit its journal, *Economía*. In the same year a Spanish translation of his *Population* was published in Chile. Yet whatever Wagemann's role may have been in propagating Manoilescu's ideas, it seems highly unlikely that the former's activities directly influenced Raúl Prebisch. True, the Argentine economist published his thesis on trade and industrialization in Santiago the year Wagemann returned to Chile, but he had worked out most of his major theses in 1948, the previous year.

Across the Andes in Argentina, where Raúl Prebisch directed the Central Bank from 1935 to 1943, Manoilescu's economic theories were unknown to industrialists in the 1930s and 1940s, if one may judge by the absence of his name and ideas in the trade journal of the national manufacturers' organization, the Unión Industrial Argentina.[41] The pro-clerical literary journal *Criterio* favored corporatism in the early 1940s but did not single out Manoilescu's model in politics, nor did it discuss his economics.[42] It is also notable that at the Facultad de Economía at the University of Buenos Aires, only two theses on corporatism were deposited from the 1930s to the 1950s, and neither cited the Rumanian theorist's political or economic works.[43]

Nonetheless, Manoilescu was known to Argentine economists. The University of Buenos Aires published South America's best journal of economics, the *Revista de Ciencias Económicas*, and the doyen of Argentine economists, Luis Roque Gondra, cited Manoilescu's work in that journal in negative terms in

1937. A somewhat more extensive treatment of the protectionist case in the same journal by Mario Pugliese two years later was only slightly more sympathetic.[44] Probably nowhere else in Latin America was the belief in a benign international division of labor so strong as in Argentina, at least until the late 1930s, because the export-driven Argentine economy had expanded so impressively in the half-century before the Great Depression.

There is still another possibility of an influence of Manoilescu on Prebisch—the professional activity of Florin Manoliu, who had been Manoilescu's assistant when the latter held the chair of economics at the Polytechnic School of Bucharest in the 1930s and had published a "biobibliography" on Manoilescu and his work.[45] From December 1940 through June 1947, Manoliu served the Rumanian foreign ministry in Bucharest and elsewhere in Europe as an economic adviser. He apparently emigrated to Argentina in the late 1940s and became an Argentine citizen in 1951. From 1958 until his death in 1971, Manoliu was professor of economics at the Universidad del Sur in Bahía Blanca, Argentina. In some of his publications in the 1960s he cited Manoilescu on trade and industrialization and attempted to popularize his mentor's ideas. Manoliu held no academic position in Argentina before 1958, however, nor, according to his curriculum vitae in Bahía Blanca, did he publish anything in Spanish before 1959. Therefore it is impossible to prove, and indeed seems highly unlikely, that he influenced Prebisch, who had formed his basic propositions by 1948–49.[46]

Beyond Manoilescu, another writer who became a corporatist in his later years and who forms a link between Rumania and Latin America, as well as one between the German Historical School and dualism as a development issue, is Werner Sombart. Before Fernand Braudel, no one in his own time was more often considered the foremost authority on the history of capitalism than Sombart. Indeed, he made the word "capitalism" an indispensable term in modern economic discourse[47]—Marx did not know the term, and Alfred Marshall, Gustav Cassel, and Charles Gide did not use it in their well-known texts. Moreover, Sombart's historical periodization of capitalism into "early," "high," and "late" stages (roughly corresponding to 1500 to 1750, 1750 to 1914, and the post-1914 period), enjoyed wide currency in European social thought between the two world wars.[48] During the preparation of his monumental study, *Modern Capitalism*, the publication of which spanned the years 1902 to 1928, Sombart changed his views, adding the "late" phase. The erstwhile "red professor" by 1902 had already perceived "the spirit of capitalism" and the role of the entrepreneur as its driving forces. Moving away from a quasi-Marxist position long before the publication of the last volumes on high capitalism in 1928, Sombart had adopted some elements of idealism. Like Max Weber, Sombart stressed the role of the will, culture, and social psychology, seeing the Jews (rather than Weber's Protestants) as the pioneers of capitalism. Yet Sombart's explanation had a racial element which Weber's lacked.

In certain respects Sombart can be associated with the third and last generation of the German Historical School of economics, though he was too much a
maverick to be a member of the group. In his youth he had followed his father
into the Verein für Sozialpolitik, an association of conservative but reformist
intellectuals, including Gustav Schmoller, Adolf Wagner, and Lujo Brentano,
men who accepted the epithet *Kathedersozialist* as a badge of honor during Bismarck's empire. In the 1890s the left wing of the Verein included Max and Alfred
Weber and Friedrich Naumann.[49] One of the Verein's abiding concerns was the
position of modern Germany's *Mittelstand*, the intermediate strata of artisans,
better-off peasants, and shopkeepers who were threatened by modern technology and business organization.[50] Here too Sombart was less than consistent,
initially taking a great interest in the *Mittelstand* as part of his *Gemeinschaft* set of
values, virtually abandoning it in mid-career as doomed to extinction,[51] and
returning to champion it in his old age. But "consistency was clearly not one of
Sombart's virtues," in the phrase of one student.[52] Like so many other European
intellectuals, Sombart became an ardent patriot during World War I, and after
Germany's defeat he remained wedded to a nationalist position, though he was
more careful to distinguish his politics from his scholarship than he had been
during the war—until the 1930s.

Sombart enters our story in part because of his conception of global economic
organization. In the last part of *Modern Capitalism*, "High Capitalism," Sombart
envisioned the world as organized around an industrial Center and an agricultural Periphery, with the latter dependent on the former. He wrote: "We
must . . . distinguish a capitalist Center—the central capitalist nations—from a
mass of peripheral countries viewed from that Center; the former are active and
directing, the latter passive and serving. England constituted the capitalist Center
in the first half of the nineteenth century; later, in the longer period of High
Capitalism, Western Europe [joined England]. . . . Finally, in the last generation,
the eastern part of the United States has moved up [to the Center]."[53] Sombart
also wrote of the "dependency" of peripheral countries and even of the servitude
of the peasantry of the Periphery, in part caused by western European capitalism.[54] But this treatment was purely descriptive, and the attempt to model the
relationship between Center and Periphery would come twenty years later, in a
Latin American context.

Another way in which the German economic historian would influence
Third World development theory was his perception of dualism in early capitalism. In the first part of *Modern Capitalism* (1902), he noted that overpopulation
existed in regions of Europe during the sixteenth to eighteenth centuries in areas
where manufacturing was developing, in part because of lack of relevant skills but
primarily because of the lower classes' precapitalist mentality, which, seen
through capitalist lenses, appears to be laziness, sloth. Meanwhile, the upper class
was already inspired with capitalistic values associated with profit maximization.[55]

If we substitute "colonial elites" for "upper classes" and "colonial peasants" for "lower classes," we approach Julius H. Boeke's model of dualism in the Indonesian economy.[56] As noted in Chapter 4, Boeke's was the first widely recognized formal statement (in publications between 1910 and 1953) of the dualist problem, in which the supply of labor is unresponsive to higher wages above a certain level. And in fact Boeke speaks of "early," "high," and "late" capitalism, identifying the village economy of Asia as a precapitalist economy and citing Sombart's dualist model of the early modern economy as apt for the Dutch East Indies.[57] Whether or not the term "dualism" was introduced by Boeke into the postwar discourse, it was already being used in Rumania in the interwar period,[58] and Ştefan Zeletin noted Sombart's contribution to the idea in his *Rumanian Bourgeoisie* in 1925.[59]

After World War I Sombart was principally concerned with the present and future of late capitalism. He addressed the subject in the 1920s and 1930s, with particular application to his own country in *German Socialism* (1934).[60] "Late capitalism" was a term that connoted the routinization of management, the decline of the profit rate, sustained state intervention in the economy, and "rationalization." Rationalization in cost accounting, "scientific management," and cartelization were phenomena that had advanced rapidly in Germany in the 1920s, and Sombart himself had written a book in 1927 called *Rationalization in the Economy*.[61] Late capitalism was apparently a transitional regime to a distant and unspecified form of socialism before the publication of *German Socialism*.[62] The term did not imply the replacement of capitalism by Bolshevism, which for Sombart had little to do with Marxism and was nothing more than "pure Blanquiism."[63]

German Socialism revealed some gruesome elements in the values of the former Kathedersozialist. Still loyal to the military he had supported in Wilhelmine Germany, he wrote that the size of the population was an issue for the General Staff.[64] Further, there were blatantly anti-Semitic elements in Sombart's *German Socialism*, published one year after Hitler came to power as an apology for the new regime, including the view that the "Jewish spirit," which Sombart believed lay at the base of modern capitalism, would have to be eliminated: it was "not enough to exclude all Jews, not even enough to cultivate an anti-Jewish temper."[65] Sombart had in mind reforming "institutional culture," which was affected by the Jewish spirit. Such sentiments, however vague on details, would have significant repercussions in Rumania.[66]

Our chief concern with the book is its corporatist doctrine. For the Sombart of 1934 the self-regulation of cartels might eventually result in a fully corporatist system, Sombart believed.[67] The state was to be "autonomous," and the author favored autarky—a not uncommon view after the failure of the World Monetary Conference in 1933. The rise of a "colored capitalism" in Asia and Africa, as Sombart put it, would make it more difficult in the future for the industrial West to place its manufactures, and the newly industrializing countries would increasingly use their own raw materials for industrial purposes. Capitalism was in decline, and state planning was necessary. Finally, Sombart had now returned to his view that the *Mittelstand*, including the peasantry, had to be saved; in a period of universally depressed agricultural prices, the plight of the peasant class could be redressed in part by the demechanization of agriculture, seemingly a kind of state-controlled Luddism.[68]

A concern for the decline of the *Mittelstand* was also present in Rumania, and the situation of artisans was the starting point for Virgil Madgearu's dissertation at Leipzig (1911).[69] Madgearu was only one of many Rumanian economists and sociologists who cited Sombart, then and later. The prestige of the professor from Berlin was enhanced by his occasional personal appearances in Rumania, owing to the fact that his Rumanian wife was the daughter of a professor at the University of Iaşi. Every major writer from Stere and Gherea in the first decade of the century to Madgearu and Manoilescu in the fourth would appeal to the authority of Sombart.

In an interview in Bucharest in 1929, Sombart spelled out his belief that late capitalism involved the dethroning of the profit motive, achieving a minimum of social welfare, diminishing tensions between labor and capital, decreasing the intensity of competition, and effecting the "rational organization of business enterprises." In the same interview he advocated the modernization of Rumanian agriculture, quite the opposite recommendation he was to make for Germany in 1934. In 1929 he opposed forced industrialization and autarky, at least for Rumania.[70] Two years later the onetime Marxist professor again appeared in Bucharest, presenting a refutation of Marx's predictions—he preferred to call them "prophecies"—to an audience of economists.[71] In 1938 Sombart offered a new message for the Rumanian public: western Europe—presumably excluding the Third Reich—had forced the rest of the world to become buyers of its industrial products and suppliers of raw materials and was still using the violence that characterized the early history of capitalism, as well as commercial policy, to obtain its ends.[72] By implication, the *Grossraumwirtschaft* was a solution to the trading problem for countries like Rumania.

Sombart died in 1941, when Nazi power was near its apogee. After the war his support for the regime, like Manoilescu's, left his work in bad odor in the triumphant liberal and neoclassical world of economics. And yet Sombart's views on dualism probably influenced postwar development economics through Boeke, his periodization of capitalism would appeal to Boeke and some Marxists, and his (unelaborated) perception of capitalism as a system consisting of an active industrial Center and a passive agricultural Periphery probably influenced Raúl Prebisch, who would attempt to model the relationship as a dynamic process. And last, was German Socialism as Sombart defined it a precursor of "African Socialism" and other postwar neopopulisms? The values and instrumentalities of *Gemeinschaft,* with an emphasis on peasant agriculture, economic self-sufficiency, and *Planwirtschaft* (the planned economy) would find their standard-bearers in the Third World proper.[73]

Seen from another angle, Sombart can obviously be associated with other corporatist and fascist writers (e.g., Manoilescu, Enrico Corradini, the Italian proto-fascist, and Ramiro Ledesma Ramos, the founder of the Spanish fascist JONS), who opposed the imperialism of Britain and France. Sombart fits into this set only because of the exceptional position in which Germany found itself in the interwar period. It was potentially the leading European power but was a defeated, and for a time had been a partially occupied, country, stripped of its colonies. Yet Sombart was not blazing a new trail—German politicians and economists had appealed for solidarity with central and southeastern Europe in a continental trading bloc against their nation's great rivals and their overseas empires long before the Nazis came to power, and, as Virgil Madgearu observed, the idea of *Mitteleuropa* can be traced back to the social reformer Friedrich Naumann in 1904.[74]

A corporatist economist who had a greater influence than Sombart in postwar development theory—and a direct one—was François Perroux, who included development theory among his postwar specializations.[75] The French writer's impact in Latin America came in two waves—the first as a theorist of corporatism, the second as a structuralist; Manoilescu's influence as corporatist and structuralist had been simultaneous. For the Perroux of the 1930s, the state would balance opposing monopolies of labor unions and capital in a corporatist economy. Planning would correct the distortions produced by the play of market forces. Workers and employers would be organized in the same producers' corporations, and class collaboration, rather than class conflict, would characterize the new economy. The state would eliminate excessive profits. Joint boards of workers and capitalists, subject to state controls, would set prices and wages. Inspired by social Catholicism, Perroux repeatedly used the metaphors "community of labor" and "family" to emphasize class collaboration.[76]

In 1937, Perroux taught in Brazil, at São Paulo and Pôrto Alegre, and wrote about corporatism in a variety of Brazilian forums, thereby laying a foundation for the subsequent reception of his structuralist economics.[77] Perroux knew Manoilescu through international economics meetings and cited the latter's work in his corporatist writings,[78] though the Frenchman developed his corporatism independently and largely before the Rumanian's *Century of Corporatism* appeared in 1934. Perroux was also the leading French economist of his generation. In his postwar study of the "domination effect," Perroux abandoned the standard assumption of roughly equal power of two or more economic agents in the exchange process and a tendency toward market equilibrium, the absence of which he had stressed as empirical facts in a corporatist treatise in 1938.[79] In fact, his work on monopolistic and oligopolistic markets in the 1930s had prepared him for his postwar study of economic domination, in which actor A exercises an asymmetrical and irreversible effect on actor B, in a relationship of domination-subordination, as opposed to one of "pure [and equal] exchange."

In 1948, based on lectures he offered at Oxford University in 1947, Perroux published his "Sketch of a Theory of the Dominant Economy,"[80] a study focusing on differences in size, bargaining power, and one-way transformations between the United States and its trading partners. "The income- and price-elasticity of the American demand for imports from the rest of the world and the income- and price-elasticity of the demand of the rest of the world for imports from the United States are such that the disequilibrium of trade balances is persistent, and the devaluations of European currencies of doubtful efficacy," he wrote in a summary article of his treatise.[81] Perroux was principally interested in the "dominated" economies of pre–Marshall Plan Europe, but he also argued that agricultural exporters had deteriorating terms of trade, owing to the import patterns of the dominant economy.[82] Perroux's approach was obviously similar to the one Prebisch was employing in the late 1940s. Nevertheless, Prebisch had worked out his basic scheme by 1948, as his unpublished class notes prove, so it seems unlikely that there was any direct connection between the French economist's ideas and those of Prebisch, and it is notable that Perroux's emphasis on differential elasticities of demand is closer to the formulation of Hans Singer (see next chapter) than to that of the Argentine economist.

Yet the main impact of European structuralism on Prebisch and the emerging school of Latin American structuralism did not derive from Perroux but was a consequence of the Keynesian revolution and the way it was developed by Central and East Central Europeans. Keynes's own influence was direct and "genetically" connected to Prebisch's work from the beginning—inter alia, Prebisch wrote a widely used primer on Keynes—whereas Perroux's theories were probably only analogous to the Argentine economist's, at least in the early years. In fact, the connection between Prebisch and Keynes has caused Hans W. Arndt to apply the term "structuralism" to the work of Keynes and his students and allies at Cambridge, Oxford, and London (of whom several hailed from East Central Europe).[83] But Arndt employs the word in a different, though related, sense to the Latin American usage. Whereas Prebisch and the Latin American structuralists used the term in a way that applied to the international capitalist system, with the major consequences flowing from the distinctive properties of Center and Periphery—a scheme of which Dobrogeanu-Gherea and Manoilescu would have approved—Arndt refers to structuralism in a more general sense as "the doctrine of market failure." This view, also shared by Perroux and other corporatists, consisted of three arguments related to interwar capitalism: prices often give the wrong signals to economic actors because they are distorted by monopoly; labor and other factors of production "may respond to price signals inadequately or even perversely" (cf. Boekean dualism); and factors may be immobile. Working at the Oxford Institute of Statistics and at London's Royal Institute of International Affairs were several "structuralists" from Central and East Central Europe who expanded on this perspective—Paul Rosenstein-Rodan, Michal Kalecki, Kurt Mandelbaum, Thomas Balogh, and Nicholas Kaldor. They agreed that the price mechanism worked even less well in underdeveloped countries.[84] Rosenstein-Rodan would write what is generally acknowledged as the first study in "development economics" in 1943, and Kurt Mandelbaum would write the first book-length treatment of the problem in 1945.[85] These works focused on the problems of East Central Europe, as did development studies of the Political and Economic Planning group and the Royal Institute of International Affairs in London.[86] As noted in Chapter 1, the Canadian trade theorist Harry Johnson, who taught at Chicago and London, saw the exiled continental economists as concerned with developing the Balkan economies on the German model; the British-based group (in his view) therefore tended to emphasize industrialization as a solution to underdevelopment.[87]

At the theoretical level, Rosenstein-Rodan traced his inspiration to an article by the American economist Allyn Young in 1928, who had argued that Adam Smith's rule—that the extent of the division of labor depends on the size of the market—needed to be revised. The contrary was also true, asserted Young, and this observation put the emphasis on the role of capital, the key to further division of labor and therefore economic growth. Increasing returns at the societal level required "that industrial operations be seen as an interrelated whole"[88] because particular industries and firms continually divided into more specialized operations. Rosenstein-Rodan noted that this perspective emphasized both economies of scale (to the firm) and external economies (in the larger industrial complex). Following Young's extension of Smith, Rosenstein-Rodan not only pointed to "indivisibility in the production function" in industry but "indivisibility of demand" in the global market. The latter implied that investment decisions were interdependent, and investments could take advantage of complementarities (and external economies) if pursued on a broad front—thus the notion of the Big Push. On the production side, markets did not function correctly as long as these economies were not fully taken advantage of, and industry by its nature had far more external economies and economies of scale than did agriculture.[89]

Later, the Pole Michal Kalecki, leader of the group at Oxford, would have a direct influence on the Latin American structural theory of inflation (from which the school got is name), and Kaldor, Balogh, and Dudley Seers, another "British structuralist"—this one in fact English—would collaborate with ECLA economists in Santiago, Chile.[90] Still another Central European exile adopting British structuralism, Hans W. Singer, in 1950 would independently develop a model similar to Prebisch's and would interact with ECLA economists as well.

According to Harry Johnson, one of the two major sources of Keynes's influence on postwar development theory in general derived from the implicit notion of disguised unemployment,[91] worked out by Joan Robinson, but used, as we have seen, in a different sense in the postwar literature. In the post-1945 meaning, the disguised unemployed had little or no measurable productivity, but they had not been dismissed from occupations with higher productivities. Furthermore, the notion was developed in the Rumanian and other East Central European literatures with statistical estimates (e.g., Grigore Manoilescu's study considered in Chapter 4) before Robinson published. Therefore, Johnson appears to be wrong on the signal importance of Keynes's influence, though the theory of the great Cambridge economist must have reinforced the importance of the concept of disguised unemployment already known to Rosenstein-Rodan and others familiar with the development literature in the succession states of East Central Europe.

Not only was the concept of massive disguised unemployment fundamental to the analyses and prescriptions of Rosenstein-Rodan and Mandelbaum but so was the notion of moving workers from areas of lesser marginal productivity—or in its strongest form, "zero marginal productivity"—in agriculture to more productive activities and industry in particular.[92] This "Manoilescu argument," in a subfield of economics in which there was very little accepted orthodoxy, nonetheless achieved a stamp of international professional approval in the widely circulated report by the UN's Department of Economic Affairs in 1951, titled *Measures for the Economic Development of Under-developed Countries*, subtitled *Report by a Group of Experts*, among whom were the future Nobel Prize winners W. Arthur Lewis and Theodore W. Schultz. The notion of disguised unemployment was approved in the report, which relied for an empirical confirmation on a study of the phenomenon in East Central Europe by the Royal Institute for International Affairs, in which the lowest estimate was 20 to 25 percent of the labor force.[93] Moving surplus agricultural population into manufacturing industry was seen as the most important measure to be undertaken in densely populated under-developed areas, though both industrial and agricultural development were necessary, the report stated.[94] That the notion of disguised unemployment and the 25 percent estimate based on prewar studies in southeastern Europe were highly influential in the postwar development literature is also shown in a famous essay by one of the originators of the "doctrine of balanced growth," Ragnar Nurkse. In *Problems of Capital Formation in Under-developed Countries* (1953), Nurkse, himself from East Central Europe—Estonia—and a former League economist, noted that estimates of 25 to 30 percent "have been widely used in recent literature," and he endorsed the growing orthodoxy of transferring the disguised unemployed from agriculture to projects in capital formation.[95]

Nurkse's former employer, the League of Nations, has generally been regarded as hostile to heterodox views on the international division of labor. If the institutional settings in which Raúl Prebisch did his postwar work helps account for the enormous influence of Latin American structuralism—the UN's ECLA and later, through Prebisch's leadership, UNCTAD—one must note the much greater accommodation of nonorthodox ideas in the United Nations than in its predecessor, the League. The latter, whose European founders hoped would help reconstruct the relatively smooth-functioning international system of trade and payments that existed before 1914, was committed to the ideal of free trade and implicitly to a traditional international division of labor, dependent as the League was on member European states. Its staff economists and authors of special studies worked with other international agencies and national governments to reestablish the gold standard and make workable the reparations system that tended to cripple general recovery after World War I. The League's concerns were Eurocentric in a world in which the colonial revolt was still largely in the future. And though League economists favored free trade and international specialization, it is important that its special reports blamed the developed West for the failure to restore the prewar economy. To review some of this material: Gustav Cassel's study for the League in 1927 scored the Western nations for their growing protectionism, as well as for establishing trade union monopolies and production cartels. Monopolistic pricing had adversely affected metropolitan and colonial producers of agriculture and raw materials, "the chief sufferers" from combines and protectionism, who saw the terms of trade turn against them.[96]

The League's Economic Committee in 1935 again cited trade unions and oligopolies as responsible for much of the price-scissors gap between industry and agriculture and, among other things, found fault with efforts by European countries to protect and stimulate their own agricultural establishments to achieve self-sufficiency for strategic reasons.[97] In an appended study to the 1935 report, Sir Frederick Leith-Ross, the British financial expert, noted that European agricultural production, excluding that of the USSR, had risen faster than world farm output between 1929 and 1933; this development owed largely to the protectionism of Germany, Italy, and France. Overseas producers reacted by stepping up output, trying to maintain total sales at a lower price per unit, and thereby aggravating the problem. Ultimately agricultural exporters could not sell their products and consequently could not import European manufactures. Thus they began to produce their own industrial goods. This sequence resulted in a general impoverishment, wrote Leith-Ross, implicitly suggesting that "agricultural" countries could not efficiently produce the industrial goods they had formerly imported, just as "industrial" countries were inefficient at farming.[98] Therefore, by implication, the developed nations had themselves to blame. But the object of the analysis remained that of restoring the traditional international division of labor.

Meanwhile, the League had been assigned a financial task that produced resentment in some of the succession states and elsewhere: its economic "policing power" to make and supervise loans to states in the process of reconstruction[99]—a function that would not burden the United Nations after its creation in

1945 because the responsibility for emergency and longer-term lending became the respective tasks of the International Monetary Fund (IMF) and the International Bank of Reconstruction and Development (World Bank), both created in 1944. In the interwar years, activities of foreign financial experts who dispensed unpalatable medicine, such as Charles Rist of France and Sir Otto Niemeyer of Britain, sometimes represented the League, sometimes not, and the League often bore the political onus unjustly. Both Rist and Niemeyer visited Rumania at the request of its government in 1932. Rist wrote a scathing report on Rumanian finances and urged the administration to obtain technical assistance from the League in reforming the country's finances. But the French professor also censured Rumania's "artificial" (heavy) industries, supported by the state, and urged the development of agriculture and agriculture-related industries as a solution to the nation's dire financial and economic plight in the depths of the Depression.[100] In 1933 an agreement was signed at Geneva putting Rumania's finances under League supervision for four years, and Manoilescu attacked foreign financial experts as "New Phanariots," alluding to the eighteenth-century Greek princes who served as satraps of the sultan when the country labored under indirect Ottoman rule.[101] The League was part of a complex of international organizations, and another attempt to limit the nation's sovereignty, in the view of the president of the Rumanian industrialists' association, UGIR, was the International Labor Office's "directive" to implement the eight-hour day and related social welfare measures in Rumanian factories. Thus one more Geneva-based international organization was seen as interfering in the country's economic affairs.[102]

By World War II, League of Nations economists had become more understanding of the industrial aspirations of backward countries. As early as 1937, a League committee report had judged that because emigration from overpopulated countries was blocked by post–World War I restrictions in most of the prewar recipient nations, the former countries would have to industrialize.[103] Five years later, League economists recognized that much of the effort to achieve import-substitution industrialization by agrarian states in the Depression years was a reaction to surplus rural population, huge commodity price swings, and balance-of-payments difficulties. Furthermore, "the problem constituted by the multiplicity of small and poor economic units in Central and Eastern Europe, heavily indebted to the Western World, was extremely complex."[104]

In 1945, the last full year of its existence,[105] the League's Economic Department had arrived at the view that in the period 1875 to 1930, manufacturing nations had traded with each other more than with agricultural exporters and that agricultural prices on a worldwide basis had fallen over the long term relative to prices of manufactures. Furthermore, "non-industrial countries can profit from [the international] division of labor only to the extent they enjoy a surplus of their production that can be exported in exchange for foreign manufactures. . . . In the majority of non-industrial countries, the surplus is not large enough to ensure them a plentiful supply of imported manufactures."[106] Consequently, though the League's economists retained a faith in the importance of trade for the development of the international economy, they acknowledged that specialization in agriculture had not been a beneficial arrangement for most agricultural countries. League economists were succumbing to an "export pessimism," that is, pessimism about trade as an engine for growth, and this view was to characterize the thinking of the UN Economic Commission for Latin America in its formative years after the war.[107]

Structural problems in international trade had interested League economists more than they had the Keynesian refugees from the Continent during the interwar and war years, though that group would subsequently turn to them in their reincarnation as "development" economists. Such concern in the League was traceable at least as far back as Cassel's report in 1927 on the price-scissors problem. But other propositions that would anticipate the initial Latin American structuralist thesis appeared in a variety of quarters during the interwar years. One such instance was found in the work of Louise Sommer, an economist at the University of Geneva, in the same city where League and ILO headquarters were located. In the mid-1930s Sommer was sympathetic to agrarian Europe's aspirations for an intra-European trade preference system and noted the defense of that project by Manoilescu and the Yugoslav economist Otto Frangeš in League of Nations meetings in the 1920s and 1930s.[108] In 1938 Sommer published an article, though forgotten today, which anticipated what would survive World War II as Manoilescu's chief contribution to development theory and, beyond that, would anticipate part of the argument of Raúl Prebisch and Hans Singer for pursuing a policy of industrialization in underdeveloped countries.

In reviewing Manoilescu's position, Sommer wrote that the Rumanian author could modernize his argument and put it in neoclassical terms by focusing on marginal rather than average productivity.[109] She proceeded to observe what Raúl Prebisch had noted for Argentina the previous year, that in the upswing of the international business cycle, prices of agricultural products rose faster than those of industrial products, but in the downswing, they fell faster.[110] The reason for this phenomenon had been explained in 1928 by the Soviet economist N. D. Kondratieff, the discoverer of "long waves" or "Kondratieff cycles."[111] Kondratieff had observed that the buying power of agricultural goods falls faster than that of industrial goods in times of depression and noted that agricultural supply is inelastic with regard to price, compared to the supply of industrial goods. Further, he noted that the consumption of foodstuffs was price-inelastic but that agricultural producers as a rule are poorly organized and therefore relatively unable to defend themselves on the world market, vis-à-vis sellers of industrial goods.[112] (Hans Singer would emphasize this feature of international trade two decades later.)

Sommer also cited a recent article by the American trade theorist Charles Kindleberger, who pointed out that agricultural and industrial exporters have different income-elasticities of demand over the course of the international business cycle. The former would expand their demand for industrial goods more than proportionally to the cyclical rise in income and contract it more than the fall in income in the cyclical slump. The industrial countries had a relatively income-inelastic demand for agricultural countries' exports over the course of the cycle.[113]

Sommer misread Kindleberger, however, because she cited him in support of the idea of a differential *price*-elasticity of demand.[114] In the Prebisch-Singer thesis that would emerge in 1949–50, both types of elasticity were relevant to explain why the terms of trade over the long term turned against agricultural exporters. In any case, Sommer used these theoretical points to explain the differential cyclical behavior of agricultural and industrial prices on the world market, showing why agricultural prices were less stable in conjunctural terms, rather than examining the long-term consequences.[115]

Oddly, perhaps, no one cites Sommer, Kondratieff, or Kindleberger as precursors of the Prebisch-Singer thesis. This could be true in Sommer's case because she drew the "wrong" conclusion. She noted that in Central Europe, industrial countries were developing their agriculture, while agricultural countries were industrializing. Given the limited European context in which she treated the issue, Sommer wrote that a more efficient division of labor could be achieved with a continental preference system, implying one in which primary exporters continued their roles, but one that would allow them to move away from monoculture and pursue some degree of industrialization.[116] Thus Sommer did not urge a policy of industrialization as the centerpiece of a solution for the market constraints agrarian countries faced, a plight Singer in 1950 would call "the worst of both worlds": as international income rose, agricultural exporters wanted more industrial goods (as a share of world income) from their trading partners, while the latter wanted fewer agricultural goods.[117]

In the following chapter we shall examine how the various currents of thought and policy prescriptions considered above—corporatism, Keynesianism, and neoclassical economics—as well as the changing international environment, affected Latin American structuralism in its original expression by the Argentine economist Raúl Prebisch. Having considered structuralism's theoretical and institutional foundations, we can turn to Brazilian ideas in Part III.

1. Constantin Dobrogeanu-Gherea in the portrait accompanying *Neoiobagia* (Neoserfdom), 1910. (Photo courtesy of Editura Politică, Bucharest)

2. Mihail Manoilescu as Rumania's Minister of Industry and Commerce, 1931. (Photo courtesy of Valeriu Dinu)

3. Raúl Prebisch as Executive Secretary of the U.N. Economic Commission for Latin America, 1962. (Photo courtesy of United Nations)

4. Celso Furtado in exile, 1973. (Photo courtesy of Celso Furtado)

5. Fernando Henrique Cardoso giving an interview in Brasília, 1976. (Photo courtesy of *O Estado de S. Paulo*)

8

Prebisch and Structuralism

If the history of ideas is notoriously international, the observation is especially apt for economic structuralism in postwar Latin America because of the interaction of personnel and institutions at the region-wide level with those at the national level in Brazil. Brazilians were studying and publishing at the Economic Commission for Latin America in Santiago, Chile, where the structuralist school was born; conversely, ECLA personnel were traveling to, and teaching in, Brazil. ECLA, a regional entity of the United Nations established in 1948, was controlled by Latin Americans; by contrast, in the League, economists concerned with the problems of underdeveloped areas, even East Central Europe, had enjoyed almost no influence.[1] The League was in general an instrument of western Europe, and Brazil had even left the organization in 1926 (effective in 1928), when it failed to get a permanent seat on the governing council.

To understand the rise of structuralism in Latin America, ECLA, and the Brazilian contribution to structuralism, we must consider the early evolution of the thought of Raúl Prebisch, the founder of the structuralist school, who based his heterodox position partly on the doctrine of the failure of market forces to allocate resources so as to spread the benefits of economic development evenly over the entire international system.[2] This endeavor involves a brief look at economic ideas and attitudes in Latin America at large and the Argentine context in more detail because of Prebisch's close association with economic policy in Argentina from the late 1920s to the early 1940s and the ways in which policy matters influenced his theoretical views.

By the 1940s, the central issue that concerned Prebisch and many other writers on economic issues was industrialization, both as fact (at first a consequence of the decline of export-led growth) and as desideratum (for ECLA, at least at the outset, a "solution" to the problem of economic underdevelopment). From the Great Depression of the 1930s until 1949, one finds a defense of industrialization without the benefit of economic theory and a counterpart coherent ideology, except where Manoilescu's work was known. Otherwise, the arguments were often limited in scope to alleged special circumstances, were sometimes inconsistent, and were often apologetic. They were these things, in part, because they "contradicted" neoclassical theory; in particular, they ran afoul of the Ricardian model of the international division of labor, still very much alive in the early years of the Depression in Latin America, despite a surge of protectionism around the world in the previous decade. In the 1930s the proponents of industrialization were almost exclusively the industrialists themselves, though by the time of World War II they were joined by government spokesmen, at least in the four most industrialized countries—Argentina, Brazil, Mexico, and Chile. In the decade after 1949 came the apogee of ECLA, whose analyses legitimized and prescribed industrialization. The defense of industrialization now became much more coherent and aggressive.

Industrialization in Latin America was fact before it was policy and policy before it was theory. In the half-century preceding 1930 there seemed to be a rough correspondence between the fact of high-performance, export-led growth and the theory of comparative advantage, which "justified" Latin America's specialization in raw material production. This theory, originated by David Ricardo (1817) and elaborated by John Stuart Mill (1848), Alfred Marshall (1879), and others later, can be summarized as follows. Given an absence of commerce between two countries, if the relative prices of two commodities differ between them, both can profit by trading such commodities at an intermediate price ratio (that is, both can gain even if one country produces both traded goods more efficiently than the other); countries export commodities whose production requires relatively intensive use of factors found in relative abundance within their boundaries; commodity trade reduces (if it does not eliminate) international differences in wages, rents, and other returns to factors of production; among other things, the theory assumes the absence of monopoly power and the spread of the benefits of technological progress across the whole trading system. In Latin America, an explicit articulation of the advantages of specialization in trade occurred in the two decades after 1880, corresponding to the beginning of a half-century of unprecedented production of agricultural and mineral goods, to be exchanged on the world market for manufactures.[3]

Given the absence of a theoretical rationale for industrial development (with the notable and controversial exception of Manoilescu's work), for those Latin American countries that had made industrial advances in the 1920s, increased self-sufficiency in the period 1930–45 was a "second-best" option, in view of the sustained crisis in export markets. The dollar value of Argentina's exports in 1933, for example, was one-third the 1929 figure. Despite the importance of industrialization in the 1920s, the following decade can still be understood as a period of significant structural and institutional change for the larger Latin American economies: convertibility and the gold standard were abandoned early in the

Depression in Argentina, Brazil, and Chile. In those countries, the rise in prices of importables, because of a fall in the terms of trade and exchange devaluation, encouraged the substitution of domestic manufactures for imported goods, as did expansionary fiscal and monetary policies.[4] Argentina, Brazil, and Chile made rapid advances in industrial production during the early Depression years so that by 1935 a North American economist would hazard that "there is probably no major section of the world in which there is greater industrial activity relative to pre-depression years than in temperate South America" (i.e., Argentina, southern Brazil, and Chile).[5] When war came in 1939, manufactures in international trade became scarce again, permitting industrial advances to the extent that capital goods, fuel, and raw materials were available.

A basic characteristic of the period 1930–45 was an intensification of state intervention in the economy, in Latin America as elsewhere, and industrialists like other economic groups sought state assistance; they asked for subsidies, credits, and increased tariff protection. As noted in Chapter 7, they argued that the state should aid in "economic rationalization," by which they chiefly meant cartelization, a major theme of Rumanian and other European industrialists in the 1930s.[6] In the larger Latin American nations, governments began to heed the importuning manufacturers by the time of the war, and for those countries, state aid to industry in the form of development loans tended to converge in the early years of World War II.[7] The reasons for such a shift in state policy are clear in retrospect: a decade of wrestling with the intractable problem of reviving traditional export markets; the relative unavailability of foreign industrial goods over virtually a fifteen-year period (1930–45); and the fact that governments (and particularly their officer corps) as well as industrialists began to consider the relation between manufacturing and national defense, though the last-named process began in the late 1920s in Chile.

Governments, however, moved hesitantly and inconsistently toward addressing the problems of industry. As late as 1940, Finance Minister Federico Pinedo's plan for the economic development of Argentina still distinguished between "natural" and "artificial" industries, implying that industrial development would occur in concert with the needs of the agricultural and pastoral sectors.[8] But the Argentine economy contracted sharply in 1942–43 because of a lack of access to traditional foreign markets,[9] and by the time of the colonels' coup in June 1943, intervention for industrial development had become state policy. An industrial development bank followed in 1944. Yet even at that point support for manufacturing was far from unrestrained. The ministry of agriculture still housed the department of industry, and the minister assured Argentineans that the development of manufacturing would not threaten, but would contribute to the growth of, the country's "mother industries," stock raising and agriculture.[10] In the next few years, however, the government of Juan Perón did tangibly put the interests of industrialists above those of ranchers and farmers.[11] Similar hesitant and tentative steps to foment industrialization occurred in some other Latin American countries in the 1930s and 1940s, notably in Brazil—on which more later—Chile, and Mexico.[12]

Meanwhile, a sea change was occurring in academic and policy circles of the developed West. In 1943 the Austro-British economist Paul Rosenstein-Rodan and the American trade theorist Charles Kindleberger both called for the industrialization of agrarian countries. And at a policy level, the Hot Springs conference of the Allied nations the same year favored a degree of industrialization for the "backward" countries.[13] The economists of the League of Nations had arrived at a similar position by the end of the war. More boldly, the British economist Colin Clark had written in 1942 that future equilibrium in world trade depended on the willingness of Europe and the United States "to accept a large flow of . . . exports of manufactured goods" from India and China.[14] The somewhat "unintended" industrialization of the larger Latin American countries and a partial acceptance of it by the United States government was reflected at the Chapultepec conference of the Pan American Union (1945). The meeting's resolutions gave a qualified benediction to the industrialization process in Latin America. At the end of the war, therefore, it was clear that industrialization had greatly advanced in Latin America; and the process was characteristically import-substitution industrialization—the replacement of imported goods with domestic manufactures, based on existing patterns of demand. Economists in several countries were noting the trend and searching for a theory to legitimate it.[15]

That theory and concomitant policies would be provided by the Economic Commission for Latin America, dominated in its early years by the ideas, personality, and programs of Raúl Prebisch. Because the agency was so much the creation of Prebisch, we must consider his early career and formative experiences during the Depression and war years to learn how the ECLA theses of 1949 crystallized, for much of Prebisch's reasoning was apparently based on empirical observation and learning from failed policies.

Born in northwestern Argentina in 1901, Prebisch studied at the University of Buenos Aires, whose Department (Facultad) of Economics at the time was probably the best school for economic theory in Latin America.[16] Prebisch gave early promise of a distinguished career within Argentina's economic establishment, as an insider's insider. At the age of twenty he published his first professional study in economics. In 1923, upon completing a master's degree in that discipline, he was asked to join the staff at the university. Although Prebisch the student was an assistant of Alejandro Bunge, the foremost promoter of Argentine industrialization in his day, the young man's career followed the more direct route to success in an early and intimate association with the leaders of the pastoral industry.[17] In 1922, before Prebisch's graduation, Enrique Uriburu (his second cousin)[18] appointed him director of the statistical office of the elite Sociedad Rural Argentina, the powerful stockbreeders' association. Two years later the Rural sent

Prebisch to Australia, where he studied statistical methods related to stock raising, and where, presumably, he also obtained a broader perspective on Argentina's position in the international economy.[19] By 1925 he was both a teacher at the university and an official in the Argentine government's Department of Statistics. In 1927 he published a Rural-sponsored study that became the basis for government action on behalf of stockbreeders in the foreign meat market.[20]

Leaders of the Sociedad Rural were apparently impressed by the need for good statistical data, by the need for economic analysis, and by Prebisch. In 1928 he was again working part-time for the Rural, compiling a statistical yearbook for the organization. Thus, from the outset of his career, Prebisch was interested in policy issues, set in the context of the international trading system. In 1928, he also launched the *Revista Económica*, the organ of the government-directed Banco de la Nación Argentina, for which Prebisch established a research division.[21] The journal was concerned not only with pressing monetary matters but also with the problems of stock raising, agriculture, and international trade—not with theoretical issues in economics.

In the early 1930s Prebisch served as an economic adviser to the Argentine government's ministries of finance and agriculture and proposed the creation of a central bank (with powers to control interest rates and the money supply) to the government of General José Uriburu, who had seized power in 1930 and to whom Prebisch was distantly related.[22] In 1932, the government asked Sir Otto Niemeyer, the British financial expert who was advising the Brazilian and Rumanian governments in this period, to draw up a plan for a central bank. But the plan ultimately approved was of more direct Argentine confection, and Prebisch played the leading role in its creation. After lengthy study and parliamentary debate, in 1935 the Banco Central became the nation's first true central bank, and from its inception until 1943, Prebisch served as its director-general. In addition, the bank functioned as the government's economic "brain trust," as a member of Prebisch's group put it.[23]

In many respects, Prebisch and his colleagues in the 1930s were treading in theoretical terra incognita. Before the Depression it was considered axiomatic that Argentina had prospered according to the theory of comparative advantage. The benefits of export-led growth, based in an international division of labor, made comparative advantage a near-sacrosanct doctrine. In the words of Carlos Díaz-Alejandro, "From 1860 to 1930 Argentina grew at a rate that has few parallels in economic history, perhaps comparable only to the performance during the same period of other countries of recent settlement."[24] But the 1920s were a period of disequilibrium as well as expansion in world trade, and though Argentina prospered, the country experienced the same problems as did other primary-producing nations in the final years before the October 1929 crash—falling export prices, rising stocks, and debt-payment difficulties. Argentina and Uruguay were the first nations in the world to abandon the gold standard in the

Great Depression, before 1929 ended. Following Britain's departure from the gold standard, in October 1931 Argentine authorities introduced exchange controls to try to stem the outflow of capital and facilitate the repayment of loans negotiated in hard currencies. Prebisch later wrote that "exchange control was not the result of a theory but was imposed by circumstances."[25] The Depression thus brought about the abandonment of many hallowed economic doctrines and practices.

In the crisis, Great Britain exploited her monopsonist position against her many suppliers. As a rule, she attempted to purchase less abroad and thereby got her imports cheaper. In the case of Argentina, Britain's trading power was magnified by the South American nation's loss of dollar investments. The United States had become a major supplier to Argentina in the mid-1920s, but the latter country had chronic difficulties in paying directly for U.S. imports with her own noncomplementary exports. Therefore, Argentina had depended on U.S. capital exports, but during the Depression, North American lenders disinvested in Argentina.[26] Excluded from the U.S. market by high tariffs and other regulations and cut off from continental markets as well in the early 1930s, Argentina feared above all the loss of the British market; indeed, it was already partly closed by the Ottawa Conference agreement (1932) among Great Britain and her dominions, several of which were Argentina's export competitors. Britain's trading power was further enhanced because in these years she bought much more from Argentina than she sold to her: in the four years 1930–33, Britain took over 40 percent of Argentina's exports but supplied only about 20 percent of Argentina's imports.[27] Consequently, Argentine statesmen and government economists—among them Raúl Prebisch—were willing to enter into the Roca-Runciman Pact of 1933, an arrangement more to Britain's advantage than Argentina's, whereby the United Kingdom agreed to keep up a certain level of meat purchases in exchange for regular debt service payments and tariff reductions for British manufactures. Thus beef exports, the traditional preserve of the Argentine oligarchy, were favored over wheat.[28] A bilateral agreement in 1936 was even more favorable to British interests. After war broke out in 1939, the British government played its monopsonistic position to yet greater advantage in negotiations between the Bank of England and Argentina's Central Bank, led by Raúl Prebisch.[29] One can easily surmise that Argentina's protracted and notorious dependence on her major trading partner left a lasting impression on Prebisch.

The Depression brought about not only bilateral negotiations but also a series of international economic meetings. In 1933 Prebisch, as an invitee of the Council of the League of Nations, attended a gathering of the Preparatory Committee of the Second International Monetary Conference in Geneva. From Switzerland Prebisch reported to the *Revista Económica* that the assembled monetary experts believed that one basic blockage in the international economic system derived from the facts that the United States had replaced Great Britain as the world's chief creditor country and that high American tariff schedules (especially Smoot-Hawley, 1930) did not permit other countries to repay U.S. loans with exports. Consequently, the rest of the world tended to send gold to the United States, and the bullion was not recirculated in the international monetary system.[30] Prebisch soon went to London to help negotiate the Roca-Runciman Pact as a technical adviser. Later in 1933, he attended the World Monetary Conference in the same city, but the conference broke up in failure. Meanwhile, Prebisch represented Argentina in negotiations with trade officials of the United States, Canada, and Australia to limit the world supply of wheat, but the experiment was no more successful than the contemporaneous effort to improve grain prices by Virgil Madgearu's Agrarian Bloc in East Central Europe. The tendency toward bilateralism in world trade continued.

Back in Argentina, Prebisch sought to understand another vexing problem wrought by the Depression—declining terms of trade. In 1934 he published an article pointing out that "agricultural prices have fallen more profoundly than those of manufactured goods" and that in 1933 Argentina had to sell 73 percent more than before the Depression to obtain the same quantity of (manufactured) imports. In the same article Prebisch attacked as "scholastic" the orthodox equilibrium theories of his senior colleague at the University of Buenos Aires, Professor Luis Roque Gondra, because such doctrines ignored the stubborn fact of sustained depression.[31]

After a period of improvement in Argentina's economy, severe depression returned in 1937–38. Originating in the United States, the problem had its major spread effects in the agriculture- and mineral-exporting areas of the world because Europe and Japan were "pump priming" through their armaments programs. Wheat was one of the commodities for which prices fell sharply in 1937.[32] As other countries introduced new trade controls, so did Argentina, in 1938, in the form of quantitative restrictions on imports. In the next two years, Argentina's banking officials, among them Raúl Prebisch, were trying to keep international credits and debts in balance "in the strictest short-run sense." Thus trade policy was not yet consciously used to foster industrialization.[33] Yet manufacturing in Argentina grew impressively in the 1930s and early 1940s, as was recognized by contemporaries at home and abroad. In particular, the Central Bank's *Revista Económica* noted an increase in output of 85 percent (by value) between the industrial census of 1913 and that of 1934–35.[34] In its annual report for 1942 (published in 1943), the bank followed through on its changing economic emphases by championing industrialization. The report, reflecting Prebisch's views, argued that exports and industrial development were by no means incompatible; rather, the issue was to change the composition of imports from consumer to capital goods.[35]

Prebisch the policy maker interests us less than Prebisch the emerging economic theorist, though the two can hardly be separated. In the latter capacity he was beginning to formulate a theory of unequal exchange by 1937. In that year the *Revista Económica* noted that agricultural production was inelastic compared to industrial output and that its products' prices tended to rise and fall faster than industrial prices in the trade cycle. The *Revista* also noted the related problem of the lack of organization of agricultural producers and concluded: "In the last depression these differences manifested themselves in a sharp fall in agricultural prices and in a much smaller decline in the prices of manufactured articles. The agrarian countries lost part of their purchasing power, with the resultant effect on the balance of payments and on the volume of their imports."[36]

The emphasis was thus on the elasticity of supply of industrial production, and implicitly on monopoly, and not on wage contracts in the industrial countries, which element was later to be a focal point of Prebisch's analysis. In the same comment the *Revista* noted that Argentina's industrial complex made its greatest gains in two periods, World War I and during "the worldwide recrudescence of the policy of economic self-sufficiency during the years 1929–1936."[37] Thus Prebisch seemed to be considering the possibility that export-led growth was no longer a viable path to economic development.

Prebisch was also intensely concerned with the trade cycle in Argentina. The Central Bank began its effort to conduct countercyclical monetary policy in 1937 by decreasing the public's purchasing power through the sale of bonds in that boom year; in the following period of contraction, it would attempt to expand purchasing power by lowering the rediscount rate.[38] In 1939, in its annual report for the previous year, the Central Bank—representing Prebisch's thinking on the matter—argued that the nation's trade cycles were primarily a reflection of those of its principal (industrialized) trading partners. It held that Argentina's internal credit expansion began with an export surplus, which led to additional demand for foreign goods because of exporters' high propensity to import; when combined with heavy import requirements, the process repeatedly produced a balance-of-payments crisis in the national business (or trade) cycle.[39]

In 1943 the military coup makers dismissed Prebisch at the Central Bank, apparently because they associated him with the ranching "oligarchy," though he later defended his services in the Depression era as those of a *técnico*.[40] Now Prebisch began to read widely in the recent economic literature.[41] Returning to teaching, he prepared a series of lectures in 1944 in which he referred, for the first time, to "Center" and "Periphery," terms he would later make famous. Prebisch developed a historical argument, with Britain as the nineteenth-century Center of the trading and monetary system based on the gold standard. (Clearly, this was a better model for the first half of the century than the second half, but Britain as Center for the whole period fit Argentina's situation well enough.) Under Britain's leadership as the cycle-generating Center, Prebisch argued, the world's economic system had equilibrated gold flows and the balance of payments over the course of the cycle for both Center and Periphery. "Gold tended to leave

Great Britain, the Center of the system, and to enter countries of the Periphery in the upswing of the cycle." Then it returned in the downswing. A problem for peripheral countries was that when gold departed in the downswing, "there was no way to diminish the gold flow except by contracting credit. . . . No one could conceive of . . . the possibility of raising the rediscount rate in competition with the monetary Center in London." Thus overall monetary stability was maintained at the cost of economic contraction in the Periphery. "The gold standard was therefore an automatic system for the countries of the Periphery, but not for the Center," where the rediscount rate could be adjusted for domestic needs. In the Periphery, the gold standard had the effect of exaggerating rather than offsetting the cycle.[42] Passing on to the post–World War I years, Prebisch concluded that New York bankers in the 1920s and 1930s did not have the knowledge or experience of the "British financial oligarchy," though of course the world situation was dramatically different after the war. By 1930 the United States had sucked up most of the world's gold. Consequently, "the rest of the world, including our country, [is] forced to seek a means of inward-directed development [*crecer hacia adentro*]"[43]—a phrase that ECLA would later diffuse broadly.

The Argentine business cycle, Prebisch continued, had depended on exogenous factors operating through the balance of payments. In the upswing, exports and foreign investment produced an influx of gold and exchange credits, creating new money and therefore imports. Such changes also expanded credit to the agricultural and pastoral industries; but because of inelastic supply, during the downswing, credit was immobilized in the rural sector. Additional imports were paid for with reserves, producing a monetary crisis.[44]

In seeking a solution to Argentina's problems, Prebisch began to think in more general terms about Latin America and its relations with the United States; his first concern in that area had involved the previously mentioned plan in 1940 (probably drafted by Prebisch but presented to Congress by Finance Minister Pinedo) "to link the Argentine economy to the surging power of the United States and to growing Latin American markets," in part by exporting manufactures.[45] After being fired at the Central Bank, Prebisch was twice in Mexico during the mid-1940s at the invitation of Mexico's central bank (Banco de México). On both occasions he participated in international meetings: once in 1944 at a gathering of intellectuals from Latin America at the Colegio de México on problems the region would face in the postwar era[46] and again in Mexico City at an inter-American meeting of central bankers in 1946. During these Mexican sojourns, his concerns moved beyond banking and foreign trade to industrialization.

Prebisch's interest in industrialization as a solution to Latin America's economic problems originally arose from a desire, shared by many other Argentine contemporaries, to make Argentina less economically "vulnerable," a vulnerability painfully evident throughout the period 1930–45. The Argentine Central

Bank, under Prebisch's leadership, had begun to advocate industrialization in its 1942 report. By implication, Prebisch was recommending similar policies to other Latin American governments in his Colegio de México lecture of 1944.[47] In his "Conversations" at the Banco de México in the same year, Prebisch again noted that the period of greatest industrial development in Argentina had been the Great Depression and times of world war, periods when the nation had to produce for itself what it could not import.[48] Later, ECLA theorists would elaborate extensively on this proposition when they devised the concept of "inward-directed development."

In a 1944 article in Mexico's *Trimestre Económico*, Prebisch noted that the United States, unlike Argentina, had a low propensity to import (defined as the change in the value of imports generated by a given change in the national product). Because other countries, he implied, had high propensities to import, and the United States had replaced Britain as the chief industrial trading partner of the Latin American states, Prebisch expanded on the League experts' argument in 1933 and warned that the postwar international trading system faced the danger of permanent disequilibrium.[49]

Prebisch first used the terminology Center-Periphery in print in 1946, at the meeting of the hemisphere's central bankers, who convened at the invitation of the Banco de México. He now identified the United States as the "cyclical Center" and Latin America as the "Periphery of the economic system." The emphasis, as indicated, was on the business cycle, whose rhythms the U.S. economy set for the whole international system. Fiscal and monetary authorities in the United States could pursue a policy of full employment without producing monetary instability, Prebisch argued; furthermore, such authorities did not need to be especially concerned about the impact of full employment policies on the exchange rate of the dollar in other currencies. By contrast, Prebisch asserted, the nations of the Periphery could not apply the same monetary tools as the Center did. Extrapolating from his 1944 argument with reference to Argentina, Prebisch contended that the money supply in peripheral countries could not be expanded in pursuit of full employment because, with a high propensity to import, any expansion of income would quickly exhaust foreign exchange, assuming no devaluation.

This 1946 statement and previous writings of Prebisch implied that peripheral countries faced three options, all with undesirable consequences: they could have strong currencies and maintain high levels of imports at the cost of high unemployment; they could fight unemployment with an expansionary monetary policy but would thereby create inflation and put pressure on the exchange rate, thus raising the cost of repaying foreign debts; or, if they used monetary policy to maintain high levels of employment but failed to devalue, their reserves would disappear. When prices of the Periphery's products fell during the downswing of the cycle, furthermore, governments of peripheral countries, at least in isolation, could not affect world prices for their goods as the Center could for its goods. Thus equilibrium theories in international trade were not acceptable.[50] This was an assault on the policy prescriptions of neoclassical economics. Prebisch's message at Mexico City was in tune with the pessimism then prevailing in Latin America regarding international trade as a long-term engine of growth, at least for traditional income-inelastic exports. Even the improving terms of trade of the early postwar years was widely viewed as transient.[51]

At the University of Buenos Aires in 1948, Prebisch specifically attacked the theory of comparative advantage, noting that its precepts were repeatedly violated by the industrialized nations, especially through tariff walls and immigration restrictions; nonetheless, economists of the developed world used neoclassical trade theory as an ideological weapon. He also implied that industrial countries acted as monopolists against agricultural countries in the trading process. Prebisch then asserted that historically, in both the United States and Britain, technological progress did not result in a decrease in prices but in an increase in wages. "The fruits of technical progress tended to remain in Great Britain" in the nineteenth century; yet because Britain had sacrificed its agriculture, part of the benefits of technological progress had been transferred to the "new countries" in the form of higher land values. Britain's nineteenth-century import coefficient (defined as the value of imports divided by real income) was estimated by Prebisch as 30 to 35 percent, whereas that of the United States in the 1930s was only about 5 percent. All this implied a blockage to growth for the agriculture-exporting Periphery under the new largely self-sufficient Center.[52]

This Center-Periphery theory even *in nuce* implied a single system, hegemonically organized.[53] To appreciate the significance of the terms "Center" and "Periphery," we should bear in mind that the idea that there was something fundamentally different about the economies of the "backward" areas was still novel in the 1940s. The concept of "underdevelopment" as a syndrome was elaborated in that decade, chiefly after the creation of specialized United Nations agencies in 1947–48. The euphemisms "developing countries" and "less developed countries" were still in the future.[54] Although a few Marxists and others preferred to retain the older term "backward" rather than "underdeveloped," even "backward" among these non-Center-Periphery terms did not in itself imply hegemony; nor did "backward" necessarily put the central emphasis on the international capitalist system. Rather, such a term could imply that the problem was largely one of leads and lags—the modernization thesis in its ahistorical setting.

Despite the fact that some of the key ideas of Prebisch's later analysis were set forth in international meetings in 1944 and 1946, there was no discussion on these occasions of an Economic Commission for Latin America, the UN agency that was subsequently to be Prebisch's principal theoretical and ideological vehicle. Rather, it resulted from a Chilean initiative in 1947 at UN headquarters in

Lake Success, New York. The agency was approved by the UN Economic and Social Council in February 1948, and ECLA held its first meeting in Santiago, Chile, in June of that year. Alberto Baltra Cortés, the Chilean minister of the economy, presided at the occasion. At the opening session, Baltra, who was already familiar with Prebisch's ideas, stressed Latin America's need to industrialize, an attitude to which representatives of the United States and the European colonial powers professed not to object. For the future of ECLA, or at least its most famous thesis, the chief outcome of the meeting was a resolution calling for a study of Latin America's terms of trade.[55]

But without Prebisch's leadership, ECLA was not yet ECLA. His personality, theses, and programs so dominated the agency in its formative phase that it stood in sharp relief to the Economic Commission for Asia and the Far East (established in 1947) and the Economic Commission for Africa (1958), agencies with more purely technical orientations. The year of ECLA's founding, 1948, seemed propitious for obtaining Prebisch's services: in Perón's Argentina he was excluded from official posts, perhaps because of his long and close association with the nation's traditional economic elite. Meanwhile, his reputation as an economist in Latin America had been enhanced by the publication in Mexico of his *Introduction to Keynes* in 1947.[56] Prebisch turned down the first offer to direct the Santiago-based ECLA in 1948 because he feared an international organization like the United Nations would not permit underdeveloped countries to analyze economic problems from their own perspectives. In this regard, he had in mind the League of Nations' lack of interest in underdeveloped areas,[57] although we saw in the preceding chapter that League economists in the later interwar years were beginning to question the traditional international division of labor. Meanwhile, substance for this concern was revealed in the failure of the U.S. Congress to take action on a UN-sponsored International Trade Organization (ITO), proposed in 1948 as a third leg—along with the World Bank and the IMF—of an international economic system. The ITO was to have dealt with an issue of great concern to the Latin Americans, commodity price stabilization.

In any case, Prebisch was again invited to go to Santiago to work on special assignment as editor and author of the introduction to an economic report on Latin America, authorized at the initial ECLA meeting. In Santiago he elaborated his theses on the deterioration of the terms of trade in *The Economic Development of Latin America and Its Principal Problems*, published in Spanish in May 1949 and later termed the "ECLA Manifesto," by Albert Hirschman.[58] Prebisch had already formed his opinions about the secular trend of Latin America's terms of trade; he had argued in the classroom in 1948 that the benefits of technological progress were absorbed by the Center. Now, a new study, *Relative Prices of Exports and Imports of Underdeveloped Countries*, by Hans W. Singer of the UN Department of Economic Affairs, provided an empirical foundation for Prebisch's thesis. This work was an examination of long-term trends in relative prices in the goods traded by industrialized and raw-materials-producing countries and concluded that the terms of trade from the late nineteenth century till the eve of World War II had been moving against the exporters of agricultural goods and in favor of the exporters of industrial products: "On the average, a given quantity of primary exports would pay, at the end of this period, for only 60 percent of the quantity of manufactured goods which it could buy at the beginning of the period."[59]

ECLA explained this finding in part by arguing that gains in productivity over the period in question were greater in industrial than in primary products, thus challenging basic assumptions of the theory of comparative advantage. If prices of industrial goods had fallen, this development would have spread the effects of technical progress over the entire Center-Periphery system, and one would expect the terms of trade for agricultural goods to have improved. They did not do so, and the significance of this fact, ECLA asserted, had to be understood in terms of trade cycles. During the upswing, the prices of primary goods rise more sharply than those of industrial goods, but they fall more steeply during the downswing. In the upswing the working class of the Center absorbs real economic gains, but wages do not fall proportionately during the downswing. Because workers are not well organized in the Periphery (least of all in agriculture), the Periphery absorbs more of the system's income contradiction than does the Center.[60] Thus in today's jargon, Prebisch, like Manoilescu before him, focused on the "double factorial terms of trade"—domestic labor's compensation versus that of its foreign counterpart in the trading process.

In the *Economic Survey of Latin America, 1949* (Spanish ed., 1950), Prebisch expanded in greater detail on these arguments. He held that there were two distinct sources of the potential deterioration of the terms of trade, those from technological productivity gains in the Center and those in the Periphery. He assumed the Center's gains would be greater, and if the system worked normally, these would, to some extent, spread to the Periphery. In that case, over the long run the Center's terms of trade would deteriorate and the Periphery's would improve. If the Periphery's terms deteriorated, that would indicate that it was not only failing to share in the Center's presumably larger gains but was transferring some of its *own* productivity gains to the Center.[61] Since *Relative Prices* had established a deterioration in the Periphery's terms, protection for industry was a sine qua non to arrest the concentration of the fruits of technological progress in the Center.

The basic cause of the deterioration was the surplus labor supply (and the underlying population pressure) in the precapitalist and largely agricultural sector of the Periphery's economy. As modern agricultural technique penetrates and reduces the size of the precapitalist sector, the *Survey* stated, a labor surplus develops. It then adduced historical data to show that the export sector in Latin America could not absorb this surplus. Industrialization, in part to absorb the labor surplus which export agriculture could not employ because of its slow growth,[62] had to be the centerpiece of a policy of economic development, the *Survey* contended. Even when protection was needed, industries were "economical in so far as they represent a net addition to real income." National income could be increased by selectively lowering components of the import coefficient.[63]

Another initial ECLA argument grew out of Prebisch's observations on Argentina's import problems in the 1930s. The United States, the principal cyclical Center, had a much lower import coefficient than export coefficient, and the former was also much lower than those of the Latin American countries. The United States tended to sell more to Latin America than it bought from the region, exhausting Latin American reserves and creating a tendency toward permanent disequilibrium. Such a tendency had not existed, ECLA averred, during the time in which import-hungry Great Britain had been the principal Center.[64] The U.S. economy even grew by closing: ECLA produced statistics showing that the United States's import coefficient had fallen from the 1920s to the late 1940s. The explanation was that technological progress in some industries was much greater than on average, allowing such industries to pay much higher wages, driving up wages in general, and in some other industries, above productivity gains. Therefore, rising costs led to greater average protectionism and a "closing" of the Center.[65]

But Prebisch and the ECLA team he organized were also interested in another dimension of the problem—monopolistic pricing at the Center. The original analysis in 1949–50 laid much more emphasis on the rigidity of wages in the downward phase of the cycle than on monopolistic pricing as such, but the latter argument was there.[66] In any event, both wage rigidities and monopoly were assumed to be nonexistent in neoclassical trade theory. Peripheral countries did not have monopolies on the goods they offered in the world market, with rare and temporary exceptions, just as they lacked well-organized rural labor forces that would resist the fall in wages during the downswing of the cycle.

The preceding analysis, taken as a whole, pointed to negative features in the Periphery's economy—structural unemployment, external disequilibrium, and deteriorating terms of trade—which problems a policy of industrialization could solve or help correct.

In 1950, the year after the appearance of the ECLA manifesto, another United Nations economist independently made a case related to the ECLA theses. Hans Singer, who had directed the UN study *Relative Prices* (the data base for ECLA's terms-of-trade argument), alleged that technological progress in manufacturing was shown in a rise in incomes in developed countries, while that in the production of food and raw materials in underdeveloped countries was expressed in a fall in prices. Singer explained the contrasting effects of technical progress in terms of different income elasticities of demand for primary and industrial goods—an extrapolation of Ernst Engel's law that the proportion of income spent on food falls as income rises—and in terms of the "absence of pressure of producers for higher incomes" in underdeveloped countries. Because consumers of manufactured goods in world trade tended to live in underdeveloped countries and the contrary was true for consumers of raw materials, Singer continued, the latter group had the best of both worlds, while the former had the worst. He also mentioned low elasticity of demand for raw materials and foodstuffs with respect to price (as opposed to income) as a related but distinct problem.[67] Singer's interpretation of the relation between trade and development was quickly linked to Prebisch's, and the two men's theories were soon dubbed the Prebisch-Singer thesis, though both economists state that there was no direct exchange of ideas at the time the related sets of propositions, based on the same UN data, were developed.[68] (Prebisch was then in Santiago and Singer in New York.) In fact, Prebisch had made *two* arguments, of which one was better stated by Singer, and Singer in turn had touched on Prebisch's theme of contrasting degrees of labor organization in Center and Periphery. The latter's central argument related to differential productivities in Center and Periphery. His other argument dealing with disparities in import coefficients was roughly analogous to Singer's more elegant argument on differential income elasticities. Finally, Singer, unlike Prebisch, did not refer to differential behavior of constituent elements of Center and Periphery over the course of the business cycle but focused on the long term.

Since ECLA's "manifesto," *Economic Development*, appeared in print in May 1949, more than six months before Singer presented his American Economic Association paper (published in 1950), Prebisch seems to have reached his position earlier than Singer; in fact, the UN study bolstered some of the conclusions he had already reached. It is notable, however, that several later writers implicitly or explicitly credit Singer and Prebisch with a simultaneous "discovery," giving 1950 as the date both men published.[69] This is because they cite Prebisch's *Economic Development of Latin America* in its English translation, published a year later than the Spanish original. In the same year that Singer's article appeared, Prebisch and ECLA elaborated a book-length study that presented a much fuller statement of the case, the *Economic Survey* for 1949 (published in Spanish in 1950 and in English in 1951).

But Singer was important to ECLA too. By 1951, the year that ECLA became a permanent organ of the United Nations, the agency was referring less to import coefficients than to disparities in income elasticities of demand at the Center for primary products and those at the Periphery for industrial goods.[70] This adoption of Singer's terms was significant because it dealt with the Central countries as a group and not just the United States, which had unusually low import requirements because of its tremendous agricultural output. Though ECLA first emphasized differential productivities, by the late 1950s Prebisch and ECLA tended to emphasize differential income elasticities of demand, possibly as a result of perceived export stagnation in Argentina and Chile.[71] Furthermore, by focusing on demand rather than Center-related monopolies, as early as its 1950 *Survey* (published in Spanish in 1951), ECLA's analysis had retreated from its more radical position in 1949–50.[72]

Such were the main lines of Prebisch's and ECLA's early development. Yet it seems useful to digress briefly on other possible (and sometimes specifically alleged) influences on Prebisch. If these were not genetically related, comparing such propositions and theories with ECLA's will at least highlight the distinctive features of the ECLA model. One possibility is the work of Werner Sombart, whose *Modern Capitalism* was the first work to distinguish between Center and Periphery in the world economic system. As indicated in the preceding chapter, Sombart specifically referred to Center and Periphery in the same sense as Prebisch did.[73] Sombart also wrote of the "dependency" of peripheral countries and even of the servitude of the peasantry of the Periphery, in part caused by western European capitalism.[74] But he did not provide any theory of relations between Center and Periphery; in particular, he offered no analysis of the relation between business cycles and the international distribution of income. Prebisch does not recollect acquaintance with Sombart's passage at the time of his initial use of the terms "Center" and "Periphery,"[75] but even if he was inspired indirectly, Prebisch would owe little more than an arresting phrase because Sombart used the terms only in a few scattered paragraphs.

Another possible source of inspiration for the Center-Periphery terminology was the work of Ernst Wagemann, the German-Chilean economist whose relations with Manoilescu and role in Chile as a possible propagator of the Rumanian's ideas were treated in the preceding two chapters. In *Structure and Rhythm of the International Economy* (1931),[76] Wagemann, a specialist in business cycles, used "central cycle" [*zentrische Konjunktur*] to designate money income movements *within* a given country and "peripheral cycle" [*periphere Konjunktur*] to designate capital movements at the international level.[77] Thus Wagemann employed a Center-Periphery scheme in connection with a cyclical movement but not in the sense Prebisch shared with Sombart. The terms "Center" and "Periphery" were already in the international banking literature by 1940, and Prebisch may have simply given them a Sombartian meaning in building his theory.[78]

Apart from the specific Center-Periphery terms, more plausible as a theoretical influence on Prebisch than the writings of Sombart or Wagemann, however, is the work of Manoilescu himself. Jacob Viner linked the theses of Manoilescu with those of ECLA as early as 1950. Over the next twenty years, others in Latin America, the United States, and Rumania would concur in Viner's judgment, though they seem to have been unaware of his earlier opinion.[79] In the previous chapter I showed that Manoilescu was well-known in certain parts of the Iberian world during the 1930s and 1940s. Several of his economic and political works had been published in those years in Spain, Portugal, Brazil, and Chile. The most likely sources of inspiration for Prebisch were two articles appearing in Chile, one about Manoilescu and the other by him, in 1945 and 1947, respectively.[80]

Clearly, there were broad similarities between the two theories of unequal exchange which converged in the same policy prescription of industrialization. It is notable that Prebisch's focus on productivities within Center and Periphery paralleled Manoilescu's. And both shared a common theoretical perspective: the separation of the critique of imperialism from that of capitalism. Furthermore, the similarity of the two men's theories is indicated by the fact that Manoilescu in 1940 and the structuralists Celso Furtado and Hans Singer in the 1950s independently worked out models of what is now called "internal colonialism."[81]

There are no references to the Rumanian economist's works in Prebisch's early writings.[82] In 1977 Prebisch confirmed the absence of such an influence, though he probably familiar with Manoilescu from the discussions the latter's ideas received in the *Revista de Ciencias Económicas* in the late 1930s.[83] Nonetheless, Manoilescu's ideas—in the Latin American circles where they were known—helped pave the way for the acceptance of ECLA doctrines when they appeared in 1949. Ten years later, in a well-known article, Prebisch still endorsed the "Manoilescu argument"—in Prebisch's words, "transferring available manpower from . . . precapitalist forms of employment of very low productivity to exports or industrial activities of much higher productivity." For Prebisch, "it is not really a question of comparing industrial costs with import prices, but of comparing the increment in income obtained in the expansion of industry with that which could have been obtained in export activities had the same resources been employed there."[84] Manoilescu could hardly have put it better. The two economists, though in different ways, also defended both industrialization of underdeveloped countries and the effort to secure better and more stable commodity prices for their exports. Prebisch, the first director of the United Nations Conference on Trade and Development (1964–69), viewed these as *complementary* endeavors, while Manoilescu, for political rather than economic reasons, tended to oscillate between them. No wonder Viner and others linked the two men's ideas. Yet Prebisch's and Manoilescu's positions were different because the Argentinean believed that prices of primary commodities would continually fall relative to those for industrial goods over the long term, while Manoilescu believed the opposite.[85] Further, for Prebisch, changing technologies resulting in new productivities, combined with differential market imperfections between Center and Periphery, were the ultimate source of unequal exchange, not labor expended and ratios of factors of production.

In the preceding chapter we saw that other major elements of the Prebisch-Singer thesis had been laid out in the interwar years. Cassel had explained the price-scissors problem by factor (labor) and product monopolies in the developed countries. Kondratieff had noted the price-inelasticity of agricultural goods and the lack of organization of agricultural producers in the world market.

Kindleberger in 1937 had pointed to contrasting inelasticities of demand between agricultural and industrial countries for the other's products in international trade, although he did so only with reference to the action of the business cycle and not yet the long term. And Sommer had presented the Manoilescu argument in its modern form. It seems likely that Prebisch was aware of these precedents because of the publication of Mario Pugliese's article on foreign trade and industrialization in the Argentine *Revista de Ciencias Económicas* in 1939.[86] In a journal in which Prebisch himself had frequently published, and would publish again, Pugliese cited Manoilescu and Sommer on the first page of the lead article. The study appeared precisely at a time when Prebisch was wrestling at the Banco Central with the problems treated in the article. And if Prebisch did go on to read Sommer, he doubtless followed her discussion of Kondratieff and Kindleberger with intense interest. In any case, he was citing the American economist directly in 1944.

In 1943 Kindleberger had published two articles calling for the industrialization of agricultural and raw material producers on the basis of long-term deterioration of the terms of trade, and Prebisch was familiar with at least one of them.[87] In "International Monetary Stabilization," which Prebisch cited in 1944, Kindleberger argued that the terms of trade moved against agricultural products "because of the institutional organization of production" in industry, a reference to internal and external economies and possibly to monopoly elements, and also because of differences in the elasticity of demand for agricultural and industrial products (Engel's law).[88] Kindleberger, then working for the Organization of Strategic Services (the predecessor of the Central Intelligence Agency), pointed out that an agricultural country's increased productivity in primary activities under these conditions could raise real income only if the labor freed from agriculture were permitted to emigrate or found employment in industry—a proposition Kindleberger borrowed from Colin Clark.[89] Otherwise, the terms of trade would move against the country, and it would have realized no benefit from the increased output of primary goods. But domestic industry need not be as efficient as that abroad. An agricultural country's real income would be increased if, "at some level of costs, labor displaced from agriculture can produce industrial products previously imported to enable part of the proceeds of an unchanged volume of exports to be spent upon other types of imports," Kindleberger wrote. Though lacking the term, this prescription was an explicit recommendation of import-substitution industrialization.[90] Furthermore, this line of reasoning is similar to Manoilescu's, and Prebisch therefore did not require a direct acquaintance with Manoilescu to arrive at his own position.

Looking ahead to the postwar era, Kindleberger foresaw disequilibria in the international trading system. A specific instance of disequilibrium was the case of two countries with differing marginal propensities to import. For the country heavily dependent on exports and having a high propensity to import, a rise in exports (through a change in investment) could eventually produce an unfavorable balance of trade. "It may be suggested that the United States has a comparatively low propensity to import and a low ratio of exports to national income, whereas the rest of the world has a relatively high elasticity of demand for United States exports of manufactured goods and a relatively high ratio of exports to income."[91] Kindleberger's contribution to Prebisch's original structuralism thus seems large, though Prebisch used the idea of contrasting import coefficients and Singer employed disparities of income elasticities of demand. Yet to put all these elements together in a coherent argument from the perspective of the Periphery was the great contribution of Prebisch and Singer.[92] As Nathan Rosenberg has noted, in the history of economic theory, as in that of natural science, it is less insight than systematization that counts.* And the urgency for advancing the thesis was a postwar phenomenon, arising from the publication of the United Nations study *Relative Prices*, directed by Singer, which noted deteriorating terms of trade for primary commodities. This process demanded an explanation because it was in conflict with the Ricardian premises of the international trading system the United States government had constructed in the mid- and late 1940s.

Were the Prebisch-Singer thesis and the structuralist school at ECLA that soon emerged "neocorporatist"? The similarities of the corporatist theses of Manoilescu and Perroux have been considered and rejected as direct influences in the 1940s. Given that structuralists did not consider corporate groups as elements of analysis (as opposed to their use of standard neoclassical categories such as capital and labor), the validity of such a notion depends on how much importance in assessing structuralism is assigned to the treatment of monopoly elements as central features of the "real" national and international economies; how much importance in assessing structuralism is attributed to the role of the state as a factor relatively independent of dominant social classes, to correct imbalances, inefficiencies, and inequities; and whether these assignments are necessarily and uniquely associated with corporatism. Although I think Latin American structuralism does make the existence of monopolies and an efficacious and reformist state central to its argument, I reject the third point because neither would I consider Keynes a corporatist, though some perhaps would.

In any case, ECLA's theses, from their initial appearance in 1949, were hotly contested by neoclassical trade theorists such as Viner. The economics profession in 1948–49 had just been treated to a formal demonstration by economist Paul Samuelson of the Massachusetts Institute of Technology that, under certain con-

---

*Rosenberg (1976), p. 79. As an example, Rosenberg cites Nobel Laureate Wassily Leontief's input-output table, enormously useful in economic planning because the table can determine the required kinds and amounts of inputs for a given output. François Quesneau's *Tableau économique* (1758) appears in retrospect as a primitive input-output table, but this was not obvious in the eighteenth century. In the words of the Argentine poet and essayist Jorge Luis Borges, every writer creates his own predecessors.

ventional (but unrealistic) assumptions, trade could serve as a complete substitute for the movement of factors of production from one country to another, indicating that international trade could potentially equalize incomes among nations. Thus the less rigorous (but empirically grounded) arguments of Prebisch and Singer burst upon the scene just after Samuelson had raised neoclassical trade theory to new heights of elegance, and against this theory the new ideas would have to struggle.[93]

At the empirical level, furthermore, the terms of trade were improving for many Latin American countries in the late 1940s, a process that, when perceived, offered another potential impediment to the effective diffusion of the ECLA doctrine. "Thus it was necessary to invoke long-term and inevitable trends and normative arguments, to counteract the immediate force of market signals."[94] At the same time, the Prebisch-Singer (secular) terms-of-trade thesis came under severe attack from neoclassical economists, who challenged the validity of the historical data on a variety of grounds.

Examining the long controversy on terms of trade a generation after the appearance of the Prebisch-Singer thesis, the Anglo-Greek economist John Spraos has provided empirical and theoretical grounds for reviving the unequal exchange thesis in a modified and more sophisticated form.[95] Spraos writes that the "empirically meaningful" question is whether patterns of trade and specialization are "incrementally inequalizing," that is, increasing disparities relative to "an identifiable earlier point in time."[96] Net barter terms of trade (the unit costs of goods against goods by value), used by economists in the 1940s and 1950s, is a "one-dimensional concept" for Spraos because the deterioration of these terms of trade, if combined with job creation and productivity increases, could have an ambiguous outcome on welfare in a given society.[97] That is, a policy that resulted in deterioration of net barter terms of trade might nonetheless have merit if it offered offsetting gains in employment and labor productivity. Spraos proposes instead a quantitative measure that takes into account three indices of welfare— (net barter) terms of trade, employment, and productivity—the "employment-corrected double factorial terms of trade."[98] Using this definition and applying econometric tests to world trade data for 1960–77, Spraos finds that because of agricultural exports' pronounced deterioration of terms of trade, there was, over the period, "unmistakable incremental inequalization for developing countries with respect to the entire pattern of traditional specialization."[99] In essence, Spraos finds substance in the arguments that disparities exist in elasticities of both income and supply between primary commodities and manufactures, coupled with pressure for increasing the supply of commodities owing to the "unlimited supply" of labor.[100] The policy implications are that industrialization should be pursued, but diversification of both production and exports is also needed.[101]

For the simpler problem of net barter terms of trade, Spraos confirmed the Prebisch-Singer conclusion of a deterioration in primary commodities' terms for

1870–1939, but found that for 1900–1970, the data were trendless.[102] More recent econometric studies, using long-term data continuing into the 1980s, have tended to support Prebisch and Singer.[103] Finally, extrapolating from Colin Clark's argument in 1942 that primary producers' terms of trade would improve if they followed up productivity gains in export agriculture with the employment of the redundant labor force in industry, one could argue counterfactually that the terms of trade for primary exporters might have deteriorated much more without the industrialization in primary-exporting countries that *did* occur after World War II, a policy that was defended so passionately by Raúl Prebisch.

The structuralist school, which formed around Prebisch at ECLA, had its greatest impact on economic thinking and policy in two countries—Brazil and Chile—in the 1950s and 1960s. Brazil underwent a kind of "big push" toward industrialization in the 1950s, analogous to Rumania's effort twenty years earlier. To assess the work of Celso Furtado, the country's leading structuralist, we first need to consider corporatism and the rise of professional economics in Brazil from the Great Depression to the late 1940s.

Part III

BRAZIL

9

From Corporatism to Economics
as a Profession

Although Brazil's "outward-directed growth," in Prebisch's phrase, was less un-questionably successful than Argentina's before 1930, the former country's econ-omy had advanced impressively under the prescription of tropical export special-ization implicit in the Ricardian doctrine of comparative advantage. By one estimate, in the 30 years from 1902 to 1931, Brazil's Gross Domestic Product grew at an average annual rate of 5.4 percent and its per capita income at 3.3 percent, though during the period the economy became perilously dependent on a single export, coffee, which provided almost three-fourths of the country's foreign earnings by the late 1920s.[1]

A corollary of Ricardo's thesis was that for each country there are "natural" and "artificial" economic activities, based on its (implicitly static) factor endow-ments. The policy implication statesmen drew was that government should dis-courage, or at least not encourage, "artificial" industries that required foreign inputs in production because their development would result in a misallocation of resources. As early as 1853 a Brazilian parliamentary commission made the distinction between natural and artificial industries, and one of the leading social and political essayists of the Brazilian Empire, Aureliano Tavares Bastos, wrote nine years later that "factories in Brazil are an accident; agriculture is the true national industry."[2] Following this line of reasoning in the financial crisis of 1901–2, Minister of Finance Joaquim Murtinho would do nothing for "artificial" industries. Government aid to them, he had asserted in 1899, would amount to "socialism."[3] Such was the policy that the Brazilian government, like those of other Latin American nations, generally tried to follow until the latter 1930s or later.

Brazil's was not a laissez-faire policy, however, because government provided direct and indirect support, for example, through artificially low exchange rates or through exchange rate deterioration, for exports and the interests behind them.[4] Indeed, support for agriculture went much further, as the state of São

Paulo, beginning in 1906–8, and later the federal government, actively inter-
vened in the international coffee market, successfully endeavoring until 1929 to
sustain prices. Thus before 1930 Brazil, much more than Argentina, had a tradition of state intervention in the economy, even if it yet had nothing to do with
industrial protection.[5]

In Rio de Janeiro, the industrialist Serzedelo Correia had parried the argument of "artificiality" in 1903 with the observation that England imported cotton for its textile mills, and no one in Brazil or elsewhere deemed British textile
manufacture an artificial activity—an argument Rumanian industrialists would
later make with regard to continental cotton textiles. At the Industrial Center of
Brazil (CIB), with which Correia was associated, Luís Vieira Souto argued in
1904 that Brazil had not been "essentially agricultural" but "essentially poor."[6]
Vieira Souto, who held the chair of political economy at the Polytechnic School
in Rio de Janeiro (1880–1914), was among the relatively few Latin Americans of
the era influenced by List and the American defender of protection, Henry
Carey.[7]

At all events, Brazilian industrialists in the succeeding years generally advanced "practical" arguments. A pseudonymous article published in 1925 in
Brazil's most important business daily, the *Jornal do Comércio* of Rio de Janeiro,
made the following arguments on behalf of manufacturing: that such industry would provide urban employment; that it would save on foreign exchange
through import substitution; that it would help agriculture by consuming local
inputs such as cotton; and that it would provide government with more reliable
sources of revenue, through consumption taxes, than the export sector could.
Beyond these considerations, however, the writer implicitly pointed to a process
of unequal exchange, when he alleged that industrial countries could impose
prices for the primary goods they purchased from their agricultural trading
partners.[8]

Leadership for the manufacturers' cause soon passed from Rio to São Paulo
state. The city of São Paulo and its hinterland had become Brazil's leading manufacturing complex by the end of World War I, and the state's most important
manufacturers' organization was the Center of Spinning [Fiação] and Textiles. In
1928 other Paulista industrialists, who had previously been content to form a
component of the state's Commercial Association, joined the textile mill owners
to establish the Center of Industries of the State of São Paulo (CIESP), partly in
response to workers' militancy.[9]

São Paulo's most active industrial propagandist in the 1920s was Otávio Pupo
Nogueira, the secretary of the mill owners' organization and, after its creation in
1928, a spokesman for the Center of Industries. A shift from circumstantial and
practical arguments to a theoretical defense of manufacturing can be noted in
Pupo Nogueira's articles, originally published from 1925 to 1931 and collected in
his book, *Concerning the Customs Tariff*.[10] Still defending manufacturers against

the epithet of "artificiality" twenty years after Correia and Vieira Souto had done so, Pupo radically altered his argument upon discovering Manoilescu's *Theory of Protectionism.* For Pupo, Manoilescu provided the winning argument against the artificiality of the burlap sacking industry, frequently attacked by coffee growers, who nonetheless used the product; they complained of its allegedly higher costs than the foreign equivalent, owing to its imported raw material, jute. On the contrary, held Pupo, the sacking industry was legitimate and beneficial because of its high productivity, which should be the measure of the value of all economic activities, as Manoilescu wrote. Moreover, Pupo alleged, the industry employed 10,000 workers making coffee bags.[11]

In the same collection, Pupo announced his intention to translate Manoilescu's book from French into Portuguese.[12] In correspondence with CIESP officials, Manoilescu offered to write a special introduction treating the problems of Brazil, using Brazilian data on productivity, but the Center for Industries was not able to provide them. Undeterred, the organization published *Theory* in Portuguese in 1931, together with the Rumanian's letter.[13] In the words of a contemporary critic, Eugênio Gudin, the book was "distributed as a kind of bible of protectionism" by the Center.[14]

In the early 1930s, three Paulista spokesmen for industry—Pupo Nogueira, Roberto Simonsen, and Alexandre Siciliano, Jr.—took the Rumanian's work to be proof of the legitimacy of their interests. Adding a touch of racism in 1931, Siciliano neatly adapted Manoilescu's thesis to tropical agriculture by contending that Brazil could not continue to rely on traditional exports because of the lower wages that Africans and Asians would accept in those activities, thereby raising their labor productivities; thus agriculture in Brazil did not possess any intrinsic superiority over industry.[15] In turn, Simonsen reworked the argument for another purpose, alleging that because Brazil had to compete in export markets with Africa and Asia, employers in the South American country could not pay high wages.[16] Although industrialists still had only a weak voice in government circles, they had some influence on the tariff of 1931. Pupo had written that the newly created tariff commission should study the work of Manoilescu, and both he and Siciliano were appointed to it by the provisional government of Getúlio Vargas. Manoilescu himself, apparently on the basis of correspondence with CIESP officials, believed that he did influence the 1931 tariff law.[17]

Over the course of the 1930s, Simonsen and other industrial spokesmen used whatever arguments suited their momentary purpose, but their main thrusts were compatible with Manoilescu's views. For instance, Simonsen helped found the Institute for the Rational Organization of Labor (IDORT[18]) in 1931, the same year *Theory* was published in Portuguese; its president was the future governor of São Paulo, Armando Sales de Oliveira, who, like his associate Simonsen, was an engineer and industrialist. IDORT was formed around the values of organizing, controlling, and maximizing the efficiency of industrial labor.[19] Its underlying assumptions included the necessities of social stratification and leadership by an industrial elite. IDORT championed the labor-efficiency principles of Frederick W. Taylor on the factory floor, combined with the assembly-line division of labor of Henry Ford. It also defended "rationalization," which concept included class collaboration under the aegis of the state.[20] In its manifesto the organization's journal stated, "Rationalization, in one word, expresses our program."[21] Another goal of IDORT, and of the industrial bourgeoisie more broadly, was the abolition of tariff barriers within Brazil's national territory. Surprisingly, this matter remained an issue throughout the 1930s, despite repeated efforts by the national government to abolish such impediments to trade, a process that extended back to the nineteenth century.[22] Other institutions to promote the development of a technically and ideologically qualified industrial elite included the School of Sociology and Politics created in 1933, under Simonsen's inspiration, and the University of São Paulo in 1934, founded by Armando Sales in his first year as governor of the state.[23] Moreover, in a special report to President Vargas in 1937, Simonsen and the other directors of the Federation of Industries of the State of São Paulo (FIESP), successor of the CIESP, specifically endorsed "the formation of elites."[24] São Paulo's industrialists therefore tended to support the values of organization, elitism, industrialization, and, increasingly, as the 1930s unfolded, state intervention in the economy. After 1937, they also supported Vargas's Estado Nôvo dictatorship (1937–45). Therefore, it is hardly surprising that they found Manoilescu's theses, values, and attitudes attractive.

Another foreign economist whose views had a broad projection in São Paulo and Brazil at large in the 1930s was François Perroux, who had a personal connection with the country and, like Manoilescu, was a theorist of corporatism. The young French professor helped develop the social science program at the new University of São Paulo in 1936–37; he was a member of a French mission there, which also included Fernand Braudel and Claude Lévi-Strauss, underwritten by the Rockefeller Foundation.[25] During his stay in Brazil, Perroux not only lectured at the university level but also sought a larger audience in law journals and in the *Estado de S. Paulo*, the Brazilian newspaper with the widest circulation at the time. In the diffusion of his corporatist message, which continued after his departure, Perroux combated both Marxism and totalitarian versions of corporatism.[26] His "social corporatism," like Manoilescu's, would have had corporations independent of the state. In Perroux's system, representative labor unions faced capital with roughly equal power, in a situation of bilateral monopoly. This permitted a "socialization of the product," he told Brazilians, which was not possible in fascist or Nazi corporatism, where the state held down wages. Publishing in a law journal where one might question whether the targeted group of Brazilian readers could follow the intricacies of his argument, Perroux used Pigouvian welfare economics, including Pareto indifference curves and Edgeworth boxes, to show how state arbitration could achieve a maximum welfare for a society in which strikes and lockouts were not permitted. Perroux seemed to think this "scientific" demonstration of the validity of his corporatist economics was more than a metaphor, although the economic analysis itself only showed that, under certain assumptions and within a certain margin, welfare gains and losses between opposing parties were not necessarily a zero-sum game. "Social corporatism," unlike socialism, still respected prices and markets, Perroux continued, but it was a regime of the "organized market." Excess profits would be eliminated by the state in the "third solution" to the problems of twentieth-century economics, "neither pure capitalism nor planned socialism."[27]

Manoilescu's corporatism was more easily separated from his economic theories than Perroux's, and among the Latin American and Iberian countries where Manoilescu's books had the greatest resonance, in Brazil alone did the diffusion of the Rumanian's economic ideas unambiguously precede that of his political writings. Yet in the late 1930s, *Century of Corporatism*, which summarized Manoilescu's economic theses, not only had an impact on Brazil's fascist party, the Integralists,[28] but also influenced the authoritarian modernizers who were constructing and articulating the ideology of the Vargas government. Such influence is not a central concern of this work, but since the Rumanian's political treatise simplified and diffused his economic message, it may be noted that *Century* helped shape the work of at least two of the ideologues of the Estado Nôvo regime, Francisco Oliveira Vianna and Inácio Manuel Azevedo Amaral, who translated the book into Portuguese.[29] Other European writers figuring in the concoction of Oliveira Vianna's eclectic corporatism included François Perroux, Gaetan Pirou, and Sergio Pannunzio.[30]

For Oliveira Vianna, Azevedo Amaral, and Francisco Campos, another ideologue of Brazilian corporatism, the state was to organize civil society, so Manoilescu's "pure and integral" corporatism, in which the corporations were free from state controls, did not figure—but neither did they for Manoilescu himself after he wrote *Single Party*. The three Brazilian writers all wanted a strong state, rationalization of the economy, and economic planning.[31] They believed that an authoritarian, though not totalitarian, state was necessary to achieve these ends. Azevedo Amaral in particular wanted to expand the domestic market and to create an industrial elite. Like Simonsen, Azevedo used Manoilescu's work to link industrial development and nationalism.[32] In this respect, he and other modernizing corporatists were combating the ruralism of Alberto Torres, a statesman and proto-corporatist writer of Brazil's First Republic (1889–1930).[33] Azevedo Amaral published *Century of Corporatism* in translation under the Estado Nôvo dictatorship of Getúlio Vargas in 1938, presumably as an ideological justification of the regime. But the state had help from the private sector too: in a tract sponsored by the FIESP, the industrialists' association whose predecessor CIESP had published *Theory* in Portuguese, Manoilescu's *Century* was cited in justification for Vargas's authoritarian regime.[34]

As Salazar used Manoilescu's *Century of Corporatism* to justify the dictatorship in Portugal while pursuing pro-agrarian policies, the Vargas government's conversion to the Rumanian's thesis on industrialization was gradual. Brazil in the 1930s, like Argentina and Rumania, had an enormous foreign debt burden; Sir Otto Niemeyer, backed by British financial interests, visited the country as an official adviser in 1931. (In 1932 he would have similar missions in both Rumania and Argentina.) Niemeyer recommended orthodox financial policies, the creation of a central bank, and implicitly a continued reliance on international trade for Brazil as a stimulus to economic growth. Though Niemeyer's specific institutional recommendations were not implemented, the new Vargas government viewed Brazil's meeting foreign debt obligations as intimately related to reviving the coffee economy.

In Depression-era Brazil, Getúlio Vargas was pro-industry—was he not the friend of all established economic interests? But he opposed "artificial" industries (manufacturing) in his presidential campaign in 1930, and government loans to "artificial" industries were still prohibited in 1937. Osvaldo Aranha, Vargas's minister of finance in 1933, had even termed industries "fictitious" if at least 70 percent of their raw materials did not come from domestic suppliers.[35] Vargas became committed to rapid industrial expansion during the Estado Nôvo; even then, the conversion was not without vacillation. Although the dictator said he could not accept the idea of Brazil's remaining a "semicolonial" economy in 1939, as late as 1940, when the coffee market was still depressed after a decade of attempts to revive it, Vargas wanted to "balance" industrial and agricultural growth. In 1941 a division for industrial development of the Bank of Brazil began to make significant loans, but from 1941 through 1945 the bank disbursed an annual average of only 17.5 percent of its private sector loans to manufacturing concerns.[36]

Yet there could be no doubt that the government's position was changing, and part of Vargas's price for joining the Allies in World War II—Brazil was the only Latin American country to send troops—was U.S. aid for building a state-owned steel mill, by far the largest in Latin America when it went into operation at Volta Redonda in 1946. Moreover, as Brazil began a program of rapid industrialization, some of Vargas's speeches from 1937 onward seem to reflect the influence of Manoilescu's *Theory of Protectionism*, as opposed to his *Century of Corporatism*. For instance, in announcing his support of the creation of "basic industries" before the Brazilian congress in 1937, Vargas spoke of the conflict of individual interests with the "superior interests of the collectivity." On November 10, 1938, the first anniversary of the coup d'état creating the Estado Nôvo, Vargas stated, "Every agrarian country sells what it produces cheaply, in order to acquire [abroad] what it consumes for a high price."[37] In any event, Manoilescu's *Theory* was cited as a justification for the regime's economic policies in the Federal Council of Foreign Trade seven weeks before the Estado Nôvo coup.[38] By the time Brazil broke relations with the Axis in 1942, *técnicos* on the council as well as some military and political leaders were probably more committed to state intervention to establish capital goods industries than were the industrialists who had cited Manoilescu earlier.[39]

Yet the Rumanian's theory as a "scientific" rationale for Brazil's industrialization did not survive the war, possibly because of the attacks on his work by Jacob Viner and other neoclassical theorists. It is also likely that Manoilescu's association with the Estado Nôvo, inasmuch as the regime's leaders viewed *Century* as a rationalization of the dictatorship, and his support for the Axis in World War II (to the degree this was known) helped cause his eclipse as a source of intellectual and ideological authority. In the 1940s Manoilescu's ideas were abandoned for more practical and circumstantial arguments, to which the Brazilian industrialists had resorted before the 1930s. Simonsen, who had frequently cited Manoilescu in the early 1930s, apparently still considered the Rumanian's thesis on unequal exchange valid a decade later[40] but had ceased referring to the master. In the debate on national planning in 1945 between Simonsen and Eugênio Gudin, a neoclassical economist, it was the latter, not Simonsen, who referred to Manoilescu, viewing him as a discredited charlatan.[41] Years later, Gudin remarked that for Simonsen, the very existence of manufacturing industries, rather than their ability to compete with overseas producers, constituted a boon for Brazil.[42] If this was so, Simonsen's view may well have remained akin to that of Manoilescu, who, contrary to List, held that such enterprises formed a gain for a national economy from their first day of operation if their productivity exceeded the national average of economic activities.[43]

Nevertheless, industrial spokesmen remained defensive when confronting agriculture, and perhaps this tendency even increased when Manoilescu went out of fashion during the war years. At the first Brazilian Economic Congress in 1943, Simonsen preached the harmony of agricultural and industrial interests.[44] The first national Congress of Industry followed in 1944, opened by dictator Vargas and Simonsen, now president of the National Confederation of Industry. Though Simonsen on the occasion endorsed government intervention in the economy, the most noteworthy aspect of the proceedings came in the resolutions concerning agriculture. Not only did the congress declare that the "harmonious development" of industry and agriculture was "necessary" for "economic expansion," but it urged on the government specific measures for farmers and planters, including price supports, silo-building programs, and agricultural loans.[45] Part of the explanation for the industrialists' lack of a "hegemonic political vocation," as Fernando Henrique Cardoso later characterized their hesitations and ambivalences,[46] can be found in their diversified portfolios and those of their families. Simonsen, for instance, had major business dealings with a British coffee export firm, Brazilian Warrant. His brother Wallace, a banker involved in coffee exports, was a local partner of Lazard Frères, which had been one of the major foreign lenders in the pre-Depression valorization program.[47]

At the same industrialists' congress in 1944, however, Pupo Nogueira sounded a more aggressive note in a speech in which he alleged that the interruption of the international trading system in World War I had been the most important factor in the industrialization of Brazil.[48] Pupo noted that during World War II, Brazil had even been able to export industrial products—textiles—but the markets for such goods were now threatened by the prospect of peace and the return of a "normal" international division of labor. Government aid was now needed to reequip obsolete plants, Pupo asserted.[49] At the end of the war, Heitor Ferreira Lima, a younger writer in the employ of the FIESP,[50] was able at last to provide a riposte to the hoary charge of artificiality, on the basis of an industrial survey carried out in São Paulo during 1942–43: Paulista industry had effected more than 80 substitutions, he wrote, for previously imported inputs.[51] One could readily infer that much greater progress in import-substitution industrialization would be made before the international trading system was again operating on a normal basis in the postwar era.

In the defense of industrial development in interwar and wartime Brazil, it is notable that economists, in the more or less professional sense then in use in Rumania, did not play a large role. At the end of the Estado Nôvo, Gudin, an engineer by training who had taught himself neoclassical economics, could put Roberto Simonsen on the defensive for the latter's earlier citations of Manoilescu. In fact, although neoclassical economics had been taught at the São Paulo Law School before the turn of the century,[52] it was only after World War II that economics as a discipline in Brazil and in Latin America at large was professionalized. Until the 1940s "economics" in Brazilian universities had largely meant monetary problems, not issues in economic development, employment, or measurement of the national product.[53]

Yet the creation of a professional economics in Brazil was not simply a matter of a modern curriculum. There were broader cultural and institutional problems that had impeded the development of social science in Brazil. The intellectual traditions of Brazil and other Latin American countries revolved around the *pensador* (lit., thinker), a man who prided himself on his broad culture and who eschewed specialization. He often wrote as readily about contemporary sociology and politics as he did about literature, and his studies frequently crossed disciplinary lines. The *pensador*'s vehicle was the essay, a literary form which in Latin America retains the prestige it has all but lost in the English-speaking world. The style perhaps was appropriate to highly stratified, preindustrial societies; in any case, the writer on social matters usually wrote without reference to monographic studies, which were being cited in Rumania before World War I and were common by the 1920s. The Brazilian essayist's judgments tended to be definitive, his treatment historical. Before 1900, and even later, few Brazilian social writers were academics, and fewer still had studied in Europe. If they had, they almost never took research degrees, as opposed to diplomas in law, engineering, or medicine.

One feature distinguishing Brazilian society from that of Rumania in this period is a relative lack of an intelligentsia, in the classical sense of an under-employed intellectual community radically at odds with prevailing power structures.[54] This fact owes chiefly to the limited number of university students in Brazil, compared to employment opportunities in law, journalism, and civil service. More conventional intellectuals in university posts, for example, were usually less radical, though often reformist in orientation. In any event, seldom could the *pensador* be Antonio Gramsci's "organic intellectual," a spokesman for the interests of a well-defined class or class fraction, because social classes were still relatively inchoate.

A sociological reason for the persistence of the *pensador* tradition is that Brazilian academic institutions were seldom oriented toward research. Brazil suffered from a dearth of social research institutions as such: there was no interwar institution in Brazil comparable to Dimitrie Gusti's Institutul Social Român (Rumanian Institute of Social Science—ISR), founded in 1918–21. The Brazilian counterpart to the ISR was the Instituto Superior de Estudos Brasileiros (Higher Institute of Brazilian Studies—ISEB), founded in 1955 and closed by the military dictatorship in 1964. Both the ISEB and the ISR held multidisciplinary research seminars seeking to illuminate aspects of respective national realities.[55] Rumania also boasted an Economics Institute (established in 1921) and a Business Cycles Institute, modeled in 1932 on those at Harvard and Wagemann's at the University of Berlin.[56] The only analogous institutes in Latin America before World War II were the research division of the Argentine Central Bank, which Raúl Prebisch had organized in 1928,[57] and the Instituto de Economía, founded at the National Autonomous University of Mexico in the same year. Thus the impediments to social research in Brazil were hardly unique in Latin America. In Charles Hale's survey of Latin American social and political thought over the half-century ending in 1930, only one intellectual of some 90 treated, the Mexican Manuel Gamio, held a Ph.D.[58] Such a fact might serve as a proxy for the weakness of a research tradition, as opposed to the abstract theorizing and indifference to the systematic collection of data so characteristic of the *pensador* style. There was, for example, little to compare with the Rumanian community studies of the 1920s and 1930s carried out by Gusti and his students.[59]

One of Brazil's early institutional efforts at professionalizing economics came in 1944 with the organization of the Fundação Getúlio Vargas (FGV) in Rio de Janeiro, under the guidance of the neoliberal and self-trained economists Gudin and Otávio Bulhões. In 1947 the FGV established a professional economic policy and data-reporting journal, *Conjuntura Econômica* (Business cycle), organized by an eclectic and development-oriented group but taken over by Gudin five years later. In the same year, 1947, Gudin also began a research journal, the *Revista Brasileira de Economia*,[60] which quickly established its reputation as one of Latin America's leading reviews in economics.[61] Gudin and Bulhões furthermore set up a research unit, the Instituto Brasileiro de Economia, at the FGV in 1950. A member of the research staff was Richard Lewinsohn, a Viennese exile who became the first director of *Conjuntura Econômica*.

In the 1940s no Brazilian institution offered a doctorate in economics, and before World War II, there had been no tradition, in contrast to that of Rumania, of seeking foreign research degrees. Only in the 1950s would Brazilians earn significant numbers of research doctorates. Celso Furtado, the leading postwar structuralist in Brazil, was among the first Brazilians to earn a Ph.D. in economics, a degree he completed at Paris in 1948.[62] Even Furtado later wrote that he did not want to be a "professional," that is, a technical, economist.[63] In any case, he became the most widely read Brazilian economist of the century and the one who, with his mentor Prebisch, would provide the industrialists with a scientific rationale for their project better than any economist since Manoilescu. We must now address his work.

10

Furtado and Structuralism

If judged by the diffusion of his works, there can be little doubt that Celso Furtado was the most influential Brazilian social scientist of the century. In Latin America, where books are usually printed in editions of 1,000 to 2,000 copies, Furtado's works had *sold* some 200,000 copies in Spanish and Portuguese by 1972. World sales of his works had reached a million copies by 1990, and half these books were published in Latin America.[1] He was the first, most original, and most prolific of the structuralist writers in Brazil. Furthermore, he is arguably the first of the dependency analysts in Latin America and the first specifically to assert that development and underdevelopment were part of the same process of the expansion of the international capitalist economy.

Because so much of his early work was done in direct or indirect association with ECLA and Raúl Prebisch, Furtado's opus forms the strongest link between the continent-wide school of structuralism and the Brazilian national school, which he founded. Indeed, it is difficult to separate some of Furtado's earliest contributions from those of Prebisch, and in the 1970s their views began to converge again, focusing on the consumption patterns of Latin America's upper strata as the motor force in the allegedly nonaccumulating, dependent economies of the region. Throughout their careers, both men believed the state was the leading force in economic development and thought it could provide the leadership that market signals, feeble or distorted by monopoly in backward economies, could not. Like Prebisch, Furtado was by profession a public servant, who, over the course of his career, was intermittently associated with both his national state and international organizations. Like Prebisch, too, Furtado was a "nonpartisan politician," in the phrase of the Brazilian economist Francisco de Oliveira.[2] Though Furtado may have lacked the finely honed diplomatic skills of the more expansive Prebisch, his large head gave him the appearance of a profound thinker.

Furtado, again like Prebisch, hailed from a remote region of his native country, a "Periphery of the Periphery"—and for the Brazilian, his native region would remain a lifelong focus of writing and action. Furtado lived in Brazil's backward Northeast until age twenty and spent his childhood in contact with the arid and violent *sertão* of the small state of Paraíba, where his father was a judge. Like Prebisch, who was almost twenty years his senior, Furtado would pursue his university studies not in the provinces but in the national capital. He arrived in Rio de Janeiro in 1940 to enroll at the University of Brazil. At the time, economics was not yet a permissible specialization there, and Furtado chose the traditional curriculum in law.[3] The young man did, however, have contact with the French economist Maurice Byé, a disciple of François Perroux; Byé had been teaching in Rio at the time of Germany's defeat of France in June 1940 and remained in Brazil until 1942.[4] While at the university, Furtado switched from law to administration, and at age 23 he entered the Brazilian civil service. He soon joined Brazil's expeditionary force to Europe, where he served as an officer in the Italian campaign.[5]

After the war Furtado made his way to Paris, where he began his study of economics in 1946, working under Byé, his thesis adviser, and François Perroux. At the time, Furtado was still an "autodidact" in economics.[6] He had come to that discipline by a circuitous intellectual route—from law to organization and administration, from organization to planning, and from planning to economics. He later wrote: "I regarded planning as a social technique of the first importance, capable of increasing the degree of rationality of the decisions governing complex social processes by preventing the setting in motion of cumulative and irreversible processes in undesirable directions."[7]

His penchant for planning and his apprenticeship under Byé and Perroux led Furtado into contact with Perroux's structuralism-in-formation (and a retreating corporatism[8]) before Prebisch had worked out his initial version of Center-Periphery relations. But Furtado, more than Prebisch, was also interested in economic history. In 1948 Furtado presented a dissertation at the Faculté de Droit in Paris on the Brazilian economy during the colonial era.[9]

Furtado now returned to his native land, where he was employed by the Ministry of Finance to help produce *Conjuntura Econômica*, one of the two new journals associated with the Fundação Getúlio Vargas,[10] to which he had contributed while in Europe. Through an introduction provided by Otávio Bulhões, a cofounder of the Fundação with Eugênio Gudin, Furtado later in 1948 joined the staff of the UN Economic Commission for Latin America, with which he would be associated for a decade. In Santiago, Furtado met Ernst Wagemann, who arrived from Germany in 1949 to direct the Institute of Economics at the University of Chile. Furtado was already familiar with Wagemann's work because *Conjuntura Econômica* had been based on the German-Chilean's business cycle analysis.[11] But far more important in the development of Furtado's economics was the work of John Maynard Keynes. Though Furtado had studied Keynes in France, the English economist had little influence on the Brazilian's doctoral thesis, and it may be that Furtado's major exposure to Keynes came through Prebisch. The latter arrived in Santiago in February 1949—after Furtado—but had published his *Introduction to Keynes* two years earlier. In any event, the influence of Keynes was obvious in Furtado's first essay at ECLA, "General Characteristics of the Brazilian Economy" written in 1949 and published the following year.[12]

Furtado worked under Prebisch, who published the Spanish version of his "manifesto"—*The Economic Development of Latin America and Its Principal Problems*—in 1949, and the Brazilian soon became one of the older man's leading collaborators. Furtado prepared the data—though he denies credit for the accompanying analysis[13]—for the Brazilian section of the famous *Economic Survey of Latin America* for 1949. Prebisch and Furtado worked in tandem to marshal Brazil's government behind ECLA. They received critical support from Getúlio Vargas in 1951, his first year as a popularly elected president, to make ECLA a permanent UN agency.[14] The two economists also courted industrialists, participating in the debates of the National Confederation of Industries (CNI) in 1950. The organization and many individual manufacturers received Prebisch's thesis warmly.[15] In the same year *Estudos Econômicos* (Economic studies), the CNI journal, ran an article explaining and implicitly endorsing ECLA's position, and in 1953 the Industrialists' Confederation financially supported a regular ECLA session in Brazil.[16] A later CNI review, *Desenvolvimento e Conjuntura* (Development and the business cycle), founded in 1957, endorsed ECLA's interpretations and proposals in its first editorial.[17] In general, industrial leaders in Furtado's Brazil accepted state intervention and the "developmentalist" ideology associated with structuralism in the 1950s much more readily than did their counterparts in Prebisch's Argentina.[18]

In the early 1950s most of Furtado's energy was devoted to the projects of ECLA, which produced its works without individual attribution. Over his own name he did find time to publish several essays that would foreshadow his later development. Although remaining a UN employee until 1958, Furtado lived most of the decade of the 1950s elsewhere than Santiago; in 1953 he moved to Brazil, where he headed a project jointly sponsored by ECLA and Brazil's Banco Nacional de Desenvolvimento Econômico (National Bank of Economic Development—BNDE). The major task of the joint committee (Grupo Misto) was to introduce planning into the economic process, and Prebisch and Furtado defended the techniques of "programming" at ECLA's meeting at Petrópolis, Brazil, in the same year. In the meantime, Furtado became widely known in the "developmentalist" movement through his collaboration with the Instituto Superior de Estudos Brasileiros in which an interdisciplinary group of intellectuals was trying to forge a new economic nationalism in Brazil. In 1955 Furtado went to Europe and subsequently on to Mexico to conduct a study of that nation's economy for ECLA, and then to Venezuela, with a similar purpose.

Following an invitation by Nicholas Kaldor, Furtado received a Rockefeller fellowship to work at King's College, Cambridge, where Keynes once held court and where other luminaries of macroeconomics such as Kaldor, Richard Kahn (the inventor of the Keynesian multiplier), and Joan Robinson (the oligopoly theorist) then taught. Furtado left the United Nations after ten years of service and at Cambridge wrote his best-known book, *The Economic Growth of Brazil*.[19] The essay would quickly take its place beside a handful of others as a classic study of Brazilian economy and society. Moreover, it opened a debate on the character and rhythm of Brazil's industrialization that has yet to be resolved. Returning home in 1958, Furtado became a director of the BNDE, with special responsibility for the poverty- and drought-stricken Northeast, his native region.[20] At the outset of the new year, he was invited to a brainstorming session with President Juscelino Kubitschek, who was presiding over an unprecedented wave of economic expansion. Furtado persuaded the president to set up a special development program for the Northeast,[21] and this endeavor led to the creation of a permanent regional autarky, the Superintendency for the Development of the Northeast (SUDENE). He also was among those who successfully urged Kubitschek not to introduce recessionary measures recommended by the International Monetary Fund to contain inflation.[22]

At the turn of the decade, the Northeast was the focus of political unrest and rural union organization, magnified in importance by international news media, which associated the Peasant League spokesman Francisco Julião with the Cuban Revolution. Furtado himself was frequently called a communist and was investigated by Brazil's National Security Council.[23] After SUDENE was approved by the Brazilian Congress at the end of 1959, Kubitschek named Celso Furtado as its first director; he was reappointed by Presidents Jânio Quadros (1961) and João Goulart (1961–64). Under Quadros, Furtado's position was raised to cabinet rank, and the younger man would soon do battle with the emerging development scheme of the Alliance for Progress, whose North American directors had a different set of priorities for the Northeast.[24] Despite his intense administrative and political activity, in 1961 Furtado published one of his major works, *Development and Underdevelopment*, which would form the bridge between structuralism and dependency.

By 1963 Furtado began to champion agrarian reform as necessary for the progress of the Northeast.[25] He found himself in an increasingly polarized situation when a (perceived) radical, Miguel Arraes, became governor of Pernambuco, the Northeast's most important state, and Goulart's presidency drifted toward the left, while right-wing forces began to conspire against the president and the regime. Meanwhile, Furtado has been appointed extraordinary minister of planning, and in 1962 he prepared a three-year development plan which is better remembered for the orthodox short-term anti-inflation measures it contained than for its long-term structuralist features. When the coup d'état ousting

Goulart came at the end of March 1964, Furtado was immediately dismissed from his post at SUDENE. Under the military dictatorship of Marshal Humberto Castelo Branco, he quickly lost his political rights as well.

Furtado now began a long exile. In 1964 he briefly worked in Chile, where he contributed signally to the emergence of dependency analysis; after a year at Yale University, he returned to his alma mater, the University of Paris, as professor in 1965. He had held a post there ever since, despite protracted stays in Brazil, beginning in 1975. At Paris Furtado wrote *Underdevelopment and Stagnation in Latin America*[26] in 1966, arguing that the region's economies were headed for a permanent slump because of the exhaustion of import-substitution industrialization, based on narrow national markets; this situation in turn owed to the maldistribution of income within the Latin American nations. Such analysis was quickly proven wrong for the Brazilian case by the country's rapid growth in 1968–73, but Furtado continued to write prolifically on other themes. He sophisticated his analysis of dependency and applied it in a region-wide context in *The Economic Development of Latin America* (1969).[27] In 1985, when Brazil returned to a civilian and constitutional regime, President José Sarney named Furtado the Brazilian ambassador to the European Economic Community. He returned to Brazil to serve as minister of culture from 1986 to 1988. Throughout the 1980s Furtado continued to plead for public support and funds for the development of his beloved and scourge-ridden Northeast.

The preceding sketch of Furtado's career should suffice to demonstrate that engagement in politics and policy formation did not preclude a fecund scholarly output, our main concern. All three major thrusts of Latin American structuralism discussed in Chapter 8—the tendencies within the Periphery toward unemployment, owing to structural (technological) heterogeneity; disequilibrium in the foreign sector; and deteriorating terms of trade—were developed inventively in Furtado's early work.[28]

Following the publication of Prebisch's *Economic Development of Latin America and Its Principal Problems* (1949), which Furtado translated into Portuguese the same year, the Brazilian quickly drew further conclusions from Prebisch's analysis of the business cycle and high import coefficients (see Chapter 8). Furtado argued that income tended to concentrate in Brazil during the upswing of the cycle, owing in part to a highly elastic labor supply that held down wages; in this manner, Furtado adumbrated by four years W. Arthur Lewis's celebrated analysis of an infinitely elastic labor supply as the source of wage rigidity in underdeveloped countries. Further, the Brazilian hypothesized that much of the effect of the Keynesian multiplier "leaked" abroad, owing to the exporting groups' high propensity to import.[29] Such analysis pointed again to the importance of an industrialization policy.[30]

One of Celso Furtado's best-known ideas, which combines economic and social analysis, was introduced in the same essay of 1950. "The socialization of losses" concerned the interaction of changes in exports, the exchange rate, and imports.[31] Furtado, like Prebisch, was much interested in the effects of the business cycle on the Periphery, which the Brazilian preferred to call a "colonial structure";[32] but unlike the Argentinean, Furtado dealt not with differential consequences of cyclical swings for Center and Periphery but with the differential effects of the cycle among the latter's socioeconomic groups. Furtado focused on the Great Depression, when coffee interests induced the government drastically to devalue the Brazilian currency. Thus the collapse in coffee prices to planters in hard currencies was partially offset by a considerably smaller drop in their receipts in Brazilian milréis; the rest of the loss was passed on to Brazilian consumers in the form of higher import prices. From 1929 to 1931, the dollar price of coffee fell 60 percent. But the greater quantum of exports combined with the fall in the exchange rate made the domestic value of coffee exports only 14 percent less in 1931 than in 1929.[33] In addition, the Great Depression called into existence an unplanned but effective effort by the government to sustain aggregate demand, and the Brazilian economy, in Furtado's view, made a decisive shift to growth based on industrialization for the domestic market rather than on exports.[34] Prebisch had noted earlier that the most economically advanced Latin American nations had made their largest strides toward industrialization when the international economy was in crisis, but Furtado supplied the term— development by "external shocks."[35]

Two years later, in 1952, Furtado authored an essay that offered a response to the theses on development defended by one of the eminent authorities of the era, Ragnar Nurkse, an Estonian who had studied in Vienna and England. In his 1951 lectures at Gudin's Institute of Brazilian Economics,[36] Nurkse, a former League economist then at Columbia University, propounded his famous "doctrine of balanced growth," published in 1953 as *Problems in Capital Formation in Under-Developed Countries*. Nurkse held that a series of vicious circles blocked economic development, and a major coordinated effort by the state would be required to overcome them. For example, low real income was a reflection of low productivity, owing principally to lack of capital. The latter in turn was a consequence of a small savings capacity, which resulted from low real income. Furtado inferred that Nurkse's doctrine took its point of departure from Schumpeter's *Theory of Economic Development* but that Nurkse had reversed the thesis of the Austrian theorist, replacing the latter's "circular flow" with "automatic stagnation."[37] Furtado himself reflected the influence of Schumpeter when he wrote, "The process of development involves either new combinations of existing factors at the current technical level, or the introduction of technical innovations."[38]

For Nurkse, investment opportunities in underdeveloped countries were limited by a small domestic market, but for Furtado, a problem of equal importance was the absence of an expanding foreign market—an implication of the doctrine, or assumed fact, of deteriorating terms of trade for commodity exporters in world commerce.[39] For Furtado "the aim of economic development must be to increase the physical productivity of labor," and to do so beyond the export sector, where it was typically higher than elsewhere in the early stages of underdevelopment. Like Nurkse and other economists of the period, Furtado believed labor's physical productivity was "in the main" explained by capital accumulation.[40] Such accumulation was difficult to achieve in the export sector, where the benefits of an increase in the physical productivity of labor might suddenly be transferred abroad by a fall in commodity prices. The export sector was also important on the demand side, especially when income was concentrated in a small group. This group (class?) emulated the consumption patterns of inhabitants of developed countries, and demand might not diversify, owing to a sharply skewed distribution of national income.[41] A similar point had been made by Nurkse, based on an extension of James Duesenberry's interpretation of Keynes's "consumption function." The Harvard economist had established that, from one period to another, the percentage of income consumed in the United States depended not on absolute income but on consumers' positions in the income pyramid; thus the consumption function was stable over time for a given stratum of income receivers. This fact was accounted for by a "demonstration effect" of the wealthiest groups on those of lesser affluence. Nurkse extended Duesenberry's concept not to explain "size-distribution" (roughly, class) behavior from one generation to the next in developed countries but the emulation of consumption patterns of such nations by the upper classes in underdeveloped countries. Furtado endorsed this extension. He wrote that Brazil lacked "not incentives to invest, but incentives to save," a problem exacerbated by "powerful stimuli to consume exercised by more advanced economies."[42] The notion of "demand-driven" and "demand-distorted" patterns of growth would later gravitate to the center of Furtado's vision of underdevelopment. At the time Furtado, like Nurkse, believed in the power of fiscal policy to shape economic development, and for the former this included some (unspecified) form of compulsory savings. The state, Furtado contended, could more effectively ensure an adequate rate of savings and investment than could the conspicuous consumption–oriented private sector.[43]

Celso Furtado, a professional civil servant, saw in economic planning the advantages that had been proclaimed by Rosenstein-Rodan and Nurkse, namely, that because of indivisibilities in large-scale investments and potential external economies not realizable by private firms, a state-directed development effort was necessary. Private investors would maximize the private, not the social, marginal net product. In underdeveloped countries, where markets did not function properly, the price mechanism was not a reliable guide for investment; in those areas, the utilization of factors of production (as expressed, for example, by wages) varied widely across sectors. The rate of development could be accelerated, Furtado confidently believed, if investments were made "according to a coordinated comprehensive plan."[44]

Beginning in 1955, Furtado and Prebisch worked for official acceptance of "programming," the ECLA version of planning, in Brazil. ECLA's programming used techniques similar to Vassily Leontief's input-output analysis—starting from a given rate of growth to be achieved by the economy and estimating the necessary structural changes needed as well as specific inputs to meet the target. Echoing Pigou, Manoilescu, and Rosenstein-Rodan, but citing Keynes, Furtado later repeated that the interest of the entrepreneur and the collective interest do not always coincide. State investment had to focus on "strangulation points" (bottlenecks) and "germination points" (growth poles), which would diminish sectoral disequilibrium, a basic feature of underdevelopment.[45] But planning was a matter of degree, and Furtado's BNDE-ECLA commission advocated a comprehensive form in 1957; this proposal contrasted with the more limited and bottleneck-oriented planning contemporaneously defended by Roberto de Oliveira Campos, head of the BNDE and a highly influential figure in the Kubitschek government.[46]

In any event, Kubitschek was listening, and if Campos was more influential in formulating the administration's Target Program, the president (1956–61) largely embraced the ECLA analysis of underdevelopment. In his first message to Congress, Kubitschek noted the vital role of government in economic development in infrastructural investment. He mentioned ECLA and BNDE specifically as participating in the planning process and endorsed "programming." He voiced approval of ECLA's thesis on deteriorating terms of trade for primary producers and the consequent and persistent balance-of-payments problems. For the president, this problem could be rectified by government promotion of import substitution and new exports. Industrialization permitted both this substitution and the diversification of exports; industry would also absorb excess labor from agriculture. Industrialization for Kubitschek was an "essential condition" for the "rapid economic development" of Brazil.[47] Furtado later wrote that the government's "Target Program" (*Programa de Metas*) was directly inspired by ECLA, and a student of economic thought in Brazil credits Furtado himself with introducing programming in the country.[48]

If the government could in some manner plan development, why could it not stanch the perennial and seemingly simpler problem of inflation? From his debut as a structuralist theorist in 1950, Furtado was interested in inflation as a persistent feature of Brazil's economy. Along with the terms-of-trade issue, the most widely debated matter at the continental level between structuralists and their opponents was their thesis on inflation, and in fact the term "structuralist" was first applied to the school's treatment of that issue in the late 1950s. The basic idea was that structural features of the Latin American economies created sustained or long-term inflationary pressures (e.g., owing to inelastic supply in agricultural production because of inefficient latifundia, or owing to rising import prices because of the secular decline in terms of trade), quite apart from, or in addition to, incompetent or irresponsible monetary policy.[49]

The thesis was not wholly a Latin American construct. In a broad sense, "structuralism," which received its name in the context of the analysis of inflation, owed something to the "doctrine of market failure" that led to Keynesianism in Britain in the 1930s.[50] More directly, the Polish economist Michal Kalecki, who had been at Oxford in the 1930s and 1940s, published a seminal article on inflation in Mexico's *Trimestre Económico* in 1954; its influence on the structuralist school was acknowledged by the leading Latin American contributors to the thesis, the Mexican Juan Noyola Vázquez and the Chilean Osvaldo Sunkel. Kalecki emphasized the "inelasticity of agricultural supply and monopolistic tendencies in industry" in inflationary patterns in underdeveloped countries. Inflation was caused by "basic disproportions in productive relations," and it could not "be prevented by purely financial [monetary] devices," wrote Kalecki.[51]

Though Furtado was not a major contributor to the final structuralist thesis as presented by the Chilean Osvaldo Sunkel in 1958,[52] the Brazilian was one of the earliest Latin American economists to ascribe inflation to structural distortions. As early as 1950, four years before Kalecki's pathbreaking essay, Furtado had pointed to deteriorating terms of trade as one cause of inflation because of the effect on prices of imported goods.[53] Furthermore, in 1952 he had asserted that inflation in Brazil was not basically a monetary problem but the result of "the disparity between the growth in income and the capacity to import," that is, a structural imbalance in the nation's international payments.[54] Beyond this, wrote Furtado, when the rate of economic growth is high, the demand for capital goods increases faster than national income, and this phenomenon, together with the tendency toward stagnation in the international markets for Brazil's (traditional) exports, causes a deterioration of terms of trade.[55] It was therefore "indispensable . . . to modify the structure of production so as to increase exports or to find substitutes for imports."[56] Despite the much greater international attention to the debate on inflation in Chile, in Brazil as early as 1955 Furtado was involved in a debate with Dênio Nogueira in which "structuralist" and "monetarist" positions were defined. Nogueira and later monetarists emphasized the need for proper monetary and fiscal management traditionally defended by orthodoxy.[57] Three years later, Furtado took a different tack, viewing diversification of demand, which outpaced diversification of the supply of industrial goods in Brazil's growth process, as "the basic cause of chronic inflation." Although trade would have been an obvious solution, Furtado focused on the diversification of production. He believed inflation could be overcome by development, which was possible through planning to make the supply of goods more flexible, elastic.[58]

When Furtado was charged with constructing a three-year development plan in 1962, inflation, a hot political issue, was one of his major concerns. The plan included both structuralist and monetarist features, basically corresponding to the long and short terms. The monetarist array of measures included budget balancing through higher taxes and lower outlays. Furtado also hoped to develop an efficient capital market, an objective favored by both schools. Elsewhere in a summary of the plan, the "deficient agrarian structure" was cited as a cause of the rapid rise in food prices.[59] Though the three-year plan was also designed to redistribute as well as increase income and remove institutional obstacles to growth (especially in agriculture), its immediate effects were recessive. Goulart was deposed and Furtado exiled before any structural reforms could be implemented.[60]

If Furtado was not among the formulators of the final structuralist position on inflation in Santiago, Chile, he was the leader in the effort to historicize structuralism.[61] True, Prebisch's *Economic Survey, 1949* had treated in brief the economic history of Latin America as a whole from the 1880s to the mid-twentieth century·and had considered individually the four most industrialized nations— Argentina, Brazil, Chile, and Mexico. In some respects this volume was a model for the country case studies to be carried out between 1959 and 1963—Furtado on Brazil, Aníbal Pinto on Chile, Aldo Ferrer on Argentina, and later, Osvaldo Sunkel and Pedro Paz on the whole region, as well as René Villareal on Mexico.[62] But Prebisch's interest was focused on the business cycle, not long-term historical development.

Furtado's *Economic Growth of Brazil* derived principally from his pre-ECLA interest in defining the features of colonial Brazil. Although "The Economy of Colonial Brazil," his pre-ECLA dissertation at the University of Paris (1948), does not contain much formal economic analysis of any kind, *The Brazilian Economy* (1954) and *A Dependent Economy* (1956), a briefer work, are structuralist treatments of Brazil's economic history.[63] These early historical essays offer evidence that Furtado's contribution precedes Pinto's, even though their "classic" studies both appeared in 1959—*Chile, A Case of Frustrated Development*[64] and *Economic Growth of Brazil.* The latter work covered the whole sweep of Brazilian history, and the colonial and nineteenth-century sections compare and contrast the structures of the Brazilian and U.S. economies, showing how Brazil's monoculture and latifundia impeded the high savings and investment rates characteristic of the American economy. Focusing on the distribution of income and the size of the domestic market, Furtado provides one of the first uses of modern income analysis in a historical framework and demonstrates the weak relationship between income and investment in an economy based on slavery.[65] The work throughout is written from the point of view of a development economist, emphasizing the heterogeneity of technologies and production functions (including the vast subsistence sector) in the Brazilian economy.

Turning to the problem of Brazil's economic cycles, examined in earlier studies by João Lúcio de Azevedo (writing on the Portuguese Empire), Roberto Simonsen, and John Normano,[66] Furtado saw in the weak monetization of the slave economy a grim resilience in that export stagnation or decline could be sustained as the free but plantation-oriented population moved toward the backlands: the subsistence economy absorbed the excess labor supply after the exhaustion of successive export booms. For example, when the sugar economy declined in the seventeenth century, the ancillary livestock economy became increasingly subsistence-oriented, and average labor productivity, by inference, fell.[67] This economic "involution," as Furtado called it, was the opposite of development because each historical export boom until coffee (brazilwood, sugar, gold, and—contemporaneous with coffee—rubber) led to retrogression, not to sustained growth.[68]

The apparent aberrations in Brazilian financial policy in the period since independence could be explained in part by the fact that the structure of "dependent economies" was different from that of the industrial economies. In times of depression, the former suffered plummeting export prices, worsening terms of trade, a reduction in capital inflow, together with rigid requirements in foreign capital servicing. In trying to adhere to the gold standard, Brazilian statesmen had failed to understand the nature of their predicament and viewed their nation's inability to keep to the standard as the result of bad management, rather than a problem with deeper causes.[69]

Differences in the growth and diversification of the production structure of the Brazilian and U.S. economies in the first half of the nineteenth century were not chiefly accounted for by the greater degree of tariff protection in the United States, Furtado believed, but by the differences in social structure and income distribution and therefore the size of the domestic market. Furtado estimated that Brazil's continually falling exchange rate provided more protection for domestic industries than high tariffs would have.[70] But more important, Brazil suffered from a small domestic market, lack of modern technology, entrepreneurship, and capital, and its small capacity to import.[71] For Furtado, Brazil's national market dated from the last quarter of the nineteenth century, when a modern working class came into existence. Beginning in the late 1880s, when immigrant wage labor replaced slave labor in São Paulo's coffee fields, Brazil began to experience a significant home market. For Furtado wages paid in the coffee sector permitted the "nucleus of a domestic market economy," with the implication of an attendant multiplier effect.[72]

The big change in relative market size, however, occurred after the crisis of 1929, in which the coffee economy, which had risen to 70 percent of the value of national exports, collapsed. In Furtado's estimation, the decisive shift toward an economy based on the stimulus of domestic demand took shape in the early 1930s. The American economist Werner Baer has noted that Furtado's analysis of events in the Great Depression accounts for only 7 percent of the space in *Economic Growth in Brazil*, but it is the theme of the book that has generated by far the greatest scholarly controversy.[73] We have already seen that Furtado's earliest treatment of the issue, the thesis in embryo, goes back to his "General Characteristics" in 1950.[74] Furtado shared the view of Prebisch and ECLA in the *Eco-*

nomic Survey, 1949 that industrialization had historically occurred in periods of crisis in the larger Latin American economies.

Elaborating on his analysis of 1950, Furtado pointed to Brazil's rapid industrial growth during the Great Depression, partly caused by the "socialization of losses" of coffee producers through exchange devaluation; this process helped maintain domestic demand by keeping up the employment level and purchasing power in the coffee sector, which permitted the rise of a significant domestic demand for industrial goods when foreign products were unavailable, owing to the absence of foreign exchange. The stockpiling and destruction of coffee in the face of grossly excess supply were financed through credit expansion, which in turn exacerbated the external disequilibrium and caused new exchange depreciation and a further socialization of losses.[75]

Furtado viewed the expansionary fiscal and monetary policies related to coffee as a form of unwitting Keynesianism because the wealth destroyed in coffee beans was considerably less than that created by maintaining employment.[76] Furtado then noted that output of capital goods in Brazil by 1932 was 60 percent greater than in 1929. Furthermore, net investment in 1935, at constant prices, was greater than that in 1929 and the level of aggregate income of the latter year had been regained, even though imports of capital goods were only half of the 1929 figure.[77] Therefore, the economy was undergoing profound structural change. Furtado's views on Brazilian industrialization in the Depression touched off a long debate.[78] In this exposition, it seems clear that Furtado was influenced by his Keynesian background, especially with regard to government intervention to sustain demand and the significance of the domestic market in dynamizing production and income.[79] Yet it now seems the case for Brazil, as for the other most industrialized countries in Latin America, that the world wars and the Depression were less important in producing "inward-directed growth," in Prebisch's phrase, than was believed by some contemporaries to these events and by ECLA economists later.[80] A now widely held view is that investment in industry (capacity) grew in line with export earnings for the period 1900 to 1945, while output (but not capacity) tended to rise during the "shocks," when imports had to be curtailed. Capacity could not grow appreciably during the Depression for lack of exchange credits to buy capital goods and inputs or during the world wars because of the unavailability of capital goods and fuels from the belligerent powers.[81]

In addition to his historicizing efforts, Furtado explored structuralism's potential in another direction, as did Hans Singer, the coformulator of the Prebisch-Singer thesis. This was the problem now known as "internal colonialism," treated in Chapter 6. Like the Rumanian economist Manoilescu, the two UN economists, Furtado and Singer, built their analysis in the 1950s around unequal exchange between industrial centers and agricultural peripheries.[82] I will focus on the Furtado version, which was published first and in a fuller form, though Singer's work was completed earlier.

As Rumania and East Central Europe as a whole formed the locus for early ideas on economic backwardness, it is hardly surprising that after 1945, when underdevelopment/development became a recognized subdiscipline of economics, the idea of regional disparities in growth would appear as a major development issue in Brazil. That nation accounts for almost half the area of the South American continent and is noted for tremendous differences in wealth between regions as well as between urban and rural areas. Of the 24 countries for which the American economist Jeffrey Williamson made estimates of regional inequalities in the 1960s, Brazil had the greatest disparity,[83] principally owing to the differences in wealth and income per capita between the dynamic Center-South of the country, containing São Paulo and Rio de Janeiro, and the retarded Northeast. Brazil and Chile were also Andre Gunder Frank's two original case studies linking internal colonialism with unequal exchange at the international level.[84]

The international models of the trading process on which Singer and Furtado drew were those of the UN Economic Commission for Latin America (developed by Prebisch in 1949) and Singer's very similar one, independently arrived at and published a year later.[85] According to Prebisch and Singer, at the international level unequal exchange derived from differential productivities between industrial Center and agricultural Periphery in the world market, combined with different institutional arrangements in capital and labor markets. Technological progress in manufacturing, in any case, was shown in a rise in incomes in developed countries, while that in the production of food and raw materials in underdeveloped countries was expressed in a fall in prices relative to industrial goods. The explanation of contrasting effects of technological progress was found in the disparate income elasticities of demand for primary and industrial goods.

To reiterate, this analysis pointed to negative features in the Periphery's economy: structural unemployment, owing to the inability of traditional export industries to grow and therefore to absorb excess rural population; external disequilibrium, because of higher propensities to import industrial goods than to export traditional agricultural commodities; and deteriorating terms of trade—all of which could be corrected or mitigated by a well-executed policy of industrialization.[86]

Furtado addressed the issue of internal colonialism in the late 1950s, when he became more deeply involved in the problems of the Northeast, just as Brazil's Center-South was expanding rapidly. His analysis was inspired by the Prebisch model but was not directly extrapolated from it. Like Prebisch, Furtado assumed the existence of market imperfections—particularly the administered pricing of industrial goods—and an "unlimited supply" of labor in the backward region at the going wage in the industrial sector.[87] (One hardly need add that most students of economic development consider these assumptions realistic.) But the Brazilian's model was more complex than Prebisch's because it purported to measure the deterioration of terms of trade between the international price of agricultural goods sold abroad by Northeast Brazil against the domestic price of industrial goods which the region had to buy from the Center-South. Furtado did not explicitly claim, as Prebisch had, that the terms of trade he was interested in deteriorated secularly, but this could be inferred.

Furtado focused on the relationship between the agrarian, latifundium-dominated Northeast, which in 1956 had an annual per capita income of less than U.S.$100, and the Center-South, where incomes were more than three times higher in the dynamic industrial economy organized around the cities of São Paulo and Rio de Janeiro. The gap between the Northeast and the Center-South was larger than that between the latter region and per capita incomes of western Europe.[88] Moreover, the distribution of income within the Northeast was highly skewed, making the situation even more desperate for the masses. Although the drought-plagued Northeast had experienced economic growth in recent decades, its growth was slower than that of the Center-South, so the income gap between regions was widening. Furtado estimated the relationship between the growth rates of the lagging and the leading regions was of the order of one to two for the decade after 1948.[89]

Furtado, like Manoilescu in Rumania, analyzed the Northeast in terms of a triangular trade between the backward region, the foreign sector, and the developed area (in Furtado's case a region rather than urban areas as such).[90] Like Manoilescu, Furtado viewed the state as an essential element in the process. Brazil's Northeast had a surplus in its commercial balance abroad but a deficit in its balance of payments with its domestic trading partner, the Center-South. Because of the country's policy of import-substitution industrialization, the central government was subsidizing industrialists and penalizing agricultural exporters. This support took the form of differential exchange rates for importers of manufacturing-related capital goods and importers who would use foreign exchange credits for other purposes. A related policy, the *confisco cambial*, also adversely affected the Northeast. The government "confiscated" a share of the earnings of traditional exporters (sugar and cocoa planters in the Northeast, coffee and cotton growers in the Center-South) by maintaining an overvalued exchange rate—in effect, collecting a tax.[91] That the central government gave exporters poorer exchange rates than importers not only effected a sectoral transfer of income; the action induced a regional transfer as well because of the size of the export sector relative to real (national) income in the Northeast, compared to that of the Center-South.[92] Furthermore, economies of scale and external economies in the industrial heartland of the Rio–São Paulo area made the hitherto large industrial advantages of the region, relative to the Northeast, even greater as development proceeded. Finally, the government stimulated industrial development by its financing of private enterprise. Thus central government policies designed to stimulate industrialization had a major inequalizing effect on the regional distribution of income in the country. Furtado estimated that in the period 1948–56, the Northeast transferred U.S.$24 million annually to the Center-South, although a more accurate figure may be $15–$17 million yearly.[93] Because of Brazil's protectionist tariffs and related exchange policies, the Northeast was in no position to seek alternative supplies abroad for its manufacturing needs. It offered a captive market for the Center-South, and its foreign exchange earnings gave it purchasing power in that region. But the relevant terms of trade now entered the picture: overall, prices of the Center-South's industrial goods rose more rapidly from 1948 to 1956 (the years studied by Furtado) than the exchange rate fell, that is, the rate at which northeastern exporters gained more cruzeiros per unit of foreign currency.[94] Furtado's model, though based on monopolies in factor and consumer markets, was in a sense more dependent on institutional and structural distortions than Prebisch's original because of government intervention in currency and commodity markets. Yet elements of the original model remained because the forces of "cost-push" inflation were still present in the form of high-wage industrial goods sold in oligopolistic markets.[95]

Nonetheless, partly because of constitutional provisions, the federal government did make a net transfer of its own tax revenues (i.e., apart from the exchange and tariff policies) to the Northeast, much of it in the form of drought relief.[96] Yet this infusion of funds into the Northeast was more than offset by private disinvestment in the region, as owners of capital sought better rates of return in the Center-South.[97] Consequently, in Furtado's view, private capital was more important in real capital formation than public spending; in any case government income transfer in the form of relief was largely consumed, not invested.[98] Beyond these considerations, federal aid to the region was partly offset by regressive taxation in the Northeast. That is, the Northeast paid more in taxes, relative to its per capita level of income, than did the Center-South.[99] Therefore, by the same measure, it contributed more than it should have to federal coffers. After doing an algebraic sum of the flows, Furtado thought the Northeast's situation was one in which on balance the central government put its own money into the region (as opposed to the consequences of its exchange and tariff policies). Thus the situation differed from that in Rumania, where, according to Manoilescu, the trading pattern *and* the fisc moved income in the same direction—toward the cities.[100]

Like Manoilescu, Furtado proposed industrialization as a solution.[101] The Brazilian's industrialization, however, was to take place in the urban zones of the depressed region, whereas Manoilescu would have had the currently "exploiting" urban sector accelerate the pace of its industrial development, a process that would eventually raise the value of rural labor and diminish urban–rural income inequalities. Furtado also stressed the need for agricultural development because the cost of wage-goods, that is, foodstuffs, in the largest city of the Northeast, Recife, was greater than that of São Paulo. Thus if wage differentials were narrowing between São Paulo and Recife to meet rising costs of living in the latter, there would be little incentive for private capital to invest in the Northeast.[102]

Without specifically advocating land reform (for political reasons?), Furtado called for restructuring agricultural production in the Northeast as a "prelimi-nary requirement for industrialization."[103]

Agrarian reform has yet to occur, however, and in the years following Fur-tado's analysis, development strategies favoring the Center-South continued. Using later studies of regional inequality, Werner Baer has assessed the longer-term effects of official policies. Despite the continuing efforts of the federal government to offset regional income concentration, Baer concluded, the overall effect of development programs continued to favor the industrial Center-South over the agrarian Northeast in the three decades following Furtado's analysis.[104] Therefore, regional inequality in Brazil and, by implication, internal colonialism, persist as major national issues in the closing years of the century.

In his two regional studies of 1959 surveyed above, Furtado had already per-ceived a relationship which he, Osvaldo Sunkel, Fernando Henrique Cardoso, and Andre Gunder Frank would develop in the mid-1960s: that a structural and perverse relation existed between the growth of developed capitalist economies (and regions) and the growth of underdeveloped countries (and regions): "[There exists] . . . a tendency for industrial economies, as a result of their form of growth, to inhibit the growth of primary economies: This same phenomenon is occur-ring within our country."[105] It is notable for the history of dependency analysis that Furtado's first published statement of the alleged link between development and underdevelopment appeared in the context of internal colonialism, rather than at the international level.[106]

Furtado's analysis of internal colonialism seemed to contradict the implica-tions of neoclassical economics. Five years after the Brazilian economist's studies in 1959, Jeffrey Williamson elaborated an explicit neoclassical model of regional development that would have major currency in development studies. According to Williamson, in the early stages of economic growth, income disparities among leading and lagging regions typically intensify because of the disequilibrating effects of growth. For instance, the migration of skilled labor and the flow of capital to the developed region occurs in the initial stage of growth because there, both wages and interest rates are higher and financial institutions are better devel-oped, owing to larger markets and better infrastructures—for example, transpor-tation and communications grids within the region. Furthermore, the central government may manipulate the external terms of trade through commercial policies in favor of the more developed, industrial region (as was the case in Brazil). The spread effects predicted by neoclassical theory in income multipliers and technological and social change may be minimized in the short and inter-mediate runs by a lack of economic integration of the advanced and retarded regions. But Williamson hypothesized that the income and growth differentials among regions tend to disappear over the longer term, as interregional markets are linked and labor migration to the leading region becomes less selective. He suggests a process consisting of three stages in which regional differentials at first increase, then stabilize, and finally decrease, in an "inverted-U" pattern. Williamson's hypothesis, he wrote, finds support in the history of Sweden, France, and the United States, where the process, beginning in 1840, spanned 120 years.[107]

Furtado's findings cannot eliminate the possibility that Williamson and the neoclassical school are right. The inverted-U hypothesis of greater regional inequality, stable inequality, and diminishing inequality over more than a century cannot be refuted because the time horizon is too long for underdeveloped countries, where industrialization and the availability of relevant data are largely twentieth-century phenomena. Yet because the hypothesis is untestable in the context of underdevelopment (for which Williamson had prepared it), it does not meet Karl Popper's well-known criterion of falsifiability: scientific propositions are meaningful, wrote Popper, only to the extent that conditions are specified which, if met in a testing procedure, will prove them false.[108] Furtado would reject the Williamson approach because of what he perceives to be the fundamentally different experience of underdeveloped countries, characterized by heterogeneous levels of productivity—the very definition of underdevelopment for structuralists—unknown in the West at the beginning of its industrial revolution. In any event, given the structural differences that currently exist between highly developed and underdeveloped countries, a time span of a century or more offers a wide margin for the intervention of variables whose role in Western development was different from that of underdeveloped countries at the outset of modernization. In particular, the modernization-industrialization process began in western Europe with population growth rates half of what they were in underdeveloped countries at the "same stage" of industrialization. Thus the "unlimited supply of labor" and heterogeneous productivities cast doubt on the predictive value of Williamson's inverted-U pattern of regional growth—or at least on the possibility that major income inequalities among regions could be eliminated in the 120-year period required by the United States.[109]

At the end of Chapter 8 we saw that recent research by John Spraos and others on the hoary issue of the deterioration of terms of trade, with appropriate qualifications, seems to vindicate the analysis of Prebisch and Singer in 1949–50; this is so in both the simple net barter version and in the more sophisticated form proposed by Spraos that takes into account employment creation and productivity increases.[110] It is obvious that, if Spraos has revitalized a metamorphosed Prebisch-Singer hypothesis, his more complex measure also has implications for internal colonialism. All the essential elements in international trade inequalization are, in principle, present within underdeveloped countries. In such nations, as Manoilescu noted, per capita incomes are more disparate between city and countryside than in developed countries, and, as Furtado pointed out, incomes between regions are sometimes more disparate than those between mean figures for "developed" countries and those for developed regions of "underdeveloped" countries.

Within-country gauges of productivities and employment between regions—concepts presenting daunting measurement difficulties between countries—should be more manageable empirically than international ones because of uniform within-nation accounting conventions; in addition, fewer commodities would need to be weighted. Finally, because prices for commodities and services would be quoted in a single currency, such fact would obviate thorny measurement problems at the international level, including the distortions produced by nontraded goods in international comparisons of per capita wealth and income. Of course, for cases—probably the majority—in which foreign trade significantly affects the differential growth of regions, Spraos's procedure at the international level would also have to be undertaken. And the qualifications noted by Grilli and Yang that an analysis of terms of trade for a given country must include sector-specific data; that falling terms of trade may indicate productivity gains; and that income terms of trade[111] may be positive in the face of negative net barter terms of trade—would have to be taken into account.[112] Consequently, the overall exercise would be more difficult than international comparisons because it includes them, yet the additional intranational effort is less fraught with problems. As a result, though the sociologist Robert Hind's judgment may be correct that models of internal colonialism have been unsatisfactory to date, it seems that the approach pioneered by Furtado and Singer could have a future, not only in states characterized by a "cultural division of labor," on which the American sociologist Michael Hechter has focused, but in relatively ethnically homogeneous states, such as Brazil, as well.[113]

The late 1950s and early 1960s were extremely productive for Furtado as a theorist of development. Not only did he write *The Economic Growth of Brazil* and develop a thesis on internal colonialism *avant la lettre*,[114] but he wrote the essays that would constitute his book *Development and Underdevelopment*,[115] which has probably been more influential than any of his other works, excepting *Economic Growth of Brazil*.[116] It is notable that except for a year's research at Cambridge in 1957–58, Furtado in this period was intensely involved in work for ECLA in Brazil and other Latin American countries, followed by service in high positions in the Brazilian government from 1958 through 1964.

In one essay in *Development and Underdevelopment* (a collection published in 1961), Furtado reviewed the major theories of growth, beginning with the classical British economists. Furtado wanted to revive the use of the classical concept of economic surplus—that portion of the social product beyond the level required for the maintenance and reproduction of members of a society and their goods and services, that is, total revenue less total costs.[117] In the same essay, Furtado critiqued neoclassical economics for its emphasis on equilibrium (as opposed to growth), while also highlighting the school's ideological features. For instance, the idea of surplus has been discarded in the neoclassical synthesis between 1870 and 1890. For the neoclassical school, "the social product was to be conceived in terms of 'costs of factors' [land, labor, and capital], savings being viewed no longer as a result of an existing surplus but as the result of an act of restraint or abstinence."[118]

In retrospect, it can be said that this set of essays established Furtado as having a claim to have been the first analyst of dependency. His passing reference to the problem in *Operation Northeast* (1959) had been explicit, but in *Development and Underdevelopment* he described how the European industrial economy by the nineteenth century had penetrated and transformed precapitalistic economies. Underdeveloped economies were "hybrid structures" and not simply *unde*veloped economies beginning to trace the path that Europe had already defined. Consequently, underdevelopment was a "discrete historical process through which economies that have already achieved a high level of development have not necessarily passed."[119]

Structuralism was one of the two most important Latin American contributions to Third World development theory, and the other was dependency analysis. Furtado's structuralism provided a heterodox but non-Marxist path to dependency. There was a Marxist path as well—one which derived in significant degree from the work of Caio Prado, Jr., whose break with communist orthodoxy is considered in the following chapter.

11

Marxism in the Postwar Periphery

Until the 1960s Marxism in Brazil revolved around the Brazilian Communist Party (Partido Comunista Brasileiro—PCB), which for four decades was directed by Luís Carlos Prestes, the charismatic former army officer who, before becoming a communist, had led a guerrilla force across Brazil in the 1920s. Prestes was in exile during much of the recent military dictatorship, but in July 1985, at the close of the regime, he participated in a nationally televised debate, dramatically illustrating the end of censorship. The debate took place in three hour-long sessions, and the issue was whether Brazil would benefit more from a capitalist or a socialist program of development. Prestes engaged Roberto de Oliveira Campos, the former "developmentalist" of the Kubitschek government and, since 1964, the market-oriented economist who had liberalized the national economy in the first three years of the dictatorship. The two men agreed that the country had grave problems, but they sharply disagreed on whether the nation's poverty, backwardness, and waste resulted from the *existence* of capitalism in Brazil (Prestes's position), or its insufficient development (Campos's). But Prestes's views as leader of the PCB in the 1950s and 1960s had been less distant from those of Campos than was apparent in 1985. *Within* the Marxist tradition, as we shall see, this debate was no less important. As in Rumania, different interpretations of fundamentals arose, including the nature and "viability" of a local bourgeoisie, but in Brazil the debate came much later than in the Balkan country. The late arrival of Marxist discourse in Brazil is a matter that requires explanation.

Before the Third International, Marxism was anemic in Latin America as a whole, as were other traditions of social thought of the German-speaking world, so important in Rumania, such as the German Historical and the Austrian schools of economics. Germanic social science would begin to transform social thought in Latin America after the arrival of Spanish exiles fleeing the Franco regime in the late 1930s. Many of these men, of whom José Ortega y Gasset was only the most famous, had studied in Germany and promoted the translation of German works into Spanish.[1] Before World War II Latin Americans' greater familiarity with French, British, and Spanish than German thought probably tended to limit their knowledge of Marxism, if one can accept Perry Anderson's judgment that there were no significant contributions to Marxist theory in France, Britain, or Spain before the 1930s.[2] Rudolf Hilferding's *Finance Capital* (1910), which was so influential in Ştefan Zeletin's *Rumanian Bourgeoisie* (1925) and in Rumanian social thought more broadly,[3] was not available in Spanish, English, or French until the 1970s. Generally speaking, there were considerably fewer Marxist works available in Portuguese than Spanish—partly because Spanish texts were easily understood by Portuguese speakers—and the first full text of Marx's *Capital* translated directly from German into Portuguese appeared only in 1968.[4]

Marxism was thus poorly understood and poorly diffused in Latin America before Lenin founded the Third International in 1919, though the assertion is somewhat less valid for Argentina than for other countries.[5] Radicalism in most of Latin America, like its Iberian counterparts, tended to revolve around anarchism more than socialism at least until the 1920s and in many nations, including Brazil, perhaps until the early 1930s.[6] In addition, most socialist parties were not exclusively or predominantly Marxist-oriented until the Third International forced the issue in the early 1920s.

Examining the Brazilian case, Edgard Carone has noted that before World War I, Marx and Engels were mentioned primarily in journalistic works and that there were no Portuguese translations of their books or even their articles. Furthermore, the PCB published little of theoretical interest before 1930.[7] Caio Prado, Jr., the leading Marxist intellectual of the quarter-century after World War II, retrospectively noted that in 1930 he was unable to obtain works by Marx—presumably in any language—in São Paulo bookstores.[8] In the 1920s and 1930s Marxist-Leninist works were generally only available in French, and one PCB militant, Heitor Ferreira Lima, who studied under Comintern auspices in Moscow, later wrote that Brazilian communists of the period knew little directly of Marx and Engels. Further, they had no knowledge of Lenin's *Development of Capitalism in Russia*.[9]

An underlying reason for the slow penetration of Marxism and a certain positivist distortion of it into the 1930s[10] was the lack of a Hegelian foundation in the Brazilian intellectual milieu. Just as Hegel's philosophy had opened the road for Marx in Russia, it had deeply influenced the Junimea circle in Rumania, preparing the way for Dobrogeanu-Gherea's Marxism (see Chapter 3); but in Brazil the dominance of Comtian and Spencerian traditions left little space for the work of Hegel in the decades before World War I. Even in the early 1930s the idealist philosopher's work was poorly known, so the few attempts to reason national problems dialectically, such as that of PCB leader Otávio Brandão in the

1920s, resulted in crude and mechanical triads (thesis, antithesis, synthesis)[11] perhaps inferior to those of Nikolai Chernyshevsky, the nineteenth-century Russian populist.[12]

The cultural traditions and institutional weaknesses impeding the development of neoclassical economics in Brazil, discussed in Chapter 9, applied a fortiori to Marxist thought because its practitioners were denied university posts and public forums more generally. One indication of the thinness of the Marxist tradition is that before World War II Brazil had no "legal Marxists" like Peter Struve of the Russian Empire or Ştefan Zeletin of Rumania; there were no revisionists who argued that capitalism in backward countries would develop through Marxist stages but that the rise of a local bourgeoisie was both inevitable and beneficial. Ironically, despite earlier twists and turns, the official position of the PCB in the 1950s would come very close to "Zeletinism," because the party's support for the national bourgeoisie was identified with anti-imperialism and antifeudalism.

One result of the weakness of Marxism as a school in Brazil, it would seem, was the fact that the creative Marxists of the years before the military regime of 1964 all worked in the tradition of historical materialism, not in that of formal Marxist economics.[13] At the end of our period a vigorous debate on modes of production took place, stimulated in part by a prior and continuing debate in France and cross-fertilized by a contemporaneous one in Spanish America. The modes debate in the Brazil of the 1970s was more sophisticated than that of Rumania in the interwar years, involving Zeletin, Voinea (defending Gherea), Rădăceanu, and Pătrăşcanu; but such a controversy within the Brazilian Marxist tradition before 1945 on a par with its Rumanian counterpart is difficult to imagine. In any event, there was none.

In both Brazil and Rumania, however, precisely because of their peculiar features of underdevelopment, Marxists sought to adapt the classical theory to the reality they perceived. It would not seem a great distortion to speak of a "structural Marxism," in the same sense in which ECLA structuralists adapted neoclassical and Keynesian theory. That is, though Marxism by definition considers a series of relations of changing structures, European theory had to be altered to fit local circumstances. Classical Marxism did not explain the local social transformations under way in the Periphery or blockages to full transformations. Revisionism in the West had begun no later than the publication of Eduard Bernstein's *Evolutionary Socialism* in 1899,[14] and some would say it began with Engels himself, who outlived Marx by twelve years. One of the unanticipated new phenomena to be explained after 1880 was the rise of imperialism, but in the works of Hilferding, Luxemburg, Kautsky, and even Bukharin and Lenin, the new phase of capitalist expansion was still examined from the point of view of the Center rather than the Periphery. Meanwhile, in that Periphery, those who had some acquaintance with Marxism—but not necessarily a sound knowledge of, or a commitment to, such a philosophy—began to adapt and revise. At a simple level, consider, for example, the notion of "proletarian nations"—the metamorphosis of exploited classes into exploited peoples. The idea was "discovered" and re-discovered by Marxist and Marxist-influenced intellectuals who viewed their nations as peripheral to the capitalist Center, such as Enrico Corradini in Italy (1910) and Li Ta-chao in China (1920).[15] Lenin had come close to adopting the notion in "Imperialism and the Split in Socialism" (1916).[16] In Rumania, Con-stantin Dobrogeanu-Gherea skirted close to the idea, and Cristian Racovski and Constantin Stere "discovered" it; but its most insistent exponent was Mihail Manoilescu, who called for a "socialism of nations" to replace a "socialism of classes."[17] Much more recently (1969), Arghiri Emmanuel has endorsed Lenin's notion of a labor aristocracy in the rich countries and further perceives the rise of proletarian nations, whose goods exchange, as in Manoilescu's scheme, for those embodying much less labor-time per unit of value.[18]

In the Center, where economists sought to explain the Periphery's problems in the 1950s, a notable departure from orthodoxy was the use of the notion of "surplus" (not surplus value) by Paul Baran, the Russian-born American Marx-ist, in the sense that classical economists had used it. His notion of the "potential surplus" focused on the waste of "feudal" regimes in Third World countries. In Brazil, the notion of surplus was developed not by Marxists but by the structural-ist Furtado, whose use of the term was contemporaneous with Baran's; yet the latter's *Political Economy of Growth* (1957) was widely read in Portuguese transla-tion among Brazilian students and intellectuals in the early 1960s.[19] All the same, "official" Marxism in Brazil—that of the PCB—was far from eager to embrace the political implications of Baran's analysis, which denied the transforming power of Third World bourgeoisies.

Marxism in Brazil, unlike Rumania, essentially made its appearance as the product of the Third International, when the PCB was organized in 1922. We need not consider the shifts—sometimes abrupt—in the party's postures; it is sufficient to say these changes before World War II generally followed Com-intern "periods" based on strategies and tactics designed to advance Soviet inter-ests in Europe and Asia.[20] The Brazilian Communist Party attempted to seize power once, in 1935, in a putsch against Vargas that failed disastrously. The PCB's leader, Luís Carlos Prestes, was soon apprehended and tortured, to be released from prison at the end of World War II. In 1950 Prestes formally appealed for a "struggle" (without definition) against the "feudal-bourgeois dictatorship in the service of imperialism," to achieve a "popular," but not socialist, revolution; this position was moderated at the PCB congress in 1954, and the possible implica-tion of violence was formally abandoned in 1958.[21] The fifth party congress in 1960 reaffirmed the call for an alliance with the national and petty sectors of the bourgeoisie to achieve a "democratic" revolution against "feudal" latifundism and imperialism,[22] and this thesis was widely shared by Latin American CPs of the era. In fact, the Brazilian party's stance in 1960 was not radically different from that ten years before[23] and would have included nonimperialist merchants and industrialists in its popular coalition. The PCB held fast to its position even after Fidel Castro demanded revolution, not reform, in Latin America in the early 1960s.[24] Brazil's military coup and repression after 1964 caught the party still supporting the national bourgeoisie.

In brief, though there were shifts in the postwar era in PCB strategy, it supported the national bourgeoisie, albeit with varying degrees of enthusiasm, because of the party's hypothesized struggle between the national bourgeoisie and the reactionary alliance of foreign capital (or, in shorthand, U.S. imperialism) and the "feudal" (sometimes "semifeudal") landlord class. Communists in Brazil, or anywhere else in Latin America, could not realistically expect to achieve a proletarian revolution in the foreseeable future, PCB leaders believed. But they could support a "bourgeois democratic" revolution that would strengthen the national bourgeoisie against its foreign and domestic rivals for control of the national economy. Agrarian reform would break the power of latifundists, and nationalization of key industries would break that of imperialist groups. When these elements were defeated, the national bourgeoisie could pursue the project assigned to it by PCB and Soviet theorists, viz., unimpeded industrialization, which would necessarily mean the rise of a large working class. Only when the process was completed could socialist revolution be contemplated.

Yet industrialization was proceeding apace in an unanticipated and not altogether welcome fashion. For most socialist writers, including Caio Prado, Jr., who was influenced by Prebisch and the early ECLA, the problem of foreign capital as late as the Kubitschek years (1956–61) focused on the "old imperialism," which had discouraged Third World industrialization.[25] The internationalization of industrial capitalism had not yet been perceived by most PCB or other socialist writers in the 1950s as the new driving force in Brazil's economic growth.[26] An exception could be found in the work of Aristóteles Moura, whose *Foreign Capital in Brazil*[27] (1959) anticipated arguments of the late 1960s and early 1970s against multinational firms. He charged that multinationals used transfer pricing to disguise their true level of profits and that such companies relied on local capital rather than the home office for investment funds,[28] thus denying scarce financial resources to domestic entrepreneurs. On the role of foreign capital in the industrialization process, Moura is the only Marxist whose analytical sophistication might be compared to that of Lucreţiu Pătrăşcanu in Rumania: there was no one in Brazil in the interwar period with such skills. That other socialists fell short of the sophistication of Moura's critique of foreign investment did not mean they ignored, or approved of, the palpably huge influx of foreign capital during the Kubitschek administration. The PCB in 1958 called for industrialization under a capitalist regime but denied its support to those Brazilian businessmen and government officials who were closely allied with foreign capital. Such persons were labeled *entreguistas*, those who would "hand over" the country to imperialist interests.[29]

Much of the Marxist critique in the 1950s and 1960s addressed agriculture. To repeat, if Brazil was to become a modern nation, it had to industrialize under the leadership of the national bourgeoisie. Therefore, the power structure that prevented the unfettered domination of this progressive class would have to be examined critically, and special attention was given to the role of latifundium owners. In PCB writer Moisés Vinhas's *Agrarian-Peasant Problems of Brazil*,[30] the national bourgeoisie—as distinct from the sector of the bourgeoisie allied with foreign capital—would support agrarian reform to unloose productive forces in a country with one of the world's highest concentrations of land ownership; such reform would greatly expand agricultural output, thereby lowering the wage bill for capitalists, and create a potentially vast rural market for national industry.[31]

For Vinhas, the abolition of slavery in 1888 had meant a shift from a slave-based system of agriculture to a precapitalist or semifeudal one, which he also styled "backwoods feudalism" (*feudalismo caboclo*).[32] Elsewhere in the same work he refers to the latifundium as "semicolonial" and makes clear that the phrase refers to production for export,[33] which would imply a capitalist mode at the level of circulation. But for Vinhas the lower classes resident on latifundia toiled in conditions of serfdom, rendering traditional services, including the corvée and the *cambão* (personal services in exchange for usufruct), and frequently not participating in the monetary economy. The great estate was the leading impediment to capitalist penetration into the countryside for vast areas of the country.[34]

Another well-known Marxist study of the 1960s, Alberto Passos Guimarães's *Four Centuries of the Latifundium*,[35] also supported a modified "feudal" thesis. Though colonial Brazil participated in an international capitalist economy, relations of production were either those of slavery or serfdom, both based on extraeconomic coercion, as opposed to the purely economic form of a wage-labor system. Extraeconomic coercion survived from feudalism and continued down to the present in many areas dominated by latifundia. Passos believed the monopoly of land ownership was the basis for such compulsion.[36] Passos and Vinhas agreed that relations of production in São Paulo and other southern states were more fully capitalist than those of the traditional Northeast. This was an advance over the view of PCB militant Otávio Brandão in 1926, who insisted that the southern coffee planter was a "feudal lord" just as much as the northern (i.e., northeastern) sugar baron, and even affirmed that the *colono* of the coffee fields, the immigrant rural worker who enjoyed usufruct, was a serf.[37]

Contesting the position of Roberto Simonsen in his economic history of Brazil that colonial agriculture had been capitalistic[38]—a thesis which Passos noted had been applied to all Latin America by Sergio Bagú in 1949[39]—the Marxist writer asserted that efforts to deny the feudal nature of colonial society amounted to disguised apologies for the status quo. The objective of most Marx-

ists was to create a progressive and roughly egalitarian capitalist agriculture so
Passos asked, "If the agrarian structure of Brazil had a 'capitalist configuration,'
why revolutionize it? Why reform it?" Thus the thesis of "colonial capitalism" in
Brazil was "conservative, reactionary."[40] To progress, Brazil needed a "democratic agrarian reform" that would simultaneously break the bonds of dependency on imperialism (i.e., on the export market) and destroy the "semifeudal
links of subordination to the extraeconomic power" of latifundium owners.
Meanwhile, Passos Guimarães believed the latifundium system, though an archa-
ism, had a tendency to expand, and an ongoing conflict still pitted estate owners
against the landowning or -occupying peasant class.[41]

Moisés Vinhas denied that there was a peasant class and argued that the groups
Passos identified as peasants (those who controlled farms up to 100 hectares,
mostly worked by family labor) were too heterogeneous to form a class.[42] Vinhas
appears to have the more proper Marxist perspective, just as the Rumanian
communist theoretician Pătrăşcanu had denied the Peasant Party's contention
that there existed a single "peasant class" in his country.[43] At all events, Vinhas
and Passos Guimarães agreed that feudal elements could still be found in major
portions of Brazil's agrarian complex. The "feudal" or "semifeudal" thesis was
probably useful for political ends because it identified the latifundium, at least the
traditional one, as archaic. But it contained a confusion, which identified force
and monopoly of land ownership with the social and political arrangements
known as feudalism. By this term Passos and Vinhas meant a form of production
and social control that reduces to manorialism, a system that included extraeconomic compulsion, and that, as Marc Bloch pointed out, antedated feudalism
and survived its demise.[44]

But Marxism had become a house of many mansions, and Caio Prado, Jr.,
hailing from one of the richest and most aristocratic families in São Paulo,
produced the most novel interpretation of Brazilian agriculture during the years
1930–70. Indeed, despite his concern with the "old" imperialism (which had
impeded industrialization) until the 1960s, he was the most innovative Marxist of
his generation. Educated in the Jesuits' Colégio São Luís, a British public school,
and the São Paulo Law School (graduating in 1928), Prado joined the PCB in
1931, four years before the communist-sponsored uprising that provoked a ruth-
less repression by the Vargas government.[45]

Earlier the same year, 1935, Prado had found himself in a strange camp by
agreeing with planters who charged that Brazilian industry was artificial. Prado
condemned the collusive and monopolistic practices of Brazilian industrialists,
for example, securing government prohibition of imports of new machinery in
the textile and paper industries, as an indication of the artificiality of manufacturing, which lacked a mass market. Prado parted company with coffee planters,
however, when he argued that Brazil had to become an industrial nation and
with the industrialists as well when he asserted that the first step was to create a

domestic market through the redistribution of wealth, particularly in the countryside; only then could industry thrive. Prado emphasized that in both cotton and coffee cultivation, the large plantation was a dynamic phenomenon, that the creation of great estates was a continuing process. The redistribution of land would also eliminate one partner in the alliance between imperialism and the latifundium.[46]

In the same article of 1935, Prado distinguished between "settler" and "exploitation" colonies in Western history, placing Brazil in the latter category. He saw the tropical colony as a producer of raw materials, a mere appendage of the European economy—hinting, perhaps, that the Brazilian colonial experience was a capitalist undertaking from the beginning, a point he would not develop until after World War II.[47] It was not a Marxist but Simonsen, the follower of Manoilescu and corporatist spokesman of industry, who first held that colonial Brazil had been a capitalist enterprise. Yet it was Prado who cast the argument in Marxist terms, developed it, and drew political implications. As early as 1947, two years before the publication of Sergio Bagú's *Economy of Colonial Society*, Prado explicitly maintained at a PCB congress that Brazilian agriculture had not been feudal but capitalist in the colonial era, thus contradicting the official stance of the party at the time.[48]

Prado's position of course depended on a definition of capitalism in the colony. It focused on the allegation that agricultural production in colonial Brazil had always been chiefly market-oriented and that the latifundium was not a feudal demesne but a large, profit-seeking enterprise. Therefore, the distribution of land to peasants, advocated by the PCB, was "reactionary."[49] The point was not elaborated, but presumably Prado meant that the rural farming population consisted primarily of wage workers or sharecroppers, who preferred better pay, working conditions, or share of the product to plots of land.[50] Thus Prado's analysis of rural society had policy implications that contradicted the PCB's program of agrarian reform to remove feudal remnants and develop rural capitalism. Although still a Marxist militant in 1954, Prado criticized the "passive obedience" of the PCB to Soviet directives at any given moment.[51]

Between 1960 and 1966 he elaborated his argument. From the outset Brazilian agriculture had been capitalist in its essential features, that is, the Portuguese colony was a mercantile enterprise in which there existed, at a theoretical level, legal equality among the settlers, implying the right of employers and employees to negotiate contracts in a wage labor regime. The latifundium was associated with the scale of the commercial enterprise, not with feudal traditions. For the nonfree population, slavery was a form of labor control associated with commercial capitalism, not feudalism. Sharecropping (*parceria*), which some writers believed was a vestige of the feudal economy, was, on the contrary, a capitalist relation between employer and employee, as its continued existence in São Paulo cotton culture during the 1930s exemplified, Prado wrote in 1960. Cotton cultivation was undertaken with a level of technique superior to that of the older coffee plantations in the region, where wage labor prevailed, a fact that bore witness to the modernity of the sharecropping arrangement in cotton, Prado held.[52]

In *The Brazilian Revolution* (1966), Prado flatly contended that a "feudal or semifeudal system, or even simply one related to feudalism in the proper sense, [had] never existed" in Brazil, which had been part and parcel of the international capitalist system from the sixteenth century.[53] Here he explicitly contended that rural workers generally do not want direct ownership of farmland, as peasants do; rather, they want better wages and working conditions. Great landowners were "a legitimate agrarian bourgeoisie." Further, at no other time than the last twenty years, during which "imperialist capital literally submerged our economy," had the Brazilian bourgeoisie enriched itself more. There was no meaningful "national bourgeoisie,"[54] a chimera so long the cynosure of Communist Party strategy.

In the increasingly polarized national and international politics of the late 1960s, the obvious implication of Prado's book was that his country, as fully capitalist, was ripe for revolution, contrary to the official position of the nation's Communist Party, of which he had long been a member. To put the proposition another way, after 450 years of capitalist development, how long did one have to wait for the inevitable contradictions to occur? The time was now. Prado thus provided an answer for Passos Guimarães's question, "If the agrarian structure of Brazil had a 'capitalist configuration,' why revolutionize it?" Having authored *The Brazilian Revolution* was the unstated reason for Prado's incarceration in 1969 because the book had, in the dictatorships' view, inspired a new generation of urban guerrillas.[55] In the tension in Marxist theory between ascribing the primary motor of historical change to contradictions in forces and relations of production on the one hand, and ascribing it to class struggle on the other, Prado implicitly opted for the latter course.[56]

Few students of Latin American agrarian structures, however, now accept the view associated with Prado and Bagú that a sempiternal capitalism characterized Latin America from the Conquest onward. One reason for rejecting this interpretation is that it does not allow for a *transition* to capitalism,[57] however one may characterize precapitalist structures and practices. One way of resolving the conflict has been suggested by the Peruvian Pablo Macera, who argued the great estate could be seen as poised between two worlds—the inner one of dependency and extraeconomic coercion of the labor force and the outer one recognizably capitalistic in its response to world markets. Generalizing to a broader dualism, the Brazilian Ignácio Rangel, a sometime structuralist, has argued that socioeconomic relations in Brazilian history have been "internally archaic and externally modern,"[58] a perspective not unlike that of Constantin Dobrogeanu-Gherea on the Rumania of 1910.

In any event, Marxists in Brazil, like social scientists of other orientations, showed little theoretical and practical interest in the middle peasants and artisan classes, rural or urban, compared to the interest shown in these problems in Rumania. In Brazil there was no concern, among Marxists or others, about the possible development of a rural bourgeoisie from a *chiaburime* or kulak group. The absence of such concern perhaps lies in the perceived centrality of a highly stratified two-class system of owners and dependents and the gulf that separated them—with the exception of São Paulo and the three southernmost states, where immigrant populations might rise to the status of middle peasants, especially in the twentieth century. Why there has been so little concern among Marxists about the larger "peasant problem" in those areas is harder to understand. At any rate, the significance of such groups, it seems, was assumed away until the 1970s.

All the same, Prado's emphasis on colonial agriculture as the key to understanding the contemporary Brazilian mode of production provided a path to dependency analysis. His thesis on capitalist agriculture was taken up by Andre Gunder Frank in Prado's journal, *Revista Brasiliense*, in 1964.[59] Two decades later, in the celebrated television debate between the conservative economist Roberto Campos and the former PCB leader, Luís Carlos Prestes, the latter had come to agree with Prado, his former antagonist within the party, on one major point: the problem was not creating a viable capitalism in Brazil by destroying its feudal remnants but the distortions and suffering created by capitalism itself.

12

Paths to Dependency

Marxism and structuralism were the discourses from which a new dependency literature would arise in the late 1960s. Though dependency analysis, like structuralism, was a continental—rather than a national—movement, Brazilian writers arguably were the single most important national group.[1] Many dependency writers and commentators from Brazil and elsewhere subsequently emphasized their central inspiration in Marxism or Leninism,[2] but I will argue that structuralism was the more important source.

"Dependent" countries and "dependency" as undefined or ill-defined terms appeared in a variety of contexts before the 1960s. One of the writers who used such terms was Werner Sombart, in the last part of *Modern Capitalism*, published in 1928. As observed in Chapter 7, the onetime Marxist economic historian wrote of the "dependency" of backward agricultural regions on the capitalist West and explicitly described (but did not model) a Center-Periphery relationship.[3] A candidate for a more immediate precursor of dependency analysis is Celso Furtado's *A Dependent Economy*[4] (1956), referring to Brazil, though the analysis is structuralist. A year later, the Marxist historian Caio Prado, Jr. wrote that underdeveloped countries were "peripheral and complementary . . . in a subordinate and dependent situation."[5] Other examples could be cited. But such terms, without specific defining properties, are ambiguous. The essential elements would seem to be a characterization of modern capitalism as a Center-Periphery relationship between the developed, industrial West and the underdeveloped, agricultural Third World; the adoption of a system-wide historical approach and the consequent rejection of Boekean dualism and Parsonian modernization theory; the hypothesis of unequal exchange, as well as asymmetrical power relations between Center and Periphery; and the assertion of the relative or absolute nonviability of a capitalist path to development, based on the leadership of the national bourgeoisies of the Latin American nations.[6] These propositions did not cohere in a single argument until the mid-1960s.

The reformism implicit in Furtado's structuralism was part of an increasing concern with social issues by structuralists in general, a concern that quickened with the growing radicalism of the Cuban Revolution from 1959, the year Furtado published his studies on the Northeast. The reformism of the 1960s in Brazil and elsewhere in Latin America was conditioned by, and for an increasing number of structuralists made irrelevant by, a long evolution of ECLA's views on its initial key policy recommendation—import-substitution industrialization (ISI). By 1957 the organization was distinguishing between two types of ISI, which in the 1960s would be seen as phases. The first involved the relatively easy substitution of simple domestically produced consumer goods for previously imported items. The second, more difficult, type involved the production of intermediate goods and consumer durables, a shift from "horizontal" to "vertical" ISI—so denominated because of the substitution of simple goods on a broad front in the first phase, and in the second, an integrated line of production of fewer final goods and their inputs. A third phase, the production of capital goods, would ensue at a later date.[7]

In 1956 ECLA had still assumed the existence of a threshold in structural changes in the economy, beyond which "dependence on external contingencies" would diminish. Yet the following year the agency first suggested that dependence on "events overseas" might even increase as ISI advanced; all the same, it still held that import substitution consisted of diminishing "the import content of supplies for the home market."[8] But by 1957, for the most "advanced" case of Argentina, ECLA acknowledged that ISI had resulted in increasing, rather than decreasing, requirements of capital good imports. The agency wondered aloud whether the Argentine experience foreshadowed the future of Latin America.[9]

Why should economic growth and industrialization in particular bring rising import requirements in their train? Michal Kalecki, the Polish economist who became a development specialist after World War II, had provided a brief answer in his article in *Trimestre Económico* in 1954, a study referred to in Chapter 10 for its impact on the structuralist thesis on inflation. Kalecki observed that rapid economic development "is apt to create a strain on the foreign balance." First, imports rise because an increase in investment requires more foreign capital goods; second, the increase in the tempo of manufacturing may involve greater imports of raw materials and semimanufactured goods; and third, because of advancing urbanization and general population growth, coupled in many cases with inelastic agricultural supply, food import requirements may rise.[10]

Furtado had already addressed the problem of the trade imbalance in 1952, making Kalecki's first point, as well as others in the context of the causes of inflation (see Chapter 10). In 1958 he elaborated on this approach. Using a simple two-sector model, he explained the problem as one in which, by assumption, the modern unit, A, had a larger import coefficient than the backward one, B, partly because the investment sector of the economy, located largely in A, had a higher propensity to import than did the consumption sector. As the economy developed, A's import coefficient grew ever larger as a share of the whole economy's coefficient, and, as a result, the average import coefficient tended to rise.[11] In the Brazilian case, the import coefficient of investments in productive capacity might be ten times higher than the average import coefficient of the consumption sector.[12] The unfortunate consequence was that any effort to increase the rate of growth tends to increase pressure on the balance of payments and therefore to be inflationary. Furtado drew the additional pessimistic conclusion that for a country at an intermediate phase of underdevelopment, such as Brazil, "any attempt at correcting disequilibrium through devaluation soon leads to a reduction in the growth rate, for the simple reason that it increases the prices of capital goods in relation to consumption goods' prices."[13] If the terms of trade were deteriorating, the pressures on the balance of payments became even more acute: stability in domestic monetary income combined with a diminishing capacity to import could put immense pressure on the balance of payments.[14] Thus for Furtado and other structuralists in the late 1950s, the import requirements in the later stages of ISI, unless offset by capital inflows or rising exports, could cause "strangulation"—a favorite ECLA metaphor for stagnation caused by insufficient imports of capital goods and other industrial inputs. In 1961 Prebisch himself wrote, "It remains a paradox that industrialization, instead of helping greatly to soften the internal impact of external fluctuations, is bringing us a new and unknown type of external vulnerability."[15]

The agonizing reappraisal of ISI came in 1964. In that year an ECLA study, though blaming Latin America's declining rates of growth on deteriorating terms of trade in the 1950s, also noted that 80 percent of regional imports now consisted of fuels, intermediate goods, and capital equipment. Consequently, there was little left to "squeeze" in the region's import profile to favor manufacturing.[16] Meanwhile, two monographs, highly critical of ISI, appeared in the agency's *Economic Bulletin*—one on the Brazilian experience in particular and the other on Latin America in general. These articles pointed to problems that by the 1960s were beginning to affect other parts of the Third World as well.[17]

The first was by a Brazilian economist who had taken the ECLA course on structuralism and had worked with Aníbal Pinto.[18] At the Rio branch office of ECLA, Maria da Conceição Tavares examined the performance of the Brazilian economy in the 1950s and early 1960s and argued that ISI had failed because of the lack of dynamism of the export sector, coupled with the fact that ISI had not diminished capital and fuel import requirements. Other problems she noted were apparent ceilings on the domestic market, owing in part to highly skewed income distribution, which also determined the structure of demand; the constellation of productive resources (e.g., the lack of skilled labor); and the capital-intensive nature of industrialization in more advanced phases of ISI, which implied little labor absorption. In these later phases, Tavares contended, the low labor absorption of manufacturing tended to exaggerate rather than to terminate the relative dualism of Brazil's economy. Among other things, she argued that bottlenecks in the food supply, partly a result of the antiquated agrarian structure, put unsustainable pressures on the import bill. Tavares recommended agrarian reform as a partial solution.[19]

In the same number of the *Bulletin*, the Argentine economist Santiago Macario wrote a blistering critique of the way ISI had actually been practiced in Latin America, following up Prebisch's observation the previous year (1963) that the region currently had the highest tariffs in the world.[20] Macario noted that the governments of the four most industrialized countries—Argentina, Brazil, Mexico, and Chile—had used ISI as a deliberate strategy to counteract a persistent lack of foreign exchange and to create employment for rapidly expanding populations. But in those four countries, and in most of the others of the region, protectionism (primarily in the form of tariff and exchange policies) had been irrational, in that there was no consistent policy to develop the most viable and efficient manufacturing industries. On the contrary, the most inefficient industries had received the greatest protection; there had been overdiversification of manufacturing in small markets in the "horizontal" phase of ISI; and these factors had contributed, in some instances, to real dissavings.[21] Overall, his thesis was less that ECLA's policy prescriptions had initially been wrong—which Tavares's analysis in some ways did—than that the region's governments had flagrantly ignored ECLA's technical advice, pursuing, in Macario's words, "import substitution at any cost."[22] Other scholars soon added new charges, such as that ISI had increased the concentration of income with regard both to social class and to region (within countries).[23] ECLA itself had voiced its first doubts in 1956 whether industry, in the world region with the fastest growing population, could absorb surplus labor from agriculture; nine years later its survey of ISI showed that nonagricultural employment in Latin America had increased from 13 to 36 million persons between 1925 and 1960, but that only 5 million of the 23 million additional employees were absorbed in industrial work.[24]

Furtado, writing over his own signature, noted in 1966 that while Latin America's industrial output in the 1950s had risen 6.2 percent a year, industrial employment had risen only 1.6 percent annually, about half Latin America's average population growth rate. The problem in part was the labor-saving technology which the Periphery had imported from the Center.[25] Furtado explained that ISI was fundamentally different from European industrialization in the eighteenth and nineteenth centuries. In the classic phase, technology continually cheapened the relative cost of capital goods, creating the possibility of solutions to social problems. In twentieth-century Latin America, unlike nineteenth-century Europe, technology was exogenous to the region's economy and was specifically designed for the requirements of the developed countries. Factor absorption, therefore, did not depend on the relative availability of factors but on the type of technology used, and over this matter Latin Americans could exercise little choice.[26] Among other things, they had to compete in their own national markets with high-technology, multinational corporations. For Furtado, ISI was actually aggravating the distance between the modern and the backward sectors, as labor-saving techniques continually advanced in the former.[27] Thus underdevelopment, the bedrock of which was "technological heterogeneity of various sectors" of the economy, as he had written in 1961, was advancing.[28]

This tendency by the mid-1960s to take the longer view and seek lessons in history was partly the result of the fact that, for structuralists, Latin America now had 35 years of import-substituting experience; furthermore, Furtado had fully historicized the structuralist argument in the late 1950s.[29] Thus the perceived failure of ISI as a historical process—and perhaps the growing suspicion that industrial growth had varied directly and not inversely with export earnings[30]— was a leading cause of pessimism among structuralists in the mid- and late 1960s. Other structuralist criticisms of the Latin American economies in the late 1960s included the perception of a sustained balance-of-payments disequilibrium and a "debt spiral" for the most industrialized countries and of high rates of inflation, with consequent social tensions and political instability. These problems were viewed chiefly as structural matters—the agrarian pattern of latifundium and minifundium; industrial structure (indivisibilities of scale, tending to produce underutilization of capital, and high capital density, with the consequence of low labor absorption); the rigidly stratified social structure; and the consequent maldistribution of income.[31]

On the political front, another source of pessimism was the end of the "developmentalist" experiment in Brazil, where the populist President João Goulart was ousted by a military coup d'état in 1964. It is possible that reformers were not only disillusioned with particular governments based on fragile populist coalitions but that they also began to be skeptical of the transformative powers of the Latin American state, a tenet central to the structuralist doctrine. Moreover, the United States's diminished interest under Lyndon Johnson in an energetic pursuit of the reform and development goals of President John F. Kennedy's Alliance for Progress, coupled with the invasion of the Dominican Republic in 1965 (the first such action in Latin America since the 1920s), was a blow to reformism. More broadly, the intellectual and political climate in which dependency analysis would be received was radicalized by the international resistance to the U.S. war in Vietnam, of which the Dominican intervention was a consequence (to prevent a "second Cuba" and the danger of two simultaneous long-term military engagements). Resistance to the Vietnam War interacted with antiestablishment protest in a variety of countries, often led by students, and reached a peak in the demonstrations and repressions of 1968–70. In Brazil, the authorities barely distinguished the student protests of July 1968 from a real urban insurrection that gained momentum after Marshal Artur Costa e Silva's Institutional Act No. 5 and related decrees in December. These measures closed Congress and gave the military dictatorship almost limitless powers.

Yet there was a tendency, if not yet a dominant one, for official economic policy in Brazil and elsewhere in Latin America to move in a contrary direction from the radicalism of the streets. Anti-ECLA orthodoxy reappeared in the programs of "monetarists" in the antipopulist and authoritarian regimes of Brazil after 1964 and Argentina after 1966.[32] In Brazil, at the end of the decade, it was a professedly neoclassical economist—though hardly an orthodox one, because of his use of state intervention—Antônio Delfim Neto, who implemented ECLA's earlier calls for the export of manufactures. Liberal orthodoxy would assume the dominant position at the policy level under most Latin American military regimes in the 1970s, though in Brazil the state's role in the economy actually expanded. The ascending star of orthodoxy and associated policies in the late 1960s, even if less distant from structuralist policy in actual practice, as in the Brazilian case, probably contributed to a frustration in intellectual circles which prepared the way for the acceptance of dependency analysis. Meanwhile, two positive developments in the late 1960s seemed to have had little effect on the emerging vision of dependency, namely, a cyclical improvement of the terms of trade for primary producers and the efforts by Brazil and Argentina to decrease their tariffs to stimulate industrial efficiency.[33] Perhaps the former process was not perceivable in the short run, and the latter was carried out by governments having little sympathy for ECLA.

In the ISI crisis of the 1960s which had helped engender dependency analysis, were there reformist policies that might have met the challenge of sustainable growth? In Albert Hirschman's view these would have included promoting the export of nontraditional primary products and manufactures to earn precious foreign exchange and financing further industrialization through new domestic capital markets and a more effective income tax, instead of through transfers across social classes (by inflation) and across sectors (by exchange discrimination against traditional export activities). Such opportunities were not easily perceived, however, because of overvalued exchange rates.[34] In any event, these policies would doubtless have met serious political obstacles, including that of populist coalitions that had provided a constituency for ISI.

In research organizations in the United States and in international agencies its government heavily influenced, the mid-1960s also witnessed a scholarly censure of the ISI strategy, focusing on the gross distortions such policies had produced in "effective protection rates," thus misallocating scarce resources in a number of Latin American and other newly industrializing countries. But the studies in question were also biased toward export promotion instead of increasing allocative efficiencies within existing industrial processes: they focused on lowering tariffs on final goods, not on *increasing* those on imported inputs and capital goods, which measure would have had the desired effect on efficiency.[35]

The neoclassical counterattack also challenged structuralist interpretations of the capital-intensive bias in Latin American industry. Orthodox economists argued that the *actual* cost of labor was greater than that of capital, relative to respective shadow prices. Capital costs in Latin America were kept artificially low by liberal depreciation allowances, low or even negative real interest rates in periods of inflation, low tariffs on capital imports, overvalued exchange rates, and institutionally induced high wages. Therefore, according to this reasoning, choices of labor-saving techniques had been rational, given the distortions of relative prices. Finally, the neoclassical school argued that low productivity in agriculture was not necessarily caused by a lack of rural entrepreneurship—for example, owing to a traditional latifundist mentality—but derived in great measure from government programs of import substitution. By this analysis, ISI, resulting in high-cost manufactured goods, had turned the domestic terms of trade against agriculture.[36] In addition, exchange policies designed to assist industrialization had given agricultural exporters less than the full value of their foreign sales and thereby discouraged production.

Ironically enough, the perspective of the 1990s allows an even more favorable view of the economic climate in which dependency emerged. The rate of population growth in Latin America, previously highest among the world's major regions, peaked in the 1960s and began a long-term decline—a trend economists could not have foreseen in the middle of the decade. The international economy was more dynamic in the period 1960–73 (ending with the oil price shock of the Organization of Petroleum Exporting Countries) than in any other period in the postwar era, permitting unparalleled diversification of Latin American exports, including manufactures. Perhaps most ironical was that the postwar growth rate for the region reached a peak in these years (5.9 percent per annum of GDP), and in the same period manufacturing in the region grew at 6.8 percent annually. Income per capita rose at 3.2 percent in 1960–73.[37] But analysts of the mid-1960s, in the midst of these developments, had no way of knowing Latin America was experiencing its most successful period of economic growth and diversification.

In any case, structuralist theories and policy prescriptions were challenged not only by the neoclassical Right but also by a heterodox Left, some of whose exegetes had been leading figures in ECLA itself, notably Furtado and the Chilean Osvaldo Sunkel. This new Left would quickly make "dependency theory" famous.[38] Although ECLA itself had produced nothing if not a kind of dependency analysis, the new variety was set off by its more clear-cut "historicizing" and "sociologizing" tendencies in both its reformist and radical versions. In the mid-1960s Furtado had not only underscored his explicitly historical view of development, but he elaborated on an earlier contention that development and underdevelopment were linked. As stated in Chapter 10, as early as 1959 Furtado had asserted that there was a "tendency for industrial economies, as a result of their form of growth, to inhibit the growth of primary economies," and he had spelled out the idea in *Development and Underdevelopment* two years later. In 1966 he again argued that because the two processes were historically associated, underdevelopment could not be a phrase in the passage to development.[39]

In a 1964 essay Furtado had called for a return to dialectics, and "The Dialectic of Development" was the Portuguese title of *Diagnosis of the Brazilian Crisis*. He meant by this a kind of methodological holism, without which the individual parts of a social entity in continual motion could not be understood. This approach required a return to history because the tendency to focus on equilibrium concepts in neoclassical economics denied process. Even if the developed economies could roughly be described as being in dynamic equilibrium, this state did not apply to the underdeveloped Periphery, where the introduction of labor-saving techniques resulted in a surplus labor supply.[40] In this interpretation, Furtado also introduced the element of social class. He argued that class struggle had historically been the engine of economic growth in the advanced West: workers "attack" by organizing to raise their share of the national product, and capitalists "counterattack" by introducing labor-saving technology; in this manner, a dynamic equilibrium is approximated. Because labor is unorganized in the Periphery, above all in the rural sector, he asserted, the process fails to work there.[41] These *marxisant* propositions are perhaps less surprising than they appear at first glance; they might be viewed as an extrapolation or transformation of Prebisch's initial explanation of declining terms of trade (concerning trade union contracts).

As early as 1961, in *Development and Underdevelopment*, Furtado had distinguished between autonomous development, which was supply-driven, and externally induced development, which was demand-driven. ISI itself led the entrepreneur "to adopt a technology compatible with a cost and price structure similar to that . . . in the international manufactured goods market."[42] Even earlier Furtado had stressed the importance of conspicuous consumption as a driving force in underdeveloped countries' internal dynamics.[43] His several essays in the late 1960s, written largely in his Paris exile, pointed to the need for an analysis of the whole capitalist system, Center and Periphery together, a problem which Samir Amin, Immanuel Wallerstein, Johan Galtung, Arghiri Emmanuel, Andre Gunder Frank, and Furtado himself began to address in the 1970s.

In works written between 1970 and 1978, Furtado views as a central feature of underdevelopment the adoption of the consumption patterns of the developed West by the upper strata of underdeveloped areas, as these regions entered the international division of labor.[44] This process was the "result of the surplus generated through static comparative advantages in foreign trade. It is the highly dynamic nature of the modernized component of consumption that brings dependence into the technological realm and makes it part of the production structure."[45] Novel items of consumption require increasingly sophisticated techniques and increasing amounts of capital. But capital accumulation is associated with income concentration, so, as he later put it, industrialization "advances simultaneously with the concentration of income."[46] Thus, in underdeveloped countries, the consumption patterns of the groups that appropriate the economic surplus and their concomitant political power—and not the elastic labor supply, as Furtado had once believed—determine the differential between the industrial wage rate and that of the subsistence sector and keep it stable.[47]

In 1978 Furtado wrote a large statement on dependency, *Accumulation and Development*, in which he attempted to relate accumulation to social stratification and political power.[48] For Furtado the struggle against dependence usually begins with a demand for national control of nonrenewable resources, followed by a similar effort to control the home market. Victories in these areas will create the possibility of freedom from financial dependence, in permitting the accumulation of a critical mass of financial resources necessary for economic development. But only after these three conquests could the most difficult problem be attacked, the control of technological progress, currently the most important form of domination by the countries of the Center; technological innovation formed a crucial link between the Center and the Periphery, based on capital-intensive production for the consumption of the upper strata.[49]

Another Brazilian, Fernando Henrique Cardoso, played a major role in moving the dependency perspective toward an analysis of social relations in the late 1960s. Though born into a family of military officers in Rio de Janeiro, Cardoso received his secondary and higher education in São Paulo. At the University of São Paulo he became a prominent, if younger, member of a Paulista School of Sociology, forming around the French professor Roger Bastide, his student Florestan Fernandes, and Fernandes's students Cardoso and Octavio Ianni.[50] After completing his doctoral dissertation in 1960 on the problem of capitalism and Brazilian slavery, Cardoso turned to industrialization, a subject of obvious interest in São Paulo. He did postgraduate work with the labor sociologist Alain Touraine at the University of Paris, where, like Furtado, Cardoso would later teach. His special interest was Brazilian entrepreneurs, about whom he published a book in 1964, and before publication he had begun comparative work on entrepreneurs in Argentina and Brazil.

Rejecting the view that the several national bourgeoisies would bring full capitalist development to Latin America, Cardoso arrived at a pessimistic evaluation of this social group in his empirical studies of industrialists in Brazil and Argentina. His view that Latin America lacked what Charles Morazé has termed a "conquering bourgeoisie" was shared by other South American social scientists who studied the matter in the mid-1960s.[51] Cardoso had reached his position before the Brazilian coup of 1964[52]—in which Brazilian business leaders supported the generals—and before multinational corporations became so prominent, and native industrialists less conspicuous, in the more open economies of the Argentine and Brazilian dictatorships of the latter 1960s.

Cardoso left Brazil following the March–April "Revolution" against President Goulart, as did Furtado, and four other contributors to dependency analysis, Theotônio dos Santos, Rui Mauro Marini, Vânia Bambirra, and José Serra, then president of the National Union of Students. All went to Santiago, Chile, to associate with various research institutions. Indeed, Santiago, with its various research institutions through which structuralists and their leftist critics moved, became the crucible of dependency analysis, and attribution of "discovery" is as difficult to assign in dependency analysis as that for the structuralist thesis on inflation, which was also largely developed in the Chilean capital.

Cardoso was invited to Santiago by the Spanish sociologist José Medina Echavarría, then director of the Latin American Institute for Economic and Social Planning (ILPES),[53] the sociological complement to ECLA which Prebisch had established in 1962. Cardoso spent three years at Santiago-based institutions, including ILPES, where he assumed administrative responsibilities. From 1965 Cardoso and his Chilean collaborator, Enzo Faletto, began to elaborate a study of dependency in Latin America, which would be completed in 1967 and published two years later. By then Cardoso had taught a year at the University of Paris, Nanterre, witnessing the fall of President Charles de Gaulle in May 1968; had returned to São Paulo, where he had won a chair in political science; and had been summarily "retired" from teaching by the government of Marshal Costa e Silva.

In their celebrated essay *Dependency and Development*, Cardoso provided most of the theoretical perspective, and Faletto was largely responsible for the comparative historical studies in the work.[54] Though Osvaldo Sunkel, a Chilean structuralist turned dependency analyst, spoke of the international capitalist system as "a determining influence on local processes," and one which was "internal" to the Periphery's own structure, Cardoso and Faletto preferred to speak on two subsystems, the internal and the external, and emphasized that the international capitalist system was not solely determining. There was a complex internal dynamic to the system, they asserted.[55] Beyond this, Cardoso stressed the mutual interests among social classes *across* the Center-Periphery system. The interests of the bourgeoisie of the Center, and by implication, those of its proletariat, overlapped those of sectors of the bourgeoisie of the Periphery; these links became all the more intimate as multinational firms loomed ever larger in Latin America.[56] Cardoso and Faletto analyzed the development of the "populist" coalition of national and foreign capital with the working class, corresponding to the successful phase of ISI, and linked the failure of import substitution with the demise of the populist political style. In the current phase of capital accumulation, they believed, authoritarian regimes were needed to assure a political demobilization of the masses.[57]

Their treatment of dependency, despite its early appearance, was more nuanced than others, emphasizing contradiction, shifting alliances, and a range of historical possibility. Cardoso and Faletto distinguished between simple enclave economies and those controlled by local bourgeoisies. For the latter, they entertained the possibility of significant manufacturing sectors. In a scheme they called "associated development" or "development with marginalization [*marginalidad*]," which Cardoso would later term "associated-dependent" development, they noted that contemporary foreign capital was focusing its investment in manufacturing operations. Furthermore, the public sector, multinational capital, and the "national" capitalist sector were joining hands under authoritarian rule. Like Furtado, Cardoso and Faletto pointed to the international system as a whole as the proper unit of analysis; and like Furtado, they saw development and underdevelopment not as stages but as locations within the international economic system, for which they offered a schematic historical analysis of the Periphery's class dynamics.[58] This feature of Cardoso's dependency analysis, emphasizing the possibilities of growth against the theses of Furtado, Marini, and Frank, became more prominent in the midst of the "Brazilian [economic] miracle" of 1968–73. Cardoso was soon to emphasize the importance of the "internationalization of the domestic market," dominated by multinationals, as the source of dynamism in the present stage of the history of imperialism.[59]

Concurrent with the efforts of Cardoso and Faletto, another researcher in Santiago who had left Brazil after the 1964 coup was producing a radical version of dependency that was almost as widely, and perhaps more hotly, debated. This was Andre Gunder Frank, whose *Capitalism and Underdevelopment in Latin America*, has sold 100,000 copies in nine languages, compared to an equal number in the Spanish edition alone by Cardoso and Faletto.[60] Born in Berlin, Frank had received his education in the United States, earning a doctorate in economics from the University of Chicago. In the early 1960s he was in Chile, then Brazil, where he worked in Rio and Brasília. Following the Brazilian coup, he went to Santiago and, after a brief stay in Mexico, returned to Chile. During Frank's stay in Brasília, three future dependency writers had been his students and associates— dos Santos, Bambirra, and Marini. Frank's own version of dependency began to emerge while he was in Brazil, and he published a critique of dualism in Caio Prado's journal, *Revista Brasiliense*, in 1964.[61] Brazilian and Chile were to be the case studies of his *Capitalism and Underdevelopment*.

Because Frank borrowed from a Marxist tradition—probably without being decisively influenced by it—it is necessary to briefly consider the history of Latin American Marxism, which, like structuralism, was undergoing a fundamental reassessment in the 1960s. In fact, the crisis of Marxism in Latin America revolved around one of the same issues that had troubled structuralists, the role of the local or national bourgeoisies. From the 1920s to the 1960s, the Communist parties of Latin America had oscillated between the view that the local bourgeoisie was progressive and the view that it was reactionary, depending in part on Soviet instructions. Yet the prevailing doctrine in most Latin American Communist parties, from the Popular Front period, beginning in 1934, through the early 1960s, was that the local bourgeoisie was a progressive force. Contending that their continent had large feudal residues, party spokesmen argued that proletarians and bourgeois must struggle in concert, at the present phase of history, to eliminate feudal residues and to contain imperialist penetration. We have seen that the Brazilian party, the PCB, exemplified this pattern: its spokesmen concluded that capitalism could and must be developed in Brazil, and the party was in effect part of Brazil's "developmentalist" and populist coalition for much of the period 1945–64.

In Cuba, as late as August 1960, just two months before Castro's sweeping nationalization of the economy, the communist leader Blas Roca announced that the Cuban Revolution was not socialist but "bourgeois-democratic."[62] Yet the issue that the Cuban Revolution posed after October 1960 was the viability of "the uninterrupted path to socialism," a thesis long defended by Latin America Trotskyists but more audibly proclaimed as viable policy by Ernesto "Che" Guevara the same year. After Fidel Castro's public adherence to Marxism-Leninism in December 1961, the thesis that contemporary Latin America could sustain only bourgeois-democratic regimes would have to be reappraised.[63]

A preexisting historiography was now discovered—beginning with Sergio Bagú's *Economy of Colonial Society* (1949), an essay which argued that colonial Latin America had a capitalist, not a feudal, economy.[64] This view, transformed into explicitly Marxist terms by Prado in Brazil and others elsewhere, would be used to oppose communist orthodoxy on the role of the bourgeoisie *not* by asserting that capitalism had arrived too late in Latin America, as the Peruvian Marxist José Carlos Mariátegui had contended in 1929,[65] but that, on the contrary, capitalism had already prevailed too long in the region. Consequently, there was nothing to hope from the local bourgeoisie. This class, rather than overseas imperialists, would constitute the "immediate enemy," as Frank put it, for Cuba-inspired groups.

In the preceding chapter we saw that between 1960 and 1966 Caio Prado, Jr., elaborated the argument he had defended as early as 1947—before Bagú in Argentina—that the Brazilian colony had always been capitalist in its basic features. In *The Brazilian Revolution*[66] (1966), Prado reviewed the course of Brazilian history to show that his country, as fully "capitalist," was ripe for revolution, contrary to the official position of the nation's Communist Party. Prado's thesis had a major influence on Frank, who expanded Prado's argument on capitalism in Brazilian agriculture in Prado's journal, *Revista Brasiliense*.[67]

Frank's work forms an obvious point of tangency between the revisionist Marxists like Prado, who emphasized relations of exchange, and the structuralists. In the mid-1960s Frank would rework ECLA's theses to yield a radical conclusion.[68] He was explicit about at least some of his sources. From Sergio Bagú— whose work had been cited in Brazil by the Marxist historian Nelson Werneck

Sodré[69]—Frank borrowed the proposition that Latin America's economy had been essentially capitalist from the colonial era. From the American Marxist Paul Baran, Frank derived the proposition that capitalism simultaneously produces underdevelopment in some areas while it produces development in others.[70] Frank briefly worked on commission for ECLA, from which he presumably took his thesis of deteriorating terms of trade, though he was to emphasize monopoly elements in the process much more than ECLA had. Frank's antinomy "metropolis-satellite" is surely derived from "Center-Periphery," and his notion of "involution"—the development of the satellite in periods of crisis in the metropolis—is directly analogous to ECLA's historical analysis of "inward-directed" growth.[71] From Pablo González Casanova, the Mexican political scientist, Frank borrowed the thesis of "internal colonialism," whereby industrial and political centers within the satellite exploit their dependent regions through fiscal and exchange policies and by draining off capital and talent.[72] Frank linked transnational exploitation with internal colonialism, hypothesizing a concatenation of metropolis–satellite relations from Wall Street down to the smallest Latin American village, in which only the end points of the continuum would not stand in both relationships.[73]

Frank hammered away at the theme that dualism did not exist in Latin America: all areas were linked by an unequal exchange of goods and services, consequent to underdeveloped capitalism. This was an extension of his "Myth of Feudalism in Brazilian Agriculture" first published in Prado's *Revista Brasiliense* in 1964. Thus Frank attacked the traditional communist positions on "feudal residues" and non-Marxist dualism as well.[74] Frank's polemical essays in *Capitalism and Underdevelopment* paralleled the simultaneous but less didactic and less explicit efforts of Furtado to find causal links between development and underdevelopment. Frank the synthesizer was also an effective wordsmith, and he termed the plight of Latin America and, by extension, that of the Third World, the "development of underdevelopment."[75] For Frank, Latin America had been "underdeveloping" for more than four centuries, a process he divided into four phases, each defined by the principal form of monopoly exercised from the metropolis: commercial monopoly, in the age of mercantilism; industrial monopoly, during the age of classical liberalism; monopoly of capital goods, 1900–1950; and monopoly of technological innovation, 1950 to the present.[76] It is notable that the stages developed by Frank and the Brazilian Theotônio dos Santos were stages in the development of the entire capitalist system, not stages in the sense of W. W. Rostow, in whose view the underdeveloped countries would repeat the trajectory of the advanced capitalist nations.[77] A similar emphasis on the development of the whole system was also implicit in the work of Furtado and Cardoso.

For Frank, exit from the system in a revolutionary struggle, following the Cuban example, was the path to development. Only in that manner could "involution," a partial and temporary exit, be transformed into continuous development. There was an urgency in Frank's voluntarist view that the continued underdevelopment inherent in capitalism would make the breakthrough all the more difficult.[78] He argued that the gap between metropolis—the United States—and satellite—Chile, a case study—was widening "in power, wealth, and income" and that the "relative and absolute" income of the poorest classes in Chile was decreasing.[79] Frank agreed with Cardoso and other dependency writers on the existence of a single Center-Periphery system, developing historically; on the consequent error of a Boekean dualist approach; on the failure of national bourgeoisies to provide leadership in capitalist development; and on the existence of unequal exchange. But he differed with Cardoso on the political inferences to be drawn and on the extent of unequal exchange because he focused on monopoly elements and interpreted the process in "drain" terms rather than as unequal gains between Center and Periphery. Frank clearly disagreed with Marx and Prebisch, who, holding that rising productivity was the essence of capitalist development, did not believe that the development of the Center had to be *primarily* at the expense of the Periphery.

If Frank's sources are evident because of his own acknowledgments, Cardoso's are less so. And just as we examined the roots of Prebisch's Center-Periphery model, so we may ask about the origins of the dependency tradition. This is important because, as noted at the outset of the chapter, Marxist roots have frequently been ascribed to dependency.[80] One who makes the attribution is Fernando Henrique Cardoso, for many students the most important dependency writer. This interpretation has been reinforced by the English edition of *Dependency and Development* (1979) by Cardoso and Faletto, in which preface, postscript, and parts of the text show a strong Marxist orientation. By contrast, the first Spanish edition (1969) is far less obviously influenced by Marxism, and the original draft (1965) is recognizably a structuralist product. In this first version the authors challenge the Parsonian categories of modernization theory, and they are pessimistic about the reformism of local bourgeoisies, but from an eclectic perspective. No Marxist studies were cited in the draft, and Marxist categories are almost completely lacking. The theme receiving most attention in the 1965 version was the inadequacy of the bourgeois-directed project of development, partly resulting from increasing market domination by multinational corporations.[81]

The issue of lineage—structuralist or Marxist—is clouded, however, by elements in Cardoso's 1964 study of Brazilian entrepreneurs. That work adumbrates one of his most important contributions to the dependency tradition—namely, his denial of the adequacy of Parsonian-derived "modernization theory," although in the limited context of the role of entrepreneurs.[82] In that work, Cardoso, though eclectic in methodology, cast his major conclusions within a Marxist paradigm.[83] Thus the sources of Cardoso's contribution were various, and a safe conclusion would seem to be that he could make his statement in either a structuralist or a Marxist idiom. Yet it was initially made in the former, as dependency emerged in Santiago.

In Chile three other Brazilian dependency analysts, Rui Mauro Marini, Theotônio dos Santos, and his wife, Vânia Bambirra, entered into dialogue and debate with Cardoso, Frank, and others during the late 1960s and would continue to publish in Mexico City, where they gathered after the Chilean military coup of September 1973. The three, like Cardoso, saw dependency analysis as a region of Marxism and wrote their best-known works in the peak years of the military repression in Brazil, which fact colored their theorizing. All took the position that Latin American capitalism was nonviable, except and partially, under conditions of extreme repression. Of the three, Marini's work was probably the most widely debated, and for one student of dependency, he was the "outstanding Marxist *dependentista*" in Latin America.[84]

Having studied in France in the late 1950s, Marini did graduate work with Frank in Brasília before the 1964 coup.[85] After three years in Mexico, he went to Santiago for the latter years of the Frei government and the Allende period, leaving Chile after General Augusto Pinochet's coup. Marini then spent a decade in Mexico City before returning to Brazil. Consequently, during the ascendancy of dependency analysis, he was probably better known in Spanish America than in his native country because most of his works were not available in Portuguese.[86] Marini's Marxism was influenced by an immersion in Marx's *Capital* in a seminar at Brasília—perhaps inspired by a previous one at the University of São Paulo, in which Cardoso was active—and then another in Santiago, in which participants included the Brazilians dos Santos, Bambirra, Cardoso, Conceição Tavares, and Chileans such as Pedro Vuscovic, soon to be Salvador Allende's minister of the economy, and Marta Harnecker, a follower of the French Marxist philosopher Louis Althusser.[87]

Marini could not be accused, as the early Frank had been, of interpreting dependency as an externally imposed phenomenon, to the exclusion of class relations in the dependent areas. His two main concepts, "superexploitation" and "subimperialism," were sketched out in *Underdevelopment and Revolution* in 1969 and more fully developed four years later in *Dialectic of Dependence*.[88] Agreeing with Frank that the bourgeoisie of the Center or metropolis extracts most of the surplus (for Marini, Marx's surplus value) of the Periphery, the Brazilian writer held that the bourgeoisie of the Periphery compensates for its losses through a superexploitation of the Periphery's working class.[89] In his model, Marini built on Marx's distinction between "absolute" and "relative" surplus value: the former referred to surplus value obtained by lengthening work days or weeks and by decreasing the wages workers receive, while the latter referred to that obtained by decreasing the cost of labor inputs by raising productivity, principally through technological change. Relative surplus value was the driving force of capitalism in the Center of the world system. For dependent countries, Marini argued that the absolute form was critical, even if it required lowering wages "beyond their normal limits," that is, below the levels necessary for the reproduction of the labor force.[90] He also emphasized one form of relative surplus value he thought especially important in dependent capitalism: intensification of labor exploitation (e.g., speedups on assembly lines), a process that raises productivity without technological innovation.[91] Superexploitation was possible because, in contrast to workers in the Center, those of dependent countries were not required as consumers. Their chief products were exported to the metropolitan countries, and their wages could be driven below ordinary subsistence levels. Because workers would otherwise take industrial action against such treatment, military regimes were ultimately required.[92]

In the Center, the Marxian "law" of the declining rate of profit had forced capitalists to look beyond the metropolis to peripheral regions in the last quarter of the nineteenth century, Marini argued. Historically, he wrote, the exploitation of dependent countries through unequal exchange had contributed to the rise of relative surplus value in the Center, through the trade in cheap foodstuffs (wage goods) which lower the cost of labor, and therefore raise profits, for capital in the central countries. But the path to capitalist development was partially or totally blocked in the Periphery by insufficient accumulation, owing to such exchange, which was a stimulus for superexploitation. For the last century at least, the violence associated with "primitive accumulation" has increasingly become "superfluous"; for Marini, monopoly power is the cornerstone of the process of modern unequal exchange.[93]

In the Center, technological change raises Marx's "variable" capital, permitting higher profits and wage increases for workers, who in turn provide the mass of consumers. In the Periphery, by contrast, import-substitution industrialization, according to Marini, was demand-driven and aimed only at middle- and upper-class "sumptuary" consumption, in emulation of that in metropolitan areas—a problem that had concerned Furtado. To meet this demand, imported technologies were applied to production, raising productivity and levels of output. Cyclical crises in Brazil and other Latin American countries had historically been resolved by wage controls, in combination with inflation and taxation policies, thereby redistributing income toward the consumption-oriented upper classes, a process that enlarged the market. Governments also became partial substitutes for domestic consumers, absorbing an increasing share of total product.[94] But because mass consumption was lacking in dependent countries for the products of import-substitution industrialization, a "realization" crisis[95]— the lack of sufficient monetary demand to convert commodity production into profits—had occurred in Brazil, Marini's case study, by the early 1960s. As a consequence, a military regime came to power, and government and business elites began to look elsewhere for markets, especially those for manufactured products.[96]

For the larger Latin American countries, and Brazil in particular, Cardoso had allowed for an "associated-dependent" form of growth; it accounted for Brazil's rapid economic expansion from 1968 to 1973, but Marini ascribed the phenomenon to "subimperialism." Like many others, he held that growth from the mid-1960s in significant measure was the result of the successful search for foreign markets[97] because capitalist accumulation was constrained by the narrowness of the home market. The Brazilian coup of 1964 represented an unprecedented "fusion of military and big capital interests. That scheme was subimperialism, the form which dependent capitalism assumes upon reaching the stage of monopolies and finance capital." For Marini, therefore, Brazil's subimperialism was an instance of a general phenomenon.[98] For him, armed struggle and revolutionary socialism offered the only path to development.[99]

In a view similar to Frank's, Marini believed that in the Brazilian case, dependent capitalism had resulted in a "absolute pauperization of the great masses" of the population.[100] It is notable that Marini's vision of dependent capitalism is such a deformed version of the European prototype that he refers to it as a "monstrous formation," and the monster metaphor appears repeatedly in his work,[101] recalling Constantin Stere's notion of Rumanian agrarian society in 1906 as "abnormal," or Dobrogeanu-Gherea's "monstrous regime," Neoserfdom, which combined the worst features of capitalism and Rumania's precapitalist labor regime. Teratology, the study of monsters, becomes a branch of economics.

Cardoso and his younger ally, the economist José Serra, who had studied economics in Santiago and took a doctorate at Cornell University, denied the validity of Marini's theses and some similar ones of Frank. To begin with, Cardoso argued in 1974, dependent capitalism was not "unviable" because of its "internal contradictions," which existed in any capitalist society. Brazil's domestic economy, which had been the focus of Marini's realization crisis, had expanded vigorously in the late 1960s and early 1970s, despite a decrease in workers' salaries.[102] Moreover, the expansion of industrial exports, Cardoso argued, had more to do with the reorganization of the international division of labor by multinationals than with the collusion of the Brazilian military and big capital, because that expansion was region-wide and included countries with constitutional regimes.[103] Consequently, the associated-dependent model of dependency provided a better explanation for Brazil's recent history than did subimperialism.[104]

Second, Cardoso rejected the superexploitation thesis, arguing that it was un-Marxist because it ignored the rising productivity levels of capitalist production, which derived from technological innovation induced by competition in the Center, and provided the dynamism of the whole system. Investments by multinationals in Brazil also introduced new technology, which lowered the total cost of industrial labor, quite apart from superexploitation.[105] In addition, Cardoso believed that Marini and Frank had carried the thesis of the failed project of the national bourgeoisie too far by arguing that local capitalists were increasingly marginalized in economy and polity. He believed the two writers had confused the ideological retreat of the bourgeoisie from "developmentalism," including an alliance with the working class, with a genuine marginalization—for example, Frank had identified a "lumpenbourgeoisie"[106]—a process that had not in fact occurred. Cardoso offered data to show that national capital, not just foreign-owned firms, had expanded its operations in several sectors of the Brazilian economy from 1960 to the early 1970s. For him, the national or local bourgeoisie was still an important part of the power structure.[107]

Cardoso furthermore rejected Marini's subimperialism thesis, which Marini had chiefly linked to multinational capital, pointing to data that showed traditional national capital had also profited from industrial export expansion—in shoes, textiles, and clothing. These industries, like those of the high-technology multinationals, had received state subsidies.[108] Serra and Cardoso also pointed out that productivity and employment had increased in Brazilian industry in the 1960s and 1970s, even in the wage-goods sector, and that workers did consume industrial goods in that country, contrary to the superexploitation thesis.[109]

Without further comment on the Marini-Cardoso-Serra debate, one can see from the vantage point of the 1990s that Marini's model was a schematic interpretation of the Brazilian military dictatorship of the 1960s and 1970s, a regime from which he unduly generalized across space and time. Cardoso's version of dependency has weathered better. In Heinrich Rickert's classic distinction between "nomothetic," law-giving sciences and those which are "ideographic" or descriptive, Cardoso's version of dependency was much closer to the latter, and he rejected Marini's effort to derive social laws from the Brazilian case.[110] The viability of Brazilian capitalism, denied by Marini, may still be a matter of debate, but the real level of wages in Brazil has risen since the 1970s, despite the near stagnation of per capita income growth in the 1980s. The dictatorship, if not a military role in governance, ended in 1985 and so was not "necessary" for the operation of the economy, as it obviously was not in Colombia and Venezuela, whose constitutional and bourgeois-led governments coexisted with the authoritarian regimes of Brazil and the Southern Cone.

One source of the much greater impact of Cardoso's version of dependency within Brazil, compared to those of Marini, dos Santos, and Bambirra, was its institutional base in São Paulo City; there Cardoso and other antiregime social scientists, presently or formerly of the University of São Paulo, founded a research organization in 1969. This was the Brazilian Center of Analysis and Planning (CEBRAP),[111] where Cardoso and others would articulate and elaborate dependency analysis. CEBRAP arguably became Brazil's leading institution of social science research during a time when the universities were being purged, as Cardoso's own case illustrates. With support from the Ford Foundation, Cardoso was the man to lead such an undertaking, having an international academic reputation and an unusual degree of "cover" with the military, because his father had been a general and a great-uncle, minister of war. All the same, he was subjected to interrogation by military authorities.

Meanwhile, "orthodox" Marxists, as we shall see, attacked dependency for focusing on relations in the international market and neglecting class analysis—an allegation only partly justified in the case of Cardoso and unjustified for Marini's work of the early 1970s. Furthermore, non-Marxist social scientists, especially in North America, charged dependency writers with vagueness, inconsistency, and an inability to specify the conditions under which dependency's propositions, if untrue, could be falsified (Karl Popper's "methodological monism" for bodies of knowledge seeking the status of science).[112] Cardoso's frequently repeated affirmation that dependency did not offer a formal theory, but rather a perspective for contextual and historical analysis,[113] was seen as elusive. Dependency's inability to provide unambiguous solutions, or at least programs in the Cardoso version, also weakened its appeal. A key dependency claim, the failure of Latin America's national bourgeoisies "to fulfill their historic mission" in building a new state and recasting hegemonic value structures in the almost-mythical manner of the French revolutionaries, should also be put into historical perspective. Were the dependency analysts aware of the censure of the bourgeoisie for failing to construct its own hegemonic values in England by Friedrich Engels or in Germany by Robert Michels?[114] Aware or not, they tended to view such matters as unproblematical and largely assumed the historical achievement of bourgeois revolutions in Europe.

Was dependency a school? For the purposes of historical exposition, I have presented it as such because of the broad agreement on defining propositions set forth at the outset of this chapter, even though there is an obvious fault line between non-Marxist and Marxist versions, plus sharp differences among Marxist theorists. To reiterate, as the 1960s yielded to the 1970s, many writers on dependency in Brazil and elsewhere adopted an exclusively Marxist perspective, impelled in part by the thesis of the failed bourgeoisie.[115] Dependency analysis for this group matured as a "region" of Marxism: it offered a perspective on imperialism which the classical Marxist theorists of the subject had ignored, that is, the view from the Periphery. For some, a respectable Marxist pedigree was apparently required to validate the dependency perspective after its radicalization, and a fortiori after it was challenged by those claiming to represent an orthodox Marxist tradition, a group considered in the next chapter. In any event, dependency became widely influential outside Latin America in the 1970s. The best-known historical model of world capitalism developing the implications of dependency was Immanuel Wallerstein's Modern World System.[116] As Wallerstein had a major impact on Anglophone scholars, so Samir Amin extended dependency perspectives in Francophone areas and to Africa more broadly.[117] Both used Marxist categories.

Although Marxist versions of dependency predominated, three of its four defining elements—the historical Center-Periphery perspective, unequal exchange, and the denial of Boekean dualism—derived more directly from Latin

American structuralism than from Marxist theories of imperialism.[118] The first two theses flowed directly from structuralism. The third was compatible with structuralism, Marxism, and neoclassical economics and, when adopted by Marxists, set them against Marxist orthodoxy as defined by the Partido Comunista Brasileiro. However, the fourth thesis—the absolute or relative nonviability of the national bourgeoisie—was incompatible with Prebisch's structuralism. This was so even if some who perceived that nonviability, such as Furtado, emphasizing the consumption-driven nature of underdeveloped economies, did not cast their findings in a Marxist framework.

13

Modes of Production and Late Neopopulism

The rise of dependency analysis was coeval with the appearance of new efforts to theorize hitherto undiscovered or improperly specified modes of production in Brazil and Latin America; if it is debatable whether there was a dependency "school," the participants in the modes debate could even less accurately be described as a school. Like the structuralists who adapted neoclassical concepts, those who wished to specify a mode of production in backward economies adapted Marxist concepts to perceived amalgams and "deformations." In fact, the mode of production was an issue of long standing for peripheral Marxism, as Dobrogeanu-Gherea's creative adaptation of Marxism in *Neoserfdom* had shown. And what was at stake, if not the mode of production, in the disagreement between Alberto Passos Guimarães and Caio Prado, Jr., on the proper way to characterize Brazilian agriculture? Among the dependency writers, Rui Mauro Marini implicitly viewed dependent capitalism, based on "superexploitation," as a mode of production because he wrote that there "corresponds" a "mode of circulation" to it.[1] Though Marini's work remained within a dependency framework, he, like Fernando Henrique Cardoso and other dependency writers, was affected by the "modes" debate that roughly coincided with the dependency exchanges between 1965 and 1980.

The modes-of-production controversy, like structuralism and dependency analysis, cannot be understood in a national context alone; on the contrary, it had direct European antecedents. Latin American intellectuals in the late 1960s and early 1970s were affected by the modes-of-production debate in France, notably that concerning an "African" mode in the Marxist journal *La Pensée*.[2] In this discourse Paris, then Santiago, and then Mexico City were the nodes of communication for Latin Americans of different nationalities, much as Santiago alone had been for structuralism and dependency. The modes-of-production issue in France had derived largely from controversies within the French Communist Party, influenced by the publication and translation in the 1950s and 1960s of

Marx's *Grundrisse*[3] and the de-Stalinization of Soviet Marxism, dating from the twentieth congress of the Communist Party of the Soviet Union in 1956.

For the historical development of the West, Marx had defined five "modes of production," which were complex assemblages of the relations of production between producer and nonproducer and of the forces of production. These were the primitive collective, slave, feudal, capitalist, and socialist modes, which corresponded to past, present, and future of the West. He had also defined an Asiatic mode, in which a despot skimmed all but a negligible surplus. Therefore, this mode included no investment or technological change; it was cyclical and historyless. Stalin directed Soviet ideologues to strike the Asiatic mode from the catalog in 1931 because it implied the impossibility of revolution in Asian societies, and Soviet ideologues proclaimed the inevitability of the sequence of the five others in the late 1930s. All existing societies were reinterpreted by communist theorists as falling into the Western stages, even though it was obvious to specialists that such sequences were inadequate for many societies. The Comintern's linear view of national histories was, in fact, a counterpart to modernization theory. Thus the rehabilitation of the Asiatic mode in the 1950s was an element in the revitalization of Marxist research in Europe.[4] It was in this context that Marxist students of Africa began to search for contemporary and historical modes of production unknown, and unknowable, to Marx and Engels.

The modes-of-production debate in Latin America was conditioned not only by French writings specifically directed to the issue but by the broader current of structuralist Marxism[5] associated with the work of Louis Althusser and Etienne Balibar. On the modes problem, Balibar had written in their coauthored work *Reading Capital* (1968)[6] that two or more modes could be articulated in a single "simultaneity," during a period of transition from one mode to another, provided that one was dominant.[7] Althusser's rereading of *Capital* and his defense of the mature "Leninist" Marx against the young "humanist" Marx inspired seminars on Marx's magnum opus in several Latin American cities during the mid-1960s. One of these was held in Santiago, as noted in Chapter 12. Among those present was Marta Harnecker, who did more than anyone else in Latin America to diffuse the work of Althusser, her mentor in Paris. Harnecker's Althusserian primer, *The Elementary Concepts of Historical Materialism*, was first published in 1969 and had reached its thirty-fifth edition eight years later.[8] Other Latin Americans, of course, were in direct contact with French Marxist ideas through study in Paris or acquaintance with *La Pensée* and other French Marxist publications.

Yet for Latin Americans, French Marxism was not the only source; national elements were also at work. The modes-of-production discourse was a response to dependency analysis, in that it questioned the capitalist nature of the Latin American past, asserted by Frank. Viewed from a different perspective, the "modes" debate was an extension of an increasingly formally Marxist dependency literature. It dealt with the same basic problem, viz., how "backward" structures are related to an advancing capitalist order. Furthermore, it addressed issues of special interest to the dependency group—the relation between the dominant class and the state and the place of the local economic system in international capitalism. The interest in modes of production also had to do with the increasing role of the state in capital accumulation. In Brazil, the state's share of Gross Domestic Product had risen dramatically in the 1960s and 1970s. By 1979, 28 of Brazil's 30 largest nonfinancial firms were publicly owned.[9] Under these circumstances, the hoary Marxist issue of the "relative autonomy" of the state from the dominant class, first explored by Engels, gained new significance. In that regard, the work of the Althusserian political philosopher Nicos Poulantzas, especially his treatment of the "exceptional state," that is, authoritarian, corporatist, and fascist forms of regime, seemed especially pertinent.[10]

Dependency might properly be seen as the opening phase of the modes-of-production debate because the conventional thesis of "feudal residues" was challenged by Frank in his polemic in 1965 with Rodolfo Puiggrós, a former leader of the Argentine Communist Party. Among other things, Frank had argued that Latin America's so-called feudal estates were not related to a subsistence economy but were the decadent residues of a previous phase of capitalist expansion.[11] The issue was reframed when Ernesto Laclau attacked Frank in two articles in 1969 and 1971. Laclau, who had read the debate on an "African" mode in *La Pensée*,[12] charged Frank with "circulationism"—putting primary emphasis on relations of exchange rather than relations of production, whereas, for Marx, capitalism was defined by a (free) wage labor market. Only when labor power had become a commodity could capitalists maximize relative surplus value, and this process occurred in the Center long before it appeared in the Periphery. Laclau further argued that students of the Latin American economy, a congeries of disparate elements, did not have to choose between capitalism and feudalism: the region could have more than one mode of production, as long as a dominant, structuring mode—capitalism—established the laws of motion for the whole system. Feudal elements were intensified, or even invented, by the international market, but were subordinated to it, Laclau argued in "Feudalism and Capitalism."[13]

In 1973 a collection of studies strongly influenced by French Marxism, *Modes of Production in Latin America*,[14] authored by Carlos Sempat Assadourian and others, revealed that Latin America, like Africa, offered fertile ground for theorizing. Laclau's essay "Feudalism and Capitalism" was republished there. The introductory essay by another Argentinean, Juan Carlos Garavaglia, argued that Latin America had experienced several analytically distinguishable modes of production in the colonial era. The University of Paris-trained Ciro F. S. Cardoso, a Brazilian who wrote more articles for the collection than any other contributor, called for an effort, in which he participated, to build a theory of a slave-based "colonial" mode. Other writers for the collection identified highly specific modes, such as Garavaglia's "despotic village" mode in the Jesuit missions of

Paraguay. Yet Garavaglia asserted that the main proposition of the group was that the dominant mode, capitalism, was exterior to the "dominated space" of colonial Latin America. Or, as Ciro Cardoso formulated the proposition more in accord with French thinking, dominant and dominated modes coexisted in the same "social formation."[15] The latter term was understood in its Althusserian sense, a concrete historical whole, defined by specific economic, political, ideological, and theoretical processes of production.

In 1973, the same year the Sempat collection appeared, a seminal article appeared in *La Pensée*: Balibar had revised his conception of the mode of production. The philosopher now argued that "mode of production" was necessarily an ahistorical abstraction and that class struggle determined the mode. Because class struggle occurred only in a given social formation, the latter, in effect, determined the mode, not vice versa, as the contributors to the Sempat volume had posited.[16] This reformulation apparently affected the thinking of participants at an international conference the following year in Mexico City, which after the coup in Santiago became the chief venue of exchange on modes of production.[17] One contributor was the Ecuadorian Agustín Cueva, who contended that there could be no colonial mode because colonialism and mode of production were concepts at different levels of abstraction. In other words, a concept at the level of theory, mode of production, was being fused with an empirical category, colonialism. The symposium on modes of production in which Cueva participated revealed a growing dissensus on the utility and proper use of the concept of precapitalist modes.[18] Other problems with any sort of colonial mode, first proposed by the Althusserian Pierre-Philippe Rey, are the issues or who constitutes the ruling class—local or overseas groups—and how class struggle under such conditions can be specified.[19]

In Brazil, despite the vogue of Althusser's structuralist Marxism for a decade or more after 1965, by no means was there a universal acceptance of the French philosopher's doctrine. José Artur Giannotti, the leading academic philosopher of his generation, opposed Althusserianism, as did his colleague at CEBRAP, Fernando Henrique Cardoso.[20] In any case, the modes debate continued in two forms; the first and larger stream of publications returned to the field in which Caio Prado had begun his criticism of the feudal thesis, historiography. Many contributors continued to focus on colonial issues, but one reviewer of the Latin American debate lamented that an adequate general definition of feudalism was still lacking.[21] Nevertheless, Brazilian historiography was enriched by debates in a modes-of-production discourse concerning, for example, the nature of slavery: consider Ciro Cardoso's examination of the "peasant breach" in which slaves sometimes controlled the sale of commodities they had produced and, at the limit, constituted a "proto-peasantry."[22] Another innovative interpretation of labor systems was José de Souza Martins's notion of the *colonato* (the combination of usufruct, subsidized housing, and wages in the late nineteenth-century coffee industry of São Paulo) as an articulated form of production. Because workers (*colonos*) were not fully separated from the means of production and therefore not exclusively dependent on wages, Souza Martins denied that the arrangement was fully capitalist. He began a debate that was relevant to the situation of coffee workers into the postwar era.[23] But in the 1960s rural wage laborers known as *bóias-frias* replaced *colonos* in the coffee fields and later became the subject of a variety of Marxist monographs and essays.[24]

The second arena of the debate, concerning contemporary precapitalist forms of production, had a greater urgency in Brazil, where the agricultural frontier seemed to exhibit a variety of precapitalist relations symbiotically attached to capitalist expansion. Violence by ranchers and their agents against squatters and peasants with insecure land titles in Amazonia was reported daily in Brazilian newspapers throughout the 1970s, when Brazil's military governments offered subsidies to companies and individuals who would help incorporate the Amazon region into Brazil's national economy. Yet this was also a moment of rising resistance, and what became Latin America's largest labor union, the National Confederation of Agricultural Workers (CONTAG), arose across the country under a political regime manifestly hostile to independent workers' associations.[25] As Amazonia began to be incorporated into the national economy, Brazil continued to exhibit its age-old concentration of land tenure. The rural census of 1975 showed that properties with fewer than 20 hectares accounted for 52 percent of the total holdings but only 3 percent of land in agricultural or pastoral use, while fewer than 1 percent of all holdings, all over 1,000 hectares, occupied 43 percent of the land. These facts doubtless understated concentration because owners of large estates often held more than a single property. Many peasants (including squatters) were being forced off their lands, and one writer estimated that Brazil had some 40 million migrants in the late 1970s. A large number headed not for the cities but for lands on the agricultural frontier.[26]

One group investigating frontier processes were anthropologists at the Museu Nacional (National Museum), housing a research institute in the former imperial palace in Rio de Janeiro. Among them Otávio Guilherme Velho, observing the contemporary expansion of the national economy into the Amazon Valley and other Brazilian frontiers, held that capitalism was dominant and structuring but continued to interact with precapitalist modes, as the Argentinean Laclau had argued earlier. The national bourgeoisie in Velho's scheme was not hegemonic, in the sense of shaping state activity toward its own ends. Focusing on the role of the state on the pioneer frontier, Velho argued that it plays a decisive role in integrating a national market system with precapitalist agricultural labor relations, which involve violence and coercion. Influenced by Nicos Poulantzas's case for the "relative autonomy" of the state from the ruling class, Velho argued that the Brazilian state displays far greater autonomy from its relatively weak bourgeoisie than its counterparts in the original European form of capitalism.

The state collaborates in the expropriation of the peasantry through land-title fraud and eventual expulsion of that class to a new frontier region, as the land and its produce become integrated into the national market. Velho termed the local Brazilian system "authoritarian capitalism."[27]

Velho, like several other "modes" theorists, emphasized the reproduction of noncapitalist relations of production. For him, the peasantry is continually reproduced rather than turned into a rural proletariat, and primitive accumulation takes place at its expense. These processes occur in part because the bourgeoisie must still share power with precapitalist landholders and because capital-intensive manufacturing industries have an attenuated need for Marx's "industrial reserve army."[28] Velho asserted, like Althusser, that the economic element is still ultimately determining because of the structural limits on state autonomy set by the international capitalist system.[29] Despite its later appearance, this formulation, of course, was subject to the same criticism as those in the Sempat collection, that is, it conflated "mode of production" with historically specific (empirical) conditions.

In *Grievous Modernization*,[30] a set of essays written between 1976 and 1980, José Graziano da Silva, another analyst of the Brazilian frontier, also placed emphasis on the reproduction of precapitalist forms of production in agriculture, articulated with a controlling combination of traditional and modern capitalist actors. But fully capitalist forms of agriculture with mechanized and large-scale production were discouraged by low food prices, held down by the highly skewed distribution of income in Brazil and (one could add) by consequent price controls. Like Marini, Silva denied that the expansion of Brazilian capitalism depended on the buying power of the masses.[31] For Silva, unlike Velho, the system was explained less by the collusion of the state and latifundists than by a combination of latifundists, rural merchant monopolists and monopsonists (representing usury capital), and an urban, industrial bourgeoisie. Capitalist modernization of agriculture was "grievous" because it was slow and restricted: peasants, unlike those in Velho's scheme, were proletarianized as agricultural workers, facing monopolies in the control of land, agricultural inputs and equipment, and marketing. Proletarianization remained incomplete, however, because of obligatory personal services, usufruct, sharecropping, and other traditional but still dynamic forms of controlling peasantries.[32]

As most of the literature in the modes debate was closely tied to the issues of land tenure and use, Velho, who had studied populism and Chayanov's neopopulism in Britain under Peter Worsley, perceived the emergence of a Brazilian populism both in efforts to specify a "peasant" mode of production and in some articulated schemes. "Classical" populism, it may be recalled, personified by Constantin Stere in turn-of-the-century Rumania, was totally lacking in the Brazil of the early twentieth century, though a Soviet ideologue perceived it in the heterodox Marxism of the Peruvian *pensador* Mariátegui.[33] Among the reasons for populism's lack of reverberations in Brazil one might cite the weakness of collective property traditions, or even closely knit and relatively egalitarian peasant communities outside the southernmost states, where German and Italian settlers became smallholders. In addition, Brazilians did not have access to the nineteenth-century Russian debate about capitalism, as did the Rumanians, and the late appearance of Hegelianism and then of Marxism in Brazil also impeded any expression of classical populism before the doctrine's demise with the Russian Revolution.

Velho's reference to populism alluded to currents within the progressive wing of the Catholic Church, whose members, in Velho's estimation, viewed the "peasant" or "small producer" in the late 1970s as "external to capitalism" and opposed to its advance. According to this view, because small peasants did not use paid labor, they were not capitalist. Furthermore, peasants tended to conceive of land not as a commodity but simply a location for the application of their labor. They sought free land in Amazonia, where they resisted capitalist penetration and their violent expulsion; in this understanding, according to Velho, the peasant constituted a "transforming potential" for the whole society.[34] Though Velho overstated the tendency toward classical populism, there were currents of thought in the Catholic church, whose social views were authoritatively enunciated by the National Conference of Brazilian Bishops (CNBB), providing some evidence for his position. The CNBB was much affected by the Marxist debate about the nature of Brazilian agriculture. Kautsky's *Agrarian Question*, employed by the Rumanian Stere in his articles of 1907–8, was frequently cited in a recent Portuguese translation in the CNBB's *Pastoral of the Land* (1976).[35] Contrary to Caio Prado's view, the document asserted that the notion of private property was deeply rooted in the mentality of the Brazilian "rural worker," making him strive to defend his land against capitalist landlords, whether as a squatter (*posseiro*) or owner.[36] At the CNBB's eighteenth assembly (1980) in Itaici, São Paulo, the bishops drew a distinction between a "property of exploitation" and a "property of labor."[37] The former was based on profit seeking and "permits the enrichment of some at the expense of the whole society," while the latter, worked by the farmer and his family, included both private and community property, "alternatives to capitalist exploitation." Such properties of labor were being "destroyed or mutilated by capital."[38] The bishops' distinction between the two types of rural holdings was that of the Paulista sociologist José de Souza Martins,[39] who saw an inevitable struggle between tenures legitimated, in peasants' eyes, by their own labor, and capitalist tenures, in which rural workers' labor was exploited. He believed Brazil had several "anticapitalist" property regimes—peasant smallholdings, community property, and untitled occupation (*posse*).[40] Yet in Souza Martins's own work, Velho's "populist" charge does not ring true: *Peasants and Politics in Brazil* (1981) does not suggest any possibility of a successful resistance to capitalism by peasants outside modern forms of political struggle.[41] Nevertheless,

Velho suggests there were clergy and laity among Catholic radicals and progressives who believed it possible. Church leaders in the 1970s in any case seemed ripe for populism in their convictions that the creation of a small property regime in Brazil was urgent and that the federal government was an ally of large capital in the struggle for land.[42] In this understanding, the state was a driving force for the advancement of capitalism, as it had been in imperial Russia a century before.

Among the several possible interpretations of a "peasant" mode of production, Brazilian writers avoided the contention of the Rumanian populist Stere and the neopopulists in the National Peasant Party such as Virgil Madgearu that peasants formed an undifferentiated class,[43] as Souza Martins's definition of "property of labor" illustrates. All the same, Chayanovian interpretations of peasant behavior made their first significant appearance in the 1970s. Whereas the medium of Alexander Chayanov's influence in Rumania had been his German (and possibly Russian) publications in the 1920s, his impact in Brazil and the Third World at large was based on the rediscovery of his theories through an English-language compendium of his work edited by Daniel Thorner and others in 1966.[44] Chayanov's model can be understood, of course, as a peasant mode of production; it is based on rational calculations, and it is market-related but noncapitalist. The basic unit of production is the family farm, which does not function in capitalist terms of profits, wages, and rents. Unlike the capitalist, the peasant exchanges surplus production to obtain what he cannot produce and seeks to balance consumption and labor expended or "drudgery" to obtain it, much as Boeke's Asian peasant balanced leisure and consumption. For Chayanov, as for Kautsky, the peasant family did not count its labor as an expense of production and therefore could accept remuneration lower than that of capitalist farmers, who had to incur labor costs. Granted, the literature cited in Chapter 4, challenging Boeke's dualism on the basis of empirical studies that peasants do attempt to expand their consumption of commodities without obvious limits, can also be used against Chayanov. But Chayanov also considered another variable, the demographic cycles of the peasant family. Based on research in Russia, he believed that economic activity depended less on capitalist profitability than on family size and the need to balance consumption and "the drudgery of labor."

In Chayanov's sense, the peasant mode of production was explored fruitfully by Afrânio Garcia, Jr., who like Velho, was a researcher at the Museu Nacional in Rio. Garcia began a series of studies in the latter 1970s culminating in *The South: The Road from the Peasant Clearing* (1990),[45] a work richly informed by the theory of peasant economy but firmly grounded in an empirical study of peasant existence in the Northeast. Examining economic conditions, the portions of product consumed and marketed, noncapitalist economic calculations, family patterns, and the social differentiation of peasants, Garcia saw the migration of landless youth from the northeastern state of Paraíba as an open-ended strategy. Though many became proletarians, others returned to Paraíba to become independent producers and, occasionally, even petty merchants.[46] Garcia wrote without the advantages of the systematic teamwork that characterized the Rumanian peasant studies of Dimitrie Gusti and his associates in the 1920s and 1930s, but he produced a monograph of distinction. The empirical investigations in Garcia's book set it apart from the earlier and more speculative array of works attempting to specify the mode(s) of production in Brazilian agriculture.

Yet the modes literature was not entirely about rural society. A fruitful effort to theorize about articulated modes concerned a less totalizing problem than Velho's "authoritarian capitalism"—namely, urban underemployment, for which the notion of "marginality" was the subject of academic debate among students of dependency in the decade after 1965. Francisco de Oliveira, Lúcio Kowarick, Paul Singer, as well as Fernando Henrique Cardoso himself—all researchers at CEBRAP in São Paulo during the early 1970s—took issue with Aníbal Quijano of Peru and José Nun of Argentina, who had worked at ECLA and other Santiago-based institutions. The latter two writers viewed marginality, in the sense of huge numbers of urban un- and underemployed, as a specific deformity of dependent capitalism; Nun saw marginality as something distinct from Marx's "industrial reserve army," the unemployed workers who served the purpose of holding down wages. He held that marginality as a Latin American social phenomenon exceeded any necessary dimensions of a reserve army, in an age of monopoly capitalism and labor-saving technology. Though some marginals directly contributed to capitalist accumulation, for example, in the construction industry, Nun's "marginal mass" was partly dysfunctional for the capitalist system because of its great strain on urban services.[47]

CEBRAP scholars took a different view. As early as 1968, Cardoso, in collaboration with the Mexican sociologist José Luis Reyna, had argued that modern industrial workers and the "marginalized population" did not constitute a polarized or dualist system. Rather, their coexistence and continuity was a peculiar feature of dependent development, one characterized by ambiguity. The "resulting amalgam," they wrote, "expresses the way in which it is possible under the particular condition of underdevelopment and dependency, for Latin American countries to move ahead in the industrialization process."[48]

The CEBRAP group, Cardoso among them, denied that marginality constituted a social problem for which classical Marxian categories were inadequate. Accusing Nun and Quijano of introducing a new dualism, CEBRAP researchers saw marginality as a phenomenon that was linked to dependent capitalist accumulation through the articulation of capitalist and precapitalist modes or the precapitalist relations of production derived from them; this articulation was dominated by the logic of the former system, locating the precapitalist elements largely in the service sector.[49] Not only did newly urbanized peasants hold down the wage level as an "unlimited supply of labor,"[50] but poorly paid hawkers helped realize profits on industrial goods with their intensive sales techniques; moreover, urban services such as car washing, or, one might say, even shoe shining, indirectly contributed to the realization of surplus value in the industrial sector by distributing and maintaining its products at low cost.[51] That these new members of the "informal" sector were not totally divorced from the means of production, and therefore in the Marxist understanding remained "precapitalist," wrote Oliveira, is shown in the fact that many built their own ramshackle housing, lowering the cost of their employment.[52] Thus CEBRAP analysts tended to identify marginality with the economic contributions of the informally employed or underemployed, whereas Nun had a less sanguine view of marginals' productivity and emphasized the precarious nature of their employment and even their superfluity or negative contribution.[53] Whether influenced by the articulation approach or otherwise, the issue of marginality generated a variety of empirical and theoretical studies of the informal sector, contributions that questioned the adequacy of the concept of underemployment in Third World countries.[54]

To conclude, the modes discourse was vexed by the lack of a general definition of "mode of production" in Marx's own writings and by his use of "society" and "social formation" interchangeably.[55] Still further confusion was inherent in the inconsistent use of the concept "Asiatic mode of production" in the works of Marx and Engels, for whom the term was, in the last analysis, "a generic residual category for non-European development," in the words of the British Marxist Perry Anderson.[56]

In Brazil the modes-of-production debate did not end in any general agreement about proper ways to characterize the agricultural economy or its components, contemporary or historical, as feudal, capitalist, or something else. In 1980 one observer of the debate compiled a list of 60 works on modes of production in Brazil, divided into four types of interpretation—feudal, capitalist, and unique modes, and works revising the others.[57] Like Otávio Guilherme Velho, other researchers "discovered" uniquely Brazilian modes of production, and the prospect loomed that every case would yield its own mode; where, then, was Marxist science, if every instance was unique? And one might well question whether the laws of motion of the proposed modes, their forms of reproduction, and their internal contradictions, were adequately specified.

Nevertheless, though the modes-of-production debate had no resolution, it was not barren. One result was the admittedly modest conclusion that precapitalist relations of production after European colonization gained their significance from their *relation* to capitalism, not from any inherent "feudalism"; another was the rejection of the thesis of an omnipresent and sempiternal capitalism. Scholars who examined combinations of precapitalist and capitalist economic relations in Brazil had charged dependency analysts with ignoring local production processes, especially in agriculture. Whereas in Rumania Dobrogeanu-Gherea had combined an examination of a local mode of production, *neoiobăgia*, with that of international dependency, in Brazil the analysis of agrarian relations came after dependency writers had first considered international market relations and local manufacturing processes. In comparison with the Rumanian debate, it is note-worthy that the issue of a rich peasantry seems not to have concerned those who contributed to the Brazilian discourse, presumably because of its absence or near absence in frontier areas where, several writers argued, the latifundium some-times appeared even before human occupation. Like Gherea, the Brazilians who looked at agriculture in a "modes" framework (e.g., Silva, Velho, and the British Marxist Foweraker) sought to explain the dynamism of the latifundium.

The character of the modes debate of the 1970s was more academic and perhaps less overtly policy-oriented than the first Marxist exchange on Brazilian agriculture between Alberto Passos Guimarães and Moisés Vinhas, espousing the "semifeudal" thesis, on the one hand, and Caio Prado's upholding the "ever-capitalist" thesis, on the other. Yet the issue of the character of the agrarian regime was far from trivial because, as the French economist Christian Topalov has remarked, each theoretical position on contemporary Brazilian agriculture implies a doctrine of economic development.[58] The modes exchange further resulted in significant contributions to Brazil's historiography, as noted in the debate over the *colonato* and explorations of the "peasant breach." If the ap-pearance of a classical populism (or at least the appropriate mentality) in Church circles was a "negative" outcome, a positive result of the modes controversy, or at least a development associated with it, was the establishment of a neo-Chayanov-ian research tradition in Brazil. Another significant result was the discovery at CEBRAP of an urban "informal" sector in which precapitalist elements were integrated into the production and reproduction of Brazil's urban capitalist re-gime; in the process CEBRAP's social scientists explicitly challenged José Nun's notion of a "marginal mass" and implicitly downgraded the importance of urban disguised unemployment. The fact that CEBRAP analysts understood the artic-ulation between precapitalist and capitalist modes of production as a characteris-tic feature of dependent capitalist accumulation showed that dependency analysis and a modes-of-production approach were not necessarily incompatible.

14

Conclusion

This book has examined components of a large set of problems: how the Third World was fashioned as a set of ideas and how it was diffused among economic theorists and their sometime allies in business and government. I have used the word "crafting" in the title to indicate a conscious effort to reify the Third World. For its creators, that notion encompassed a majority of the human race, having in common, despite enormous differences in culture and social structures, certain problems (of which poverty was only the most salient) and interests that were distinct from the First World of developed capitalist countries, the West. Most, but not all, of the writers treated in the preceding pages believed the Third World shares many, but not all, of its economic interests with the West. All were structuralists by the broad definition that in their theories they tried to specify, analyze, and correct economic structures that impede or block the "normal" development and functioning of modern economies. Many of them used historical analysis—the Marxists in this study necessarily so because their method was dialectical materialism rather than formal Marxist economics—while others combined a historical approach with economic analysis. In the case of Celso Furtado, he moved beyond Prebisch's interest in Latin America's economic cycles to fully historicize the structuralist perspective.

When was this Third World "created" or "crafted"? It is implicit in this work that the answer is a process, not an event. Although the world division of labor began in the late fifteenth century, the intellectual construction of the Third World occurred much later. The French Revolution set off a train of events leading to the rise of other European and extra-European nationalisms and aspirations for a vaguely defined "civilization," which included economic well-being. Friedrich List argued the case for a medium-term exception to David Ricardo's international division of labor—the infant industry argument—in 1841, and, by labeling the work of the classical economists "the English School," he implicitly denied that the theories of Adam Smith, Ricardo, and their successors were strictly scientific. List was read and debated in East Central Europe and Latin America in the nineteenth century, as recently formed states pondered paths to (Western) civilization and development.

Disillusion with economic liberalism began earlier in East Central Europe than in Latin America, as primary exports as an engine of growth stuttered against those of new "overseas," lower-cost competitors in the world market. In Rumania economic writers from Xenopol to Manoilescu denounced and attempted to analyze an alleged unequal exchange between an advanced industrialized Center and a backward agrarian Periphery. The tradition was reinvented in the postwar era by structuralists and dependency writers in Latin America. The terms "Center" and "Periphery," made famous by Raúl Prebisch and probably introduced into the twentieth-century debate by Werner Sombart, conceivably have their roots in *The Isolated State* (part I, 1826) by the German economist J. H. von Thünen.[1]

In Marxist discourse as well, non-Western writers in Russia, Rumania, and elsewhere imported, assimilated, and adapted Western theory to fit local circumstances. In 1910 Constantin Dobrogeanu-Gherea began a long debate among Marxists on the nature of capitalism in Rumania, as did Caio Prado, Jr., at midcentury in Brazil. Populism, a third school, might be considered a Marxist heresy, but it had its own independent and evolving tradition (in its Chayanovian incarnation), stressing peasant exceptionalism to both Marxist and neoclassical propositions. Populism denied that the capitalist path to development was possible for agrarian countries because of the West's enormous technological lead by the late nineteenth century. Its centrality in Rumania in the early twentieth century and its absence in Brazil at the time not only had to do with Rumania's access to the Russian development debate but also with the respective configurations of demography and land tenure in Rumania and Brazil, as well as Rumania's great peasant revolt of 1907 and the mobilization of peasants as a political force in the Balkan nation by World War I.

At a political level, the reification of the Third World began with the decay of the Ottoman Empire, a process begun long before the partitioning of Africa at the Berlin Conference of 1885, an event that marked the high tide of European imperialism, the "scramble for Africa." Europe's ascendancy began to falter with World War I, which destroyed four great empires and resulted in new or enlarged, and allegedly national, states in East Central Europe at the end of the conflict. During the war the Second World arose in 1917, as the Soviet Union appeared to offer an alternative route to development and modernity. In the interwar years, I have argued, the newly independent or newly configured nations of East Central Europe constituted a "proto"–Third World in which the problems of economic and social backwardness were first confronted and formally theorized, against a range of development options, which included Soviet socialism.

World War II vastly accelerated the process of decolonization, with the military occupation or relative decline of most of the Great Powers in Europe and Asia, as well as smaller European colonial empires. In the years after 1945 the United Nations and other new international forums, global and regional, including a myriad of commodity-marketing associations, facilitated the formation of a Third World identity, as did the rise of "development economics" in academic institutions and UN agencies. Meanwhile, the Cold War opened a breach between the two superpowers that statesmen in underdeveloped areas could sometimes use to advantage. The emergence of a self-aware Third World is often dated from the Afro-Asian Conference of newly independent states at Bandung, Indonesia, in 1955, but the term itself had been coined three years earlier by the French demographer Alfred Sauvy.[2] Latin America "joined" Asia and Africa in the Third World by increments, of which Raúl Prebisch's assumption of leadership of the UN's Economic Commission for Latin America in 1949 was arguably a significant moment. A related institution that reinforced Latin America's identification with the Third World was the United Nations Conference on Trade and Development (UNCTAD), directed in its initial years (1964–69) by Prebisch, who used the organization to propagate his message of unequal exchange. Contemporaneously a shift at the political level occurred with the Cuban Revolution, as Fidel Castro used international forums to denounce U.S. imperialism. In 1966 he held a Tricontinental Conference in Havana, identifying the Latin American poor with the wretched of the earth.

That the Third World is still a dynamic concept is shown by the destructuring and reordering of the former Second World; parts of the former Soviet Bloc are apparently falling to Third World income levels, while a few countries on its western fringes can realistically aspire to First World status in a few decades. East Central Europe is thus becoming more internally differentiated with the advance of capitalism, as radically different policies in the region produce divergent rates of growth, along with rising income disparities within each nation. In this context, the restructuring of the Rumanian economy, however incomplete, has been traumatic. By one estimate, the Gross Domestic Product per capita of Rumania in 1993 was below that of 1989, as measured by the country's international exchange rate. The 1993 figure was a mere $1,080, compared to Brazil's contemporaneous $2,883 per person, and almost $1,500 below Rumania's level in 1982 (though Rumanian data for the early 1980s may have been inflated). The same source nonetheless estimates Rumania's domestic purchasing power per capita at $2,600 in 1993, when services and non-traded goods are taken into account.[3] At all events, Rumania's poor economic performance in part reflects the middle-term chaos of attempting to transform the socialist economy, but the country's reforms had been far less radical than Poland's.[4] To the extent that the liberal model prevails in Rumania, the high regard which economists and other social scientists of the former regime accorded Mihail Manoilescu's theories of state-sponsored industrialization may disappear.[5]

As a history of ideas, this book has been concerned with three processes—the borrowing or importation of ideas, their adaptation and transformation, and their independent discovery or rediscovery. I have argued that the second and third processes are as important as the first. The traditions in question were originally Western ones—neoclassical economics and Marxism—but were quickly adapted and acclimatized in backward areas. The borrowing, adaptation, rejection, discovery, rediscovery, and reformulation of ideas were ongoing processes, in a continual dialogue between heterodox and orthodox ideas. Beyond these abstractions, I have tried to locate the ideas in historical situations, emphasizing not only the lives and times of the writers and their interactions with one another but also the "consumption" of ideas by two major constituencies of economic theorists, government and industrialists' associations. Such consumers were also institutions. Institutions are themselves important in the story as facilitators and transmitters of ideas—not only governments, business associations, and foreign and domestic universities, but also the League of Nations and UN agencies, even nongovernmental development organizations. For example, the Rockefeller Foundation sent several Rumanian economists and other social scientists to study in the United States; it assisted in establishing a national statistical service in Rumania; and it subsidized a French mission, which included François Perroux, to the University of São Paulo, as it had earlier sent Perroux to study in Vienna. Later Rockefeller sent Celso Furtado to Cambridge, and the Ford Foundation underwrote Fernando Henrique Cardoso's social research institute, CEBRAP, in São Paulo.

Institutions as instruments for the reform and restructuring of backward economies had spotty success, as ECLA's record illustrates. Sometimes international efforts were patent failures: Virgil Madgearu's ten-nation Agrarian Bloc in East Central Europe collapsed in the mid-1930s under the weight of surplus wheat supplies in "overseas" granaries, for which Raúl Prebisch's contemporaneous efforts on behalf of Argentina likewise proved ineffective in negotiations with the United States, Canada, and Australia. Efforts by Prebisch and others in the latter 1940s to establish an International Trade Organization for commodity-exporting countries as a "third leg" to the world trading system—along with the World Bank and the International Monetary Fund—failed to gain the approval of the U.S. Congress. Leaders of Third World countries succeeded in establishing a UN Conference on Trade and Development in 1964 with Prebisch at its head, but the Argentine economist was more effective in propagating his doctrine of unequal exchange in African and Asian venues than in securing multilateral commodity price-support agreements, and he left UNCTAD five years later. The organization foundered on the rocks of resistance to such trading conventions in the First World and to conflicting interests among commodity producers in the Third World. A cynical interpretation had it that UNCTAD was an acronym for "Under No Condition Take Any Decisions."[6] Somewhat more effective were specific commodity associations, but even the most successful, the Organization of Petroleum Exporting Countries, seems to have passed its apogee, as supplies become uncontrollable in the short run and the substitution of other forms of energy seems likely in the long run. The international economic institutions most successful in meeting their objectives were those controlled by the First World: consider the financial missions of the League in East Central Europe, and recall Manoilescu's denunciation of fiscal controls in Rumania imposed by "the new Phanariots." In the postwar years, think of International Monetary Fund missions to Latin America and elsewhere, even though Furtado scored a temporary success in urging President Kubitschek to resist IMF policies in 1959.

This history necessarily began with a consideration of liberalism. Smithian economics introduced the idea of a world division of labor, and from it flowed the notion that Brazil and Rumania were "essentially agricultural." Liberalism, the explicit ideology associated with classical and neoclassical economics, was the first set of West European ideas and values to be imported into the emerging states of Brazil and Rumania. It was also the first to be extensively adapted, in the "statist liberalism" that prescribed government intervention in Rumania's economy to foster industrialization and a counterpart intervention in Brazil's to valorize the nation's chief export, coffee.

Yet the relationship between shifts in the world market and ideas on economic development in Brazil contrasted sharply with that in Rumania before World War I. In Rumania, market failure, social upheaval, and access to the continuing Russian debate led to new theoretical responses, in both Marxist and non-Marxist discourses. In the interwar years Rumanians had firmer philosophical and theoretical bases and techniques for understanding the gap between rich and poor countries, owing to stronger academic traditions (requiring the Ph.D., obtainable abroad) and the existence of research institutions, such as the Rumanian Institute of Social Sciences and the Rumanian Business Cycles Institute. In Brazil and elsewhere in Latin America, the perceived success of export-driven economies, combined with institutional factors, cultural patterns, and the feebleness of certain critical traditions known in Rumania and neighboring states, significantly delayed theoretical challenges to growth based on the Ricardian thesis of comparative advantage. Industrial development was under way in Brazil before government policy pushed in the same direction. A theoretical justification of industrialization came last, in the structuralism of Raúl Prebisch in 1949, endorsed by the Vargas and Kubitschek governments in Brazil during the following decade.

Identifying capitalism was the first issue in the great debate for Marxists and others, and there was little consensus, even within Marxism in Brazil and Rumania, about capitalism's viability. Whether it would work, and, if so, how it could be made to work, were issues debated throughout the period considered. Directly linked to this issue was the nature and viability of a local capitalist class and its potential for a capitalist restructuring of precapitalist societies. Was there no reformist bourgeoisie in Rumania, but only a *pătură cultă* (cultured stratum), as Dobrogeanu-Gherea held? Yet might an *Ersatzklasse* of state bureaucrats, or, put more positively, technocratic elites, as Brazilian corporatists in the 1930s and even structuralists in the 1950s might have it, substitute for, or decisively buttress, an authentic national bourgeoisie? Was the development of the Rumanian bourgeoisie abnormal, aberrant, as Gherea argued, or "normal" in the quite different senses that Ştefan Zeletin and Lucreţiu Pătrăşcanu viewed the process? The former excused the bourgeoisie's corruption and rapacity as normal in its early development, while the latter saw its drive toward monopoly and imperialism as normal. In postwar Brazil, could the bourgeoisie lead the national economy toward an autonomous development if imperialism and latifundism could be contained, as the Brazilian Communist Party would have it, or was that bourgeoisie fatally linked to foreign capital, consumption patterns, and culture, as the dependency analysts and some modes-of-production theorists contended? For Ruy Mauro Marini, Brazilian imperialism was "subimperialism," with its peculiar features, not the standard variety Pătrăşcanu ascribed to wartime Rumania. In Latin America's structuralist school, the role of the bourgeoisie was not explicitly treated as a theoretical problem, but that class implicitly played a decisive role, assisted by foreign capital, in the development process. For all schools the peasantry was as difficult to characterize as the bourgeoisie, and in both Rumania and Brazil there was little agreement whether it consisted of a single class or a composite of classes.

In the Marxist tradition, two of the Rumanian figures mentioned in the previous paragraph, Zeletin and Pătrăşcanu, had earned doctorates in Germany, and this fact set them apart from the Comintern-directed Marxist writers of Brazil in the 1920s and 1930s. There were patently many differences between the Marxist discourse in Rumania and that in Brazil, given the dissimilarities in social and political conditions in the Rumania of the interwar years and the Brazil of the postwar period. Yet there were some instructive likenesses in the several positions defended in each national debate. Ştefan Zeletin's evolutionary Marxism—the view that capitalism would eventually triumph over a precapitalist past—paralleled that of the postwar Brazilian Communist Party. Dobrogeanu-Gherea shared with Brazil's modes theorists the conviction that local, precapitalist modes of production were subordinated to a dominant, structuring capitalism, though such modes and forms nevertheless exploited the peasantry in ways unanticipated by Marx.

Dobrogeanu-Gherea also shared perceptions and theses with Latin American structuralists and dependency analysts—most notably his vision of a Center-Periphery relationship between the industrialized West and its agrarian suppliers of foodstuffs and raw materials. Furthermore, Furtado's emphasis on consumption of Western goods and culture as the driving force of dependency was anticipated by Gherea in his analysis of the *boieri*, though the Rumanian denied they were bourgeois and emphasized the importation of values more than commodities.

In Rumania, grosso modo, Marxism preceded corporatism, but in Brazil, the opposite occurred. The "socialism of classes" in the Balkan nation preceded what Manoilescu termed the "socialism of nations." In Brazil, Marxist analysis was feebly developed before World War II, and the corporatism of the interwar years had paved the way for the structuralist thesis on unequal exchange before an indigenous Marxist discourse began to question the formulae of the Comintern and Cominform.

An obvious difference between the Rumanian and Brazilian debates over economic development was the absence of the populist and even neopopulist voices in Brazil virtually until the 1970s. Partly as a consequence, just as Rumanian populists had argued that the West's huge technological lead resulted in market monopolies that precluded the rise of an authentic capitalism in backward countries, so the argument was reinvented by Brazilian dependency analysts 60 years later. Furthermore, the Rumanian populist Constantin Stere, like Furtado and dependency analysts, noted that labor-saving technology also meant a smaller number of consumers in the national market. Like dependency writers, Stere also stressed the international character of modern capitalism—its "vagabond" nature, putting large firms outside the control of the national state. Yet again, the Rumanian neopopulist Virgil Madgearu anticipated dependency analysts by more than three decades by noting that foreign firms could leap across tariff walls to establish their operations within backward countries. More fundamentally, the agenda of neopopulists and other students of peasant economy in Rumania during the interwar years included a wide array of scientific studies unparalleled in Brazil; among other things, social scientists in Rumania and elsewhere in East Central Europe tried to measure "disguised unemployment" long before the idea became a building block of development economics in 1945–50.

The absence of populist and neopopulist discourses in the South American nation in the first half of the century, as well as that of the German Historical School, meant that Marxism was less likely to be critically examined by its early advocates than it was in Rumania. It is debatable whether populism ever had any authentic voice in Brazil, as opposed to being an epithet. Beyond that particular ideological construct, there was relatively little interest among Brazilian researchers in rural freeholders and dependents until peasants, broadly defined, became more important in the political process and contested frontier occupation with speculators and latifundists in the decades after 1970. Modes-of-production writers turned their attention to "archaic" relations of production in the informal economy of the cities, where rural migrants had recently arrived, and to larger processes in the countryside. By the 1970s as well, Chayanovian neopopulism, which in Brazil owed its original appeal in part to addressing the "modes" question, formed a small but growing and empirically grounded tradition. To date, however, studies of peasant economy in Brazil do not approach the breadth and depth of Rumania's peasant studies in the interwar years.

The backwardness which all theorists tried to explain began with a perception of contrast. Intellectuals of underdeveloped countries seeking to understand the economies of their own lands could hardly avoid comparing local poverty to the wealth of the Western countries with which they traded. To intuit unequal exchange as an explanation for that contrast was natural enough. Consider Falstaff's speech in *The Merry Wives of Windsor:*

> . . . she is a region
> in Guiana, all gold and bounty.
> I will be cheater to them both, and they shall
> be exchequers to me: They
> shall be my east and west
> Indies, and I shall trade to them both.[7]

A corollary of unequal exchange for a number of Marxist, populist, and corporatist writers, including Manoilescu, was the international division of labor between exploiter and exploited countries, plutocratic and proletarian nations. This notion, invented and reinvented in the early twentieth century in Rumania and elsewhere, was politically linked to rising nationalisms, first in Europe and then more broadly. But it represented a vulgarization of the concept of unequal exchange, and the latter notion did not necessarily entail it.

The perception of unequal exchange was a common thread through classical populism, Manoilescu's theory of protectionism, Latin American structuralism, internal colonialism, dependency, and even the modes-of-production literature, which ostensibly stressed relations of production rather than relations of exchange. But there the role of intermediaries (commercial capital) was sometimes crucial, and in articulated modes the immediate exploiter of labor did not necessarily receive the largest portion of the surplus value produced. For example, the exploitation of rural workers and peasants by market mechanisms or by force—the latter means still widely observable in rural Brazil in 1993[8]—held down the cost of wage goods for urban industrialists.

For the Marxist tradition, it may help to think of the unequal exchange relationship as a multiple one in any complex or "real-world" form of production because the value of labor as a commodity is, in Marxist theory, exchanged unequally in the first instance with a capitalist employer who pays a wage. Every phase of production involves an exchange of labor for less than its full value, in a serial process of unequal exchange. Production processes often traverse international boundaries, so labor exploitation and unequal exchange are multiple, concatenated processes. This does not necessarily imply that exploitation of colonial or Third World labor is the *principal* source of capitalist wealth—though Manoilescu and some dependency writers did draw this conclusion—because for Marx, relative surplus value, based on rising productivities, is the chief source of expanding wealth. In turn, productivity increases in relative surplus value are achieved though organizational improvements in the production process and technological change, especially the latter.

In non-Marxist traditions, the differing labor productivities between Center and Periphery in world trade were at the heart of both Manoilescu's and Prebisch's analyses. For Prebisch, however, productivity differences were ultimately driven by changing technologies and organizational innovations, combined with differential market imperfections between Center and Periphery, and not labor expended and capital per worker, as in the static model of Manoilescu. The Rumanian nonetheless anticipated the double-factorial considerations (costs of traded goods in terms of labor expended to produce them) introduced into the postwar debate by Raúl Prebisch and developed by John Spraos. At any rate, in modern economic theory Mihail Manoilescu is primarily remembered for the "Manoilescu argument" that when the marginal productivity of labor in agriculture is below that in other sectors, surplus labor should be moved to manufacturing or other higher-productivity activities. The prescription is still controversial because it directs emphasis away from raising productivity in farming.

Manoilescu not only wrote about trade and development but also theorized about corporatism. There was a historical if not a direct analytical relationship between corporatism and Latin American structuralism; Manoilescu and François Perroux prepared the way for the reception of the latter school in Brazil in the 1930s. Perroux was sequentially associated with both schools and a contributor to both. Manoilescu's thesis of unequal exchange yielded a model of internal colonialism similar to those of Furtado and Hans Singer for Brazil. But the analytical similarities are broad ones, and Keynesianism shares many features with both schools, trying to account for and correct or offset market failures, real-world oligopolies and oligopsonies in product, capital, and labor markets.[9] At all events, I believe Manoilescu's theory of corporatism and his theory of protectionism, which preceded his corporatist treatise by five years and is the chief concern of this study, are separable: Manoilescu himself once stated that there was only a "limited" connection between his economic and political theories.[10]

Like Perroux, an economist who was neither Rumanian nor Brazilian, but whose work is an essential element in this narrative, is the Argentinean Raúl Prebisch. The literature on Prebisch is large and often hagiographic, partly because he directed an institutional forum, ECLA. The major contribution of this book to evaluating Prebisch's work has been to place him in the shifting currents of orthodoxy and heterodoxy, arguing that his initial and defining position was eclectic. To establish that proposition, I have shown how he was influenced not only by Keynes, possibly by Sombart, Wagemann, and Manoilescu, but also by Nikolai Kondratieff, Louise Sommer, Gustav Cassel, and notably by the trade theorist Charles Kindleberger. In Chapter 8 I showed how his thesis on unequal exchange differed fundamentally from Manoilescu's. Yet the third part of this book has not been concerned primarily with Prebisch, but rather with the structuralist school in Brazil and the elaboration of its doctrine, as well as varieties of Marxism—contestations to structuralism—which in dependency analysis tended to fuse with it. Indeed, I argued in Chapter 12 that Latin American structuralism rather than Marxism was the primary source of dependency analysis.

Do the doctrines examined in this book have a future as well as a past? In the wake of the collapse of the Soviet Union and its satellite regimes in 1989–91, there can be little doubt that Marxist programs of development[11] now seem much less relevant than at any previous time in our century, or even appear irrelevant to the hard choices the Third World faces. Less sudden but still manifest is the degree to which state-directed solutions to the problems of economic backwardness have fallen from favor in the last two decades. In the economic historiography of Latin America, the mounting evidence that twentieth-century industrial growth has been positively correlated with that of foreign trade has undermined faith in "delinking" solutions. On the state as fomenter of development, Celso Furtado, whose theses on the centrality of government action have been examined in these pages, concedes in a recent memoir that the Brazilian state is in need of regeneration, though he still maintains that its role is indispensable in passing from backwardness to development. Furtado alludes rather vaguely to abusive forms of corporatism in the Brazilian state,[12] meaning perhaps military corruption during the institutional dictatorship of 1964–85. Yet anyone familiar with Brazilian or other Latin American bureaucracies would also be concerned with incompetence and "rent-seeking behavior," problems which Furtado presumably would concede and which Hernando de Soto has so eloquently if tendentiously exposed in the Peruvian state.[13]

The Indian economist Deepak Lal is equally persuasive in his attack on the "*dirigiste* dogma" of economic development. Yet he aims his darts at an extreme form of *dirigisme*, one that supplants rather than merely supplements the price mechanism. Looking primarily at the postwar experience of India rather than that of Latin America, Lal holds, for example, that protectionist exchange rates and trade policies made scarce foreign exchange "even scarcer," for two reasons: first, by importing only "essentials"—capital goods, foods, and fuels— government and private agents became insensitive to changes in the relative prices of these goods; and second, trade controls were biased against exports in general, including innovations. Consequently, the "foreign exchange gap" became a self-fulfilling prophecy.[14] The same criticism could be leveled against the statist industrialization policies of Manoilescu and others in Rumania in the 1930s and the structuralism of Furtado and Prebisch in the 1950s. In the Indian case Lal contends that government intervention led to more rather than fewer distortions, imbalances, and deformations. It is not the case, however, that Latin American structuralists were indifferent to the matter of government-induced economic distortions. State-created distortions in exchange, capital, and labor markets were the centerpiece of Furtado's analysis of internal colonialism in Northeast Brazil, and Prebisch was among the first economists, in 1963, to perceive and decry the protectionist excesses of Latin American governments.[15]

Liberalism was the first formal economic doctrine considered in this work, and it is fair to ask, Have we come full circle? Some commentators refer to "neoliberalism" and others call it "neoconservatism," but both groups have in mind the liberal doctrine of freeing the market from constraints and seeking to reinstate an international division of labor, while allowing Third World countries to develop new export markets. Though neoliberalism has shown its great power in recent years, it would be wrong to conclude that the role of the state in the developed economies or those striving for development has been, or should be, abandoned. In fact, there is still enormous controversy about the proper role of the state.

In Brazil and Latin America, structuralism during the 1980s yielded to a "neo-structuralism." The new version would avoid the mistakes of import-substitution industrialization and incorporate lessons from neoliberalism, seeking, for example, export opportunities, in a flexible policy to develop both internal and external markets: Prebisch's "inward-directed development" would be replaced by "development *from* within." The state would remain interventionist, seeking to collaborate with the private sector, but would concern itself as well with social development, environmental problems, and equity issues.[16] Another avenue for research would be formal analyses of various types of market failure.

For one neostructuralist, the Brazilian Winston Fritsch, the recurrent external disequilibrium that concerned Prebisch and Furtado in the 1940s and 1950s could be overcome in the 1990s not by less trade but more, given the ever-rising share of manufactures in the world market and the limits of a strategy of the compression of imports. According to Fritsch, Latin American nations should follow a policy of generalized liberalization of trade combined with protection of nascent industries, especially manufactures, based on criteria of efficiency and competitiveness in the international market.[17] Here neostructuralism reconciles the structuralist tradition, emphasizing industrialization, with the mounting evidence linking economic growth with international trade.[18]

There can be little doubt that equity is still a central issue in development economics (for example, in the work of Amartya Sen, the Harvard-based Indian economist[19]), and, indeed, widening and even obscene inequalities characterize much of the growth process in Latin America. Mexico's decision to pursue neoliberal domestic policies and hitch its star to the United States market in the North American Free Trade Association may have been the correct one, but the equity issue (and the need for the intercession of the state) was raised immediately by the revolt in Chiapas. That a resurrected and tempered structuralism has a future may derive in large part from its attention to issues of equity, which also affect the size and nature of demand.

In addition, a promising thrust of the structuralist tradition was the research on the informal sector at the Regional Employment Program of Latin America and the Caribbean (PREALC),[20] a structuralist-suffused division of the International Labor Office associated with the UN regional headquarters in Santiago. Focusing on the microeconomy of the streets, PREALC economists and sociologists have sought to understand the positive and negative features of Latin America's informal economy, so important, yet so difficult to measure—partly because of its heterogeneity—in the region today. Such interest is perhaps a late Latin American counterpart to the study of artisans and small peasants in East Central Europe before 1945. In any case, the literature on the informal sector, whether from the perspective of PREALC in Santiago, Hernando de Soto's Instituto Libertad y Democracia in Lima, or the CEBRAP Marxists in São Paulo, raises the important issue of where disguised unemployment or underemployment ends and where (efficient) informal sector employment begins. Underemployment in fact seems to prevail.[21]

Despite the current tide of privatization, directed at the waste and mismanagement of state bureaucracies, it seems unlikely that a basic appeal of structuralism in Latin America—the state's role as economic actor to correct imbalances and distortions—will soon disappear. At a world level, there may be historical cycles of state growth and shrinkage; at any rate, it is clear that a vigorous state is essential to the creation and maintenance of effective markets.[22] Furthermore, state intervention will have its defenders among those who believe in population and environmental policies. The power of the modern state has advanced symbiotically with the development of capitalism over the last five centuries. More concretely, it is notable that the most developed countries have governments, on the average, with much greater extractive powers than those of Third World countries, which fact seems to indicate the large government is inherent in "mature" development. Of 24 industrialized countries in 1990, government tax collections ranged from 30 percent of the national product in the United States and Japan, to 37 percent in Germany, to 43 percent in France, to 58 percent in Sweden.[23] Furthermore, as Eastern Europe and Latin America were privatizing, the United States was socializing, following the collapse of the nation's savings-and-loan institutions. By early 1991 the American government had taken over $200 billion in private assets, and another $100 billion was deemed likely before the crisis was resolved.[24] Nor, despite the undeniable waste caused by "rent-seeking" behavior in Third World bureaucracies, has state intervention in the development process been repudiated. Although orthodox economists point to the "high-performing" countries of East Asia—Japan, Korea, Malaysia, Indonesia, Singapore, Thailand, and Taiwan—as successful examples of the application of liberal policies, a revisionist monographic literature has established that governments played important roles in development through market intervention in Japan, Korea, and Taiwan.[25] Moreover, the same seven "high-performing" countries that achieved three times the growth rates of Latin America and South Asia between 1960 and 1985—and five times those of Sub-Saharan Africa—also performed considerably better than the latter areas with regard to income distribution among social groups, partly because of state policy, including land reform in Japan, Korea, and Taiwan.[26] One of the themes development economists now stress is the importance of human, as opposed to physical, capital, and the extension of primary education in the East Asian high performers was, for the World Bank, "by far the largest single contributor to . . . [their] predicted growth rates."[27]

In Brazil, a country with an interventionist tradition and one where the signs of the exhaustion of "easy" import-substitution opportunities were perceived by Conceição Tavares in 1964, the longer-term postwar record of growth was nonetheless impressive until the sustained recession of the 1980s. In the 30 years after 1950, Brazil's portion of the total product of Latin America rose from one-quarter to one-third. Even in the 1980s, Brazil was one of only four Latin American countries, and probably the most interventionist among them, for which 1989 per capita income was not below that for 1980.[28] In foreign trade, Brazil was the only Latin American nation in the 1980s to produce a surplus in the manufacturing sector,[29] a fact that owed significantly to parastatal enterprises. Yet Brazil's growth depended in good measure on the performance of the postwar world economy, and Brazilian growth was not accompanied by gains in equity. The contrary was true, as Furtado and others emphasized. The enormous disparities in income distribution and the sumptuary consumption by upper-income strata in Latin America remained a major concern of neostructuralists and others, in part because of the adverse implications for long-term growth.[30] Controversy about the role of the state in economic development will continue. In Brazil statesmen until recently have been much more resistant to sweeping neoliberal policies than their counterparts in Chile, Argentina, and Mexico; yet a sign of the times was the evolution of the position of Fernando Henrique Cardoso, who in 1995 no longer sought "paths toward socialism"[31] but as the new president of Brazil, sought to increase the rate of privatization of the national economy while maintaining a minimum social safety net. One wonders whether this shift is simply that of a pragmatic politician or whether a theoretical revision will follow.

Last, for the ideas discussed in this book, it is not the intention of the author to decide whether they were ultimately true or false. This is chiefly the task of

Reference Matter

Notes

Chapter 1

1. Arndt, *Economic Development: The History of an Idea* (1987). A recent history and critique of early development theory from a postmodernist perspective is found in Escobar (1995), chap. 3.

2. If this definition seems too broad, compare that of Hollis Chenery: "The structuralist approach to development attempts to identify specific rigidities, lags, and other characteristics of the structure of developing economies that affect economic adjustments and the choice of development policy." Chenery (1975), p. 310. For H. W. Arndt, structuralism originates in "the doctrine of market failure." Arndt, "Origins" (1985), p. 151. A more restricted definition of structuralism, associated with the work of Raúl Prebisch, is found in the footnote on p. 12.

3. In fact, neoclassical theory could be adopted to "special circumstances" more readily than some of its critics were ready to concede, as the concept of backward-sloping labor supply curves illustrates. But the theory as a whole applies only to economies in which markets clear, equilibria are attainable, relatively full employment of factors is possible, and so on.

4. See Knight (1930).

5. Arndt, "Economic Development" (1981), p. 465. Melvin Knight had also used the term "backward" to refer to human populations as well as regions: "From an economic standpoint a backward people might be defined as one which makes ineffective use of its resources." "Backward Countries" (1980), p. 380.

6. See Arndt, "Economic Development" on the evolution of the meaning of the term and, on euphemisms, Myrdal (1970), pp. 35–36. Charles Kindleberger used the term "underdeveloped countries," apparently in the postwar sense, in "Planning" (1943), p. 350.

7. In the broad sense used here, not in the Althusserian sense.

8. The best known of these debates took place in the developed world—between Maurice Dobb and Paul Sweezy. See Dobb, *Studies in the History of Capitalism* (1963 [1947]), and Hilton, ed., *Transition from Feudalism to Capitalism* (1976), containing Sweezy's essay of 1950, Dobb's reply, a further exchange, and the comments of other Marxist scholars.

One should note that such a debate, if usually only implicit, was present in non-Marxist discourses as well. Like Adam Smith, Karl Polanyi in *The Great Transformation* (1957 [1944]) stressed the importance of the market in the creation of the modern world economy, whereas David Landes in *Unbound Prometheus* (1969) stressed changes in the technology and organization of production. Both dimensions were essential, and as early as 1928, Allyn Young had altered Smith's famous dictum that the division of labor is limited by the extent of the market, to point out that "the extent of the market also depends upon the division of labor," thereby emphasizing the role of capital in economic development. Young, p. 539.

9. From these brief remarks it may be noted that the relevant Marxist tradition was that of historical materialism and not that of formal Marxist economics, which had little influence in the cases examined in this work.

10. Szlajfer (1990), pp. 1, 2.

11. These historians are Franciszek Bujak, Ludwik Landau, Marian Malowist, and Witold Kula. Ibid., pp. 4, 5.

12. Szlajfer notes that Kemmerer dispensed financial advice in Poland and five Andean countries, while Sachs directed missions to Argentina, Bolivia, and Poland (ibid., p. 4). Niemeyer's work as foreign adviser included trips to Argentina, Brazil, and Rumania.

13. On the history of the term and concept of a "Third World," see Love (1980).

14. For Ignacy Sachs, the early appearance of theorizing on underdevelopment in East Central Europe between the wars merits a systematic analysis of the work in the several national contexts; he mentions specifically Poland, Hungary, and Rumania. See his *Découverte* (1971), p. 133. In a phone conversation in June 1994, he remarked to me that the project was still to be undertaken.

15. East Central Europe, like other world regions, is not uniformly defined in the literature, as exemplified by the fact that Berend and Ranki define its boundaries differently in *Economic Development* (1974) and *East Central Europe* (1977). My definition includes the three new Baltic nations—Estonia, Latvia, and Lithuania—plus Poland, Hungary, Rumania, Yugoslavia, Bulgaria, Albania, and Greece. I exclude relatively industrialized Austria and Czechoslovakia. "The Balkans" in this work refers to a subset of East Central European countries, namely, those of the Balkan Peninsula—Rumania, Bulgaria, Greece, Yugoslavia, and Albania. "Eastern Europe," used in Chapter 2 in the discussion of populism, includes Russia.

16. Rosenstein-Rodan, "Problems" (1958 [1943]); Rosenstein-Rodan, "International Development" (1944); and Mandelbaum, *Industrialisation* (1945); [Political and Economic Planning], *Economic Development* (1945). The Economic Research Group of Political and Economic Planning was established in 1941.

17. Mandelbaum, "Portrait" (1979), p. 510; Rosenstein-Rodan, "Natura" (1984), p. 207; Rosenstein-Rodan to author, Boston, 13 May 1981.

18. In addition, two non-native authorities on backwardness in interwar East Central Europe later became students of the Third World proper: the economist Doreen Warriner and the economic demographer Wilbert Moore.

19. Schumpeter, *Theory* (1934 [Ger. orig. 1912]).

20. Ibid., p. xi.

21. Schumpeter claims to have worked out his ideas for the book in 1909, his first year in Czernowitz. Ibid., p. ix.

22. The Brazilian economist Celso Furtado (see Chapter 10) has pointed out that Nurkse reversed Schumpeter's "circular flow" to posit an "automatic stagnation" in the economies of underdeveloped countries. Furtado, "Capital Formation" (1953 [Port. orig. 1952]), p. 127.

23. Johnson, "Ideology" (1967), pp. 131 (quotation), 132.

24. See Chapter 12 on the relationship between structuralism and dependency.

25. Both Rumania and Brazil were territorial states whose leaders strove to create nation-states. The problem was more formidable in Rumania, where ethnic minorities were proportionally larger, economically more important, and perhaps less willing to be assimilated.

26. I refer to the impact of Mihail Manoilescu's work (see below). Again, Chile, where Manoilescu's work was also published, was a close second in this regard.

27. One might further speculate that Rumania and Brazil's former metropolis, Portugal, shared formative experiences as Christian nations on a Muslim frontier and that Muslim institutions, attitudes, and patterns of behavior that had once prevailed in those countries at the level of the state had long-term consequences that were inimical to modernization. Nevertheless, the Rumanian principalities formally retained an internal autonomy under the Ottoman Empire, at the price of heavy tax burdens and a sharp reduction of actual self-government in the eighteenth century.

28. Stahl, *Traditional Romanian Village Communities* (1980 [Fr. orig. 1969]), pp. 216–20.

29. Mouzelis (1986), p. xiii. For the other Iberian Empire, in 1854 Marx and Engels had compared Spain to Turkey, denying that either country had ever known absolutism in the European sense. "Spain, like Turkey, continued being an agglomeration of badly administered republics with a nominal sovereign above them." *Revolución* (N.d. [Eng. orig. 1854]), p. 12.

30. "Essentially [or eminently] agricultural": e.g., see Soutzo (1840), p. 78; Ion Ionescu de la Brad, quoted in Demetrescu, p. 268; Dobrogeanu-Gherea, *Neoiobăgia* (1977 [1910]), p. 99. Also note the title of Constantinescu's *Critica teoriei "România—țara eminamente agricolă"* [The critique of the theory of "Rumania—the eminently agricultural country"] (1973), a review and refutation of the nineteenth- and twentieth-century literature asserting that the country had an agricultural vocation. In Brazil Luís Vieira Souto denied, with no great success, that Brazil was "essentially agricultural" in 1904. See his "Apresentação" (1977), p. 54. As late as 1947, Brazil's minister of finance referred to his country as "essentially agrarian"—an exaggeration by that time—and recommended that it continue to specialize in agricultural exports. Skidmore (1967), p. 70.

31. See the comparison between Russian boyars and the Brazilian titled elite in Uricoechea (1980), p. 25. The Rumanian *boieri* relied on serfdom (de jure or de facto) in agriculture, whereas the Brazilian land-based titled elite and Russian boyars both relied on slavery (ibid., p. 25). The *boier* stratum in Rumania probably had its origins in a service nobility, and the term *boier* became a synonym for "large landowner" in popular language.

32. As well as chattel slavery for Gypsies in Rumania until 1851. The personal service associated with serfdom was legally abolished in the mid-eighteenth century in Wallachia and Moldavia, which were brought together as Rumania in 1859. Dues and labor services of peasants to their lords were abolished only in 1864. Yet even after that, the peasantry remained economically dependent on landlords or leaseholders, and corvée requirements actually increased in the late nineteenth and early twentieth centuries. Residual aspects of

serfdom even survived until the Communist-directed land reform after World War II (see Chapter 3).

33. Probably originally applied to formal, rather than substantive, efforts by the Brazilian government to meet its treaty obligations to the British to abolish the international slave trade after 1830.

34. An expression associated with Titu Maiorescu and the Junimea movement. See Chapter 3.

35. Marc (1890), p. 440; Racovski, *Roumanie* (1909), p. 1.

36. Prado, *Evolução* (1969 [1933]), p. 52. As Maurice Dobb has pointed out, slavery and wage labor regimes in theory shared a feature which serfdom lacked—the separation of the worker from the means of production; but only wage labor was based on contracts freely entered into. Dobb, p. 35.

37. Marcu, "Dezvoltarea" (1970), p. 161; Racovski, *Roumanie* (1909), pp. 10–11.

38. Mouzelis, pp. 3–4, 72.

39. Marc (1890), p. 439; Graf ([1927?]), p. 132.

40. Douglass North even calls this transformation the "Second *Economic* Revolution," comparable to the first, the Agricultural Revolution of 10,000 years ago; this, because of the enormous productivity gains and sharp upward thrust of the "supply curve of new knowledge." North (1981), chap. 13 (quotation on p. 172).

41. Walicki (1969).

42. Maier (1975), p. 567.

43. Steven Topik contrasts the interventionism of Brazil's government in the Old Republic (1889–1930) with the relatively laissez-faire posture of Porfirio Díaz's dictatorial regime in Mexico, usually viewed as a "strong state." Topik (1988).

44. See Hartz (1964), esp. pp. 3–6.

45. This was only an enabling condition, however, as the orthodoxy of other UN regional economic agencies in Asia and Africa, ECAFE and ECA, illustrated in their early years.

46. E.g., the Chilean Aníbal Pinto, one of the leading theorists at ECLA, offered a course on structuralist economics while directing the ECLA office in Rio de Janeiro from 1962 to 1965. Furthermore, his text on structuralism written with Carlos Fredes, another Chilean, was published in Portuguese, as was another structuralist economic primer, this one also widely used in a Spanish edition, by the Brazilians Antônio Barros de Castro and Carlos Francisco Lessa. See Pinto and Fredes (1970 [1st Sp. ed. 1962]); Castro and Lessa (11th ed., 1973 [1st Port. ed. 1967]).

47. See Chapter 9 for an extension of these considerations.

48. See Clark, *Conditions* (2d ed., 1951). Clark defines the "international unit" for comparing purchasing power among countries as "the quantity of commodities exchangeable for $1 in the USA over the average of the period 1925–1934" (p. 19).

49. See Morris (1979), including an extensive explanation and defense of weighting and other techniques employed; and Todaro (1985), pp. 102–5 (a brief description and critique of Morris's index).

50. Clark, *Conditions*, pp. 46–47, 158–59. The 1913 figure includes territories annexed by Rumania in 1919 and is therefore comparable to later figures. The Old Kingdom alone had a real per capita product of 400 in 1913 (p. 159). Clark provides no interwar estimates for Rumania after 1929.

51. The apparent losses in production associated with the agrarian reform were to some degree a transfer of income to the nonmonetized (and unmeasured) subsistence sector, rather than a real loss of efficiency in agriculture.

52. In 1982 Rumania's national product per inhabitant was estimated at $2,560 and Brazil's at $2,240. The U.S. figure was $13,160, so the relationship of Rumanian to U.S. product per capita was roughly the same 1-to-6 ratio as Clark indicated in product per worker for 1929. Data in Todaro, pp. 54, 58. However, a recent study of Rumanian economic growth views data from the early 1980s as exaggerated. Economist Intelligence Unit (1994), p. 18.

53. In 1982 Rumania's PQLI was 91 and Brazil's only 72, so the spread was relatively greater than that in per capita income at the time (see preceding note). The U.S. registered 96, while Iceland and Sweden led the world at 98. Todaro, pp. 54, 58.

54. The service sector is a residual, however, and includes persons in the "informal sector"—street hawkers, bootblacks, ticket collectors, and the like, who may be underemployed, if their product is measured at all.

55. Data in this and the following two paragraphs are found in, or derived from, Merrick and Graham (1979), p. 162, and Mitchell (1975), p. 160. Workers in commerce, finance, transport, and communications were grouped in the service sector. Another source for Brazil—Brazil: IBGE, *Estatísticas* (1990), p. 75—shows higher percentages of the work force in industry in 1940 and later than do Merrick and Graham. By the IBGE source, in 1950 Brazil had reached the share in industry attained by Rumania in 1956.

56. Statistics in this paragraph are from Merrick and Graham, p. 327; Ludwig, p. 57; Şandru (1980), p. 107; Lampe and Jackson (1982), p. 334. Both the Rumanian and Brazilian definitions of "urban" depended on administrative criteria.

57. Figures refer to Gross Domestic Product rather than Gross National Product in both countries.

58. Lethbridge (1985), 1: 536.

59. Industry's share in national income in Brazil for 1939 (including mining, utilities, and construction) was estimated by Cláudio Haddad at 22 percent. He makes no mention of handicrafts, but some of his "industries" implicitly include small shops. See Haddad (1974), p. 14 and the Appendix.

A comparison of shares of GDP and shares of national income is legitimate because both are measures of the same set of goods and services, one from the side of expenditures or consumption (GDP) and the other from the side of income generation (national income).

60. Lethbridge, pp. 592–93; Brazil: IBGE, *Estatísticas*, p. 125. For a single year, 1949, Haddad (p. 14) shows industry as providing a larger share of product than agriculture (27 and 22 percent, respectively).

61. Lethbridge, p. 595; Haddad, p. 14.

62. Jackson (1986), p. 78.

63. See data in Brazil: DGE (1927), 5: 6–12, 48–59, 72–87; Rumania: Ministerul de Industrie şi Comerţ (1921), pp. 28–31, 116.

64. That is, using the nearest data interval in the Brazilian census to the Rumanian definition.

65. For data, see Rumania: Zentralinstitut (1942), p. 99; Brazil: IBGE, *Recenseamento* (1950 [1940]), 3: 170–71.

66. Madgearu, *Evoluția* (1940), pp. 256–57; Merrick and Graham, pp. 18–19.
67. Ludwig, pp. 317–18.
68. Roberts (1969), p. 380.
69. Ludwig, pp. 323–26; Berend and Ranki, *Economic Development*, pp. 149, 281–82.
70. See Merton (1961), esp. p. 477.

71. In choosing which writers to consider, I faced some "boundary" issues of chronology and nationality. Though I cite his work, I have excluded consideration of the émigré Nicholas Georgescu-Roegen—the best-known Rumanian economist of the postwar period—whose major contributions lie outside the period under study. Most of his research in any event did not deal with development issues. Likewise, I have omitted individuals who were born in Rumania but made their intellectual lives elsewhere, such as Carl Grünberg, an early contributor to Austro-Marxism and the first director of the Frankfurt Institute of Social Research, and Lucien Goldmann, the philosopher and critic. Neither was principally a student of the type of problems considered here. On the Brazilian side, I exclude Ignacy Sachs and Michael Lowy. Both received university degrees in Brazil but made their careers in Europe. As with Georgescu-Roegen, I cite their studies.

72. "Ideology" in this study is a set of propositions which implicitly justifies social values or social configurations. Though many economic theorists have argued that the scientific project of economic analysis can be successfully separated from ideology, Ronald Meek is persuasively skeptical. See his *Economics and Ideology* (1967), esp. pp. 196–224.

73. See Kuhn (1970 [1962]); Blaug (1980).

Chapter 2

1. Transylvania, the third major region of contemporary Rumania, remained under Hapsburg rule until the end of World War I.

2. E.g., in the work of Alexandru Moruzi. See Demetrescu ([1940]), pp. 264–68.

3. Stahl, *Traditional Romanian Village Communities* (1980 [Fr. orig. 1969]), pp. 29–30.

4. Pătrășcanu, "Curs" (mimeo., 1947), p. 192.

5. Demetrescu, pp. 270, 274 (quotation). The Paris peace conference of 1856, ending the Crimean War, had begun the process of uniting the two principalities.

6. Named for the Greek district of Phanar in Constantinople, whence the overlords originated.

7. Berend and Ranki, *European Periphery* (1982), p. 42. Such lands were distributed to peasants under the agrarian reform of 1864.

8. Stahl, *Traditional Romanian Village Communities*, p. 83. Meanwhile, in 1830 *boieri* had become hereditary nobles under the Organic Regulation, but this legal status was to last only until the Convention of Paris in 1858. The Rumanian constitution of 1866 reaffirmed the abolition of their special legal standing and privileges.

9. According to Marcu (1979), p. 148, 3.8 million hectares went to the *boier* group and 3.1 million were retained by the peasants.

10. Ibid., p. 149.

11. Marcu and Puia (1979), p. 264.

12. Murgescu, *Mersul* (1987), p. 272–76; Chirot, *Social Change* (1976), pp. 94–103.

13. Murgescu, *Mersul*, p. 277; Soutzo (1840), p. 78.

14. Soutzo (1840), p. 122, cites Ricardo. Ricardo had demonstrated that, given two

countries and two goods, it was to the advantage of both countries to specialize in the production of one good and trade for the other, even if one country produced *both* goods more efficiently (i.e., at lower cost) than the other. (For a more rigorous exposition of the thesis, see Chapter 8.)

15. Constantinescu (1973), pp. 53–57; Academia Republicii (1960), pp. 227–28.

16. Dobrogeanu-Gherea, "Ce vor" (1976 [1886]), pp. 101–2.

17. Demetrescu, p. 270.

18. Cf. the importance of Smith in Brazil in works published by the future Visconde de Cairu in 1809 and 1811, as noted in Rocha (1989), pp. 55–56.

19. The phrase, which he applies in a Latin American context, is Tulio Halperín's. Personal communication.

20. Lampe and Jackson (1982), p. 265.

21. Zeletin, *Burghezia* (1925), p. 95. See also Ercuţă (1941), p. 46.

22. See List ([Ger. orig. 1841]).

23. Jackson (1986), p. 61. Cf. John Montias's opinion that "there can be little doubt . . . that the 1886 tariff stimulated the growth of domestic industry." Montias (1978), p. 63, n. 26.

24. Relatively inefficient compared to "overseas" grain exporters, Rumania could not compete in the British market with Argentina and the Dominions, but it could still sell grain on the Continent.

25. Berend and Ranki, *European Periphery*, pp. 83, 115, 123, 156. The authors define the Periphery as countries in Eastern Europe, Scandinavia, and the Mediterranean region (excluding France), all of which were relatively backward at the beginning of the period.

26. "Populism," defined below, is used in the European or "Russian," and not in the Latin American, sense; the latter primarily refers to urban mass politics, in which the inchoate proletariat is manipulated by "developmentalist," often demagogic, politicians from traditional ruling sectors.

27. With the controversial exception of an appearance in the 1970s.

28. On the penetration of capitalism, see Racovski, "Poporanism" (1908), p. 331 ("vortex"); and Stere, "Fischerland" (1976 [1909]), pp. 365–66. A decade earlier, Lenin had referred to precapitalist economies as being drawn into "the whirlpool of the world economy." *Development* (2d ed., 1956 [Russ. orig. 1899]), p. 652. On the exploitation of peasants, see Racovski, *Roumanie* (1909), pp. 17, 60; Stere, "Fischerland," pp. 369–70.

29. Racovski, *Roumanie*, pp. 8–9. Stere, "Ţara" (1979 [1906]), pp. 379, 387; "Fischerland," p. 369.

30. Racovski wrote that rents doubled on 70 percent of the lands where cereal crops were grown in Rumania between 1870 and 1907 and rose four times on 6 percent of these properties (*Roumanie*, p. 170). A new form of calculating corvée requirements substantially increased the number of days per year the peasant owed to the lord, rising under the Organic Regulation to about 56 days per year at mid-century. De facto corvée requirements continued to mount after corvée's formal abolition. Chirot, *Social Change*, pp. 97, 133.

31. See Kitching (1982).

32. The Verein für Sozialpolitik, many of whose members would be influential in Rumania, was concerned with this problem. See Chapter 7.

33. On Herzen, see Venturi (1960 [Ital. orig. 1952]), chap. 1.

34. The Junimea, which might be construed as a "nativist" movement, was based on an interpretation of Hegel, not a reaction to his philosophy. See Chapter 3.

35. Gerschenkron, "Economic Development" (1966), p. 190; Walicki (1969), p. 132.

36. Not to be confused with the Rumanian region Moldavia, as used in this study.

37. The issue of reform vs. revolution was not inescapably posed until the October Revolution, when Cristian Racovski joined the Bolsheviks and Constantine Dobrogeanu-Gherea remained a reformist. See below on Racovski.

38. There were communal properties in Rumanian agriculture, but most peasant communes were divided up after the agrarian reform of 1864; some, despite government intentions, still remained communal. Stahl, *Traditional Romanian Village Communities* (1980 [Fr. orig. 1969]), pp. 85, 90.

39. For biographical data in this paragraph, see entries on Stere in Diamandi ([1936?]), pp. 212–22; *Minerva* (1930), p. 893; "Stere, Constantin," *Dicţionar enciclopedic romîn* (1962), 4: 508.

40. Hurezeanu, "Revue" (1986), pp. 331, 337.

41. Roberts (1951), p. 153; interview with H. H. Stahl, Bucharest, 28 October 1981 (on Stere's charisma).

42. "Poporanism," *Dicţionar enciclopedic romîn*, 3: 823–24.

43. Stere, "Ţara," p. 379.

44. Ibid., 387. But in "Fischerland" Stere says it controlled 90,000 ha. (pp. 365–66).

45. Stere, "Fischerland," pp. 369, 371.

46. Stere, "Causele" (1907), p. 435; "Mizeria" (1908), p. 464.

47. Stere, "Mizeria," pp. 454–55, 459.

48. Stere, "Fischerland," p. 371. Stere relied on data furnished by the Chamber of Commerce of Botoşani in 1906, and it was in Botoşani county that the peasant uprising began in February 1907.

49. Hurezeanu, "Revue," p. 337.

50. Twenty percent of the factories in this group had fewer than ten workers. Stere, "Socialdemocratism" (1907–8), 2, no. 9: 320–21.

51. Ibid.

52. Ibid., p. 323.

53. See note 23 for evidence to the contrary.

54. Stere, "Socialdemocratism," 2, no. 10: 32.

55. Ibid., pp. 17–19. On the necessity of foreign markets, Stere cites Gherea, "Din ideile," pp. 21–23, in ibid., p. 19.

56. Ibid., pp. 25–27. "Rumania . . . cannot find a path between peasant upheaval and voting at the command of Domnul Subprefect" (p. 26).

57. Ibid., pp. 30–31.

58. Ibid., p. 31.

59. For example, on the estates he called Fischerland. See "Fischerland," pp. 366, 370.

60. Stere, "Socialdemocratism," 2, no. 11: 199, 202; 3, no. 1: 69–70 (quotation). Jews could not own land and were not full citizens until after World War I.

61. See note 72.

62. Stere, "Socialdemocratism," 2, no. 8: 188–89; 2, no. 9: 313; 3, no. 1: 72–73. Stere did not mention, however, that Kautsky remained an orthodox Marxist and showed in *Die*

Agrarfrage (The agrarian question, 1899) how capitalism had revolutionized agriculture, albeit in more complex ways than industry. See Chapter 4.

63. Stere, "Socialdemocratism," 3, no. 4: 60, 62, 63, 68.

64. Ibid., 2, no. 10: 15, 36. Cf. the opinion of Garabet Ibrăileanu in *Viaţa Românească* in 1906: If socialism had a future in Rumania, it was only because it would triumph first in the West, permitting Rumania to avoid or skip (*ocoli*) capitalism. Until then, it was necessary to fight for the interests of the vast majority, the peasantry. Thus a populist gave a surprising twist to Gherea's argument on the West's determining role (see Chapter 3). Ibrăileanu (1906), p. 138.

65. Stere, "Socialdemocratism," 2, no. 9: 330; 3, no. 4: 61.

66. Ornea, *Poporanismul* (1972), p. 512; Stere, "Socialdemocratism," 2, no. 9: 338; Lenin, *Development*, pp. 174, 182.

67. Racovski, "Autobiography," and Haupt, afternote, in Haupt and Marie, eds. (1974), pp. 385–403, passim; Iacoş (1977), pp. 5–6, 10–12.

68. Racovski, "Poporanism."   69. Ibid., p. 340.

70. Ibid., p. 336.   71. Ibid., p. 339.

72. Ibid., p. 331. It is notable that Stere, like Racovski, nevertheless had a vision of "proletarian nations": from 1903, he divided the world into "exploiting" and "exploited" states" with regard to their places in the international capitalist order. Rozorea (1970), p. 193. See Chapter 5 for the same notion in M. Manoilescu.

73. Racovski, "Poporanism," p. 332.

74. Ibid., pp. 333–34. That same point had been made without the benefit of Sombart's researches by Panait Muşoiu in 1892. See Stoica (1972), p. 6.

75. Racovski, "Poporanism," pp. 337–38, 350.

76. Stere, "Socialdemocratism," 2, no. 10: 17–18, 32, 36; Racovski, "Poporanism," pp. 355–56.

77. Racovski, "Poporanism," p. 363. Racovski was not entirely accurate on this point. Rumania did have a communal property tradition, but communes had become vestigial in the decades after 1864. Stahl, *Traditional Romanian Village Communities*, p. 85.

78. For a survey of other Rumanian ideologies of development of the latter nineteenth century, see Hitchins (1994), chap. 2.

Chapter 3

1. Lenin, *Development* (1956 [1899]), pp. 151, 172–74, 182, 250, 347, 555.

2. Hurezeanu, *Constantin Dobrogeanu-Gherea* (1973), p. 11; "Dobrogeanu-Gherea, Constantin" (1972), pp. 588–93.

3. Hurezeanu, *Constantin Dobrogeanu-Gherea*, pp. 1–17.

4. Ibid., pp. 26–27, 37–42.

5. Ibid., pp. 46, 50; "Gherea (Dobrogeanu-Gherea), Constantin" (1964), p. 548.

6. Dobrogeanu-Gherea, "Karl Marx" (1976 [1884]), pp. 40–164; and "Ce vor" (1976 [1886]). In *Neoiobăgia* (1977 [1910]), p. 175, Gherea admitted the influence of Russian populism when writing *What the Rumanian Socialists Want*.

7. Dobrogeanu-Gherea, "Ce vor," pp. 63–64.

8. Ibid., pp. 75, 101–2.

9. Ibid., pp. 101–2.

10. Ibid., pp. 104–7.

11. Dobrogeanu-Gherea, "Rolul" (1976 [1892]), pp. 431–32.

12. Ibid., p. 432. In this formulation Gherea came close to the transmogrification of social classes into bourgeois and proletarian nations, a proposition later advanced by Mihail Manoilescu, who in the 1930s called for a "socialism of nations" to replace the "socialism of classes." See Chapter 5.

13. Ibid., p. 433.

14. Dobrogeanu-Gherea, "Mic răspuns" (1977 [1908]), pp. 456, 458–60. This was also a response to Garabet Ibrăileanu's review of his "Din ideile" in 1906.

15. Dobrogeanu-Gherea, "Post-scriptum," pp. 498–99, 503.

16. Dobrogeanu-Gherea, *Socialismul* (1945 [1912]), pp. 8–9.

17. Ibid., p. 9. An excellent introduction to Gherea's thesis is Stahl, "Théories" (1978).

18. Dobrogeanu-Gherea, *Socialismul*, pp. 10, 17. Cf. Racovski's similar view in Chapter 2.

19. Meisner (1967), p. 144.

20. Dobrogeanu-Gherea, *Socialismul*, p. 10.

21. Boeke, *Tropisch-Koloniale Staathuishoudkunde* [Tropical colonial economic policy] (1910). Boeke's thesis, elaborated over the next 40 years, was that workers over a certain range of wages would prefer increased leisure to higher income; i.e., that the price mechanism was not an adequate allocator of resources. For a critique of Boeke, see Chapter 4.

22. Dobrogeanu-Gherea, *Socialismul*, p. 27. This idea was first expressed by Marx regarding the Germany of the 1860s and later echoed by Lenin with respect to Russia in the 1890s. Marx, *Capital* (1961 [Ger. orig. 1867]), p. 9; Lenin, *Development*, p. 659.

23. Dobrogeanu-Gherea, *Socialismul*, pp. 34–35.

24. Ibid., p. 35. This contention is not wholly consistent with the role of the *pătură cultă*.

25. Hurezeanu, *Constantin Dobrogeanu-Gherea*, pp. 172–73.

26. Unlike some of his lesser works, Gherea's *Neoiobăgia* was never translated into another language. Kautsky had wanted a German version, but the translation was never realized. Ornea, "Sociologia" (1981), p. 45.

27. Dobrogeanu-Gherea, *Neoiobăgia*, p. 64.

28. As Cristian Racovski noted in 1909, peasants had to sign formal contracts, a characteristic feature of capitalist labor relations, but these contracts contained stipulations for the payment of feudal dues such as the *dijmă* (forced payment in kind on a basis of shares). Racovski, *Roumanie* (1909), pp. 10–11.

29. Dobrogeanu-Gherea, *Neoiobăgia*, p. 281. Nicolae Stoica points out that Gherea is inconsistent in defining relations of production in *neoiobăgia*. Are they "semifeudal" (p. 68), "feudal in *fond* and bourgeois in *formă*" (no page given) or "in both *fond* and *formă* the same as before" (p. 92)? Page numbers refer to original Socec 1910 edition. See Stoica (1972), p. 119.

30. Dobrogeanu-Gherea, *Neoiobăgia*, pp. 31, 35.

31. Ibid., p. 34.   32. Ibid., pp. 35–36.

33. Ibid., pp. 33 (quotation), 38–41.   34. Ibid., p. 49.

35. Ibid., pp. 80–81.   36. Ibid., pp. 53–54.

37. Ibid., pp. 64–68, 72.

38. Ibid., p. 82. Cf. the similar analysis of Racovski in "Chestia" (1907), pp. 40–41.

39. Dobrogeanu-Gherea, *Neoiobăgia*, p. 82.

40. Ibid., pp. 91, 95. See Stahl, *Traditional Romanian Village Communities* (1980), p. 89, on the one-half share.

41. Because of de facto corvée requirements and other arrangements, by the 1880s peasants often spent two-thirds of the week on the landlord's crops. Chirot, *Social Change* (1976), p. 133.

42. Dobrogeanu-Gherea, *Neoiobăgia*, pp. 100–102.

43. Ibid., pp. 188–89.

44. Ibid., pp. 128–30 (quotation on 129).

45. Ibid., pp. 243, 253–54.

46. Ibid., p. 334. Presumably this was only physical product; services were not measured.

47. Ibid., p. 339. See below on his later views on the "oligarchy."

48. Ibid., pp. 226–31.

49. Ibid., pp. 282, 295, 308, 360.

50. Hurezeanu, *Constantin Dobrogeanu-Gherea*, p. 302.

51. Ornea, "Sociologia," pp. 54–55.

52. Compulsory universal male suffrage was first implemented under the chaotic conditions of the war-torn but greatly enlarged country of 1919, the year before Gherea died. Subsequent laws modified the original statute, but the Constitution of 1923 incorporated universal manhood suffrage. Women, however, did not win the franchise until 1946.

53. Gherea's son became a Communist and like Racovski later died in a Soviet prison camp.

54. Dobrogeanu-Gherea, "Geneza" (1920), pp. 4, 8 (quotation). This essay was written in 1914. See also his "Din urmările" (1920), stressing the parasitism of state employees and the earlier themes of maladministration, arbitrary actions, and partiality in government.

55. Had he lived two more decades, Gherea would presumably not have been surprised when public employment rolls rose from 248,000 persons in 1934 to 332,000 in 1939. Janos, "Modernization" (1978), p. 108.

56. Zeletin, *Burghezia română: Originea și rolul ei istoric* (1925).

57. Zeletin, however, was never a member of that party. Michelson (1987), p. 367.

58. Zeletin, *Burghezia*, p. 18.

59. Ibid., pp. 22–23.

60. Ibid., pp. 25–26.

61. Ibid., pp. 36–37, 45. On page 38 he says that the rapid influx of foreign goods destroyed the medieval regime. Thus Zeletin took what might currently be called a "circulationist" position.

62. Ibid., pp. 56–57.   63. Ibid., pp. 67–69.

64. Ibid., pp. 36–37, 43–45.   65. Ibid., pp. 73–75.

66. Ibid., pp. 75, 77.

67. Ibid., pp. 93–94, 104; Zeletin, "Pseudo-burghezia" (1927), pp. 119–21.

68. Zeletin, *Burghezia*, pp. 112–14, 118.   69. Ibid., p. 157.

70. Ibid., pp. 158, 165–66.   71. Ibid., p. 52.

72. Ibid., pp. 200–201, 210. In "Originea," p. 19, Zeletin says *neoiobăgia* and rural misery were "natural phenomena" at the beginning of capitalist development.

73. Zeletin, *Burghezia*, p. 241. Zeletin agreed with the socialist Racovski that populism was an exotic plant in Rumania, because, unlike Russia, Rumania had no tradition of peasant communism (pp. 237–38). In "Originea," p. 28, Zeletin argued that "peasantism," a postwar successor to populism, was analogous to physiocracy in eighteenth-century France, i.e., both were reactions against the transformations wrought by early capitalism in their respective countries.

74. Zeletin, *Burghezia*, p. 244.

75. Ibid., p. 243.

76. Zeletin, "Originea," p. 4. The term "neoliberalism," a kind of proto-corporatism, was in the air; Mihail Manoilescu had published a lecture with the same title in 1923.

77. Zeletin, *Neoliberalismul* (1927), p. 80.

78. Ibid., pp. vii–viii, 93.

79. Zeletin, "Desvoltarea," p. 56; "Pseudo-burghezia," pp. 113, 122.

80. Zeletin, "Plutocrația," p. 155. Zeletin did not want to exclude foreign investment in Rumania but to raise tariff barriers against foreign goods. Paraphrasing the National Peasant Party's slogan of "open gates" for foreign goods (as opposed to the Liberals' slogan of "[development] through our own efforts"), Zeletin offered his own formula: "Closed gates for foreign manufactures, but open [gates] for foreign capital and foreign technology [*capacități*]." *Burghezia*, p. 134.

81. Zeletin, "Acumularea," pp. 165–67.

82. Zeletin, "Naționalismul," p. 211.

83. Zeletin, "Neoliberalismul," p. 86; and "Socialism," p. 251.

84. Boeuve was the half-brother of the distinguished Marxist sociologist Henri H. Stahl, whom he introduced to Marxism. Stahl, *Amintiri*, p. 18.

85. Voinea, "Sozialismus" (1924), pp. 501–8.

86. Ibid., pp. 506–7.

87. Ibid., p. 507. Gherea had stated only that socialism as a form would precede changes in the material base. "Socialismul," p. 10.

88. Voinea, *Marxism oligarhic* (1926).

89. Ibid., pp. 66, 76. On the Zeletin-Voinea debate on development in a broader context, see Chirot, "Neoliberal and Social Democratic Theories" (1978). This exchange was a forerunner of the debate between Maurice Dobb and Paul Sweezy in the 1950s and Ernesto Laclau's critique of Andre Gunder Frank in early 1970s: all three controversies focused on the issue of production vs. circulation. See Chapter 13 for the Brazilian debate.

90. Voinea, *Marxism*, p. 28. Voinea quickly found support for his critique of Zeletin's history in the work of a young historian, Gheorghe Zane, who based his arguments on research in primary sources. For one thing, Zane argued that an exchange economy based on money existed "centuries before" Zeletin's decisive date, 1829, thus also correcting Gherea, who likewise saw a money-based economy as arising in the early nineteenth century. For another, Zane argued that English trade was less important than Greek trade in the early nineteenth century and that French commerce was then almost nonexistent. English trade was, in addition, less important than Austrian in the latter nineteenth century, contrary to Zeletin. But Zane also criticized Voinea as well as Zeletin for missing the importance of the transformation of *iobăgia*, brought about by the Organic Regulation, in increasing the number of days a peasant had to render his lord in corvée labor.

Marx himself, Zane argued, had not foreseen that money rents would be refused by the *boieri* in preference to labor payments. Further, the intensification of circulation of money did not hurt the *boieri*, as Zeletin claimed. Zeletin had greatly exaggerated the importance of the importation of foreign goods because the number of consumers was so small until the end of the nineteenth century. Zane believed the modern Rumanian state had arisen from the *iobăgie* system rather than from foreign commerce. Because Zeletin tended to ignore the importance of Turkey in the development of Rumania's institutions, as well as the parallels between Russia's and Rumania's economic and social structures, he was wrong to view the Rumanian state as a creation of the Western bourgeoisie. Zane, "Burghezia" (1927), pp. 245–51, 255–58, 325, 327, 331, 333–34. Later scholars tended to agree with Zane on most of these points and, more generally, on Zeletin's inadequate command of Rumanian history. See, for example, Michelson (1987), pp. 372–73.

91. Voinea, *Marxism*, pp. 15–16. The point was originally Gherea's.

92. Ibid., pp. 153–54. Danielson (pseud., Nicolai-On) was a correspondent of Marx and Engels and in his early intellectual career was a Marxist. He was the first person to translate *Das Kapital* into another language, and his Russian edition of volume I (Ger. ed. 1867) appeared in 1872.

93. Rădăceanu (1924).

94. Ibid., 5, nos. 3–4; 506–7, 527–28.

95. Ibid., pp. 527.

96. Ibid., pp. 529–31; 6, nos. 1–2: 179.

97. Ibid., p. 173.

98. See below for Pătrășcanu's analysis of the dictatorship. The Social Democrats also denied, for the first time, that the state was the instrument of a single social class. Roberts, p. 249.

99. Ibid.

100. His reputation was posthumously rehabilitated by the Central Committee of the Rumanian Communist party in 1968.

101. The dissertation, "Reforma agrară," was translated and published posthumously in 1978. It is interesting that in this study Pătrășcanu heartily approved of the rise of an agrarian middle class, which was developing out of the land reform. This was consistent with his later analytic work in perceiving class differentiation in the countryside but inconsistent with his political views by the latter 1920s. See "Reforma agrară," p. 112.

102. Following a similar action in Wallachia in 1746.

103. Pătrășcanu, *Veac* (2d ed., 1969 [1945), pp. 9–10.

104. Ibid., pp. 11, 14, 15.

105. Pătrășcanu, "Curs" (mimeo., 1947), p. 138 (he also implies that it circulated before the seventeenth century).

106. Ibid., pp. 139–40. The *boieri* were explicitly interested in retaining the clacă for the production of commodities. See *Veac*, p. 194.

107. Ibid., pp. 288–89.

108. Pătrășcanu, "Curs," p. 192. Citing a contemporary traveler's account for evidence, Pătrășcanu stated that two-thirds of the peasants' income was taken by the Porte. Pătrășcanu, *Veac*, p. 49. Other writers have tended to agree with Pătrășcanu's harsh judgment of the Phanariot regime. Jelavich implies that turning the Rumanian principalities over to the Phanariots virtually converted the country into a colony; the sultan sold the title of prince to the highest bidder, who was expected to extract enormous sums in levies for the Porte while amassing a fortune for himself. Jelavich (1983), p. 103.

109. Pătrășcanu, *Veac*, pp. 280, 284.

110. Ibid., p. 286.

111. Cf. Eidelberg (1974), pp. 230–31, who cites 1875, the year of the crash of the international grain market (an event followed by the rise of an alternative path to development in the form of industrialization), as the decisive date for the beginning of peasant misery that led to the uprising of 1907.

112. Pătrășcanu, "Curs," p. 205.

113. Pătrășcanu, *Veac*, p. 287. Cf. the postwar acceptance of Pătrășcanu's position by Marxist economic historians, e.g., Marcu (1979), p. 155.

114. Pătrășcanu, *Veac*, pp. 293–95.   115. Ibid., p. 304.

116. Ibid., p. 296.   117. Ibid., p. 298.

118. Ibid., pp. 304–5.   119. Ibid., pp. 305, 317–18.

120. Ibid., p. 279.   121. Ibid., p. 325.

122. Ibid., p. 335. The international bourgeoisie was divided, according to Pătrășcanu. The German and Austrian sectors were interested in expanding the Rumanian market, but their French and British counterparts were largely interested in obtaining Rumanian grain supplies, which resulted in their alliance with large property owners. Ibid., p. 336.

123. Ibid., pp. 338–39.

124. Ibid., p. 339. Pătrășcanu had argued that in 1848 the Rumanian bourgeoisie was progressive, though not revolutionary, because it could not solve the question of the *iobag* peasant. Ibid., p. 200.

125. Nonetheless, Zeletin was the first to note, and Pătrășcanu agreed with him, that "1907 had been provoked not only by the pressures of pre-industrial capitalism, but by incipient sheltered industrialization as well." But Pătrășcanu did not agree with Zeletin's contention that this was done "in an effort to further undermine the big landlord, the main opponent of industrialization." Eidelberg, p. 7.

126. A policy in fact adopted by the Groza government in 1945.

127. Pătrășcanu, *Problemele* (1947 [1944]), pp. 292–93. In 1944 Pătrășcanu did not believe that conditions existed for socialist transformation because of the small size of the Rumanian proletariat (p. 294). After the war, Pătrășcanu wrote that the land reform of 1945 had destroyed the "feudal remains" in Rumanian agriculture, giving land to 800,000 peasants. "Curs," pp. 220–21.

128. Pătrășcanu, *Problemele*, p. 7.

129. Madgearu, *Evoluția economiei românești după războiul mondial*.

130. Pătrășcanu, *Problemele*, p. 26. Only capitalism has wage labor as a "general phenomenon," Pătrășcanu wrote in his "Curs" (p. 168).

131. Pătrășcanu, "Curs," p. 205.

132. Pătrășcanu, *Problemele*, p. 79. In "Curs," he wrote that the land reform of 1918 left one-fourth of the land in the form of large properties (p. 205).

133. Pătrășcanu, *Problemele*, p. 80. The sociologist Henri Stahl confirmed this in 1945 when he observed a corvée contract situation, despite a 1910 law prohibiting it. *Traditional Romanian Village Communities* (1980 [Fr. orig. 1969]), p. 91.

134. Pătrășcanu, *Problemele*, pp. 84–86. This was a misuse of Cresin's findings, as Henry Roberts pointed out in his classic study, *Rumania* (1951). Cresin had estimated that 40 percent of middle and large properties used wage labor. Pătrășcanu "took this figure of 40 per cent of paid agricultural laborers, equated it with the fact that 40 per cent of the

arable land in Rumania in 1930 was in holdings over 10 hectares, and gave the quite unjustified impression that in effect agricultural laborers were responsible for the cultivation of all land over 10 hectares." Roberts, p. 291, n. 36. However, in the only detailed county study of the 1941 agricultural census—published in 1945 and therefore not available to Pătrăşcanu—Cresin noted that 39 percent of the individually owned farms by area used some amount of hired labor. He also noted that the county in question, Argeş, was representative of Rumania's varieties of soil and methods of exploitation. Cresin, *Agricultura* (1945), pp. 11, 16. For the country as a whole, Cresin estimated in an unpublished study that 13 percent of all agricultural units in the country used hired labor, but that this group accounted for approximately 35 percent of the total cultivated area. Cresin, "Forms," MS. (n.d.), p. 8. These considerations may be summarized by saying that although Pătrăşcanu misused his data, the thrust of his argument may not have been as wide of the mark as Roberts suggested.

135. Pătrăşcanu, *Problemele*, p. 88, citing Sombart, *Apogée* (1932 [Ger. orig. 1928]), 1: 327.

136. Pătrăşcanu, *Problemele*, pp. 88, 89.   137. Ibid., pp. 91–92.

138. Ibid., p. 98.   139. Ibid., pp. 99–100.

140. See Chapter 4.   141. Pătrăşcanu, *Problemele*, p. 101.

142. Ibid., p. 103.   143. Ibid., p. 110.

144. Ibid., pp. 111–12. Pătrăşcanu's views on the domination of finance capital were greatly influenced by Rudolf Hilferding's *Finanzkapital* (1910), on which Lenin had also drawn heavily in writing his tract, *Imperialism* (1916).

145. Pătrăşcanu, *Problemele*, p. 114.

146. Ibid., p. 237. Cf. the similar opinion of Roberts (p. 157), based on data in Golopenţia and Georgescu, eds., *60 sate* (1941–43), 5 vols.

147. Pătrăşcanu, *Problemele*, pp. 279–81.

148. Ibid., p. 282.

149. Ibid., pp. 266, 273. This fact had been noted early in the century by both Karl Kautsky and Max Weber. See Kautsky, *Social Revolution* (1903 [Ger. orig. 1902]), p. 29; Weber, "Politics" (1958 [Ger. orig. 1919]), pp. 85–87.

150. Pătrăşcanu, *Problemele*, pp. 276–78.   151. Ibid., p. 24.

152. Ibid., pp. 34, 37.   153. Ibid., p. 38.

154. Ibid., pp. 40–43, 50, 55. In 1928 Pătrăşcanu had made a study of Rumanian banks, employing methods of Hilferding's *Finanzkapital*, and concluded that post-1918 trends in state policy (in Rumania as elsewhere in Europe) had accelerated the process that the Austrian Marxist had identified—the domination of industry by banks in the imperialist phase of capitalist development. Rumanian banks appropriated an increasingly large share of national income, wrote Pătrăşcanu. Three banks, the Bancă Românească, the Bancă Marmorosch-Blank, and the Bancă de Credit Român, controlled many industrial firms, and Pătrăşcanu demonstrated that large Rumanian banks had especially high profit rates, compared to English and German banks. Furthermore, Rumanian banks' profits were superior to those in industry. Pătrăşcanu, "Băncile" (1975 [1928]), pp. 103, 105, 108, 116, 118, 132–33, 135.

155. Pătrăşcanu, *Problemele*, p. 30.

156. Ibid., p. 33.

157. Ibid., pp. 282–86.

158. Pătrăşcanu, *Sub trei dictaturi* (1970 [1944]), pp. 24–25, 35.

159. Ibid., p. 26.   160. Ibid., pp. 28, 30–31.

161. Ibid., pp. 30–31.

162. Pătrăşcanu cites a report to the Banca Naţională. Ibid., p. 35.

163. Ibid., p. 36.   164. Ibid., pp. 37–38.

165. Pătrăşcanu, *Problemele*, p. 14.   166. Ibid., pp. 60–61.

167. Madgearu, *Evoluţia* (1940), p. 361.

168. Pătrăşcanu, *Problemele*, pp. 24, 27–28, 64.

Chapter 4

1. Lupu (1967), p. 98.

2. Sollohub (1932), pp. 590–92. In the next two years the law on agricultural debt was changed several times, but the peasants remained destitute.

3. Boeke, *Economics* (1953). This work combines two earlier studies written in 1942 and 1946. Furnivall (1944), defines "plural society" as "a society . . . comprising two or more elements or social orders which live side by side, yet without mingling, in one political unit" (p. 446). Boeke himself used the phrase "segmented society" in "Dualistic Economics" (1966 [1930]), p. 170. On the modern sociological use of the idea, see Van den Berghe (2d ed., 1978), pp. 34–36.

4. The fact that Boeke's basic idea could be expressed in neoclassical terms did not imply that his views were compatible with "mainstream" economics.

5. At a theoretical level, the Rumanian-American Georgescu-Roegen has, by implication, argued that Boeke put the wrong interpretation on peasant idleness. Georgescu holds that there is more leisure in overpopulated countries than in developed countries because there is no effective choice between more leisure and more income; the economic cost of greater leisure is zero. See his "Economic Theory" (1976 [1960]), p. 131. A similar argument is implicit in Clifford Geertz's analysis of Boeke's Java; see Geertz (1963), pp. 141–42. At an empirical level, in some non-Western cultural contexts the failure of price (wage) signals in the labor market à la Boeke has been denied. In Latin America, the market orientation of Indian peasants in the highlands of Guatemala was the central subject in Tax (1953). A more recent example concerning non-Hispanicized Pervuian peasants is Figueroa (1984), especially p. 120. On the general discrediting of Boeke's views, see H. W. Singer, "Dualism" (1970), p. 70. But on the same page Singer adds that Boeke's analysis survives to the extent that many Western concepts have had to be rethought, e.g. concerning employment. In retrospect, Boeke's scheme might be thought of a special and extreme form of structuralism or institutionalism. Finally, despite the fame of his approach, it is notable that Boeke's ideas were highly controversial in the Netherlands in the 1920s and 1930s and were not generally accepted by other Dutch economic theorists; nor did his views prevail at the level of colonial policy. See Koninklijk Institut (1961), pp. 14–15, 21, 56–57.

6. Lewis, "Economic Development" (1954). But in the Rumanian case Lampe and Jackson (1982) have denied that Bucharest in the early twentieth century could draw on an infinitely elastic rural labor supply (p. 244).

7. E.g., on late imperial Russia, see Nicolas-On (1902), pp. 445–50; Stepniak (1888), pp. 17–23; on Italy, see Gramsci (1957 [Ital. orig. 1926]), p. 41, and for a discussion of the

large literature on the *questione meridionale*, see Benenati (1982); on Spain, see Ledesma Ramos (1940), p. 186; on Uruguay, see Martínez Lamas (1930).

8. In 1914 Bucharest had a population of 350,000 persons, equaling the combined total of three other Balkan capitals—Athens, Sofia, and Belgrade. Lampe and Jackson (1982), p. 239.

9. Ionescu-Şişeşti (1940), p. 618. One of the most detailed studies of relative prices, that of Florin Manoliu for the Research Office of the Higher Economic Council, used 1929 as the base year to measure the prices of agricultural goods against those of industry in the national economy. He found that the trough occurred in 1936, when primary goods would buy barely more than half of the amount of industrial goods they had commanded in 1929. Manoliu, *Politica* (1939), p. 9. Looking at the problem as one of (mostly industrial) imports vs. (largely agricultural) exports, the Rumanian Business Cycles Institute estimated that though it took 5.4 to 6.6 tons of exports to purchase 1 ton of imports in the years 1922–29, a ratio that rose to 14.8 to 1 by 1932. Institutul Românesc de Conjunctură ([1933?]), p. 122. Furthermore, the agricultural economist Roman Cresin provided detailed yearly prices of all major cereals (in constant terms) for the decade 1924–33, confirming disastrous losses for farmers. Cresin, "Puterea" (1934), p. 230.

10. Seton-Watson, item enclosed in Hankey to Visc. Halifax, Bucharest, 22 July 1940, in PRO: FO R7352/475/37.

11. Ianculescu (1934), pp. 50 (quotation), 73.

12. Manuilă (1940), p. 24.

13. See Chapter 3.

14. Popa-Vereş (1938), pp. 83, 85, 98.

15. Sombart is cited earlier in Popa-Vereş's study (p. 74).

16. Popa-Vereş, pp. 101–3.

17. M. Manoilescu, *Încercări* (1938), pp. 119–21.

18. M. Manoilescu, "Sozialökonomische Struktur" (1944), pp. 1–2, 5, citing Wagemann, *Neue Balkan* (1939), p. 104, on the progression from *Eigenwirtschaft* to *Binnenwirtschaft* to *Aussenwirtschaft*.

19. Pătrăşcanu, "Reforma" (1978 [1925]), p. 97.

20. Mitrany (1930), pp. 221–22. In these calculations Mitrany classified properties up to 100 hectares as small or peasant holdings.

21. Ghiţă Ionescu distinguishes between populism and peasantism, in that the latter was a new political movement throughout East Central Europe based on the rural masses. Ionescu (1969), pp. 98–99.

22. Roberts (1951), p. 164.

23. Kautsky, *Cuestión* (1974 [Ger. orig. 1899]), pp. 5–6.

24. Ibid., pp. 80–81, 91. Ground rent in practice was complicated by the frequent coexistence of "natural," market-governed, Ricardian rent and "absolute" rent, based on monopoly ownership (p. 91).

25. Ibid., pp. 124–26, 131–33, 201. Kautsky notes that the notion of excessive peasant self-exploitation was already present in J. S. Mill (p. 124). Kautsky ascribes the phenomenon to the existence of a (capitalist) market for agriculture coupled with backward technique (p. 125).

26. Ibid., p. 186.

27. Ibid., p. 199.

28. Ibid., pp. 203–4.

29. Especially *Lehre* (1923) and "Zur Frage" (1924).

30. Thorner (1966), p. xv.

31. Chayanov, "Peasant Farm Organization" (1966 [Russ. orig. 1925]), p. 109.

32. Ibid., p. 195.

33. Millar (1970), p. 219.

34. Kochanowicz (1988), p. 30.

35. Ernst Wagemann, head of the Institut für Konjunkturforschung in Berlin and a promoter of Hitler's Grossraumwirtschaft (Greater German Economic Space), like Chayanov believed that the peasant did not include the implicit cost of his own or his family's labor in calculating his expenses; therefore, by the accounting of capitalist farmers, the peasant farm often operated at a loss. Wagemann, *Neue Balkan*, p. 112.

36. Discounting, presumably, the value of peasant labor.

37. Kochanowicz, pp. 16, 22, 31 (quotation).

38. A study that synthesizes much of this work is Warriner (2d ed., 1964 [1939]). For other estimates on surplus agricultural population in interwar East Central Europe, based on differing assumptions, see Moore's study for the League of Nations, *Economic Demography* (2d ed., 1972 [1945]), passim.

39. Egoroff (1936), pp. 135 (citing Chayanov), 152–53. Egoroff was pessimistic, however, that significant numbers could be shifted from agriculture to industry (pp. 157–58). Cf. the similar view of Whipple and Toteff on Bulgaria (1939), pp. 73–75.

40. Part of this flowering of social research derived from foreign study and contacts. Not only were Rumanians taking doctorates in Germany, Austria, and France, but the Rockefeller Foundation brought at least four promising young scholars to the United States for postgraduate training—the economists Paul Sterian and Nicholas Georgescu-Roegan, the demographer Sabin Manuilă, and the agricultural economist Roman Cresin. On the organization of national statistical services and the role of the Rockefeller Foundation in the interwar period, see Şandru (1980), chap. 1. In chapter 8, Şandru surveys the interwar literature on rural overpopulation and labor redundancy.

41. E.g., see Gusti (1936).

42. See Vulcănescu (1937), pp. 5–94.

43. *Arhiva pentru Ştiinţa şi Reforma Socială.*

44. Stahl, "Şcoala" (1937), pp. 172, 181, 184–85; Stahl, *Amintiri* (1981), p. 32.

45. Golopenţia and Georgescu, eds., *60 sate româneşti*, 5 vols. (1941–43). Vol. 2 includes an extensive economic analysis by P. Stănculescu and C. Ştefănescu. They offer information by region, crops cultivated, and size of plot, providing detailed family budget studies by size of holding and region.

46. Cornăţeanu (1935), pp. 37, 97. Racovski had argued before the war (and postwar land reform) that real incomes of peasant families were negative, while Stere, as noted in Chapter 2, had believed landless peasants had net negative incomes. Racovski, "Poporanism" (1908), p. 350; Stere, "Fischerland" (1909), p. 371.

47. Ornea, *Ţărănismul* (1969), p. 164.

48. See budget tables in Niţescu (1928), pp. 181–255. (Vlaşca no longer exists, and the area studied now lies in Ilfov, the *judeţ* or county containing Bucharest.)

49. Institutul de Cercetări Agronomice (1936), p. 97.

50. Stănculescu and Ştefănescu, 2: 292.

51. J. Robinson, "Disguised Unemployment" (1936), p. 226.

52. Rosenstein-Rodan, "Natura" (1984), p. 212.

53. See Boeke, "Dualistic Economics" (1930), pp. 188. In the same passage Boeke attributed the phenomenon to the displacement of traditional economic practices and crafts by industrialization. As a solution, he recommended "simple cottage industry meeting general, primary needs," such as Gandhi's spinning wheel (p. 189).

54. Kalecki, Review of M. Manoilescu, *Nationale Produktivekräfte* (1938), p. 711. Later, Kalecki made clear that "unemployment" in the context of underdevelopment was a different problem than that for the economically advanced countries; in the latter, the problem was a lack of effective demand and could be dealt with by deficit spending. In the former, the problem was caused by a shortage of capital equipment, owning in turn to basic factor disproportions. Kalecki, "Unemployment" (1976 [1960]), p. 17. In the postwar period, the first use of the term "disguised unemployment" may be that in [Political and Economic Planning] (1945).

55. G. Manoilescu, "Şomuri" (1933), p. 104.

56. G. Manoilescu also cites a study with a very similar estimate by A. Alemănişteanu. Ibid., p. 109.

57. Ibid., pp. 109, 110 (quotation).

58. Frunzănescu (1935), pp. 11–14. Cf. G. Manoilescu's estimate, above.

59. Madgearu, "Teoria" (1936 [1925]); Stahl, *Amintiri*, p. 30. For more on Madgearu's opinions on agriculture, see his "Curs" (n.d.). He cites Chayanov's *Lehre* (1923) on p. 137.

60. On Madgearu's life and work, see Malinschi (1975); Predescu (1940); "Madgearu, Virgil" (1965), 3: 194. On his theoretical eclecticism, see Malinschi, p. 36. On his place in the development debates of the interwar years, see Hitchins (1994), chap. 7, esp. pp. 320–34.

61. *Evoluţia economiei româneşti după războiul mondial* (1940).

62. Ibid., p. 377.

63. Member states of the Agrarian Bloc were Rumania, Yugoslavia, and Czechoslovakia (the original Little Entente group from which the idea for the Bloc arose), plus Bulgaria, Estonia, Hungary, Latvia, Poland, Greece, and Turkey. Bussot (1933), pp. 1544–58, esp. 1553 (on Madgearu).

64. This is not to argue that the UN agencies, such as the Conference on Trade and Development (UNCTAD), were highly effective from the Third World's viewpoint, nor to accept the prevailing view that the League was altogether insensitive to the needs of the nonindustrialized world (see Chapter 7).

65. Shanin (1972). On the problem of defining the peasantry as a class, see esp. pp. 204–7, 212–13.

66. Dore (1983), p. 363.

67. Marx, *Eighteenth Brumaire* (1959 [1852]), p. 338. On the same page Marx observes that "most numerous class in French society" is "small-holding [*Parzellen*] peasants" and makes his famous assertion that "the great mass of the French nation is formed by simple addition of homologous magnitudes [i.e., such peasants], much as potatoes in a sack form a sack of potatoes."

68. Ornea, *Ţărănismul*, p. 351.

69. Ene (1932), pp. 4, 9, 10. Another Peasantist, Scutaru, would have supported "true" national industries. Scutaru ([1935]), p. 21.

70. Scutaru, p. 11. Scutaru's book had a kind of official Peasantist approval, because Ion Mihalache, the party leader, wrote a preface to it.

71. Ibid., pp. 15–16.

72. Ibid., pp. 17, 23.

73. Pătrăşcanu, "Statul" in his *Texte* (1975 [1936]), pp. 239, 241, 244.

74. Myrdal (1970), p. 543 (Rosenstein-Rodan quoted).

75. Warriner, pp. xxvii, xxx.

76. Myrdal, pp. 521–22, 544. Gerald Meier agrees with Myrdal that moving labor to industrial employment is not a costless activity. Meier emphasizes capital formation with surplus agricultural labor more than industrialization as such. Meier (1968), pp. 186–87, 190–91.

77. Schultz (1964), chap. 4, esp. pp. 55–58. It should be noted, however, that W. Arthur Lewis's model of the "unlimited supply of [agricultural] labor" does not require zero marginal productivity in agriculture, but only "an excess supply of labor at an exogenously given wage." Findlay (1980), p. 68.

78. For a discussion, see Bhaduri (1989 [1987]), pp. 109–13.

79. The historian and former prime minister Nicolae Iorga was assassinated at the same time.

Chapter 5

1. E.g., see Xenopol (1967 [1882]), pp. 101–2.

2. A Rumanian from Transylvania who was perforce a subject of Austria-Hungary.

3. Among the several summaries of their views, see Nicolae-Văleanu, "Istoria gîndirii economice" (1982), pp. 54–67; and Constantinescu (1973), pp. 65–83. A selection of their writings, as well as those of men who defended other views, is found in Academia Republicii (1960). Many of the nineteenth-century economic writers have also been anthologized in individual volumes.

4. E.g., see Răzmiritza (1932), pp. 92, 301–2.

5. Ioţa (1968), p. 303. According to Ioţa, Xenopol also influenced I. N. Angelescu, who likewise failed to cite Xenopol. Ibid., p. 303. (See below on Angelescu.)

6. On the Junimea, see Chapter 3.

7. For a brief biography and critical study of Xenopol's works, see Veverca (1967), pp. 7–71.

8. Ioţa, p. 19.

9. The tradition had deep roots. As early as the 1820s Dinicu Golescu [Constantin Radovici din Goleşti] had condemned the practice of selling raw materials abroad cheaply and buying them back at a price "thirty times greater." Murgescu, *Mersul* (1987), 1: 269.

10. In the words of Iranyi, leader of the party in 1873, "trade between unequal parties always favors the stronger and hence does not deserve the designation 'free.'" Quoted in Janos, *Politics* (1982), p. 139.

11. Xenopol, pp. 79–80; Veverca, p. 49.

12. Demetrescu ([1940]), p. 264.

13. Ioţa, p. 154. Haşdeu also associated industrialization with civilization, progress, and national independence. Haşdeu (1960), pp. 271–82.

14. Xenopol, pp. 85, 189.

15. Iota, p. 238; Xenopol, pp. 189, 193. In his polemical efforts to dismiss agriculture, Xenopol weakened his argument, however, by asserting that Rumania could not compete with the United States, Russia, or even Hungary, all of which presumably had higher labor productivities. Xenopol, pp. 91–92. Clearly, this interpretation ignores the "income terms of trade," which takes into account the quantity of goods exchanged as well as unit prices. Incredibly, in 1979, a Rumanian economic historian wrote that in the late nineteenth century five tons of his country's exports were required to equal the value of one ton of imports, which fact "demonstrates the economic exploitation" of Rumania at the time by its more developed trading partners. By this logic, England, the world's largest exporter of high weight-to-value coal in the last century, was presumably being exploited in international trade. Perhaps this allegation shows the staying power of the tradition in economic thought which Xenopol represented. See Cherciu (1979), p. 186.

16. Veverca, p. 24. Unlike Xenopol, however, Manoilescu attributed the difference to the capital per worker invested in a given economic activity.

17. "The political economy [i.e., economic theory] of France and England does not deserve the name of science; it is theory at the service of a practice [which is profitable for those countries]," wrote Xenopol, p. 95.

18. Ibid., pp. 97–98, 177.

19. Iota, p. 174; Xenopol, p. 178.

20. Xenopol, p. 180. The Rumanian phrase is *industria mare*, which means both "heavy" and "large-scale" industry, but by the examples he gave, it seems Xenopol had in mind highly capitalized firms with large numbers of workers, rather than capital goods industries. He cites the textile, leather, and paper industries, all of which the state could easily subsidize through purchases for the army and the bureaucracy.

21. In the 1890s, Xenopol retreated from this position and argued that Rumania could feasibly develop only light industries, such as brewing, and, in general, those without huge capital investments and the most advanced technology. In particular, he promoted those industries using domestic raw materials. Like the Populists, Xenopol contended that foreign markets were closed to Rumanian industries by Western monopolies. Iota, p. 111.

22. Ibid., p. 151.

23. Ibid., p. 148; Xenopol, p. 181.

24. Within Rumania, Xenopol added, foreigners had taken over commerce and industry, leaving only the bureaucracy and agriculture for Rumanian nationals. Iota, p. 161.

25. Xenopol, p. 189.

26. Iota, pp. 162–63. Xenopol seems to have had a mercantilist view of foreign trade, by which Rumania imported more than it exported, thus sending capital abroad to cover its import bill.

27. Veverca, p. 11.

28. Xenopol, pp. 192–93.

29. *Viitorul nostru economic.*

30. Aurelian (1890), pp. 19–21.

31. Ibid., pp. 39, 44.

32. Ibid., pp. 9, 43.

33. Angelescu was minister of finance in 1919 and held the same position in 1920–21—undersecretary (i.e., assistant minister) of finance—that Manoilescu would hold in 1926–27.

34. Angelescu, "Dependența noastră economică" (1915), pp. 724, 727. In 1919, Angelescu argued, as Manoilescu would four years later, that class representation through corporate organization was necessary in the modern postwar economy. The state was to

"harmonize" class interests. This in part was an extension of his earlier advocacy of a central economic commission. See Angelescu, *Politica economică a României Mari* (1919), p. 29.

35. Angelescu used the 1901–2 census definition of "large" industrial firms, which were those employing mechanical means of production and machines using water, gas, gasoline, oil, or electricity as sources of energy; in addition, the largest artisanal workshops were included. See Rumania: Ministerul Agriculturei (1904), p. viii.

36. Angelescu, "Avuția" (1915), pp. 305–7.

37. Angelescu, "Politica," pp. 24–26.

38. Angelescu, "România" (1927), esp. pp. 2, 5.

39. Sir R[eginald] Hoare to Foreign Office, 21 June 1940, FO 371.24992.

40. M. Manoilescu, "Memorii" MS. (1946–48), p. 6; Manoliu, *Bibliographie* (1936), p. 9. The most comprehensive bibliography of and about Manoilescu's works is Nechita, ed., *Mihail Manoilescu* (1993), pp. 268–303.

41. Manoliu, *Bibliographie*, p. 10.

42. Averescu had been the minister of war who directed the repression of the peasant revolt of 1907.

43. Diamandi ([1936?]), pp. 260–67; M. Manoilescu, "Memorii," p. 247.

44. Whether Manoilescu was motivated by anti-Semitism or sound financial judgment in letting the Bancă Marmorosch-Blank fail is debatable, but a recent study has supported the latter view. See Popișteanu et al. (1982), esp. p. 42. In his memoirs Manoilescu says the French financial expert Charles Rist advised him that the bank should be allowed to fail. "Memorii," p. 420. If this is true, Manoilescu respected the foreign adviser's opinion then more than in 1933, when, no longer in office, he decried foreign financial experts, and implicitly Rist. (See Chapter 7).

45. M. Manoilescu, "Memorii," p. 486.

46. Ibid., pp. 106–13.

47. Ibid., pp. 532, 610, 612, 618. Manoilescu had a private audience with Salazar (p. 614). For more on the Rumanian's relations with the Portuguese dictator and his successor, see Chapter 6.

48. Diamandi, pp. 266, 271. The sociologist Henri H. Stahl, who as a young man knew Manoilescu, also believed him to be an impressive personality—less charismatic than Stere, but more so than Madgearu. Interview, Bucharest, 28 Oct. 1981.

49. Diamandi, p. 268. Similar opinions were held by French and British diplomats. The French minister in Bucharest reported a rumor that Manoilescu had secretly sent government funds to Switzerland while he was minister of commerce. French Minister in Bucharest [G. Puaux] to Foreign Minister, 29 June 1931, Quai d'Orsay, vol. 170, p. 28. The British embassy reported in 1939, "He [Manoilescu] is said to be venal." "Records of Leading Personalities in Rumania," Bucharest, 31 July 1939, FO 371.23855, p. 17.

50. French Minister in Bucharest [G. Paux] to Foreign Minister, Bucharest, 18 Oct. 1930, Quai d'Orsay, vol. 169, p. 163; M. Manoilescu, "Memorii," part VII, p. 328.

51. Diamandi (p. 266) suggests he left Averescu's People's Party in 1927 because a ministerial portfolio was not enough for him. Manoilescu himself said it was because of the general's rapprochement with Ion Brătianu, the Liberal leader. "Memorii," pp. 165–66.

52. Hoare to Sir Anthony Eden, Bucharest, 12 Jan. 1938, [FO 371] R533/250/37.

53. M. Manoilescu, "Prefață" ([1940]), pp. 8–9.

54. In the 1920s, at least, Manoilescu had had no objections to working with Jewish partners in a Transylvanian mining venture in which he had invested his wife's fortune. "Memorii," pp. 41, 499, 576.

55. Hoare to Foreign Office, Bucharest, 21 June 1940, FO 371.24992; Hoare to P. B. B. Nichols, 5 July 1940, Bucharest, FO 371.24992 (quotation). Cf. Ciano's observation on 27 July 1940: "I received the Rumanians [Prime Minister Ion Gigurtu and Foreign Minister Manoilescu]. They are simply disgusting. They open their mouths only to exude compliments. They have become anti-French, anti-English, and anti-League of Nations." Ciano (1946), p. 279.

56. Ciano (1946), p. 289 (entry for 30 Aug. 1940). In his apologia, Manoilescu argues that in mid-1940, following the fall of France and the USSR's seizure of Bessarabia and northern Bucovina, there was little Rumania could do to oppose Hitler's designs. If he had refused German-Italian "arbitration," Manoilescu contended, Rumania would have lost all of Transylvania, instead of half, and he would have exposed Moldavia to Soviet occupation because the Axis would not have defended the integrity of the remaining Rumanian territory. M. Manoilescu, "Urmare la 'memoriile mele'" MS. (1947), pp. 26–30, 55, 68, 271, 316.

57. Furthermore, the new Iron Guard–dominated government quickly ceded an area on the southern frontier to Bulgaria, another Axis satellite.

58. E.g., M. Manoilescu, "Economia" (1942), p. 50.

59. For details, see Vasile (1979). Rumania's export prices to Germany rose 123 percent from 1939 to 1944, while import prices from Germany rose 614 percent, giving the lie to Manoilescu's vision of how the *Grossraumwirtschaft* would work. See Lampe and Jackson, p. 532.

60. Dinu and Manoilescu (n.d.), p. 16. Presumably the charge referred to articles such as "Curiosități psihologice"(1942), in which Manoilescu defended the German-Rumanian alliance "in the same struggle for liberation" against the "plutocratic forces" (p. 116). His "Problematica războiului" (1942) was shrilly pro-Nazi.

61. Even the British embassy reported, "He is clearly a man of culture, knows a fair amount of English, and professes friendliness to British industry." See "Records of Leading Personalities in Rumania," 30 Sept. 1930, FO 371.14438, p. 18. M. Manoilescu, "Memorii," pp. 278, 483.

62. M. Manoilescu, "Memorii," p. 55.

63. M. Manoilescu, *La théorie du protectionnisme et de l'échange international* (1929).

64. M. Manoilescu, *Lege* (1932), p. 18.

65. M. Manoilescu, *Le siècle du corporatisme* (1934).

66. Neumark (1936), p. 51. According to Neumark, a "neomercantilism" had arisen even before the war, when the major industrial states raised tariff barriers against their competitors and established exclusive trading areas within their empires. Ibid., p. 34.

67. See Kofman, "Economic Nationalism" (1990), esp. p. 207.

68. Maier (1975), p. 567.

69. M. Manoilescu, *Imperatif* (1933), p. 5; Condliffe (1933), p. 358. Condliffe opined that it was the industrialized countries who had the most to lose by pursuing autarkic policies, a view M. Manoilescu had expressed three years earlier (see below). On the general tendency for agriculture-exporting nations to seek to industrialize in the decade after 1925 (when major European countries other than England began to seek agricul-

tural self-sufficiency), see Société des Nations [League of Nations]: Comité Economique (1935), pp. 36–37.

70. Cassel put the larger share of blame on trade union monopolies rather than on "monopolistic combines of enterprises" but argued that the two were mutually reinforcing. Cassel (1927), pp. 43–44.

71. There was also the cost of increased unemployment in the West, in Cassel's view, partly owing to labor unions' insistence on the introduction of the eight-hour day. Ibid., pp. 28, 29 (quotation), 32.

72. See below.

73. M. Manoilescu, "Criza" (1933), p. 121. In the same passage Manoilescu added that Cassel "absurdly" proposed free trade as a solution, but the Rumanian ignored Cassel's principal recommendations for the West, which were to provide greater credit and capital investment for agricultural and colonial areas. See also Christodorescu, *Problema* (1933), pp. 2–3; Société des Nations: Comité Economique, p. 9; and UN: ECLA, *Economic Development of Latin America and its Principal Problems* (1950 [Sp. orig. 1949]).

74. E.g., see Warriner (1964 [1939]), p. 35, and esp. chap. 3; Egoroff (1936), p. 152; Frangeš, "Industrialisation" (1938), pp. 44, 76; Reithinger (1937), pp. 25, 36–37, 74, 175; Whipple and Toteff (1939).

75. Delaisi (1929). M. Manoilescu became a friend of Delaisi that year. See his "Memorii," p. 347.

76. See Chapter 7.

77. Delaisi, pp. 21, 23, 26–27.

78. Ibid., pp. 81, 83, 196, 202. In fact, the idea of a Europe-wide preference scheme for wheat goes back to Jule Méline (author of the Méline tariff in France) and the first International Congress of Agriculture in 1889. See Société des Nations: Comité Economique, p. 40.

79. In buying agricultural goods from the United States or Canada, western Europe's manufactures exchanged for goods embodying more equivalent amounts of labor.

80. M. Manoilescu, "Régime" (1930), pp. 6–10. The father of the Bloc in Rumania was Virgil Madgearu, then minister of agriculture, who in 1929 had effected a 30 percent decrease in tariffs, in the spirit of the Geneva Economic Conference of 1927.

81. M. Manoilescu, *Imperatif*, pp. 6–8, 15.

82. M. Manoilescu, *Forţele* (1986), p. 125; see the same point in *Théorie* (1929), p. 177. I will refer hereafter primarily to *Forţele*, the expanded Rumanian edition of *Théorie*. The work was revised in 1946–48 but only published in 1986, 36 years after the author's death. The Rumanian edition is a reworked version of the 1937 German edition. Though the 1986 edition is the definitive one, it is necessary to refer to others, especially the original French edition (1929), because of its reception by critics and Manoilescu's attempts to answer them in later editions. Note that the first words of the title of the Rumanian version ("national forces of production") emphasize the productivity issue, as did the title of the 1937 German version. "The productivity of labor is the fundamental [*capitală*] notion in our work," he wrote in *Forţele*, p. 97. The Rumanian edition also includes arguments and data published in his "Productivitatea" (1941).

In a given economic activity or branch of industry, if C = fixed capital invested, and K = liquid capital, and A = total number of workers, then "specific capital" (or q) = $(C + K)/A$, or capital per worker. Further, if P = value of production, and S = total wages, then

p = value of output per worker, or P/A, and s = average wages, or S/A. Further, the value of output per worker or "productivity" equals average wages plus specific capital multiplied by i, the average rate of profit in that industry, or $p = s + q(x)i$, because $P/A = S/A + q(x)i$. This formula was not included in the French and French-derived editions in English, Italian, and Portuguese. *Forțele*, p. 124. See also "Productivitatea," p. 2.

83. M. Manoilescu, *Forțele*, pp. 131–32. These calculations were based on the assumption that only male adults worked in agriculture. If, said Manoilescu, one more realistically added the additional labor inputs in agriculture by women and children, the ratio of productivities would reach 9 to 1. See his "Productivitatea," p. 30; *Forțele*, p. 130. Generalizing for "backward agricultural countries" in the latter work, Manoilescu believed labor productivity in industry was four times greater than in agriculture (p. 127).

84. "Productivitatea," pp. 10–11; *Forțele*, p. 127. On this matter, Manoilescu followed in the century-old tradition of the Scot John Rae, who argued, contrary to Adam Smith, that national interests and individual interests were not identical. Rae, like Smith and unlike Manoilescu, however, focused on individual and national wealth, not productivity and profitability. See Rae (1834), chap. 1, esp. p. 62.

85. A. Robinson (1987), p. 96.

86. Rosenstein-Rodan noted that the private investors would maximize the private, not the social, marginal net product. "Natura" (1984), p. 215.

87. M. Manoilescu, *Forțele*, pp. 136–37.

88. The coefficient of quality was equal to average net production of an industry (roughly, value added) divided by the square root of the product of the number of workers times the amount of fixed capital, or $Q = \dfrac{P}{\sqrt{AxC}}$. *Forțele*, p. 147.

89. *Forțele*, p. 160. Agricultural and industrial countries were so distinguished by their exports. *Siècle*, p. 28, n. 2.

90. *Forțele*, pp. 160–61. Manoilescu thought that the price scissors of the Great Depression was a "passing" phenomenon (p. 353).

91. In 1954 Lewis "independently advance[d] the argument first made by the Rumanian writer Manoilescu . . . that protection is justified in [lesser developed countries] on the ground that wages in industry are excessive in relation to agriculture." Findlay (1980), p. 70. See Lewis, "Economic Development" (1954). Three decades later Lewis recalled no influence of Manoilescu in developing his own theory. Lewis to author, Princeton, N.J., 6 May 1986.

92. The formula in note 88 could be modified to include land, by replacing the square root of AxC by the cube root of AxCxO, where the last term represents the amount of land cultivated in a given branch of agriculture. *Forțele*, p. 149.

93. Ibid., p. 330 ("relative utility"). He had nothing to say about other components of the service sector, such as government or professional salaries and fees.

94. Ibid., p. 279; *Théorie*, p. 183.

95. M. Manoilescu, *Forțele*, p. 304; *Théorie*, p. 342. He added that there was no sacrifice by society under a protectionist regime, as List's theory had indicated; on the contrary, the whole nation benefited because of the higher productivity gained. "In that regard, the bourgeoisie, following its own interests, has helped the whole people" (*Forțele*, p. 304). Adam Smith's invisible hand worked under a protectionist regime as well as any other!

96. M. Manoilescu, *Forțele*, p. 302. They might persist, one assumes, because of greater technological change in industry over the middle term.

97. M. Manoilescu, *Théorie*, p. 161.   98. M. Manoilescu, *Forțele*, p. 234.

99. Ibid., p. 262.   100. Ibid., p. 288.

101. Ibid., p. 351.

102. Ibid., p. 365. Manoilescu did, however, momentarily defend autarky after the London economic conference of the League ended in failure in 1933. See his "Autarhia" (1934), esp. pp. 15–19.

103. *Forțele*, p. 362.

104. Ibid., p. 89.

105. M. Manoilescu, "Productivitatea," p. 2.

106. M. Manoilescu, "European Economic Equilibrium" (1931), p. 2.

107. M. Manoilescu, "Curs" (1940), p. 331.

108. *Forțele*, p. 44. Note the same notion in Stere and Racovski in Chapter 2. Elsewhere, a division of the world into plutocratic and proletarian nations had been identified by the Italian proto-Fascist Enrico Corradini (1910), and the Chinese theorist who introduced Mao Tse-tung to Marxism, Li Ta-Chao (1920). Corradini (1973 [Ital. orig. 1910]), p. 146; Meisner (1967), p. 144. Modesty aside, Manoilescu believed that just as Marx had explained the exploitation of social classes, he had explained the exploitation of peoples. M. Manoilescu, *Siècle*, p. 29.

109. As late as the 1940s, M. Manoilescu still had not abandoned the idea of "raising the purchasing power of agricultural countries," at least as a rhetorical device. *Forțele*, p. 375. This goal would be successively taken up by ECLA and UNCTAD later.

110. *Buletinul Uniunei Generale a Industriașilor din România* (hereafter *Buletinul UGIR*. The UGIR had been preceded by an emphemeral association organized by Petre Aurelian called the Societatea "Industria." From 1909 to 1928 UGIR had the same president as the Union of the Chambers of Commerce and Industry, but divergent interests separated the groups again at the end of the period. For details of UGIR's history, see speeches by Constantin Bușila, president of UGIR, and Chr. Staicovici in *Buletinul UGIR* 8, nos. 9–10 (May 1929): 122–24, 144.

111. Ștefan Cerkez, president of UGIR, *Buletinul UGIR* [manifesto] 1, no. 1 (Apr. 1922): 2.

112. Ștefan Cerkez, president, and C. R. Mircea, director general, "Memoriul rezumativ al doleanțelor industriei," *Buletinul UGIR* 2, nos. 5–6 (Mar. 1923): 375.

113. Anon., "Darea de seamă," *Buletinul UGIR* 4, no. 5 (May 1925): 287; C. R. Mircea, president of UGIR, statement on 23 November 1932, cited in Christodorescu, *Problema* (1933), pp. 31–32; Anon., "Reducerea duratei muncii la 40 ore pe săptămână," *Buletinul UGIR* 13, nos. 9–12 (Sept.–Dec. 1935): 2.

114. Anon., "Darea de seamă," *Buletinul UGIR* 4, no. 5 (May 1925): 287.

115. C. R. Mircea, "Industria națională," *Buletinul UGIR* 5, no. 1 (Jan. 1926): 2; Mircea, "Agricultura și tariful vamal," *Buletinul UGIR* 6, nos. 3–4 (Feb. 1927): 50.

116. C. R. Mircea, "Industria națională," *Buletinul UGIR* 5, no. 1 (Jan. 1926): 3.

117. C. D. Bușilă, president of UGIR, "Expunerea," *Buletinul UGIR* 9, nos. 1–4 (Jan.–Feb. 1930): 1.

118. Anon., "Drumul nostru [editorial]," *Buletinul UGIR* 6, no. 1 (Jan. 1927): 2; George D. Cioriceanu, "Noua orientare în economia națională," *Buletinul UGIR* 10, nos. 3–4 (Feb. 1931): 84.

119. C. R. Mircea, "Darea de seamă," *Buletinul UGIR* 10, nos. 3–4 (Feb. 1931): 204, 206.

120. Anon., "Drumul nostru [editorial]," *Buletinul UGIR* 14 [?], nos. 10–12 (Oct.–Dec. 1936): 1.

121. George D. Cioriceanu, "Noua orientare în economia națională," *Buletinul UGIR* 10, nos. 3–4 (Feb. 1931): 206; Gh. Brânzescu, "Cîteva constatări," ibid., 17, nos. 1–2 (Jan.–Feb. 1939): 13; Ion Veverca, "Tensiunea demografică și industrializarea," ibid., 17, nos. 7–8 (July–Aug. 1939): 6; I. Bujoiu, "Desvoltarea industriei românești în ultimii ani," ibid., 18, nos. 5–8 (May–Aug. 1940): 7.

122. Kofman makes the general point that state bureaucrats welcomed M. Manoilescu's ideas and program. "How to Define" (1990), p. 30. See Chapter 3 for Lucrețiu Pătrășcanu's analysis of the royal dictatorship.

123. In October a new Ministry of Armaments was also created, soon to be put under the direction of Victor Slăvescu, a President of UGIR with a much stronger background in economics than his predecessors. On institutional changes see Savu (1970), pp. 180–83.

124. Rumania: Consiliul (1939), pp. vii, viii (quotation), x.

Chapter 6

1. M. Manoilescu, *Forțele* (1986), p. 44.

2. E.g., see Popa-Vereș (1938); and Ionescu-Șișești (1940).

3. He estimated that a certain proportion of industrial imports, such as metal tools and cotton textiles, were destined for the countryside and villages. "Triangle," pp. 20, 21.

4. Manoilescu equated "villages" with "rural inhabitants," as did other Rumanian writers of his era. In this calculation, Manoilescu assumed that the difference in exports and imports—81 million francs, a sum that included payments for invisibles and profit remittances—mainly accrued to the cities. The assumption seems largely justified, in that agricultural surpluses in the commercial balance repaid foreign-held bonds for urban improvements. See "Triangle," p. 19.

5. Ibid., pp. 20, 22.

6. Ibid., p. 19.

7. Ibid., pp. 17, 18, 22.

8. In his "Triangle," Manoilescu based this generalization on data for only two years, 1935 and 1937; as Rumania recovered from the Depression in the latter year, foreign trade almost doubled, but the transfer of income from the countryside to the cities rose two and a half times. Ibid., p. 22.

9. Ibid., pp. 22, 26.

10. In modern economic parlance, when the marginal productivity of labor in agriculture is below that of other economic endeavors, surplus labor should be moved to industry or other higher-productivity activities. See a discussion of the Manoilescu argument in Corden (1965), pp. 60–61.

11. M. Manoilescu, "Triangle," pp. 25–26.

12. Ibid., p. 19.

13. Ibid., p. 20.

14. Cf. a similar argument for late imperial Russia in Nicolas-On (1902), p. 448.

15. M. Manoilescu, "Triangle," p. 19, note 5; p. 21.

16. He assumed that, in money terms, urban dwellers consumed at least as much agricultural production as the villagers, whose expenditure he was able to generalize from local monographs on family budgets. In fact, Manoilescu noted, urban expenditures were

probably much greater because factory workers' incomes were more than twice as large as agricultural workers'. Per capita income in the cities, moreover, was at least four times that of the countryside. Ibid., pp. 23–24.

17. Ibid., p. 24. In an accounting sense, of course, the payments between city and countryside had to balance. A presumably large but undetermined share of the difference in the accounting and real income flows owed to payments to landlords residing in the cities.

18. M. Manoilescu, "Criterii" (1926), pp. 13, 16–17.

19. M. Manoilescu, *Rostul* (1942), p. 89.

20. M. Manoilescu, *Încercări* (1938), pp. 119–21.

21. M. Manoilescu, "Sozialökonomische Struktur" (1944), p. 11.

22. M. Manoilescu, "Curs" (1933), p. 359; *Forţele*, p. 44.

23. E.g., in González Casanova (1965), and Hechter (1975). Indeed, stratification and exploitation based on ethnicity formed part of the definition of internal colonialism in the work of these two writers.

24. M. Manoilescu, "Politica" (1940), pp. 229–30. For political reasons of the moment, perhaps, Jews are the only minority in this passage he mentions by name.

25. Nicholas Bukerow argues that Manoilescu's theory can be seen as having two stages: import-substitution industrialization and the export of manufactures, "allowing goods of ever higher labor productivity to increase their export share." Bukerow does not provide a citation for this interpretation, but in his view, the Communist regime in Rumania, inspired by Manoilescu, attempted to follow this policy and switched from stage one to stage two about 1965. The reader of the 1990s may judge how successful this effort was. Bukerow (1980), pp. 49 (quotation), 183, 202, 207.

26. In *Siècle* (1934), p. 368, Manoilescu recommends a policy of exporting manufactures, but it is not clear that he is directing his advice only to agrarian countries trying to industrialize; see below.

27. In an implicit contradiction; see below.

28. E.g., in *Revue Economique Internationale* (by Léon Hennebicq), *American Economic Review* (by Leo Pasvolsky), and in a medium of *haute vulgarisation*, the *Times Literary Supplement* (anon.).

29. It may have been Manoilescu whom Oskar Morgenstern, later known as the father of game theory, had in mind when he wrote, "In the esoteric circles of 'pure theory' the division between real science and amateur economics is quite clear: The occasional outbursts from outsiders, especially people trained in mathematics and engineering, who advance monstrous ideas, does not alter this to any great extent." *Limits* (1937), p. 122.

30. With Eli Hecksher, Ohlin demonstrated how comparative advantage is derived from differences in factor endowments among countries and how a country could profit by exporting goods whose production made the most intensive use of its most abundant factor.

31. Ohlin (1931), pp. 34–35.

32. Ibid., p. 35.

33. Ibid., p. 36.

34. Ibid., p. 36. In the subsequent Rumanian edition (*Forţele*, p. 287), Manoilescu answered Ohlin by saying that certain industries would never be created in agrarian countries without artificial price incentives; this defense only amounts to List's infant

industry argument, though elsewhere Manoilescu defends new high-productivity industries from their first day of operation (see Chapter 5). Furthermore, Manoilescu misread
Ohlin in saying that the latter approved of tariffs to the extent that they maintain high
salaries, obtained through the activities of trade unions as noncompeting groups (p. 293).

35. Viner, Review of M. Manoilescu, *Theory* (1932), pp. 121–25 (quotation on
p. 125). Manoilescu responded to Viner in the Rumanian edition of his work (pp. 252–54)
but did not address the issue of trade union monopoly as the reason why wages, prices, and
productivity (by Manoilescu's definition) might be higher in those industries for which
Manoilescu found empirically higher cross-national data to support his case.

36. See Baumol and Seiler (1979), pp. 784–85.

37. Viner, *Studies* (1937), pp. 490, 492. Georgescu-Roegen, the most important Rumanian economist after 1945 and a major figure in the American profession, wrote:
"Viner kept decrying Manoilescu's thesis. . . . Yet even Viner . . . finally weakened, as
he sought to justify the classical doctrine by the difference in occupational disutilities."
Georgescu-Roegen, "Manoilescu, Mihail" (1987), p. 300.

38. On the Taşcă-Manoilescu debates, see Paiuşan and Buşa (1990).

39. Taşcă (1937), pp. 40–41. The exploitation of Rumanian peasants by urban ethnic
minorities was a process Manoilescu had condemned. In a reply to Taşcă, Manoilescu stated
that his program would benefit Rumanian agriculture—an allegation that was correct in the
long run, if workers sought jobs in industry and relative prices and wages in agriculture
rose. M. Manoilescu, "Doctrinele" (1937), p. 56. Long-run terms of trade data available at
the international level in the latter 1980s, however, seemed to indicate the predicted
process was not occurring. See Chapter 8.

40. Kalecki review of M. Manoilescu, *Nationale Produktivekräfte* (1938), pp. 708–11.
Kalecki wrote that because of "unemployment, manifest or disguised," in agricultural
countries, the supply of new savings is not fixed but is "equal to the investment undertaken," and new industries could create opportunities for investment and employment
(p. 711).

41. See the reference to Sombart implying his approval of Manoilescu's doctrine in
Forţele, p. 44.

42. Brinkmann (1938), esp. pp. 276–79. Viner had made similar criticisms. In fact,
Manoilescu inconsistently employed both the (classical) labor theory of value and the
(neoclassical) marginalist price theory, based on the utility and availability of goods (and
inversely on their scarcity). He accepted the neoclassical concept of economic equilibrium
based on a marginalist explanation of prices. Manoilescu distinguished between "internal"
and "external" values: the former were derived from the creation of goods, accounted for
costs of production, and were explained by the labor theory of value, as modified by his
"qualitative" stratification of labor inputs, based on capital per worker. "External value"
was derived from utility and expressed a quantitative relation between the utilities of two
goods; it was therefore explained by marginalist considerations. *Forţele*, p. 73; "Curs"
(1940), pp. 22–25. Also see Sută-Selejan and Sută (1972), pp. 35–36.

43. Frölich (1938).

44. Wagemann, *Neue Balkan* (1939), pp. 65–70.

45. Ibid., pp. 104, 120–22, 135.

46. See the summary of Wagemann's critique of Manoilescu and an unfavorable assessment of Wagemann's own thesis in Roberts (1969), pp. 217–18.

47. Manoilescu referred to members of the liberal professions and civil servants as a "pseudo-bourgeoisie" in *Rostul* (1942), p. 110.

48. M. Manoilescu, *Forţele*, p. 347.

49. M. Manoilescu, *Theorie* (1929), p. 103.

50. M. Manoilescu, *Forţele*, p. 350.

51. Hagen (1958), pp. 498–503, 511 (quotation), 513. Hagen also shows that a policy of subsidies will in theory raise real income higher than protection will, and the *optimum optimorum* is a combination of free trade and subsidies (p. 498).

52. Ibid., pp. 496–97.

53. Findlay (1980), p. 70.

54. See his defense of the *Grossraumwirtschaft*, with concessions to the idea of some Rumanian industrialization, in *Ideia* (1938); "Solidaritatea" (1939); and "Economia" (1942). Apparently untroubled by his inconsistency, Manoilescu continued to defend industrialization for backward countries in "Mehr Industrie" (1938); "În ce constă" (1940); "Triangle" (1940); "Sozialökonomische Struktur" (1944); and "Probleme" (1945). Another Balkan economist, Otto Frangeš of Yugoslavia, was similarly inconsistent between supporting a policy of industrialization for his country and supporting an agricultural role for it within the Greater German Economic Space. Frangeš backed the latter as early as 1933, using the "threat" of Yugoslavian industrialization if his country could not sell its agricultural goods in Germany; in 1938, he supported industrialization for southeastern Europe; and in 1941 (when Yugoslavia was under German occupation) he once again backed the *Grossraumwirtschaft*, allowing for some local industrialization, while arguing that the Danubian states (Hungary, Rumania, Yugoslavia, and Bulgaria) could meet all the agricultural needs of Germany and its dependencies. See "Wirtschaftlichen Beziehungen" (1933), pp. 133, 142–43; "Industrialisation" (1938), pp. 68, 76; "Treibenden Kräfte" (1938), pp. 327, 338–39; and "Donaustaaten" (1941), pp. 285, 287, 311–12, 315.

55. M. Manoilescu, "Solidaritatea" (1939), pp. 8–9. In fact, German trade officials did use the overvalued mark to pay prices in some instances "well above the international level" to exporters as part of a strategy to bring southeastern Europe under Germany's economic sway. But these purchases were often in the form of credits rather than goods, and the latter were not fully delivered. The end result was a strong form of unequal exchange. Berend and Ranki, *Economic Development* (1974), pp. 276–78.

56. M. Manoilescu, "Memorii," p. 601.

57. J. Castro (1960), p. 79.

58. Another important social theorist between St.-Simon and Bourgeois was Auguste Comte, who, like his mentor and employer Henri St.-Simon, visualized an industrial society free of class conflict. Comte championed a paternalist role for the state vis-à-vis the working class and made the family, rather than the individual, the foundation of society. His program of modernization without social mobilization appealed to progressive conservatives in Latin America during the latter years of the last century and may have laid a foundation there for the reception of corporatism after World War I.

59. Mladenatz (1942), p. 16; Perroux, *Capitalisme* (1938), p. 298 ("third solution").

60. Note the same title of an essay published in 1928 by Ştefan Zeletin, the pro-establishment Marxist, treated in Chapter 3. The term may be confusing today, for in the late twentieth century "neoliberalism" usually connotes an ideology supporting a market-centered economy.

61. M. Manoilescu, *Neoliberalismul* (1923), pp. 7, 8, 13, 14, 19.

62. M. Manoilescu, "Anticipare" (1932), pp. 1–9; "Memorii," p. 508.

63. See the detailed program of Manoilescu's National Corporatist League in International Reference Library (1936), pp. 208–23.

64. M. Manoilescu, *Le siècle du corporatisme: Doctrine du corporatisme intégral et pur.*

65. Ibid., pp. 7, 12.

66. Ibid., p. 16.

67. Ibid., p. 17 (quotation); "Doctrinele" (1937), p. 31. For Manoilescu, King Carol's dictatorship with corporate trappings after 1938 also failed to qualify as authentic for the same reason. Nechita, "Doctrina" (1971), p. 216 (citing Manoilescu). Cf. Othmar Spann's criticism of Austria's corporate constitution of 1934 for having no "corporate estates" as a foundation. Lebovics (1969), p. 17.

68. *Siècle*, pp. 27–33. Four years after World War II, W. Arthur Lewis took a radically different view of the reason for the decline in international trade in manufactured goods between the world wars. It was due, "not as is alleged, to the industrialization of new countries, but to the decelerated demand for primary commodities [because their production outstripped demand], and to the resultant movement in the terms of trade. World trade in manufactures would have been larger . . . if there had been more industrialization and a less rapid growth of primary production." Lewis, *Economic Survey* (1949), p. 197.

69. M. Manoilescu, *Siècle*, pp. 45, 56. He omitted the inconvenient fact, cited in successive versions of *Théorie*, that industrialized nations were each other's best customers. To export agricultural goods of low productivity was now "anticorporative" (*Siècle*, p. 368).

70. Ibid., pp. 30, 35.

71. Ibid., p. 40.

72. Ibid., pp. 45–46. "Organization" presumably meant, or at least included, entrepreneurship, a factor along with land, labor, and capital. In the same year (1934) that Berle and Means made the point with much greater elaboration (*The Modern Corporation and Private Property*), Manoilescu wrote that in large enterprises, the administrator played a more important role than the owner. *Siècle*, p. 56. His emphasis on organization in the production process is ironic because it implicitly conflicts with his exclusive concern with labor in defining productivity, at least for comparative purposes. Firmin Oulès explicitly criticized Manoilescu as an economist for ignoring "organization" (entrepreneurship) and capital in defining productivity. See Oulès (1936), p. 478.

73. *Siècle*, pp. 68, 311, 367, 373. But "rationalization," meaning principally the formation of monopoly combines, still figured heavily in "organization" (p. 296), which fact seems to conflict with the emphasis on curbing profits. In 1930 Manoilescu had defended the organization of cartels as a form of rationalization of business enterprise, in part, he asserted, because a cartel could achieve a more efficient division of labor among participating firms. "Cartelurile și raționalizarea" (1930), pp. 46–48.

74. *Siècle*, p. 368. Manoilescu argued four years later that the issue was not a "free" economy versus a planned one. The Rumanian economy was already directed by cartels of industrialists "who exploit the consumer masses." He preferred an economy directed by the state in the general interest. M. Manoilescu, *Ideia* (1938), p. 11.

75. Manoilescu did not concern himself with such matters in an essay in which one would have expected it—his last published work during his lifetime—"Autour de la définition" (1946–47).

76. Lebovics, pp. 122, 125.

77. E.g., Perroux, "Capitalismo e corporativismo: Socialização" (1939). See also Chamberlin, and J. Robinson, *Economics*, both published in 1933.

78. *Siècle*, pp. 100, 107.

79. Ibid., pp. 137–39.

80. *Le parti unique* (1936), published in outline in "Partidul unic" (1936). The author curiously averred that the transformation of Weimar into Nazi Germany showed that the one-party regime could arise with a minimum violation of judicial norms. In Rumania such a party could be instituted through constitutional reform, he wrote. See "Partidul unic," esp. pp. 319, 322. Manoilescu may have been appealing to King Carol to establish a one-party dictatorship; and in fact the dictatorship came two years later, but without Manoilescu's aid and without a real party. Ultimately, his defense of the single party became a fulsome apology for the Axis powers: "In Fascism and Naziism, nationalism emerged free from liberalism and the bourgeois spirit for the first time in history." M. Manoilescu, "Europäische Nationalismus" (1943), p. 20.

81. Taşcă (1937), pp. 6–14, 34–37.

82. M. Manoilescu, "Doctrinele" (1937), p. 27. In this article and in "Lupta" (1938), two replies to Taşcă, Manoilescu repeated many of his arguments and cited his defenders, including Mussolini ("Doctrinele," p. 68), but offered little that was new.

83. See "Memorii," pp. 42–43, and as an example, "Până când nu vom avea o elită" (1939).

84. For Schmitter, by 1936 Manoilescu had adopted "Fascistoid and Germanophilic delusions," but there is no mention of opportunism. Schmitter, "Reflections" (1978), pp. 130–31.

Chapter 7

1. Viner, *International Trade* (1952) [lectures delivered in Rio de Janeiro in 1950], pp. 61–64; Noyola Vázquez, "Evolución" (1956), pp. 278–79 (Manoilescu's influence on ECLA is implied); Murgescu, "Demisia" (1968), p. 15; Nicolae-Văleanu, "Raúl Prebisch" (1980), p. 29; Schmitter, "Still the Century" (1974), p. 119; and Schmitter, "Reflections" (1978), p. 121.

2. Spanish translations are *Teoría del proteccionismo y del comercio internacional* (1943); *Siglo del corporatismo* (1941); and *Partido único, institución política de los nuevos regímenes* (1938); Portuguese translations are *Theoria do proteccionismo e da permuta internacional* (1931); and *Século do corporativismo* (1938), both published in Brazil. In addition, Manoilescu wrote several popular articles for the *Revista Hispánica de Bucarest*, a dual-language magazine in Rumanian and Spanish, published between 1927 and 1931. In one of these (in Rumanian), he looked forward to expanded trade between Argentina and Rumania; in the same issue, the publication of his *Théorie du protectionnisme* was announced. See *Revista Hispánica de Bucarest*, no. 6 (1929), pp. 4, 13. Eight years later Manoilescu published another piece—this time in Portuguese—about his correspondence with the CIESP. It appeared in another ephemeral journal based in Bucharest and aimed at Latin America. See *Luz: Revista Rumeno-Sul Americana* (1937), 2: 19.

3. See M. Manoilescu, *Lege* (1932), p. 18; and "Memorii" MS. (1946–48), pp. 349, 617.

4. M. Manoilescu, "Memorii," p. 617.

5. "Just recently, there appeared in Lisbon a famous Romanian called Manoilescu, who upon his arrival declared, The new doctrine currently spreading throughout Portugal lured me across these frontiers, I come as a respectful disciple, as a jubilant believer." Saramago (1991 [Port. orig. 1984]), p. 173.

6. M. Manoilescu, "Memorii," pp. 612, 614–15.

7. *O sistema corporativo*. Caetano wrote that *Siècle du corporatisme* "will be a classic . . . because it is the first effort [to construct] a general theory of corporatism based on contemporary experiences . . . and it takes advantage of the whole body of thought of the several schools [of corporatism]. It is a brilliant essay, constructive and persuasive, in which the author attempts to demonstrate that corporatism satisfies the imperatives of the twentieth century." The Portuguese law professor also approved of *Parti unique*, without mentioning that the author had suddenly abandoned those theses in *Siècle* noted in the previous chapter. See Caetano (1938), pp. 30, 31 (quotation), 51, 94–95.

It must have been clear to Manoilescu by the time of his visit to Portugal, however, that Salazar's corporatism failed to meet his standard of the independence of corporations from the state, for which the Rumanian was soon to criticize the regimes of Mussolini and King Carol. On the power of the Portuguese executive to run the corporations, see Lucena (1979), p. 83; on state control of industrialists' corporations in particular, see Brandão de Brito, "Condicionamento" (1981), 1: 163, 498; and Rosas, *Estado* (1986), pp. 268–69. As late as 1952, Caetano admitted that the Portuguese corporate state was still an "intention," not a fact. Brandão de Brito, "Condicionamento," 1: 50.

8. On the importance of Manoilescu's corporatist doctrine in Portugal, see, in addition to Caetano, Soares (1946), pp. 129–37. A recent important treatment of Manoilescu's influence on Portuguese corporatism is Lucena, especially pp. 83–85. On Manoilescu's influence on the economic dimension of corporatism (i.e., apart from the trade-industrialization argument), see Brandão de Brito, "Condicionamento," vol. 1, chap. 1, esp. pp. 18, 23.

9. Caetano, p. 31.

10. In his study of Portuguese industrial policy in the 1930s, Rosas finds that rural interests were clearly favored by the regime at the ideological level; nevertheless, it is notable that the first Congress of Industry in 1933 implicitly called for a hegemonic position for industry in the Portuguese economy. Despite contradictions at the policy level, however, on balance, agriculture and colonial-commercial interests received more assistance from the Estado Nôvo in this period than did manufacturers. Rosas, *Estado*, pp. 155, 157, 159, 246; Rosas, "Idéias" (1988), pp. 191, 192–93.

11. In Rosas's view, the "autodidact" industrial bourgeoisie had few articulate spokesmen of its own and left the ideological defense of its interests to engineers. In any case, according to Armando Castro, there was no serious university-level instruction in economics in Portugal until 1949. See Rosas, *Estado*, p. 154; and A. Castro (1978), p. 8. Brandão de Brito shows how engineers wanted to run the country as a business enterprise. José N. Ferreira Dias, Salazar's undersecretary of state for commerce and industry (1940–44) and minister of the economy (1958–62), valued optimism, *produtivismo* ("productivism"), technological efficiency, and voluntarism. Development problems for Ferreira Dias were technical problems, independent of opportunity costs and the optimization of resource allocation. Brandão de Brito, "Engenheiros" (1988); and "Condicionamento," chap. 2.

12. All the same, on at least one occasion Manoilescu pandered to the Salazar govern-

ment in his defense of the regime's imperialism. "The people of the metropolis constitute the elite of the Empire," wrote Manoilescu in his "Génie" (1940), published in Lisbon (p. 637).

13. Aunos [Pérez] ([1935?]), pp. 187, 205, 239, 251, 257, 260, 261 (citations of M. Manoilescu, *Siècle*); 223 (citations of *Théorie*). Aunos had been labor minister under the dictator Primo de Rivera and had written a corporative labor code for Spain in 1926.

14. M. Manoilescu, *Partido*, pp. 9, 15. The Spanish edition also included a new chapter on the Falange and the JONS, the leading fascist organizations in Spain.

15. See the exhaustive study of autarkic theory and policy in Spain (1936–51) by Velasco Murviedro (1982).

16. Olariaga (1936), pp. 229–31 (quotation on 231). Cf. Kalecki's assessment in Chapter 6.

17. Gual Villalbí (1943 [1940]), pp. 496–549; Ros Jimeno (1941); París Eguilaz (1945), chap. 8, esp. pp. 314–28. Gual represented Catalan industrial interests.

18. Fuentes Irurozqui (1943), p. xiv (on previous serial publication by the same ministry in *Información Comercial Española*). Fuentes was sympathetic to Manoilescu's theses, despite his familiarity with Oulès' criticisms. Ibid., pp. vii–xv.

19. M. Manoilescu, "Autarhia" (1934).

20. Velasco, p. 255. Robert's book was *Problema* (1943).

21. Velasco, p. 268.

22. Modeled in part on Mussolini's Istituto per la Ricostruzione Industriale, established in 1931. Schwartz and González (1978), pp. 6, 15.

23. Velasco, p. 1014.   24. Schwartz and González, p. 27.

25. Velasco, p. 932.   26. Ibid., pp. 959–60.

27. Ibid., pp. 745, 1019–20. Autarky was never attempted in a strict sense, Buesa Blanco points out, because Spain remained dependent on foreign capital goods. Buesa Blanco (1983), pp. 483–84.

28. Buesa, pp. 465, 467; Velasco, pp. 268–70.

29. Buesa, pp. 467, 476, 485.

30. Alvarez Andrews (1936), pp. 6, 327–28 [first set of pages], 385 [second set]; Aguirre Cerda (1933), pp. 8, 51, 54, 61; Zañartu Prieto (2d ed., 1946), pp. 241–42.

31. Concha, "Balanza" (1889), pp. 327–31; Concha, *Lucha* (1910), pp. 25–27, 54, 97.

32. Palma, "Growth" (1979), p. xix.

33. M. Manoilesco [*sic*], *Siglo* (1941), translated by Hernán G. Huidobro.

34. Mahn, "Sobre los argumentos" (1945). Manoilescu's *Theory* had already been cited (but not discussed) in the same journal in 1943. See del Canto Schramm (1943), p. 4.

35. Mahn, "Sobre los argumentos," p. 69.

36. M. Manoilesco [*sic*], "Productividad" (1947).

37. Pinto acknowledges that some economists who would later work for the organization knew Manoilescu's work but believes that the influence of Rosenstein-Rodan and Keynesian and Marxian traditions was greater in the formation of structuralism. Pinto to author, Santiago, 31 Jan. 1985.

38. See Chapter 6.

39. *Der Neue Balkan; Menschenzahl und Völkerschicksal.* See *Neue Balkan* (1939), p. 66; *Población* [Sp. version of *Menschenzahl*] (1949). On Manoilescu, see pp. 133–37. Biographical data on Wagemann from Degener (1935) and *Diccionario biográfico* (n.d.), p. 1283.

40. On Wagemann, see *Neue Balkan*, esp. pp. 120–36. On Manoilescu, see Chapter 6.

41. Surveying the UIA's journal from 1930 to 1946, I did not find any references to Manoilescu's theories, in sharp contrast to the frequent citations of the Rumanian theorist by leaders of the Federação das Indústrias in São Paulo.

42. See, for example, Francheschi (1940), pp. 221–27; "Pensamiento" (1942), pp. 13–16.

43. Belaúnde (1939) and Politi (1955), both at the Facultad de Ciencias Económicas, Universidad de Buenos Aires.

44. Gondra (1937), p. 810; Pugliese (1939), p. 917. But also see the discussion of Pugliese's article in the following chapter.

45. Manoliu, *Bibliographie* (1936).

46. Manoliu, "Curriculum Vitae" (1970); Manoliu to Valeriu Dinu, Bahia Blanca, 16 Nov. 1967; and Lascăr Săveanu to author, Bahia Blanca, 30 Dec. 1982. For Manoliu's citations of Manoilescu, see his "Reflexiones" (1962), p. 19; and especially "Comercio" (1968), p. 161. Prebisch's thinking on economic development in 1948 is contained in his "Apuntes" (class notes), mimeo. (1948), located at the Facultad de Ciencias Económicas, Universidad de Buenos Aires.

47. Sombart did not coin the phrase, which dates in its modern sense from the mid-nineteenth century. Rather, according to Fernand Braudel, the German scholar made it common currency in academic milieux as the "natural opposite of socialism" by the publication of *Moderne Kapitalismus* in 1902. Braudel, *Civilization* (1982 [Fr. orig. 1979]), p. 237.

48. See Sombart, "Capitalism" (1931). The three phases or stages were apparently inspired by the conventional periodization of the Middle Ages. The last term has retained a certain popularity among Marxists; e.g., see Mandel (1975).

49. Mitzman (1973), p. 152.

50. E.g., on the subject of preserving German agriculture and the peasantry which lived off it, note the anti-free-trade positions of Adolf Wagner and Ludwig von Pohle, even after Germany had established its industrial supremacy in Europe. See Wagner (1902) and Von Pohle (1902).

51. Mitzman, pp. 237–44.

52. Ibid., p. 203.

53. Sombart, *Moderne Kapitalismus* (1928) 3 [2 vols. bound as one], erster Halbband: xiv–xv.

54. Ibid., p. 64; 3, zweiter Halbband: 1019.

55. Ibid. (1902), vol. 1, zweiter Halbband, *Die vorkapitalistische Wirtschaft*: 798–808, and especially 807 on the " 'natural' precapitalistic attitude" of the lower classes.

56. Boeke, like Sombart, whose *Moderne Kapitalismus* he frequently cites in his various publications, distinguished between two groups of natives—the dynamic elite and the unchanging masses. See Koninklijk Institut voor de Tropen (1966), p. 37. This work contains excerpts from Boeke's dissertation of 1910 and his 1930 address "Dualistic Economics."

57. Boeke, *Economics* (1953), pp. 13, 16. In "Dualistic Economics" (1930) he wrote, "Werner Sombart's description of the pre-capitalist period and his lively, brilliant sketch of economic principles obtaining in it fit the sphere of feudal dualism in the [Dutch East] Indies remarkably well." Koninklijk Institut, p. 170.

58. E.g., see Popa-Vereş (1938), pp. 101–3.

59. Zeletin, *Burghezia* (1925), p. 198, n. 1. In the same note, Zeletin also cites Weber's *General Economic History* (1927 [Ger. orig. 1923]) as making a similar point. Zeletin used Sombart and Weber in a different way from Boeke, however, to show that the coexistence of a labor shortage and overpopulation was a standard precapitalist (or early capitalist) phenomenon, and therefore that this apparent paradox in the Rumanian economy was normal.

60. Sombart, *Deutscher Sozialismus* (1934), translated as *A New Social Philosophy* (1937). Sombart had also written a book in 1932 titled *Zukunft des Kapitalismus* (The future of capitalism). See a summary of the former in Lebovics (1969), pp. 72–74.

61. Sombart, *Die Rationalisierung in der Wirtschaft* (1927).

62. Cf. his contemporary Joseph Schumpeter's view after World War II that "the march into socialism" was a regrettable but relentless development, owing to the popularity of the welfare state. Schumpeter, *Capitalism* (3d ed., 1950), pp. 415–25.

63. Sombart, "Critica" (1931), p. 20.

64. Sombart, however, did not believe population policies were very effective. *New Social Philosophy*, pp. 172–73.

65. Ibid., p. 179.

66. In 1941, the year of his death, Sombart published a foreword to a thesis by a Rumanian disciple, in which the Jews, along with foreign capital and the "liberal Rumanian state," were credited with the development of capitalism in the Balkan country. The Rumanian author wrote, however, that the *Volksgeist* of the Rumanian people had nothing in common with the (Jewish-derived) capitalist spirit. Although the dissertation is perhaps less obviously anti-Semitic than one might expect in 1941, a negative valuation of "Rumanian capitalism" may have provided a rationalization for the fiercely anti-Semitic government policies of the period. Ercuţă (1941), pp. 22, 110.

67. Lebovics, p. 73; the view is implied in Sombart, *New Social Philosophy*, p. 285.

68. Lebovics, pp. 67–68, 73–74; Sombart, *New Social Philosophy*, p. 256.

69. Madgearu, *Zur industriellen Entwicklung* (1911). Madgearu was also concerned about the greater adaptability of artisans among the ethnic minorities in his country to modern capitalism than of their Rumanian counterparts.

70. J. B. F. [unidentified] (1929), p. 3.

71. Sombart denied that Marx's predictions of the immiseration of the proletariat, the concentration of capital, and the increasing gravity of capitalist depressions were borne out by historical experience. He published in 1931 so the last point might have seemed difficult to establish, but Sombart curiously claimed the current crisis was caused by the overproduction of peasant agriculture, which was not capitalistic. See Sombart, "Critica," pp. 1–21, esp. 9–10.

72. Sombart, "Procesul" (1938), p. 2.

73. This is not to argue that the resemblance between the ideology of, say, Julius Nyerere and the elderly Sombart derives from the direct influence of the latter on the former, but is presumably a case of subsequent "rediscovery" of similar propositions or of indirect inspiration. On the populism of the Tanzanian politician, see Kitching (1982), pp. 64–70.

74. Madgearu, "Imperialismul" (1924), p. 15.

75. Perroux ran his own development institute, which published *Mondes en Développe-*

ment, and he wrote many works on development problems. His last major treatise on the matter is *New Concept of Development* (1983).

76. E.g., see Perroux, *Capitalisme* (1938), pp. 298–300; and Perroux and Madaule (1942?), pp. 7, 31. Perroux, like the Austrian corporatist Othmar Spann, favored a decentralized, nontotalitarian form of corporatism. He also made clear that the "third solution" was one *within* the capitalist system, contrary to the claims of some writers. Perroux, "Economie" (1933), pp. 1413, 1474. In his memoir, "Peregrinations" (1980), Perroux makes no mention of corporatism; and in a letter and an interview, I was unable to get him to say anything on the subject. Perroux to author, 30 July 1982; interview, Urbana, Ill., 14 Mar. 1983.

77. Shortly before coming to Brazil, Perroux briefly held the first chair of economics at the University of Coimbra in Portugal. His published lectures were entitled *Lições de economia política* (1936). See also A. Castro (1978), p. 7.

78. See, for example, Congrès International, *Travaux* (1937), vol. 1 (citing presence of Manoilescu and Perroux). Perroux cites Manoilescu in *Capitalisme*, on pp. ix, 73, 225.

79. Perroux, *Capitalisme*, p. 299.

80. "Esquisse d'une théorie de l'économie dominante."

81. Perroux, "Domination Effect" (1950), p. 203. See the same point in the full treatise, "Esquisse" (1948), p. 288. A recent translation of a section of the original French study is Perroux, "Outline" (1979). Income elasticity of demand for a good refers to the relative response of demand to a small percentage change in income, $\Delta q/q/\Delta y/y$, where q is the quantity demanded, and y is disposable income. Price elasticity of demand analogously refers to the relative response of demand to a small percentage change in price.

82. Perroux, "Esquisse," p. 297.

83. Arndt, "Origins" (1985).

84. Ibid., p. 152.

85. Rosenstein-Rodan, "Problems" (1943); a nontechnical treatment was his "International Development" (1944); Mandelbaum, *Industrialisation* (1945). Rosenstein-Rodan's two articles "may well be regarded as the beginning of modern development economics," according to Arndt, *Economic Development* (1987), pp. 47–48.

86. Arndt, *Economic Development*, p. 47.

87. Johnson, *Economic Nationalism* (1967), pp. 131–32.

88. Young (1928), esp. p. 539 (quotation).

89. Ignoring these potential economies, neoclassical economics made unrealistic assumptions that individual firms had linear and homogeneous production functions, thought Rosenstein-Rodan. See his "Natura" (1984), p. 213 (quotations); Rosenstein-Rodan to author, Boston, 13 May 1981. Charles Kindleberger in the same year, 1943, had a perspective similar to Rosenstein-Rodan's on the need for industrialization, coming at the problem from the perspective of international trade. He saw the terms of trade moving against agricultural-trading countries as world income rose and Engel's law operated. Therefore, "If the agricultural and raw materials countries want to share the increase in the world's productivity including that in their own products, they must join in the transfer of resources from agriculture, pastoral pursuits, and mining to industry." Like Rosenstein-Rodan, Kindleberger called for infrastructural development loans from the West, sums that could be repaid out of productivity gains from these large-scale investments. Kindleberger, "Planning" (1943), p. 349.

90. Arndt puts the case a little too strongly for the "British" structuralists' influence on their Latin American counterparts' theory on inflation by suggesting that Kaldor and the American Hollis Chenery wrote a structural interpretation of Latin American inflation before Osvaldo Sunkel, the Chilean economist—though Kalecki did influence the Latin American structuralists, as Sunkel acknowledged. Arndt, *Economic Development*, p. 155.

91. Johnson, "Keynes" (1978), p. 229. For Johnson the other source was the postwar Harrod-Domar model of economic growth, which focused on capital formation to the near exclusion of other factors (pp. 230–31).

92. Mandelbaum, *Industrialisation*, pp. 1–2.

93. The "disguised unemployed" were defined as "those persons who work on their own account and who are so numerous, relative to the resources with which they work, that if a number of them were withdrawn for work in other sectors of the economy, the total output of the sector from which they were withdrawn would not be diminished, even though no significant reorganization occurred in the sector, and no significant substitution of capital." United Nations: Department of Economic Affairs, *Measures* (1951), pp. 7 (quotation), 8–9, citing Committee for Reconstruction for the RIIA, *Memorandum on Agricultural Surplus Population* (London, 1943). The UN report preferred the term "disguised underemployment" because, properly speaking, "unemployment" referred to wage earners, whose unemployment was recorded in government statistics (p. 7).

94. UN: Department of Economic Affairs, *Measures*, p. 59. Later one of the experts, Schultz, would write a book to show that there was no such thing as zero marginal productivity in traditional agriculture. Oddly, in his reminiscences of his contributions to development economics, he does not mention that he once subscribed to the notion. See Schultz, *Transforming* (1964), chap. 4, esp. pp. 55–58, and Schulz, "Tensions" (1987).

95. Nurkse (1953), pp. 35–37, citing Warriner on southeastern Europe (p. 35).

96. Cassel (1927), p. 27.

97. Société des Nations [League of Nations]: Comité Economique (1935), pp. 9, 10.

98. Ibid., pp. 25, 36.

99. E.g., Austria's economy collapsed after the hyperinflation of 1922; the League arranged an international loan, with League supervision of the Austrian economy until 1926. For similar reasons Hungary was also under League economic controls from 1924 to 1926. The League granted other reconstruction loans (with attendant controls) in the 1920s to Bulgaria, Estonia, and the Free City of Danzig. Lewis, *Economic Survey* (1949), pp. 22, 36.

100. Rist (1932), pp. 38, 41. Rist did concede that traditional European markets were then largely closed to Rumanian agriculture (p. 38).

101. M. Manoilescu, "Nouii fanarioți" (1933). A Rumanian economic historian later judged that foreign experts, including those of the League, backed by Western governments, were able to obtain modifications of the agricultural debt conversion plan in 1932 because they were afraid it would affect foreign debt payments. Lupu (1967), pp. 102, 105–7, 109.

102. Christodorescu (1933), citing C. R. Mircea, the president of UGIR, pp. 31–32. Mircea did admit that the eight-hour day had been adopted by the Rumanian parliament (p. 32). Also see Chapter 5.

103. League of Nations: Committee for the Study of the Problems of Raw Materials, *Report* (1937), pp. 10, 15. The committee included well-known conservative advisers such as Leith-Ross and Rist.

104. League of Nations: Economic, Financial and Transit Department, *Commercial Policy* (1942), p. 133.

105. The United Nations Organization was agreed on by the major powers at San Francisco in June 1945, and it came into being in October. The League was formally abolished in April 1946, when its assets were transferred to the United Nations.

106. League of Nations: Economic, Financial and Transit Department, *Industrialization* (1945), pp. 5, 16, n. 2, 34 (quotation). The principal author of the report was Folke Hilgerdt (p. 6). Interestingly, page 16, note 2 argues that the data, if carried through the latter 1930s, contradict the observation of Manoilescu, who found agricultural prices in the United States to be secularly rising relative to industrial prices. Manoilescu interpreted the Great Depression as an aberration to the secular trend he had identified, but this note seems almost a gratuitous slap at the Rumanian because League economists now seemed to be conceding much to the position of their longtime detractor.

107. On Latin America, see Díaz-Alejandro, "Trade Policies" (1975), p. 116; "1940s" MS. (1982), pp. 11, 39.

108. See Sommer, *Neugestaltung* (1935), pp. 180, 188–89.

109. Sommer, "Pays" (1938), p. 90.

110. Prebisch only notes the faster fall of agricultural prices in the downswing, but the faster rise in the upswing can readily be inferred. [Prebisch], *Economic Review* [of the Banco Central de la República Argentina], series 2, 1, no. 1 (1937): 26–27.

111. See Kondratieff, "Long Waves" (1935 [Russ. orig. 1925]). Whether such long waves exist in the historical development of capitalism is still a matter of controversy. Kondratieff did not get to elaborate his thesis because he was purged by Stalin in 1930 and died in prison at an unknown date.

112. Kondratieff, "Preisdynamik" (1928), pp. 58–59.

113. Kindleberger, "Flexibility" (1937).   114. Sommer, "Pays," p. 108.

115. Ibid., p. 110.   116. Ibid., pp. 111–12.

117. H. Singer, "Distribution" (1950), p. 479.

Chapter 8

1. Though Ragnar Nurkse, from Estonia, was a League economist, at the time he was an orthodox neoclassical.

2. Fishlow (1984), p. 192. Prebisch once even wrote, "Today we recognize that it is indispensable to oppose market forces." Prebisch, "Anexo" (1963), p. 5.

3. E.g., see Reyes Gómez (1888), pp. 86, 88; Murtinho (n.d.), p. xiii; Plaza (1903), pp. 49–50, 68–69. The last-named writer, Victorino de la Plaza, served as president of Argentina, 1914–16.

4. There was less import-substitution industrialization in other parts of Latin America. Díaz-Alejandro, "Latin America" (1984), p. 25; on Peru in particular, see Thorp and Bertram (1978), p. 183.

5. Phelps (1935), p. 281.

6. See citations in Chapter 7, note 30 (on Chile); also, Pupo Nogueira, "A propósito de modernização" (1945), p. 18 (Brazil); "Industrialización" (1945), p. 6 (Mexico).

7. See Love, "Economic Ideas" (1994), pp. 400–401. The establishment of development banks was an important symbolic act, but changes in tariff structures, which have yet to be thoroughly analyzed, may have been more important for growth.

8. "Argentine Industrial Exhibition," (1933), pp. 11, 13, 15; Villanueva (1975), p. 78.

9. González and Pollock (1991), p. 484.

10. Masón (1944), p. 5.

11. Randall (1978), p. 76.

12. On Argentina, Brazil, Chile, and Mexico, see Love, "Economic Ideas," pp. 399–401.

13. See Rosenstein-Rodan, "Problems" (1958 [1943]), and Kindleberger, "Planning" (1943), p. 349; Prokopovicz (1946), pp. 278–79.

14. Rosenstein-Rodan, "Problems," pp. 246, 253–54; Kindleberger, "Planning," pp. 347–54; Prokopovicz, pp. 278–79; Clark, *Economics* (1942), p. 114.

15. Bagú, "¿Y mañana" (1944), p. 37; Ferreira Lima, "Evolução" (1945), p. 17; "Monetary Developments" (1945), p. 523; Robles (1947), p. 1.

16. In 1918, Luis Gondra introduced South America's first course in mathematical economics at the University of Buenos Aires. Gondra et al. (1945), p. 32.

17. Prebisch, "Planes" (1921), pp. 459–513; interview with Prebisch, Washington, D.C., 10 July 1978.

18. Information from Eliana Prebisch, Prebisch's widow, Washington, D.C., 26 May 1986.

19. Prebisch, *Anotaciones* (1926), p. 3.

20. Prebisch's study offered statistical proof that the meat pool's interference in the market had been beneficial for the British packinghouses but not for the Argentine cattlemen. See Prebisch, "Régimen" (1927), pp. 1302–21.

21. Banco de la Nación Argentina (1928), p. 2. Luis Duhau, the president of the Sociedad Rural, had a hand in these events as the director of the bank: Interview of Ernesto Malaccorto by Leandro Gutiérrez, Bs. As., Aug., 1971; Prebisch, "Historias" (1985), [p. 1].

22. Information from Eliana Prebisch, 26 May 1986.

23. *Who's Who* (1975), pp. 455–56; Prebisch, "Versión" (MS, 1955), pp. 23–24; Díaz-Alejandro, *Essays* (1970), p. 97; Malaccorto interview, p. 40 ("brain trust"); Banco Central, *Creación* (1972), 1: 267–69. The last-named work details the differences in the Niemeyer plan and that actually adopted by the Argentine government. The Niemeyer proposal did not attempt to reorganize the banking system, nor did his plan include a countercyclical instrument as did the one that was implemented. For a summary history of the bank's inception, see Prebisch, "Historias," 2a. sección, [p. 1].

24. Díaz-Alejandro, *Essays*, p. 2.

25. Kindleberger, *World Depression* (1973), pp. 102, 104; UN: ECLA, *Economic Development . . . Its Principal Problems* (1950), p. 29.

26. Fodor and O'Connell (1973), pp. 18, 30.

27. Data in Vásquez-Presedo (1978), pp. 253, 272.

28. Fodor and O'Connell, pp. 52–54. Britain was to eliminate tariffs on cereal imports, but the emphasis was on beef. Argentina also agreed to spend all sterling sums earned in the United Kingdom. Villanueva, pp. 65–66. At Geneva, Prebisch had been willing to make tariff concessions to British manufacturers, partly to mitigate Argentina's dollar shortage. The Foreign Office considered him an amiable sort but a tough negotiator. F. W. Leith-Ross to Sir Horace Hamilton, Geneva, 16 Jan. 1933, FO 371.16531; and "Report on Leading Personalities in Argentina," 27 Jan. 1937, 317.20598, p. 16.

29. Fodor and O'Connell, pp. 56–59.

30. Prebisch, "Conferencia" (1933), pp. 1, 3. Another reason for U.S. absorption of the world's gold supply was the overvaluation of the pound sterling, when Britain returned to the gold standard in 1925.

31. Prebisch, "Inflación" (1934), pp. 11–12, 60, 194. Later it was discovered that the purchasing power of Argentina's exports fell by about 40 percent between 1925–29 and 1930–34. Ferrer (1967), p. 162.

32. Kindleberger, *World Depression*, pp. 278–79.

33. Beveraggi-Allende (1952), pp. 219 (quotation), 246; Malaccorto interview, p. 64.

34. Phelps, p. 274; *Economic Review* (1937), 1: 69.

35. Banco Central, *Memoria, 1942* (1943), pp. 30–31. In the same year this report was published, government economists in Franco's Spain, working in a country seeking (or forced into) autarky, came to the same conclusion. Velasco Murviedro (1982), p. 344.

36. *Economic Review* (1937), 1: 26–27.

37. Ibid., p. 69.

38. Olarra Jiménez (1968), p. 13.

39. Banco Central, *Memoria, 1938* (1939), pp. 5–8; Prebisch to author, Washington, D.C., 9 Nov. 1977.

40. Prebisch, "Argentina" (1982), p. 18.

41. Prebisch interview.

42. Prebisch, "Moneda" (1944), pp. 61–65, mimeo.

43. Ibid., p. 65.

44. Ibid., summarized in Olarra Jiménez, p. 76.

45. Villanueva, p. 78. On Prebisch as probable author of the Pinedo plan, see Díaz-Alejandro, *Essays*, p. 105, n. 37.

46. At the same time Prebisch gave a series of lectures at the Banco de México on "the Argentine monetary experience (1935–1943)," covering the period in which he was the director-general of the Central Bank. See Banco Central, *Creación*, 1: 249–588; 2: 599–623.

47. Prebisch, "Patrón" (1944), p. 234; Banco Central, *Memoria, 1942*, p. 30.

48. Prebisch, "Análisis," p. 407. See the similar judgments on import-substitution industrialization by Dorfman (1942), p. 74 (on World War I and the Great Depression); Ferreira Lima, p. 17 (on São Paulo in World War II). But see Chapter 12 for the later debate on the significance of wars and depression on industrial development.

49. Prebisch, "Observaciones" (1944), pp. 188, 192–93. Even before Prebisch took charge at ECLA, his ideas on external disequilibrium had influenced the research of a young economist who would later be a leading figure in the organization: Juan Noyola Vázquez's *licenciado* dissertation explored the problem of disequilibrium in Mexico, using the analysis of Prebisch in "Patrón oro" (1944) as a point of departure. See Noyola Vázquez, *Desequilibrio* (1949), pp. 22–23 (on Prebisch). This work, along with that of Alfredo Navarrete, another Mexican, shows that Prebisch was not the only Latin American coping with external disequilibrium problems which neoclassical theory did not seem to answer. See Navarrete (1950), published in Spanish in 1951.

50. Prebisch, "Panorama" (1946), pp. 25–28; "Observaciones," p. 199.

51. Bhagwati (1984), p. 198; Díaz-Alejandro, "1940s" (MS, 1982), p. 39 (Cf. the pessimism of economists at the League of Nations in 1945, cited in Chapter 7.)

52. Prebisch, "Apuntes" (1948), pp. 88–97 (quotation on 97), mimeo.

53. Though the term "hegemony" did not appear in this early use of Center-Periphery terminology, years later Prebisch himself would specifically employ the word to characterize relations between the two elements of the world economy. Prebisch, "Critique" (1976), p. 60.

54. See Chapter 1.

55. UN ECOSOC E/CN.12/17 (7 June 1948), p. 2; E/CN.12/28 (11 June 1948), p. 6; E/CN.12/71 (24 June 1948). I consulted these documents at ECLA headquarters in Santiago.

56. *Introducción a Keynes* (1947).

57. Prebisch interview; Prebisch, "Anexo" (1963), p. 1, mimeo. For support on the League's lack of interest in underdeveloped areas, see Arndt, *Economic Development* (1987), p. 33.

58. Hirschman, "Ideologies" (1961), p. 13.

59. United Nations: Department of Economic Affairs, *Relative Prices* (1949), p. 7.

60. UN: ECLA, *Economic Development . . . Its Principal Problems* (1950), pp. 8–14.

61. UN: ECLA, *Economic Survey . . . 1949* (1951), p. 47.

62. Ibid., p. 4. In 1958 Prebisch estimated that agriculture in Latin America could absorb only 10 percent of the growth of the economically active population between 1959 and 1967, and "industry will have to absorb some 47% of it." Prebisch, "Commercial Policy" (1959), pp. 251–73.

63. UN: ECLA, *Economic Survey . . . 1949* (1951), pp. 78 (quotation), 79. At that time Prebisch believed that by changing the composition of imports from consumer to capital goods, Latin American countries could reduce their import coefficients. UN: ECLA, *Economic Development . . . Its Principal Problems*, pp. 44–45.

64. UN: ECLA, *Economic Development . . . Its Principal Problems*, pp. 15–16; UN: ECLA, *Economic Survey . . . 1949*, pp. 20, 35–38.

65. *Economic Survey . . . 1949*, pp. 35, 75.

66. Ibid., pp. 59. More ambiguously, *Economic Development of Latin America and Its Principal Problems* stated that "the income of entrepreneurs and of productive factors" in the Center increased faster than did productivity in the Center from the 1870s to the 1930s; but in another passage the document placed exclusive emphasis on the role of wages in the Center (pp. 10, 14).

67. H. Singer, "Distribution" (1950), pp. 473–85 (quotation from 479). Elasticity of demand is defined in Chapter 7.

68. Prebisch to author, 29 June 1977; Singer to author, Brighton, England, 21 Aug. 1979.

69. Wallerstein, "Periphery" (1987), p. 847; H. Singer, "Terms" (1987), p. 626; Jameson (1986), p. 224. In "Raúl Prebisch" (1988), Schwartz writes, "It was not until 1950 that the famous Prebisch-CEPAL papers began to appear" (p. 125). Arndt credits Singer with simultaneity on the basis of his article "Economic Progress in Underdeveloped Countries" (1949), which I find insufficiently developed in explaining deteriorating terms of trade to justify the claim, although the article makes a case for the "Big Push." Rather, it is "Distribution of Gains," the paper he presented in 1949 and published in 1950, that made Singer an independent "discoverer."

70. E/CN.12/221 (18 May 1951), p. 30.

71. E.g., see Prebisch, "Commercial Policy," pp. 251–73.

72. Fitzgerald, "ECLA" (1994), p. 100.

73. Sombart, *Moderne Kapitalismus* (1928), 3 [2 vols. bound as 1] erster Halbband: xiv–xv. Prebisch could also have seen the French edition, *Apogée du capitalisme* (1932), located at the FCE library. If he read the Spanish translation in manuscript, published in Mexico in 1946, it would have to have been before he used the terms in his 1944 lectures at the FCE. (This is possible because he was in Mexico in 1944 before the academic year began in Buenos Aires.)

74. Ibid., 1: 64; 2: 1019.

75. Prebisch to author, Washington, D.C., 26 June 1979.

76. *Struktur und Rhythmus der Weltwirtschaft.*

77. Wagemann, *Struktur* (1931), pp. 70–71. Prebisch might have known this work in its Spanish translation, *Evolución* (1933). Though noting the different meanings of the Center-Periphery opposition in Wagemann and Prebisch, Joseph Hodara believes the former influenced Prebisch's thinking on the international economy. Alfredo Navarrete cites Wagemann—incorrectly, I think—as the principal source of Prebisch's inspiration on the use of Center-Periphery. Hodara (1987), pp. 132–36; Navarrete, p. 115.

78. See Brown (1940), 2: 862. In 1977 Prebisch did not recall how he came to use the terms "Center" and "Periphery." Prebisch to author, 29 June 1977.

79. See citations by Viner, Noyola, Murgescu, Nicolae-Văleanu, and Schmitter in Chapter 7.

80. See Mahn (1945), pp. 59–70; M. Manoilescu, "Productividad" (1947), pp. 50–77. Of course, Prebisch might also have read Manoilescu's *Theory* (1929) in French, or in translation, before the latter's article appeared in Chile.

81. See below, Chapter 10, and for more detail, Love, "Modeling" (1989).

82. See Prebisch, *Obras* (1991).

83. Although both Prebisch and Manoilescu made appearances in different parts of Europe in 1933, I found no evidence that their paths crossed.

84. Prebisch, "Commercial Policy" (1959), p. 255.

85. See Love, "Manoilescu, Prebisch" (1980–86), p. 132. Hugo Böker was one of the early writers to contest Manoilescu's view that there was a long-term tendency to close the agricultural-industrial price scissors. Böker (1941), p. 25.

86. Pugliese (1939), p. 917. (See citations of Cassel, Kondratieff, Kindleberger, and Sommer in previous chapter.)

87. Kindleberger, "Planning" (1943) and "International Monetary Stabilization" (1943). Prebisch cited the latter in "Observaciones," pp. 195–96, though he did so to contest the American's references to the behavior of the Argentine economy. On the former article, see Chapter 7. At his seminar on central banking in Mexico in 1944, Prebisch also cited Kindleberger's thesis that the United States would have a persistent trade imbalance with the rest of the world because of disparities in demand elasticities. At the time, Prebisch was not certain the thesis was valid. Prebisch, in Banco Central, *Creación*, 1: 530–31.

88. Kindleberger, "International Monetary Stabilization," p. 378.

89. Ibid., p. 377, citing Clark, *Economics* (1942).

90. Kindleberger, "International Monetary Stabilization," pp. 378–79.

91. Ibid., p. 381. The writer was referring both to income and price elasticity (p. 380). Kindleberger later recalled that his thesis that a rise in exports could trigger a rise in imports remained controversial during the war. Kindleberger to author, Lexington, Mass., 31 Dec. 1991.

92. Though I doubt any influence by François Perroux on Prebisch in 1948–49 (see previous chapter), the French theorist's subsequent concept of "growth poles" was a Center-Periphery notion, and his *Coexistence Pacifique* had a clear Center-Periphery framework, inasmuch as he divided the world into "focal countries" (*pays foyers*) and "dependent economies," the former exercising a domination effect over the latter. See Perroux, "Notes" (1970) and Perroux, *Coexistence Pacifique* (1958), pp. 236–38. For Perroux and Furtado, see Chapter 10. In "Economic Ideas and Ideologies," I also consider and reject the theoretical influence on Prebisch of two Latin American writers, Alejandro Bunge of Argentina and Víctor Emilio Estrada of Ecuador.

93. Hirschman, "Generalized Linkage Approach" (1977), p. 68. Samuelson's articles were "International Trade" (1948) and "International Factor-Price Equalisation" (1949).

94. Fishlow (1984), p. 193.

95. Spraos, "Statistical Debate" (1980), pp. 107–28.

96. Spraos, *Inequalising Trade?* (1983), p. 3.

97. Ibid., p. 7.

98. In words, the formula is as follows: the net barter terms of trade times the ratio of the productivities of commodities and manufactures times an index of employment in the commodity-exporting countries' traditional exportables. Ibid., pp. 9–10.

99. Ibid., p. 15.

100. Ibid., p. 42.

101. A different conclusion is reached by W. Arthur Lewis, whose analysis of the terms-of-trade problem puts primary emphasis on raising productivity in food production in underdeveloped countries. Lewis, *Evolution* (1978), chap. 11, and Findlay (1980), p. 72.

102. Spraos, "Statistical Debate," p. 126. Yet even had this conclusion remained undisputed, Prebisch would still have argued that anything less than a *favorable* trend for primary products would show that the Center was benefiting more than the Periphery in the trading process (assuming greater technological productivity gains in the Center).

103. For an extensive review of the literature, generally supporting Spraos's findings and arguing that there was some deterioration of the barter terms of trade for primary commodities, although less than Prebisch originally believed, see Diakosavvas and Scandizzo (1991), esp. p. 237. Prebisch and Singer are more strongly supported in a study by Grilli and Yang, who estimate a trend rate (for 1900–1986) of −0.5 percent in net barter terms of trade a year for all primary commodities and −0.6 percent for primary commodities excluding fuels. This amounts to a 36 percent decline for all primary goods traded, and 40 percent for the nonfuel group, during this century. Grilli and Yang (1988), pp. 1, 34. The authors note (p. 7) that a country could still benefit in a situation of declining net barter terms of trade if its "income terms of trade" are improving. (Income terms of trade, which measure the purchasing power of total exports in terms of imports, is the unit price of a given good times the number of units exported, divided by the unit price of imports.)

Chapter 9

1. Contador and Haddad (1975), p. 412; Dean, "Brazilian Economy" (1986), pp. 695–96.

2. Morais Filho (1980), pp. 19, 21.

3. Murtinho (1899), p. xiii.

4. Paying their costs in local currency and receiving "hard" currencies for their exports, such groups profited by obtaining more local currency as its exchange value fell.

5. For details on valorization, see Love, *São Paulo* (1980), chap. 2, and the citations therein.

6. Correia (1977) and Vieira Souto (1977), pp. 8, 42, 54.

7. Ferreira Lima (1976), p. 108.

8. "O Brasileiro," cited in Sáenz Leme (1978), pp. 161, 163.

9. Decca (1981), pp. 141–49.   10. *Em torno da tarifa aduaneira* (1931).

11. Ibid., pp. 136, 138.   12. Ibid., p. 3.

13. "Prefacio" to Manoilescu, *Theoria*, p. 6.

14. Gudin, "Rumos" (1977 [Mar. 1945]), p. 108.

15. Siciliano, cited in Pupo Nogueira, p. 133; for Pupo's own views, see pp. 3, 131; Siciliano (1931), pp. 12, 62; Simonsen, *Crises* (n.d.), pp. 58, 91; Simonsen, speech of 8 April 1931, in *À margem* ([1932?]), p. 250. For the rubber industry, contrary to Siciliano's argument, Warren Dean has denied that Asian labor was cheaper than its Brazilian counterpart. Dean, *Struggle* (1987), p. 82.

16. Fanganiello (1970), p. 186.

17. Federação das Indústrias do Estado de São Paulo (hereafter FIESP, successor to CIESP), circular no. 152, São Paulo, 1 July 1931; Pupo, p. 119; M. Manoilescu, "Memorii" (MS., 1947–48), p. 349.

18. Instituto de Organização Racional do Trabalho.

19. Its Rumanian counterpart, the Institute for the Scientific Organization of Labor, had been created in 1927. Malinschi (1967), p. 24.

20. Antonacci (1985), p. 8.

21. Walther (1931), p. 1.

22. On the history of efforts to abolish interstate barriers to trade, see Love, *São Paulo*, pp. 195–96, 247–48. Though domestic freedom of commerce was a measure championed by liberals in the nineteenth century, by the 1930s the cause was no longer the property of liberals alone. Corporatists had similar objectives to enlarge national markets, just as mercantilists had pursued the same objective before liberals.

23. See O'Neil (1971), pp. 56–66. Sales was appointed interventor of São Paulo by Vargas in 1933 and was elected governor the following year.

24. FIESP, *Relatório* of 19 May 1937, cited in Carone, *Pensamento* (1977), p. 9.

25. Teixeira Vieira (1981), p. 362. Rockefeller fellowships were granted to four Rumanian social scientists—Manuilă, Georgescu-Roegen, Sterian, and Cresin—to study in American universities in the interwar years, and Perroux himself had received a Rockefeller grant to the University of Vienna.

26. E.g., Perroux, "Nobrezas" (1936); "Trapaça" (1937); "Contra as trapaças" (1937); "Socialismo," nos. 2 and 4 (1937); "Capitalismo e corporativismo: Economia" (1937); "Capitalismo e corporativismo: Funcionamento" (1938); "Pessoa" (1939). Some of the journal articles had originally appeared in *O Estado de S. Paulo*.

27. Perroux, "Capitalismo e corporativismo: Socialização" (1939), pp. 402–5 [orig. in *Revista do Trabalho*]. It is ironic that many of Perroux's articles appeared in the *Revista do Trabalho*, dedicated to the study of a labor regime that was anything but independent of the state.

28. Reale (1986), p. 75.

29. See Vieira (1981), chap. 2, and M. Manoilescu, *Século* [tr. by Azevedo Amaral] (1938).

30. Vieira, pp. 31, 68.

31. Diniz (1978), p. 59.

32. Ibid., pp. 62, 69.

33. On Torres's ruralism, nationalism, anti-imperialism, and general confusion, see his two main works, *Organisação nacional* (1914) and *Problema nacional brasileiro* (1914); and Marson (1979). Torres, like so many others, would have permitted only industries that used domestic raw materials. Marson, p. 173.

34. [FIESP et al.], *Constituição* (n.p., [1940]), pp. 23, 29–30, 104, 106, 108–9, 126. Also citing Manoilescu's version of corporatism approvingly in a professional journal, as well as Perroux's *Capitalisme*, was the Paulista economist Tito Prates da Fonseca. See his "Tendências" (1940), pp. 219, 222.

35. Vargas, *Nova política* (1938), 1: 26–27; Aranha in *O Estado de S. Paulo*, 8 Mar. 1933.

36. Vargas, *Nova política* (1940), 6: 91; (1941), 8: 179; budgetary data from Villela and Suzigan (1973), p. 352. In theory, the government could provide bank credit to industry from 1921, when the Rediscount Division of the Banco do Brasil was created. The Division of Agricultural and Industrial Credit was established in 1937, but it could not make loans for the expansion of industrial capacity or lend to firms in "artificial industries." In any case, funds disbursed to industrialists were not significant until the 1940s.

37. See Vargas, *Mensagem* (1937), pp. 13–14; and Vargas, "Estado Nôvo" (10 Nov. 1938) in *Nova política*, 6: 91.

38. Doc. 85, 22 Sept. 1937, in A-CFCE, processo 435, "Instituto Nacional de Mate," p. 162, Arquivo Nacional. That Manoilescu's theory of protectionism was cited to justify creating a corporate autarky shows a link between his economic and corporatist theories. For more on the relation and the context of this document, see Bak (1985).

39. Diniz, p. 105.

40. He still believed to trade goods produced with low wages for those produced with high wages was a bad bargain. Fanganiello, p. 213.

41. In Gudin's view, Ohlin, Viner, and Gottfried Haberler had "liquidated" Manoilescu's "supposed theory." Gudin, "Rumos," pp. 108–9.

42. "Eugênio Gudin" (MS., 1979), transcript of interview, Centro de Pesquisa e Documentação, p. 155.

43. As late as 1964, a similar argument was made by an economist associated with the National Confederation of Industry: if 1,000 units of capital are available to Brazil, and agriculture can only absorb 200, to apply the remaining 800 to industry will be a net gain, whatever the costs of the goods produced because agricultural output will not decrease. Almeida Magalhães, *Controvérsia* (1964), p. 133.

44. I [i.e., Primeiro] Congresso Brasileiro de Economia, *Anais* (1943–46), 2: 51.

45. Ibid. (1945), 1: 79 (Simonsen's speech), 225–26 (resolutions). What the Brazilian industrialists wanted most and received from Vargas was government control of the labor movement, in exchange for their acceptance of welfare legislation for workers.

46. F. Cardoso, *Ideologías* (1971), p. 215.

47. Love, *São Paulo*, pp. 63–64, 206.

48. Cf. Prebisch in contemporary Argentina.

49. Pupo Nogueira, "A propósito" (1945), pp. 16–18.

50. And former Communist militant. See Chapter 11.

51. Ferreira Lima (1945), p. 17.

52. Hugon ([1958?]), pp. 312–13.

53. Gudin, "Notas" (1972), p. 86. In an earlier review of the training of professional economists, Gudin had written that only in 1945 had a federal statute set the proper standards for economics as an analytical discipline in Brazil. Gudin, "Formação" (1956), pp. 54–55.

54. On Rumania, see Janos, "Modernization" (1978), pp. 107–8.

55. On the ISR, see *Roumanian Institute* (1926). On the ISEB, see Alves de Abreu (1975); Sodré (1978); and Toledo (1982).

56. Succeeded in 1936 by the Rumanian Association for the Study of Business Cycles.

57. By contrast, the Banco do Brasil was more of a commercial than a central bank. The Superintendency of Currency and Credit, established in 1945, is usually considered Brazil's first central bank, with power to control the money supply, change the rediscount rate, and establish the minimum level of reserves for commercial banks.

58. Gamio studied anthropology at Columbia University with Franz Boas. Hale (1986), p. 434, n. 138.

59. The partial exception was provided by Mexico, where Gamio and other anthropologists had begun to map out local village ethnography.

60. Bielschowsky (1985), 1: 46–47.

61. The Argentine *Revista de Ciencias Económicas*, dating back to 1913, lost its leadership under the Perón regime.

62. Sikkink traces the graduate education in the United States of several early Brazilian economists, including Roberto Campos, who would play important policy roles in the 1950s. See her "Developmentalism" (1988), pp. 117–23.

63. Furtado, *Fantasia organizada* (1985), p. 19.

Chapter 10

1. Furtado, "Adventures" (1973), p. 38; Furtado interview, Rio de Janeiro, 31 May 1990.

2. Oliveira (1983), p. 14. Furtado did not belong to any political party, according to his *Fantasia desfeita* (1989), p. 96.

3. Furtado, "Adventures," pp. 28–30, 32.

4. Furtado, *Fantasia organizada* (1985), pp. 18, 27.

5. Furtado, "Adventures," pp. 30, 32.

6. Furtado, *Fantasia organizada*, p. 14.

7. Furtado, "Adventures," p. 32.

8. See Perroux's apologetic defense of corporatism in "Domination Effect" (1950), p. 198. Byé as well was conversant with corporatist theories, which he had discussed, including M. Manoilescu's *Siècle*, in his "Congrès" (1937), pp. 143–45.

9. Furtado, "Economie" (1948).

10. Along with the *Revista Brasileira de Economia*, the professional economics journal discussed in the previous chapter.

11. Furtado, *Fantasia organizada*, pp. 46–47, 99–100.

12. Furtado, "Características gerais da economia brasileira" (1950).

13. Furtado interview.

14. Furtado, *Fantasia organizada*, pp. 120–22; Magariños (1991), p. 140.

15. Furtado, *Fantasia organizada*, p. 106. See following notes for other documentation.

16. [Confederação Nacional das Indústrias] (1950); Sikkink, *Ideas* (1991), p. 155; Sikkink, "Developmentalism" (1988), p. 406.

17. See *Desenvolvimento e Conjuntura* 1, no. 1 (July 1957): 5–15 (including ECLA's deteriorating terms-of-trade argument, the structuralist thesis that inflation is frequently caused by bottlenecks, and the need for government planning or programming). Later numbers in the period examined (through 1960) were generally favorable to ECLA.

18. Sikkink, *Ideas*, pp. 154–57. A full discussion of the relations of industrial associations and the state for 1930–61 is found in Leopoldi (1984).

19. *Formação econômica do Brasil* (1959), published in English as *Economic Growth of Brazil* (1963). The English title is slightly misleading because *formação* indicates qualitative aspects of development as well as quantitative growth.

20. He was also a member of the Working Group for the Development of the Northeast, collaborating with the BNDE.

21. Furtado, *Fantasia desfeita*, pp. 44–45.

22. Ibid., pp. 70–73. For a discussion of other individuals and groups seeking to influence Kubitschek, see Skidmore (1967), pp. 178–82.

23. He was labeled a Communist, for example, by the renowned though now reactionary social essayist Gilberto Freyre and by Carlos Lacerda, governor of Guanabara (the former Federal District, containing the city of Rio de Janeiro and replaced by Brasília as the national capital in 1960). Furtado, *Fantasia desfeita*, pp. 68–69, 133.

24. Ibid., p. 130.

25. Ibid., p. 147.

26. Furtado, *Subdesenvolvimento* (1966).

27. *Formação* (1969), published in English as *Economic Development of Latin America* (1970).

28. Palma, "Structuralism" (1987), p. 529.

29. Furtado, "Características," p. 11; Lewis, "Economic Development" (1954).

30. In this essay Furtado also employed the terms of trade in gauging the country's total buying power abroad, a notion ECLA was now calling the "capacity to import" (unit price of exports times quantities sold), a key indicator of the state of the economy and the numerator of the coefficient later known as the "income terms of trade." (Income terms of trade is defined as the unit price of a given good times the number of units exported, divided by the unit price of imports.) In *Fantasia organizada*, Furtado takes credit for pioneering the use of the idea of capacity to import (p. 70); but it is also found in UN: ECLA, *Economic Survey, 1949* (1951 [Sp. orig. 1950]), a study directed by Prebisch and published in Spanish the same year as Furtado's "Características." Presumably Furtado was a significant contributor to the ECLA product.

31. Furtado, "Características," p. 10. Again, the concept, though not the phrase, is present, though undeveloped in class terms, in the *Economic Survey, 1949*, published almost simultaneously (p. 60). Of course, the idea might still be Furtado's because he was a collaborator in writing the volume, responsible for the section on Brazil. The germ of the idea perhaps can be traced to Prebisch's observation at Geneva in 1932 that "currency

depreciation has lessened the effect on the home market [in Argentina] of the world drop in prices." Prebisch, "Suggestions" (1932), p. 3, mimeo.

32. Furtado, "Características," p. 11.

33. Ibid., p. 24.

34. Ibid., pp. 27–28. Here again Furtado probably drew his inspiration from Prebisch in *Economic Survey, 1949*, in which the latter wrote that Argentina maintained aggregate demand in the agricultural sector during the Depression by government crop purchases (pp. 171–72).

35. Furtado wrote, "The shock caused by the external crisis (1929) gave . . . the Brazilian economy the opportunity to develop its internal market." "Características," p. 28. In the *Economic Survey, 1949*, also published in 1950 (in Spanish), Prebisch affirmed that, in Argentina, the crisis of 1890 began industrialization and that World War I produced new industries, "which developed most vigorously during the Great Depression and the following war" (p. 97).

36. Jacob Viner had been at the institute the previous year and gave the lectures that were published as *International Trade and Economic Development* (1952), linking Manoilescu and Prebisch.

37. Furtado, "Capital Formation" (1954 [Port. orig. 1952]), p. 127.

38. Ibid., p. 129. Furtado later discussed Schumpeter's theory of growth in *Development* (1964 [Port. orig. 1961]), pp. 44–52.

39. Furtado, "Capital Formation," p. 126.   40. Ibid., pp. 127, 130.

41. Ibid., pp. 132–33.   42. Ibid., pp. 134, 138, 144.

43. Ibid., p. 144; Bielschowsky (1985), p. 203.

44. Furtado, "Capital Formation," p. 139. Furtado must be one of the economists whom Harry Johnson had in mind when he cites the improperly placed faith, derived from Keynes, in capital accumulation in the form of government-planned investment as the key to economic development; such a formulation underestimates the subsequently discovered importance of human capital. Johnson, "Keynes" (1978), p. 231.

45. Furtado, "Fundamentos" (1958), pp. 39, 42–44. Cf. the similar and contemporary emphasis by Albert Hirschman in *Strategy* (1958). In reviewing this book, Furtado criticized the German-born American economist for largely ignoring the work of ECLA, especially regarding inflation and external disequilibrium. But it seems clear that Hirschman followed his own path to similar conclusions, traceable to his earliest structuralist analysis. See Furtado, Review of Hirschman, *Strategy* (1959), p. 65; and Hirschman, *National Power* (1945).

46. Bielschowsky, p. 217.

47. Kubitschek (1956), pp. 47–48, 54, 275, 278, 362.

48. Furtado, *Economic Development of Latin America*, p. 208; Bielschowsky, p. 182. For Roberto Campos's view of early planning efforts, see his *Lanterna* (1994), chap. 5.

49. In Chile, where the analysis was first applied, the stagnation of the largely mineral export sector was also recognized as a structural cause: repeated devaluations to raise export earnings automatically boosted the price of imports. A related cause in this view was deteriorating terms of trade, fueled by a demand for imports that rose faster than the demand for exports. Also related to the foreign trade problem was a shift in the fiscal system: as exports stagnated, the relative weight of revenues provided by regressive domestic taxes tended to rise, allowing a smaller tax burden for the already import-oriented upper classes.

To a lesser degree the ECLA economists noted as a cause of inflation national industrial monopolies and oligopolies shielded by high tariffs, firms that could raise prices quickly. See Noyola, "Desarrollo" (1956), pp. 603–18; Sunkel, "Inflation" (1960 [Sp. orig. 1958]), pp. 107–31; Rodríguez (1980), chap. 6. In Chile, as Sunkel pointed out, agriculture was a "structural" problem because it did not respond adequately to rising prices by increasing output. By contrast, in Perón's Argentina, one would have expected a stagnating agriculture because of government price and foreign exchange controls.

  50. Arndt, "Origins" (1985), pp. 151–52.

  51. Kalecki, "Problem" (1976 [Sp. orig. 1954]), pp. 50, 62. On Noyola's and Sunkel's acknowledgments of Kalecki's influence, see Arndt, *Economic Development* (1987), p. 126. For the Latin Americans, of course, this was not the whole story, for the fact that Chile experienced major inflationary pressures while Mexico did not had to be explained. Noyola had emphasized that Chile had strong "propagating mechanisms" which Mexico lacked. The latter country had a large labor surplus that tended to depress the wage level, whereas Chile had a well-organized working class that sought to protect its share of national income. H. W. Arndt stresses that Kalecki's contribution to the structuralist analysis of inflation was reinforced by the work of several of his former associates at the Oxford Institute of Statistics, Thomas Balogh, Nicholas Kaldor, and Dudley Seers, the first two of whom were Hungarians by birth and all of whom worked at ECLA in the late 1950s and early 1960s. See Noyola, "Desarrollo," pp. 605, 608–12; and Arndt, "Origins," pp. 151–52, 156.

  52. Sunkel distinguished the several "structural" features of inflation from "exogenous" or adventitious causes (for example, natural disasters, changes in the international market), and "cumulative" causes—action by government and private groups to raise wages and prices in a climate of inflationary expectations. See Sunkel, "Inflation," p. 110. The notion of cumulative factors bore a resemblance to what was known in Brazil in the 1980s as "inertial inflation." It is important to recognize that the structuralist thesis did not deny that traditional "monetarist" explanations of inflation had some validity—for example, that some supply inelasticities were caused by distortions in exchange rates and by prices following an inflationary spiral.

  53. Furtado, "Características," p. 7.

  54. Furtado, "Capital Formation," p. 143. ECLA's *Economic Survey, 1949* had pointed out the gap between Brazil's growth of real income and its capacity to import between 1925–29 and 1945–49, resulting in "a constant tendency towards disequilibrium in the balance of payments" (p. 196). The study noted that this maladjustment created inflationary pressures; but in a perceived process of mutual causation, ECLA (i.e., Prebisch) believed "in the last analysis [external] disequilibrium derives from the inflationary process." Inflation caused a transfer of income from wage earners to profits receivers; as a result, the latter invested more, and this effect increased the demand for capital goods and contributed to the external disequilibrium (p. 261).

  55. Furtado, "Capital Formation," p. 143. When he wrote this essay in 1952, Furtado was probably unaware of the *licenciado* thesis of the Mexican economist Noyola, published two years earlier. Noyola, who was soon to be the principal contributor to the structuralist thesis on inflation (see note 51, above), had made a similar argument to Furtado's regarding the relation of exports, capital imports, and national income in his *Desequilibrio* (1950), p. 55 (items 6 and 7). Noyola did not, however, treat the inflation issue in this early work.

  56. Furtado, "Capital Formation," pp. 143–44.

57. Bielschowsky, p. 551.

58. Furtado, *Perspectiva* (1958), p. 97; Bielschowsky, pp. 207–8, 211.

59. Brazil: Presidência (1963), pp. 56, 149.

60. Bielschowsky, p. 212.

61. Furtado sees this as one of his major contributions to structuralism. Furtado to author, Paris, 22 Dec. 1982.

62. Furtado, *Formação econômica do Brasil* (1959); Pinto Santa Cruz (1959); Ferrer (1963); Sunkel and Paz (1970). Subsequently a more specialized structuralist work appeared on Mexico: Villareal's *Desequilibrio* (1976). Villareal argues, however, that structuralism accounts more adequately for Mexico's external disequilibrium in the period 1939–58 than in 1959–70.

63. "L'économie coloniale brésilienne" (1948); *A economia brasileira* (1954); *Uma economia dependente* (1956).

64. *Chile, un caso de desarrollo frustrado.*

65. Baer, "Furtado Revisited" (1974), p. 115.

66. Azevedo (1947 [1929]); Simonsen, *História* (1937); and Normano (1935).

67. Furtado, *Economic Growth*, pp. 69–71; Bielschowsky, p. 243.

68. On "involution" see Furtado, *Economic Growth*, p. 71. It may be that Andre Gunder Frank borrowed the term involution from Furtado, though he changed the meaning to emphasize the break with the international economy, a situation in his view in which some growth was possible. Frank's meaning was closer to Prebisch's "inward-directed development" than to Furtado's "involution." See Frank, *Capitalism* (1969 [1967]), pp. 174–77, and Chapter 12.

69. Furtado, *Economic Growth*, pp. 174–77.

70. Ibid., pp. 107–8.   71. Bielschowsky, p. 241.

72. Furtado, *Economic Growth*, p. 167.   73. Baer, "Furtado Revisited," p. 119.

74. The thesis also appears in later approximations and sketches of the work that would become *Economic Growth* [*Formação*] in 1959, namely, *Economia brasileira* (1954), pp. 132–43, and *Economia dependente* (1956), pp. 32, 57–66.

75. Furtado, *Economic Growth*, pp. 205–6.

76. Ibid., p. 211.

77. Ibid., pp. 218–19.

78. For the best summary of Furtado's arguments and the subsequent debate in Brazil, see Suzigan (1986), pp. 21–73.

79. Bielschowsky, p. 191.

80. For case studies of Latin American countries, including Brazil, see essays in Thorp, ed. (1984).

81. During World War II, Brazil's growth was perhaps less hampered because of the existence of a small capital goods sector. For discussion of the revisionist literature on Brazil and other Latin American countries, see Suzigan above, Love, *São Paulo* (1980), pp. 57–59, and C. Cardoso and Pérez Brignoli (1979), p. 197 (summarizing a literature on Mexico, Argentina, Brazil, and Chile), 199. See also the essays in Thorp, ed., passim.

82. Singer's work was circulated in mimeographed form in 1953 but was published (in Portuguese) nine years later. A brief English version was published in 1964. See H. Singer, "Trade" (1964). That Singer completed the work in 1953 is indicated in his memoir, "Early Years" (1984), p. 278, n. 9, and is supported by the dated preface (1954) to the Portuguese version of his *Estudo* (1962), p. 22. At least two Brazilian economists, Rômulo

de Almeida and Roberto de Oliveira Campos, also participated in this analysis before Furtado. See Bielschowsky, pp. 225, 582. For Furtado's work, see Conselho (1959). That Furtado was the principal author of this statement is indicated in Furtado, *Operação* (1959), p. 35. For later treatments of this problem, see Baer, "Regional Inequality" (1964), pp. 268–85; Albuquerque Cavalcanti and Vasconcelos Cavalcanti (1976); Merrick and Graham (1979), pp. 118–45; and Equipe PIMES (1984).

83. Williamson, "Regional Inequality" (1968 [1965]), pp. 110–15. Cf. the observation that "the degree of disparity [in income of Brazil's regions] in 1970 was about equivalent to 1940, when Brazil was one of the most regionally unequal nations in the world." Katzman (1977), p. 211.

84. Frank, *Capitalism*. Frank may have hit upon the link between international and internal underdevelopment as a result of his reading the essays of Pablo González Casanova and Rodolfo Stavenhagen in the UNESCO journal *América Latina* in 1963; Frank himself published in the same review shortly after, and he credits González Casanova as the inspiration for his views on internal colonialism. Frank, *On Capitalist Underdevelopment* (1975), p. 73.

85. UN: ECLA [Prebisch the author], *Economic Development . . . Principal Problems*, elaborated in UN: ECLA, *Economic Survey, 1949*; H. Singer, "Distribution" (1950), pp. 473–85.

86. As seen in Chapter 7, a contemporaneous effort to explain relations of domination and subordination in international trade was that of François Perroux. His analysis also focused on different elasticities of demand of the United States and "the rest of the world," a perspective similar to that of Prebisch and Singer. Perroux also contended that the domination effect existed within countries, and, like Manoilescu, he believed that state intervention was necessary to offset such monopolies. He soon developed the concept of "growth poles," which idea brought his views closer to the traditions of central place theory and regional science. See Perroux, "Esquisse" (1948); Perroux, "Domination Effect" (1950), pp. 198, 203; and Perroux, "Notes" (1970), pp. 93–103.

87. The concept of the "unlimited supply" of agricultural labor, as noted above and in Chapter 4, was developed by W. Arthur Lewis.

88. Conselho, pp. 7, 14.

89. Ibid., p. 7.

90. Conselho, p. 22.

91. This was a way of getting around the federal constitution, which prohibited the central government from levying any tax on exports. Furtado, *Operação*, p. 49.

92. Of course, any protectionist policy anywhere would have differential effects on regions with different factor endowments, so a completely region-neutral protectionism would be virtually impossible to devise.

93. Conselho, pp. 8, 29. I have discovered a mistranscription from tables 6 to 8 in the data used to arrive at the figure of $24 million. Also, a faulty procedure was followed in reaching that sum, viz., a positive transfer of income to the Northeast from the Center-South in 1952 was simply omitted, rather than subtracted, from the net outflow of resources. Taking these items into account, and using the several alternate series that *Política* provides, I calculate that the net transfer of income to the Center-South was of the order of $15 to $17 million per year for 1948–56. In the 1960s the income transfer flows favored the Northeast, according to Albuquerque and Vasconcelos (pp. 49–50). In 1995 Baer took

their findings into account but estimated that the long-term trend in government policies and trade flows favored the Center-South against the Northeast, as Furtado had argued. See note 104.

94. Conselho, pp. 27–28.

95. The element of oligopoly would have been present, to be sure, though in lesser degree, even if the Northeast could have chosen to purchase abroad as well as in São Paulo.

96. Conselho, pp. 30, 47.

97. Ibid., p. 30. In *Economic Growth*, published in Portuguese the same year (1959), Furtado added that because the flow of labor from the poor region to the rich one lowers the wage level of the latter, profits in the wealthy region tend to rise, attracting additional capital from the poor region. The concentration of investment also led to external economies in the rich area, again raising the profitability of investments there, as against that in the poor region (pp. 266–67).

98. Conselho, pp. 47–48.

99. Ibid., pp. 10, 46.

100. See Chapter 6.

101. Conselho, p. 49.

102. Ibid., p. 59; Furtado, *Operação*, p. 37. In 1957, Furtado noted, the absolute cost of food in Recife was a quarter more than that of São Paulo, and much of the food was imported from the South (Conselho, p. 60).

103. Conselho, p. 61. Hans Singer's model of internal colonialism was similar to Furtado's; in its (English) published form Singer's is far briefer, however. Both economists emphasized the "terms of trade" between the (weighted) prices the Northeast received for its foreign sales and those for its domestic purchases, the bulk from the Center-South. Singer found that the Northeast's terms of trade (as thus defined) had fallen by 39 to 42 percent between 1948 and 1952, depending on what domestic wholesale price index was used; thus regional income fell 4 to 4.5 percent. Singer had another argument: he judged that the policy of overvaluation, resulting in a discrepancy between the external and internal value of the Brazilian unit of currency, had also diminished the export quantum and further reduced the income of the region. Singer, like Furtado, argued that the Northeast unfairly bore a larger tax burden relative to its income than the rest of the country. H. Singer, "Trade," pp. 263–65.

104. Baer, *Brazilian Economy* (4th ed., 1995), chap. 12. Following Gustavo Maia Gomes, Baer notes that the Northeast grew faster than the country as a whole in the recession of the early 1980s but views this achievement as the temporary result of government subsidies and public employment—income transfers having little impact on the region's productive capacity (p. 298).

105. See Furtado, *Operação*, p. 13.

106. In the previous year, Furtado had made the connection between development and underdevelopment at the international level in an academic thesis, but *Desenvolvimento e subdesenvolvimento* was not published until 1961.

107. Williamson, pp. 102–6, 126–29.

108. Popper (1959).

109. Even in the context of the developed world, Feinstein has challenged the validity of the method, data, and conclusions of the inverted-U curve for the British case, about which Williamson wrote a book. Feinstein (1988).

110. The latter form has yet to be established, however, on a secular basis.

111. See definition in note 30.

112. Grilli and Yang (1988), pp. 7, 25–26. Barter terms of trade are the ratio of a country's (or region's) weighted average price of exports to its weighted average price of imports.

113. Hind (1984), p. 559; Hechter (1975). Of course, there are limits to the regional dispersion of industrial activities. At some point considerations of efficiency (related to economies of scale and economies external to the firm) would have to be balanced against considerations of equity among regions.

114. The term "internal colonialism" became widely known after the mid-1960s, when it was introduced in the Latin American literature by the Mexican sociologist Pablo González Casanova. For more on the history of the concept and the phrase, see Love, "Modeling" (1989).

115. Furtado, *Development* (1964 [Port. orig. 1961]).

116. Another highly-influential book at the continental level was *Economic Development of Latin America*, an essay on the economic history of the region in structuralist terms, loosely modeled on *Economic Growth of Brazil*. A larger portion of the region-wide study is devoted to an analysis of contemporary issues, by topic, including dependency. The book on Latin America is consequently a more diffuse work than that on Brazil.

117. This surplus is not Marx's surplus value. Its chief source is not the exploitation of labor but technological progress, as for Prebisch. Furtado, "Historic Process" [Port. orig. 1955], pp. 78–79.

118. Ibid., p. 79. Cf. the critique in Meek (1967), pp. 208–9.

119. Furtado, "Elements" (1961 [Port. MS. 1958]), p. 129.

Chapter 11

1. For example, the philosopher José Gaos, the sociologist José Medina Echavarría, and the economist José Urbano Guerrero, all resident in Mexico in the late 1930s and early 1940s. To be sure, Latin Americans traveled to Europe and could follow Spanish thought in journals such as Ortega's *Revista de Occidente*. Moreover, some Spanish intellectuals had visited Latin America before the Spanish civil war; Ortega, a neo-Kantian, had lectured in Buenos Aires in 1916 and 1928. *Exilio* (1982), pp. 814, 868, 975; Romero (2d ed., 1983), pp. 128, 134. Yet in our own day by contrast some German-language classics in social science, Marxist and non-Marxist, are available in Spanish but not English; still others appeared in Spanish before their publication in English. Major studies by Werner Sombart, Henryk Grossman, Otto Bauer, and Fritz Sternberg have been published in Spanish but still await their English editions. Weber's *Economy and Society*, Hilferding's *Finance Capital*, and Kautsky's *Agrarian Question* all appeared in Spanish before English. The Portuguese translation of the last-named work also preceded the first English edition (1988) by sixteen years.

2. Anderson, *Considerations* (1976), pp. 25–37. Anderson notes a new generation of French intellectuals entering the PCF in 1928 but perceives no "generalization of Marxism as a theoretical currency in France" until the German occupation (p. 37).

3. The Peasantist Madgearu and the corporatist Manoilescu also drew on Hilferding.

4. Amaral Lapa (1980), p. 23. Another reason for a relatively slow rise of Marxism in Latin America may have been Marx's own indifference toward the region, compared to his interest in Spain, India, Turkey, China, and Russia. He regarded the Latin American political process as the embodiment of Bonapartism and reaction. Furthermore, Marx had

a low opinion of the liberator Simón Bolívar, whom he privately compared to Faustin Soulouque, the Haitian dictator whose bragadoccio Marx used to parody Napoleon III. Marx's lack of concern about Latin America has even provoked a study of the reasons for it by the region's leading student of Marxism, José Aricó, *Marx* (1982). On the points mentioned, see pp. 40, 107, 116–17.

5. On the relatively early appearance of Marxism in Argentina, see Ratzer (1969).

6. On Brazil, see Dulles (1973), p. 514.   7. Carone (1986), pp. 59, 63.

8. Amaral Lapa, p. 23.   9. Konder (1988), pp. 143, 169.

10. Leônidas de Rezende (1889–1950) sought to fuse Comtian positivism and Marxism. Paim (1984), pp. 505–15. On the broader influence of positivism on Brazilian Communists, see Konder, p. 195.

11. E.g. President Artur Bernardes (1922–26) represented feudal agrarianism, the thesis; General Isidoro Dias Lopes represented the petty bourgeoisie in rebellion, the antithesis; and the future proletarian revolution in Brazil was the synthesis. Konder, pp. 146, 203.

12. Chernyshevsky believed that the *obshchina*, the most traditional institution in Russian society, could be transformed into a socialist institution: "In its form, the highest stage of development is similar to the initial stage," he wrote. Gershenkron, *Economic Backwardness* (1966), p. 172.

13. Bielschowsky (1985), p. 260.

14. Bernstein (1909 [Ger. orig. 1899]). Kautsky published *Agrarian Question*, and Lenin, *Development of Capitalism in Russia*, the same year as Bernstein's German edition.

15. See Chapter 5, n. 109.

16. Lenin wrote, "The exploitation of oppressed nations . . . increasingly transforms the 'civilized' world into a parasite on the body of hundreds of millions in the uncivilized nations." "Imperialism" (1916), p. 106.

17. As we have seen, Manoilescu was a corporatist and sometime fascist (like Corradini), but he was influenced in this regard by Marxism.

18. Emmanuel (1972 [Fr. orig. 1969]), p. xxiv; on Emmanuel, also see Andersson (1976), p. 72.

19. Baran (1957), tr. in Portuguese as *Economia política de desenvolvimento econômico* by S. Ferreira da Cunha (1960).

20. See Caballero (1986) for region-wide and country-specific relations between the Communist parties and Moscow.

21. Prestes (1982), pp. 152, 153 (quotation).

22. Partido Comunista Brasileiro (reprinted, 1980), pp. 39–40.

23. Prestes, p. 152.

24. In 1962 a minority split away, forming the "Chinese"-oriented Partido Comunista do Brasil.

25. Bielschowsky, p. 280; Prado, *Esboço* (1957), p. 201 (on underdeveloped countries' chief function as suppliers of raw materials). Prado cites Prebisch on page 213, and the Argentinean's influence is also inferred from Prado's adoption of a Center-Periphery scheme, as well as the latter's concern with foreign disequilibrium, based on an ECLA analysis of deteriorating terms of trade (pp. 201–4).

26. Bielschowsky, pp. 280–82.

27. Moura (1959).

28. Ibid., pp. 136–37, 306, 309.   29. Mantega, p. 166.

30. *Problemas agrário-camponeses do Brasil* (1968).

31. Vinhas, p. 214.   32. Ibid., pp. 39, 66, 92 (quotation).

33. Ibid., p. 17.   34. Ibid., pp. 37–45, 66, 171.

35. *Quatro séculos de latifúndio* (1964).

36. Passos Guimarães, pp. 27–28, 33, 146, 171.

37. Ibid., pp. 168–76; Vinhas, pp. 111–83; Brandão (1979 [1924]), p. 273.

38. Simonsen, the leading champion of Manoilescu in Brazil, was also the author of the now classic *História econômica do Brasil*, 4th ed. (1962 [1937]); see pp. 80–83 on colonial Brazilian agriculture as capitalistic. Simonsen in turn had been influenced by João Lúcio de Azevedo, who saw the Portuguese overseas empire as a commercial, not a feudal, venture. See Simonsen, p. 81; and Azevedo (1947 [1929]). Possibly Simonsen was also influenced—the early Furtado was—by another Portuguese historian, António Sérgio, who argued that with the rise of the Avis dynasty (1385), Portugal had developed a precocious bourgeoisie that pioneered the maritime explorations and commercial experiments of the following two centuries. See Sérgio (1949 [1928]), pp. 323–34; and Furtado, "Economie" (1948), p. 3.

39. The Argentine writer Sergio Bagú, in his *Economía* (1949), was the first to ascribe a capitalist and nonfeudal past to all of Latin America. He argued that the region had never had a feudal past at all but in broad outline had evinced fundamental features of capitalism since the sixteenth century. The Spanish and Portuguese empires in the New World, Bagú and others alleged, were basically commercial enterprises, for which "feudal" titles and trappings were but a veil. Bagú's work was not explicitly Marxist, unlike those of three later contributors to this thesis, in addition to Caio Prado (treated below)—Marcelo Segall and Luis Vitale of Chile and Milcíades Peña of Argentina, whose writings on this matter, along with those of Prado, are anthologized in Lowy (1980), pp. 243–53, 413–22.

40. Passos Guimarães (1964), pp. 24, 30 (on Bagú), 31 (quotation). Passos does not mention Caio Prado's views in this context.

41. Ibid., pp. 35 (quotation), 106–7, 134–35, 143.

42. Ibid., pp. 190–91; Vinhas, pp. 102–3.

43. The peasantry has been notoriously difficult to define satisfactorily in Marxism and other discourses. On Pătrăşcanu and the lack of consensus in the Rumanian Marxist tradition, see Chapter 3.

44. Bloch (1961 [Fr. orig. 1939]), 1: 279; 2: 442.

45. On Prado's life and works, see F. Iglésias (1982), pp. 7–44.

46. Prado, "Programa" (1983? [1935]), pp. 127, 128, 133–35.

47. Ibid., p. 125.

48. [Prado], "Três etapas" (1954), p. 127 (citing his action at the PCB congress in 1947). As early as 1942, Prado had written that the colonial economy was "a mercantile enterprise for exploiting the tropics, entirely geared to international trade in which, although an essential part, it functioned only as a source of supply for specialized commodities." *Colonial Background* (1969 [Port. orig. 1942]), p. 273. Though the book did not make the flat claim that Brazil had always been capitalist in its organization, this view could be inferred from the text. See the original, *Formação* (1942), pp. 113–21, 269, 340. The Argentinean Bagú, however, published his essay on colonial capitalism in 1949, before Prado explicitly developed his own thesis in works published in the 1960s.

49. [Prado], "Três etapas," p. 127.

50. This was his argument in 1966 (see discussion of *Revolução* below).

51. [Prado], "Três etapas," p. 136.

52. In the early 1960s Prado wrote two important articles on capitalism in early Brazilian agriculture, viz., "Contribuição" (1960) and "Nova contribuição" (1962). These and other articles of the period, originally published in *Revista Brasiliense*, are collected in Prado, *Questão* (1979), On the mercantile nature of the colony and of the latifundium, freedom of contract, the nature of slavery, and sharecropping as a modern form of labor relations, see "Contribuição," pp. 48–50, 66–68, and 70, respectively. Later José de Souza Martins would point out that coffee production in São Paulo under the *colonato* labor system was not based on wage labor alone but also on usufruct, and this complicated the matter of whether the arrangement was fully capitalistic. See Chapter 13.

53. Prado, *Revolução* (1966), pp. 51, 301.

54. Ibid., pp. 68, 166, 188.

55. Gabeira (1979), pp. 31–32. Carlos Marighela, the longtime PCB militant who broke with the party in 1967 and led an urban guerrilla campaign from 1968 until his violent death in November 1969, apparently was not influenced by Prado. His position was a voluntarist and almost antitheoretical one, arguing that bourgeois leadership had failed and that insurgency, however long the struggle, would bring about a social revolution. Six months before his death, he wrote: "What made us [his revolutionary group] grow was action: Solely and exclusively revolutionary action. Working on the principle that action creates the vanguard, we threw ourselves into urban guerrilla warfare without yet having given it a name." Marighela (1971 [Port. orig. 1969]), p. 31.

56. Perry Anderson sees an "oscillation" in Marx's own writings on this matter; for Anderson, it is the issue of structure versus subject or agency. Anderson, *In the Tracks* (1983), pp. 34, 38.

57. See Duncan and Rutledge, pp. 4–5.

58. Macera, cited in Bartra (1976), p. 81; Rangel (1962), p. 215.

59. See following chapter.

Chapter 12

1. Cf. the Brazilian writers considered in Kay (1989)—Furtado, Cardoso, Marini, dos Santos, Bambirra, and Serra (chaps. 5 and 6). Likewise, Bottomore (1983) and Gorman (1985) give more attention to Brazilian than other Latin American dependency writers.

2. F. Cardoso, "Consumption" (1977), pp. 10, 14; Muñoz (1978), p. 104; Liss (1984), p. 25; Aricó, *Cola* (1988), p. 106. Palma, "Dependency" (1978), p. 882; Packenham (1992), pp. 7–12.

3. Sombart, *Moderne Kapitalismus* (1928), 3 [2 vols. bound as one], erste Halbband: xiv–xv; zweite Halbband: 1019. In the same year the Ecuadorian Ricardo Paredes, speaking at the Sixth Congress of the Communist International, spoke of "dependent," "semicolonial," and "colonial" countries in increasing degrees of subjugation to imperialist powers. Paredes (1978 [1928]), p. 179.

4. *Uma economia dependente.*

5. Prado, *Esboço* (1957), p. 190.

6. E.g., Angotti (1982), pp. 126–27.

7. UN: ECLA, *Economic Survey, 1956* (1957), p. 116; UN: ECLA, *Process* (1966 [Sp. orig. 1965]), pp. 19–20; Rodríguez (1980), pp. 202–3.

8. UN: ECLA, "Situation" (1956), p. 30; UN: ECLA, "Preliminary Study," p. 115.

9. UN: ECLA, "Preliminary Study," pp. 128, 150.

10. Kalecki, "Problem" (1976 [Sp. orig. 1954]), p. 52.

11. Furtado, "External Disequilibrium" (1958), p. 406.

12. Furtado, "External Disequilibrium" (1964 [Port. orig. 1961]), p. 151. (This article is somewhat different from that in the previous note.)

13. Furtado, "Elements" (1964 [Port. orig., 1961]), pp. 166, 167.

14. Ibid., p. 133.

15. Prebisch, "Economic Development" (1961), p. 5.

16. UN: ECLA, *Economic Development . . . Postwar Period* (1964), pp. 14, 21. It is noteworthy that the previous autarkic experience of Spain, though its economy in the 1940s was more radically closed than any in Latin America in the following decade, had resulted in the perception that industrialization creates unanticipated trade, and therefore growth, problems. Government economists there understood in the early 1940s that large exports were necessary to sustain industrialization, and Manuel de Torres observed in 1956 that industrialization had decreased the country's capacity to export and therefore the capacity to import. Velasco Murviedro (1982), p. 343; Buesa Blanco (1983), pp. 482–83.

17. Tavares (1964) and Macario (1964). For citations of studies critical of ISI strategies in Asia in later years, see Arndt, *Economic Development* (1987), pp. 82–84.

18. Tavares interview, Rio de Janeiro, 22 July 1985.

19. Tavares, pp. 7–8, 11, 12, 55.

20. Prebisch, *Towards a Dynamic Development Policy* (1963), p. 71.

21. Macario, pp. 65–67, 77, 81.

22. Ibid., pp. 67 (quotation), 84 (formula for "uniform level of net protection"), 87.

23. On ISI failures, see the literature surveyed in Baer, "Import Substitution" (1972), esp. p. 107, and Furtado's analysis of the regional effects of ISI in Brazil in Chapter 10.

24. UN: ECLA, "Situation," p. 42; UN: ECLA, *Process*, p. 38.

25. Furtado, *Subdesenvolvimento* (1968 [1966]), pp. 9–10. Prebisch had previously made this point in *Towards a Dynamic Development Policy*, p. 27.

26. Furtado, *Subdesenvolvimento*, pp. 9–11.

27. Ibid., p. 87.

28. Furtado, *Development* (1964 [Port. orig. 1961]), p. 141.

29. Beginning with Furtado's *Economia dependente* (1956) and extended to the whole of Brazilian history in *Economic Growth of Brazil* (Port. orig. 1959).

30. See Chapter 10.

31. Rodríguez, pp. 187–88, 214–17.

32. For structuralists, the disappointing performance of the Chilean economy under the administration of Christian Democrat Eduardo Frei (1964–70) also helped stimulate a pessimism in the latter 1960s. For more details, see Love, "Origins" (1990), pp. 156–57.

33. Baer, "Import Substitution," p. 110 (on Argentina and Brazil); Palma, "Dependency," p. 908 (on terms of trade).

34. Hirschman, "Turn" (1979), p. 74.

35. Ibid., pp. 76–77. These studies were undertaken for the World Bank, the OECD,

and the Brookings Institution. "Effective protection" as opposed to "nominal protection" is a measure of tariff protection on imported inputs as well as the final product and may result in ad valorem rates well above 100 percent of international prices. Macario had made a similar point.

36. Baer, "Import Substitution," p. 105. The same point had been made by the structuralists Furtado and Singer in the 1950s. See Chapter 10.

37. Ffrench-Davis and Muñoz (1991), p. 9; Ffrench-Davis, Muñoz, and Palma (1994), pp. 177, 181.

38. I accept F. H. Cardoso's objection to the term "dependency theory" because the perspective was a partial one, not a theory in the sense of a theory of capitalist development. I therefore use the term "dependency analysis." F. Cardoso, "Teoria" (1971), p. 32. On Sunkel as an early dependency analyst, see Love, "Economic Ideas" (1994), pp. 435, 440.

39. Furtado, *Operação* (1959), p. 13; Furtado, *Desenvolvimento* (1961), p. 180 and passim; Furtado, *Subdesenvolvimento*, pp. 3–4. These statements lend credence to a claim of priority for Furtado as the first theorist of dependency, but I believe H. W. Arndt has exaggerated in tracing Furtado's dependency position back to *Economic Growth*, which in my view is more correctly described as the full historicization of structuralism. See Arndt, *Economic Development*, p. 120. At any rate, in a recent retrospective Furtado dates his central contributions to dependency analysis in books and articles published between 1970 and 1978. See his "Underdevelopment" (1987), pp. 210–11.

40. Furtado, *Diagnosis* (1965 [Port. orig. 1964]), pp. 3, 6, 13, 20.

41. Ibid., pp. 48–51, 61–62. See Furtado, *Desenvolvimento*, p. 32, for the specific term "counterattack"; it occurs again in *Subdesenvolvimento*, p. 7. Despite his judgment that the class struggle was inoperative in the Periphery, in the same work, written shortly before the military coup of 1964, Furtado saw a rising revolutionary potential in the peasantry of the Northeast. Subsequent events proved him wrong on this point. See *Diagnosis*, p. 162.

42. Furtado, "Elements," p. 135; "External Disequilibrium" (1964), p. 142 (quotation); Baer, "Furtado on Development" (1969), p. 272.

43. Furtado, "Capital Formation" (1954 [1952]), pp. 132–33; and Furtado, "External Disequilibrium" (1958), p. 406.

44. For Furtado's first statement of this position, see *Underdevelopment* (1973). A more widely accessible version appeared as "Subdesenvolvimento" (1974).

45. See Furtado's retrospective, "Underdevelopment" (1987), pp. 210–11. Technological dependence, resulting from elite consumption patterns, was ultimately an aspect of cultural dependence Furtado. *Ares* (1991), p. 35.

46. Furtado, "Underdevelopment" (1987), p. 211.

47. Furtado, *Underdevelopment* (1973), pp. 5–6. The evolution of Furtado's thought on these matters was similar to Prebisch's between *Towards a Dynamic Development Policy* (1963) and *Capitalismo periférico* (1981). On Prebisch's changing views, see Love, "Economic Ideas," pp. 455–57.

48. Furtado, *Accumulation* (1983 [Port. orig. 1978]).

49. Ibid., pp. 4, 121, 129.

50. On Cardoso's biography, see Kahl (1976), pp. 129–94, and F. Cardoso, "Autobiografia" (MS. 15 July 1991). On the Paulista School of Sociology, see Morse (1978).

51. F. Cardoso, *Empresário* (1964), pp. 170–71, 180, 184; F. Cardoso, "Entrepreneurial

Elites" (1966), p. 147; F. Cardoso, *Ideologías* (1971) [data collected in 1963, 1965–66], pp. 1, 103, 146, 158, 215; Cuneo, *Comportimiento* (1967), pp. 129, 172, 192; Véliz (1965), pp. 2, 7–8; Jaguaribe (1965), p. 182 and passim.

52. Kahl, p. 124.

53. Instituto Latinoamericano de Planificación Económica y Social.

54. Interview of F. H. Cardoso, São Paulo, 8 June 1990. Also see note 81.

55. Sunkel, "Pattern" (1973), p. 6; Cardoso and Faletto, *Dependencia* (1969), pp. 17, 28, 38. Sunkel later changed his view to include an internal dynamic of dependency.

56. F. Cardoso, "Desenvolvimento" (1969), p. 21. In 1965 the Brazilian political scientist Hélio Jaguaribe had already specified a "consular" bourgeoisie, with distinct interests from the "national" or "industrial" variety. Jaguaribe, p. 182.

57. Cardoso and Faletto, *Dependencia*, pp. 27, 143, 154, 155. On transnational class alliances, also see F. Cardoso, "Desenvolvimento" (1969), pp. 17, 21.

58. Cardoso and Faletto, *Dependencia*, pp. 28, 32–33, 135 (quotation), 142, 147, 155. For Cardoso's view on dependency in the early 1970s, see his "Associated-Dependent Development" (1973), pp. 142–78.

59. F. Cardoso, "Teoria," p. 43.

60. Frank, "Underdevelopment" [a memoir] (1991), p. 35; Cardoso interview.

61. Frank, "Underdevelopment," pp. 22–23.

62. Lowy, p. 47.

63. Guevara (1961 [Sp. orig. 1960]), p. 15; Lowy, p. 269.

64. Bagú, *Economía* (1949).

65. Mariátegui, "Point" (1980 [Sp. orig. 1929]), p. 113.

66. *A revolução brasileira.*

67. Prado, *Revolução* (1966). Frank's essay reflecting Prado's influence was "Agricultura" (1964), published in English as "Capitalism" (1967), pp. 219–77. Frank acknowledges Prado's influence in "Underdevelopment," p. 26. F. H. Cardoso in 1977 saw Prado as one of a group of Brazilian scholars trying to identify a colonial mode of production. I do not believe Prado saw the problem in that way in the early 1960s: his category was capitalism. See Cardoso, "Consumption" (1977), pp. 11–12.

68. Frank's model has the force and crudity of W. W. Rostow's "stages of growth" model, to which it has been compared. See Rostow (1960) and Foster-Carter (1976), pp. 167–80, esp. 175.

69. See the frequent citations (e.g., pp. 45, 47, 100) in Sodré (1967 [1962]).

70. Despite Frank's attribution of Baran, H. W. Arndt has pointed out that Frank went beyond Baran, who had held that capitalism was an obstacle to the underdeveloped world's progress, to argue that underdevelopment was *caused by* capitalism. Arndt, *Economic Development*, p. 127. Cf. the similar but more tentative thesis by Furtado on the association between development and backwardness in *Development*.

71. But the term may have been borrowed from Furtado, who used it in a different sense; see Chap. 10.

72. Frank, *On Capitalist Underdevelopment* (1975), pp. 11 (on Prebisch), 26 (on Bagú), 68 (terms of trade), 73 (González Casanova); Frank, *Capitalism*, pp. xi, xviii (on Baran), xii (association with ECLA); also, Frank to author, Frankfurt am Main, 1 Nov. 1977. On Frank's professional development, see his memoir, "Underdevelopment."

73. This was an independent "rediscovery," I believe, of a model Manoilescu had developed a generation earlier, and one Singer and Furtado had worked out in a structuralist framework in the 1950s. On these matters, see Chapters 6 and 10.

74. The non-Marxist dualism Frank attacked was less that of ECLA than that of J. H. Boeke, who had first developed the concept of virtually unrelated modern and peasant sectors in the Indonesian economy. Although ECLA had hypothesized the existence of a dual economy in the 1949 *Survey*, in its model the surplus labor force passed from subsistence to modern sectors, assuming a highly wage-elastic labor supply. ECLA in any event preferred the term "heterogeneous" to "dualist."

75. The phrase appeared in the second half of his "Capitalism," scheduled for the *Revista Brasiliense* in its issue of March–April 1964; but the military coup resulted in the repression of the journal.

76. Frank, *Capitalism*, p. 211.

77. Santos, "Structure" (1970), pp. 231–36, esp. 232; Rostow.

78. Revolution would be more costly in human terms because of the strengthening of capitalist institutions in the development-underdevelopment process. Frank, *On Capitalist Underdevelopment*, p. 110.

79. Frank, *Capitalism*, pp. 47–48.

80. See note. 2.

81. See Cardoso and Faletto, *Dependencia* (1969); and the original draft, "Estancamiento" (MS., 1965). Another unpublished version of the essay by Cardoso alone, dated November 1965, emphasized that dependent countries had their own internal dynamics, established types of dependent countries, noting the internationalization of the domestic market in the third type, and challenged the modernization paradigm. This version supports Cardoso's claim that the theoretical apparatus in the published version was principally his, rather than Faletto's. Again, the citations and terms were overwhelmingly structuralist. "Proceso," pp. 19, 21–32, 43.

82. Cardoso denied that the roles played by Europe's historical bourgeoisies in economic development could be replicated by Brazilian entrepreneurs in the 1960s. F. Cardoso, *Empresário*, pp. 41, 44, 183. For Cardoso, the modernization paradigm presumably did not qualify as "theory" any more than the dependency paradigm.

83. Ibid., pp. 181–87.

84. Kay, p. 144.

85. Frank, "Underdevelopment," p. 22. Other biographical information from Marini interview, Rio, 19 Aug. 1985.

86. The same was true of the works of dos Santos and Bambirra. A Portuguese version of Marini's *Subdesarrollo* (1969) appeared in Lisbon in 1975; presumably it would have been difficult to publish in Brazil because of the intermittent but effective censorship.

87. Information on *Capital* seminars from dos Santos interview, Rio, 22 July 1985.

88. Marini, *Dialéctica* (1982 [1973]); *Subdesarrollo* (1969).

89. Low wages, in turn, would keep exports competitive. Marini, *Subdesarrollo*, pp. 88–89.

90. Marini, *Dialéctica*, p. 64. Presumably, the process had its limits, but it could continue in the intermediate run because of rapid urbanization and a readily available supply of cheap wage labor.

91. Ibid., pp. 40, 92.

92. Ibid., pp. 64, 75; *Subdesarrollo*, p. 111. This interpretation was directly influenced by the decade of falling real wages for working-class Brazilians after the coup of 1964.

93. *Dialéctica*, pp. 23, 30–34 (p. 32: "superfluous"); also see *Subdesarrollo*, p. 72.

94. *Dialéctica*, pp. 65, 73.   95. Ibid., p. 73.

96. *Subdesarrollo*, pp. 85–87.   97. *Dialéctica*, pp. 75–76.

98. Marini, "Brazilian Subimperialism," pp. 14–15 (quotation); *Dialéctica*, p. 76. For an elaboration on the notion of subimperialism, see Bambirra (1974), esp. pp. 160–62, 178–80.

99. *Subdesarrollo*, pp. 152–62.

100. Ibid., p. 122.

101. E.g., Marini, *Dialéctica*, p. 77 (quotation); also see "Brazilian Subimperialism" (1972), p. 20, and his "Razones" (1978), p. 63.

102. F. Cardoso, "Novas teses" (1975 [1974]), pp. 50–51.

103. In fact, Marini notes the market-reordering forces of the central economies in *Dialéctica* (p. 68), but elsewhere he emphasizes joint action of large Brazilian capital, foreign firms, and the military regime. E.g., see *Subdesarrollo*, pp. 80–81.

104. F. Cardoso, "Novas teses," pp. 52–53, 59.

105. Ibid., pp. 32–33.

106. Frank, *Lumpenbourgeoisie* (1972 [Sp. orig. 1970]).

107. F. Cardoso, "Novas teses," pp. 34–35. Evans likewise emphasized the continuing importance of the national bourgeoisie in *Dependent Development* (1979), pp. 40, 160–61.

108. F. Cardoso, "Novas teses," pp. 35–37, 56. In addition, Cardoso rejected the thesis of Theotônio dos Santos that socialism and fascism were the only options for Brazil, his case study, and by extension for other Latin American nations. See Santos, *Socialismo* (1969). Cardoso pointed out that the social and political mobilization of fascism was missing in the military regimes of southern South America in 1974, but conceded that the authoritarian regimes had yet to be adequately characterized. "Novas teses," pp. 38–42.

109. Serra and Cardoso (1978), pp. 41–46, summarized in Serra (1979), p. 108. For their charge that Marini misused Marxist methodology by focusing on surplus value rather than the rate of profit, the central capitalist interest, see Serra and Cardoso, pp. 19–27, 43, and Serra, pp. 106–7. Marini replies to their 1978 article in "Razones," adducing further data on falling wages, extension of the workday, and the intensification of labor. For a summary and critique of this debate, see Kay, pp. 163–73.

110. E.g., see F. Cardoso, "Novas teses," p. 28.

111. Centro Brasileiro de Análise e Planejamento.

112. For a critique of Cardoso's dependency as failing to meet Popper's falsificationist criterion, see Packenham, chaps. 3 and 4.

113. E.g., F. Cardoso, "Teoria," pp. 32, 41, 44.

114. "The English bourgeoisie are, up to the present day [1892], so deeply penetrated by a sense of their social inferiority that they keep up, at their own expense and that of the nation, an ornamental caste of drones [the nobility] to represent the nation worthily at all state functions; and they consider themselves highly honored whenever one of themselves is found worthy of admission into this select and privileged body, manufactured, after all, by themselves." Engels (1959 [1892]), p. 64.

"In contemporary Germany [circa 1910], there is no socially independent bourgeoisie, proud of itself. Its highest aspiration is first to be accepted by the nobility, then to enter." Michels, quoted in Mitzman (1973), p. 280.

115. One might speculate—because direct evidence is weak—that on the failed national bourgeoisie, the Italian Marxist Antonio Gramsci had an indirect influence on dependency analysis through his notion of the *rivoluzione mancata* (the impaired or incomplete revolution) in Italy. Gramsci probably had an impact as well through his concept of bourgeois "hegemony," as applied to the relations between First and Third World bourgeoisies and the emulation characteristic of the latter group. In Brazil, Gramsci appears as a kind of totem in the scholarly citations of social scientists in the latter 1960s and 1970s. On his influence in South America, consult Aricó, *Cola* (1988).

116. Chirot and Hall remark, with some exaggeration, that World-System Theory "is in most ways merely a North American adaptation of dependency theory." See "World-System Theory" (1982), p. 90. Wallerstein's main project, *Modern World System*, a history of capitalism from the late Middle Ages to modern times, has yielded three volumes to date (1974, 1980, 1989).

117. Amin's major works were *Accumulation* (1974 [Fr. orig. 1970]) and *Unequal Development* (1976 [Fr. orig. 1973]).

118. See a fuller argument in Love, "Origins," pp. 143–68.

Chapter 13

1. Marini, *Dialéctica* (1973), p. 74. Since his model combines a modern capitalist mode extracting relative surplus value with a form of exploitation of absolute surplus value, it can be seen as an "articulated" mode of production, in the jargon emerging at the time.

2. Maurice Godelier, Jean Suret-Canale, and Catherine Coquery-Vidrovitch were the principal participants in the African debate, which occurred in several journals from the late 1950s to the late 1960s. A number of the articles in *La Pensée* on Africa and other non-Western settings were collected in Centre d'Etudes et de Recherches marxistes (1969).

3. *The Outline of the Critique of Political Economy*, written in 1857–58 and first published in Russian in 1939–41, was virtually unknown in the West until the first complete German edition in 1953. The relevant section was published in English as *Pre-capitalist Economic Formations* in 1965, with an introduction by Eric Hobsbawm.

4. Important in the international discourse on the history of the Asiatic mode of production was Sofri (1969), published in Portuguese toward the end of the modes controversy (1977).

5. Note that "structuralism" in this tradition has only a distant relation to that defined in Chapter 1. On Althusserianism in Latin America, see, for example, Harris (1979).

6. *Lire le Capital* was first published in 1965 as a multiauthored work but was reduced to the revised contributions of Althusser and Balibar in 1968. The English translation (1970) is from the second edition.

7. Balibar, "Basic Concepts," (1970 [Fr. orig. 1965]), p. 307. A Spanish edition of Althusser's *Pour Marx* was published in Mexico in 1967. Note that "articulation" in the Althusserian usage applied to modes of production in transition, at least in theory, to a full capitalism, though that transition might be long or ultimately blocked.

8. Harnecker, *Los conceptos elementales del materialismo histórico* (35th rev. ed., 1976 [1969]). She took her title from Balibar's group of essays in *Reading Capital*.

9. Trebat (1983), p. 59. For the view, contrary to Trebat's, that such firms were not profitable, see Anglade (1985).

10. Poulantzas (1973).

11. Puiggrós' essay, "Modos," and Frank's reply, "¿Con qué modo?," were twice published in Mexico City and Buenos Aires. The same issue of *El Gallo Illustrado*, the paper in which the exchange first appeared, also published a selection from Marx's *Grundrisse*.

12. Laclau interview, Urbana, Ill., 12 Nov. 1984.

13. See Laclau, "Feudalismo" (1977 [1971]), pp. 28–37, 43; and Laclau, "Modos" (1969), pp. 305–11.

14. *Modos de producción en América Latina.*

15. Ibid., pp. 14, 94, 161, 212.

16. Balibar, "Sur la dialectique" (1973), p. 47. Also see Tandater (1976), p. 154. Cf. the change in the positions of the English Althusserians Barry Hindness and Paul Hirst between 1975 and 1977.

17. General Pinochet's coup and repression in September 1973 prompted Marxists to flee Chile, and Mexico City became the home of many exiles. The Puiggrós-Frank polemic had occurred in the Mexican capital in 1965, and the new journal *Historia y Sociedad* published the modes-of-production papers of the 1974 Congress of Americanists, as well as later contributions on the problem.

18. Bartra et al. (1976); in particular, see Cueva, p. 28.

19. E.g., see Brewer (1980), pp. 200–201, 271; and Rey (1971).

20. Giannotti's major philosophical work, which conflicted with Althusser's repudiation of the young "humanist" Marx, was *Origens da dialética do trabalho* (1965). F. H. Cardoso rejects the formalist position of Althusser as against an "analysis of [concrete] situations" in "Althusserianismo" (1972), pp. 104–22, esp. p. 122. A direct attack on Althusserianism from a defender of Georg Lukács's Marxism was Coutinho (1972). A ponderous instance of the Althusserian vogue in the social sciences was Srour (1978). On CEBRAP, see Chapter 12.

21. Chiaramonte (1984), p. 265.

22. C. Cardoso, *Escravo* (1987); Cardoso's publications on the subject began in 1979 and were inspired by previous explorations of this modes-of-production issue in the Caribbean by Tadeusz Lepkowski and Sidney Mintz. See C. Cardoso, "Peasant Breach" (1988), p. 49. Empirical studies of the "peasant breach" and slaves' negotiation with masters are found in Reis and Silva (1989). Slavery and the slave trade also figured importantly in Fernando Novais's *Antigo sistema colonial* (1979), a major work on the Portuguese imperial system, emphasizing the role of metropolitan commercial capital in primitive accumulation and in directing the movement of the system. The book's impact is discussed in Amaral Lapa (1982) and its place in the modes-of-production debate in Pinheiro, ed. (1983). In Argentina the theoretical explorations of the modes debate were important in the gestation of three major economic studies of the colonial period, focusing on relations of production, the production process, and the circulation of commodities. See the mature works of Sempat (1983), Garavaglia (1983), and Tandater (1992).

23. I prefer the view of Stolcke and Hall, who see the system as capitalist without such qualification. They interpret the usufruct system as a means of minimizing planters' cash outlays and maximizing their profits. This situation occurred because prices of food were initially high, much of it being imported from other states; because usufruct would attract

immigrants and therefore contribute to labor market saturation, forcing down wages; and because peak labor demands for coffee and food crops did not occur in the same season. See Souza Martins, *Cativeiro* (1979), pp. 18–19; and Stolcke and Hall (1983), esp. p. 184. Stolcke extended her analysis of coffee labor from the *colonato* to the present-day agricultural proletariat in *Cafeicultura* (1986). Like Souza Martins, Cardoso de Mello, using a strict Marxist definition of capitalism—requiring, among other things, functioning labor markets—develops the notion of "late" or "retarded" capitalism in *Capitalismo tardio* (1982).

24. *Bóias-frias* ("cold-lunches") received their name from the fact that they had to eat lunch in the field, in a culture in which a cold meal implies a mean status and low quality of life. On the proletarianization of coffee workers, see Stolcke (1986), pp. 179–240. An important study of *bóias-frias* is D'Incao e Mello (1975).

25. See Maybury-Lewis (1991).

26. Souza Martins, *Expropriação* (1980), pp. 45 (on census data), 47.

27. Velho, *Capitalismo* (2d ed., 1979 [1976]).

28. A study much influenced by Velho's "authoritarian capitalism," with an empirical examination of three postwar Brazilian frontiers, is Foweraker (1981).

29. Velho, *Capitalismo*, pp. 43–44. Velho did not cite Althusser in this work, but he cited the Althusserians Balibar, Poulantzas, and Pierre-Philippe Rey (see below). He used Althusserian categories in his "Antropologia" (1980).

30. *Modernização dolorosa* (1981).

31. Ibid., pp. 30–31, 63.

32. Ibid., pp. 119, 124 (quotation), 126–29.

33. José Carlos Mariátegui, often viewed as Latin America's most original Marxist thinker before World War II, hinted that Peru's indigenous *ayllu*, which he viewed as an Incaic form of agrarian communism, could be the foundation for the transformation from a semifeudal stage of development directly to socialism in the countryside. Thus, like Alexander Herzen, Mariátegui would seem to be a "stage-skipper," despite his following Lenin in condemning the Narodniki. Nor was Mariátegui alone. The idea that peasant collectivism could be the basis for passing from "feudalism" to socialism was shared by a leading Latin American spokesman at the Sixth Congress of the Communist International in 1928, Ricardo Paredes of Ecuador; Paredes's views were echoed by a Uruguayan delegate, Sala. In the event, Mariátegui's praise of "Incaic socialism" seemed to a Comintern critic in 1941 a reincarnation of the Russian populist tradition. To the degree the charge is justified, Mariátegui appears to have fallen into populist "error," in part, because of the absence of classical populism in Latin America. See Mariátegui, *Siete ensayos* (1959 [1928]), pp. 9, 53, 68–71, 89; Internacional Comunista (1978), pp. 180–81, 367; Miroshevski (1980 [Russ. orig. 1941]), pp. 55–70, esp. 68.

34. Velho, *Sociedade* (1982), pp. 125–29.

35. CNBB, *Pastoral da terra* (1976), in which Velho was also cited as a contemporary authority.

36. Ibid., p. 189.

37. In Portuguese, *Terra de exploração* and *terra de trabalho*.

38. CNBB, *Igreja* (1980), p. 30.

39. See Souza Martins, *Expropriação*, chap. 3, where he uses *terra de negócio* as a synonym for *terra de exploração* (p. 60). Souza Martins takes responsibility for the theoretical

framework of the document at the CNBB's eighteenth assembly and denies that it is populist. Interview, São Paulo, 1 Aug. 1985.

40. Souza Martins, *Expropriação*, pp. 60–61.

41. Souza Martins, *Os camponeses e a política no Brasil* (1981). One is reminded of the controversy between two Rumanian writers laying claim to the Marxist method: Şerban Voinea had charged Ştefan Zeletin with populist inspiration when the latter wrote of the "contradiction" between precapitalist production and capitalist circulation.

42. Romano (1979), pp. 237–38.

43. Except Passos Guimarães, who, unlike the Rumanian populists, wanted to see peasants integrated into the capitalist economy (see Chapter 11).

44. See Chayanov (1966), and Heynig (1982) on the importance of the English-language compendium (p. 124). Spanish translations of Chayanov appeared in the 1970s.

45. Garcia, *O Sul: Caminho do roçado* (1990). An early version of the work with the same title had been defended as a dissertation in 1983.

46. Ibid., pp. 159–60, 292. The study might be called neo-Chayanovian, in that the Chayanov method is critiqued and modified on the basis of writings by later observers of the peasant economy such as Nicholas Georgescu-Roegen, Jerzy Tepicht, and Boguslaw Galeski. Garcia's *Terra* (1983) complements *O Sul* and deals with peasant family life cycles in chapter 4.

47. See Nun (1969) and Quijano, "Notas" (1977 [written in 1966]). For a summary of Quijano's and Nun's positions and a critique, see Kay (1989), pp. 100–124. Kay also discusses the CEBRAP group in this context, and I draw upon his work.

48. Cardoso and Reyna (1968), pp. 44, 53.

49. F. Cardoso, "Participação" (1972), p. 184; Kowarick (1974), pp. 79–84; Oliveira, "Economia brasileira" (1972), p. 27; P. Singer (1973), pp. 63–90.

50. In W. Arthur Lewis's sense. Kowarick, pp. 92, 96.

51. Oliveira, "Economia brasileira," p. 29.

52. Ibid., p. 31.

53. Víctor Tokman's historical comparisons of the structure of Latin American employment a decade later tended to lend support to the CEBRAP interpretation that the structure of contemporary Latin American employment was less radically different from that of developed countries a century earlier than Nun had imagined; Tokman's terms, however, were not Marxist. For contemporary Latin America, Tokman emphasized the failures of the service sector to employ people in higher-productivity jobs, rather than the lack of absorption of the industrial sector. Tokman (1982), p. 126.

54. See the literature cited in Kay, chap. 4.

55. Harnecker, p. 137; Bottomore, "Social Formation," in Bottomore (1983), p. 444.

56. See Anderson's history and analysis of the concept, "Asiatic Mode of Production" (1974), quotation, p. 494. Other conceptual problems arose as well. On the French side, not only had Balibar altered his causal sequence and emphasis in the middle of the Latin American polemics, with the social formation now determining the mode of production, but two of the most inventive of the Francophone Marxists specializing in underdevelopment revised Marx himself while the Latin American debate was developing. Pierre-Philippe Rey, who worked out a phased model of Althusserian "articulation" of precapitalist and capitalist modes, took issue with Marx's proposition that ground rent was properly a capitalist form of surplus; rather, he averred, it was feudal in essence. Samir Amin meanwhile denied that the Asiatic mode and feudalism were distinct and unrelated

types, as Marx had defined them, but rather saw them as poles of a continuum under a "tributary" mode. See Rey (1973) and Amin (1976 [Fr. orig. 1973]).

57. Amaral Lapa, *Modos* (1980), pp. 29–33. A notably rigorous exposition in the third category, with a formal model, was that of the French economist Christian Topalov, who proposed a "latifundiary" mode situated between feudal and capitalist modes of production. In this scheme, the latifundist functions as a capitalist entrepreneur, but labor does not have a fixed supply price because the workers are not completely separated from the means of production. Nonetheless, they are dependent on the latifundist for concessions of subsistence rights and must accept the wage he offers. Therefore the "mode of production" is not totally based on capitalist labor relations. The latifundist will seek to maximize the proportion of the labor force in the commercial, rather than the subsistence, sector. Topalov (1978), pp. 70–71, 80.

58. Topalov, p. 11.

Chapter 14

1. I make no claims about direct descent, but von Thünen's work and later that of Alfred Weber were the antecedents of central place theory, developed by Walter Christaller and others in the 1930s. This form of analysis may have been the inspiration for Perroux's thesis on "growth poles," which concept in turn affected Latin American structuralism in the 1950s. See von Thünen (1966 [Ger. orig., 1826]).

2. Sauvy based the term on the model of the Third Estate, alluding the celebrated phrase of the Abbé Sièyes in 1789: "What is the Third Estate? Everything. What has it been till now in the Political Order? Nothing. What does it want to be? Something." Sauvy (1952), p. 5.

3. Economist Intelligence Unit (1994), p. 18; (1995), p. 20; Todaro (1985), p. 54.

4. Poland's per capita income in international exchange terms in 1993 was $2,270. By contrast, the figure for the United States was $24,750. *World Bank Atlas* (1994), pp. 20–21.

5. For example, Manoilescu's thesis on international trade is endorsed in Gheorghiu (n.d.), p. 37. It is also approved, though without attribution, in Horovitz (1958), p. 17, and in Grindea (1967), p. 196.

6. On the politics of UNCTAD, see Nye (1973); quotation on p. 334.

7. Act 1, scene 3, ll. 64–68. Note the pun: "cheater" also means "escheater."

8. "Forced Labor" (1993).

9. The Keynesian J. K. Galbraith argued that government should act as or create a "countervailing power" in situations of relative monopoly in the postwar American economy, and this concept bears an obvious resemblance to Perroux's understanding of monopoly capital and labor markets in the 1930s. Galbraith (1956 [1952]).

10. See Chapter 6.

11. As opposed to a Marxist sociology of capitalist societies.

12. Furtado, *Ares* (1991), p. 154.

13. De Soto, *Other Path* (1989 [Sp. orig. 1986]).

14. Lal (1985 [1983]), pp. 1–6, 24–26.

15. Prebisch wrote that Latin America had, on average, the highest tariffs in the world, depriving it of economies of scale and opportunities to specialize for export. *Towards a Dynamic Development Policy* (1963), p. 71.

16. See the essays in Sunkel, ed. (1993 [Sp. orig. 1991]).

17. Fritsch (1991), pp. 407, 414.

18. On the positive association of trade and growth, see, for example, Levine and Renelt (1992), who examined data for 119 countries; and Esfahani (1991), who considered data for 31 semi-industrialized countries. Esfahani emphasizes that the correlation between export and GDP performance has mainly to do with exports' foreign exchange earnings; they mitigate import "shortages," which restrict the growth of output in these countries.

19. Among other writings, see Sen (1984).

20. Programa Regional de Empleo de América Latina y del Caribe.

21. For a discussion of the "cutting point" issue, see Márquez (1991), esp. p. 2. On the prevalence of underemployment over productive employment in Venezuela, see p. 9.

22. Bresser Pereira (1993); Biersteker (1990), pp. 488–91; Chaudhry (1993).

23. Thurow (1992), p. 269 (citing OECD figures). Obviously, gauged from the expenditure side, the role of governments is even larger, to the extent that expenditure is chronically greater than income.

24. Ibid., p. 18.

25. World Bank, *East Asian Miracle* (1993), p. 83. On the same page the bank takes a middle position, arguing for a limited "market-friendly" interventionism "to ensure adequate investment in people, provision of a competitive climate for enterprise, openness to international trade, and stable macroeconomic management."

26. Ibid., p. 2. The narrowing of income disparities in turn stimulated domestic demand and probably secured a greater degree of political legitimacy, and therefore stability, for the Asian regimes that achieved such success.

27. Ibid., p. 52.

28. The other countries were Chile, Colombia, and the Dominican Republic. E. Cardoso and Fishlow (1992), p. 197.

29. Fajnzylber (1990), p. 5.

30. E.g., see ibid., p. 61.

31. Cardoso and Faletto, *Dependency* (1979), p. xxiv.

References Cited

Archival Materials, Miscellaneous Manuscripts, Mimeographed Course Outlines, Letters to Author, and Interviews

Archival materials

Brazil, Arquivo Nacional. Rio de Janeiro.
  Doc. 85, 22 Sept. 1937, in A-CFCE, processo 435, "Instituto Nacional de Mate."

Centro de Pesquisa e Documentação de História Contemporânea do Brasil. Fundação Getúlio Vargas, Rio de Janeiro.
  "Eugênio Gudin (depoimento)" [transcript of interview]. 1979.

Columbia University: Oral History Research Collection. New York.
  Malaccorto, Ernesto: Interview by Leandro Gutiérrez, Buenos Aires, Aug. 1971 (copy; orig. at Instituto Torcuato di Tella, Buenos Aires, Argentina).

France, Ministère des Affaires Etrangères. Quai d'Orsay, Paris.
  French Minister in Bucharest [G. Puaux] to Foreign Minister, 29 June 1931, vol. 170, p. 28.

Great Britain, Foreign Office. Public Record Office, London.
  "Records of Leading Personalities in Roumania," 30 Sept. 1930, FO 371.14438 C7527/5547/37; Leith-Ross, F[rederick] W., to Sir Horace Hamilton, Geneva, 16 Jan. 1933, 371.16531 A523/48/2; "Report on leading personalities in Argentina," 27 Jan. 1937, 317.20598 A674/674/2; Hoare, Sir R[eginald], to Sir Anthony Eden, Bucharest, 12 Jan. 1938, [FO 371] R533/250/37; "Records of Leading Personalities in Roumania," Bucharest, 31 July 1939, FO 371.23855 R5695/5695/37; Hoare to Foreign Office, Bucharest, 21 June 1940, FO 371.24992 R6395/475/37; Hoare to P. B. B. Nichols, 5 July 1940, Bucharest, FO 371.24992 R7024/475/37; Seton-Watson, Hugh: Item enclosed in Hankey to Visc. Halifax, Bucharest, 22 July 1940, R7352/475/37.

United Nations, Archive of the League of Nations. Geneva.

> Prebisch, Raúl. "Suggestions Relating to the International Wheat Problem." League of Nations: Commission Préparatoire/Conférence Monetaire et Economique/E8, 11 Dec. 1932 (mimeo).

United Nations: Economic Commission for Latin America and the Caribbean. Santiago, Chile.

> Prebisch, Raúl. "Versión taquigráfica de la conferencia de prensa . . . 15 de noviembre de 1955." (Prebisch file.)
> ———. "Anexo especial" to "Noticias de la CEPAL," no. 7 (July 1963), mimeo.
> UN.ECOSOC E/CN.12/17 (7 June 1948); E/CN.12/28 (11 June 1948); E/CN.12/71 (24 June 1948); E/CN.12/221 (18 May 1951), mimeo.

Valeriu Dinu Collection. Bucharest.

> Dinu, Natalia, and Alexandru Manoilescu. "Profesorul Mihail Manoilescu: Date biografice." MS. (N.d.)
> Manoilescu, Mihail. "Memorii." MS. (1946–48); "Urmare la 'memoriile mele.'" MS. (1947) (Published as *Dictatul de la Viena: Memorii. Iulie–August 1940*; *Memorii*, 2 vols. [All ed. by Valeriu Dinu.] Bucharest, 1991, 1993.)
> Manoliu, Florin, to Valeriu Dinu, Bahia Blanca, Argentina, 16 Nov. 1967.

Miscellaneous manuscripts

> Cardoso, Fernando Henrique. "Autobiografia." MS., 15 July 1991. Cardoso papers, São Paulo. Author's copy.
> ———. "Proceso de desarrollo en América Latina." Mimeo., 1965. United Nations: Latin American Institute of Economic and Social Planning (ILPES), Santiago, Chile. Author's copy.
> Cardoso, Fernando Henrique, and Enzo Faletto. "Estancamiento y desarrollo económico en América Latina." Mimeo., 1965. United Nations: Latin American Institute of Economic and Social Planning (ILPES), Santiago. Author's copy.
> Cresin, Roman. "Forms of exploitation in Rumanian agriculture: Finding[s] of the 1941 agricultural census." MS., N.d. Cornell University Library, Ithaca, N.Y.
> Federação das Indústrias do Estado de São Paulo [FIESP]. Circular no. 152. Mimeo., 1 July 1931. FIESP Archive, São Paulo.
> Manoliu, Florin. "Curriculum vitae." MS., 25 July 1970. Universidad Federal del Sur, Bahía Blanca, Argentina. Author's copy, courtesy of Lascăr Săveanu.

Mimeographed course outlines

Academia Română, Bucharest.

> Madgearu, Virgil. "Curs de economie agrară." Academia de Înalte Studii Comerciale și de Industrie, 2d ed. (N.d.).
> Manoilescu, Mihail. "Curs de economie politică." Școala Politehnică (1933); revised and expanded version (1940).

Biblioteca Facultăţii de Drept, Bucharest.

Pătrăşcanu, Lucreţiu. "Curs de economie teoretică" (1947).

Facultad de Ciencias Económicas, Universidad de Buenos Aires.

Prebisch, Raúl. "Apuntes de economía política (Dinámica económica)" (1948).

——. "La moneda y los ciclos económicos en la Argentina." Assistant's notes, approved by Prebisch. (1944).

Letters to author

Frank, Andre Gunder. Frankfurt am Main, 1 Nov. 1977.
Furtado, Celso. Paris, 22 Dec. 1982.
Kindleberger, Charles P. Lexington, Mass., 31 Dec. 1991.
Lewis, W. Arthur. Princeton, N.J., 6 May 1986.
Perroux, François. Paris, 30 July 1982.
Pinto, Aníbal. Santiago, Chile, 31 Jan. 1985.
Prebisch, Raúl. Washington, D.C., 29 June 1977; 9 Nov. 1977; 26 June 1979.
Rosenstein-Rodan, Paul. Boston, Mass., 13 May 1981.
Săveanu, Lascăr. Bahía Blanca, Argentina, 30 Dec. 1982.
Singer, Hans W. Brighton, England, 21 Aug. 1979.

Interviews

Cardoso, Fernando Henrique. São Paulo, 8 June 1990.
Furtado, Celso. Rio de Janeiro, 31 May 1990.
Laclau, Ernesto. Urbana, Ill., 12 Nov. 1984.
Marini, Rui Mauro. Rio de Janeiro, 19 Aug. 1985.
Perroux, François. Urbana, Ill., 14 Mar. 1983.
Prebisch, Raúl. Washington, D.C., 10 July 1978.
Santos, Theotônio dos. Rio de Janeiro, 22 July 1985.
Souza Martins, José de. São Paulo, 1 Aug. 1985.
Stahl, Henri H. Bucharest, 28 Oct. 1981.
Tavares, Maria da Conceição. Rio de Janeiro, 22 July 1985.

Published Works and Dissertations

Academia Republicii Populare Romîne. Institutul de Cercetări Economice. *Texte din literatura economică în Romînia—secolul XIX.* Vol. 1. Bucharest, 1960.
Aguirre Cerda, Pedro. *El problema industrial.* [Santiago], 1933.
Albuquerque, Roberto Cavalcanti de, and Clóvis de Vasconcelos Cavalcanti. *Desenvolvimento regional no Brasil.* Brasília, 1976.
Almeida Magalhães, João Paulo de. *A controvérsia brasileira sobre o desenvolvimento econômico: Uma reformulação.* Rio de Janeiro, [1964?].
Althusser, Louis. See Balibar, Etienne.
Alvarez Andrews, Oscar. *Historia del desarrollo industrial de Chile.* Santiago, 1936.
Alves de Abreu, Alzira. "Nationalisme et action politique au Brésil: Une étude sur l'ISEB." Ph.D. diss., Université René Descartes, Paris, 1975.

Amaral Lapa, José Roberto do, ed. *Modos de produção e realidade brasileira*. Petrópolis, 1980.

Amin, Samir. *Accumulation on a World Scale: A Critique of the Theory of Underdevelopment*. New York, 1974 [Fr. orig. 1970].

——. *Unequal Development: An Essay on the Social Formations of Peripheral Capitalism*. New York, 1976 [Fr. orig. 1973].

Anderson, Perry. "The Asiatic Mode of Production." In *Lineages of the Absolutist State*, pp. 462–549. London, 1974.

——. *Considerations on Western Marxism*. London, 1976.

——. *In the Tracks of Historical Materialism*. London, 1983.

Andersson, Jan. *Studies in the Theory of Unequal Exchange Between Nations*. Helsinki, 1976.

Angelescu, I[on] N. "Avuţia naţională a României." *Democraţia* 3, no. 7 (1 July 1915): 297–308.

——. "Dependenţa noastră economică şi reorganizarea economiei raţionale." *Democraţia* 3, no. 16 (1915): 720–25.

——. *Politica economică a României Mari*. Bucharest, 1919.

——. "România actuală şi politica economică internaţională." *Analele Economice şi Statistice* 10, nos. 1–2 (1927): 1–13.

Anglade, Christian. "State and Capital Accumulation in Contemporary Brazil." In Anglade and Carlos Fortín, eds., *The State and Capital Accumulation in Latin America*, Vol. 1: Brazil, Chile, Mexico, pp. 52–138. Pittsburgh, 1985.

Angotti, Thomas. "The Political Implications of Dependency Theory." In Ronald H. Chilcote, ed., *Dependency and Marxism: Toward a Resolution of the Debate*, pp. 124–37. Boulder, Colo., 1982.

Antonacci, Maria Antonieta Martines. "A vitória da razão: O Instituto de Organização Racional do Trabalho de 1931 a 1945." Ph.D. diss., Universidade de São Paulo, 1985.

"The Argentine Industrial Exhibition." *Review of the River Plate*, 22 Dec. 1933, pp. 11–17.

Aricó, José. *La cola del diablo: Itinerario de Gramsci en América Latina*. Buenos Aires, 1988.

——. *Marx y América Latina*. 2d rev. ed. Mexico City, 1982 [1980].

Arndt, H[einz] W[olfgang]. "Economic Development: A Semantic History." *Economic Development and Cultural Change* 29, no. 3 (Apr. 1981): 457–66.

——. *Economic Development: The History of an Idea*. Chicago, 1987.

——. "The Origins of Structuralism." *World Development* 13, no. 2 (Feb. 1985): 151–59.

Aunos [Pérez], Eduardo. *La reforma corporativa del Estado*. Madrid, n.d. [1935?].

Aurelian, P[etre] S. *Viitorul nostru economic*. Bucharest, 1890.

Azevedo, João Lúcio de. *Epocas de Portugal econômico: Esboços de história*. 2d ed. Lisbon, 1947 [1929].

Baer, Werner. *The Brazilian Economy*. 4th ed. New York, 1995 [1979].

——. "Furtado on Development: A Review Essay." *Journal of Developing Areas* 3, 2 (Jan. 1969): 270–80.

——. "Furtado Revisited." *Luso-Brazilian Review* 2, no. 1 (Summer 1974): 114–21.

——. "Import Substitution and Industrialization in Latin America." *Latin American Research Review* 7, no. 1 (Spring 1972): 95–122.

——. "Regional Inequality and Economic Growth in Brazil." *Economic Development and Cultural Change* 12 (1964): 268–85.

Bagú, Sergio. *Economía de la sociedad colonial: Ensayo de historia comparada de América Latina.* Buenos Aires, 1949.

——. "¿Y mañana, Qué?" *Revista de Economía* [Mexico] 7, nos. 5–6 (30 June 1944): 36–39.

Bak, Joan L. "Political Centralization and the Building of the Interventionist State in Brazil: Corporatism, Regionalism and Interest Group Politics in Rio Grande do Sul, 1930–1937." *Luso-Brazilian Review* 22, no. 1 (Summer 1985): 9–25.

Balibar, Etienne. "The Basic Concepts of Historical Materialism." In Louis Althusser and Balibar, *Reading Capital* [tr. by Ben Brewster], pp. 199–308. London, 1970 [Fr. orig. 1965].

——. "Sur la dialectique historique: Quelques remarques critiques à propos de *Lire le Capital*." *La Pensée: Revue du Rationalisme Moderne*, no. 170 (Aug. 1973): 27–47.

Bambirra, Vânia. *El capitalismo dependiente latinoamericano.* Mexico City, 1974.

Banco Central de la República Argentina. *Memoria, 1938, Memoria, 1942.* Buenos Aires, 1939, 1943.

——, ed. *La creación del Banco Central y la experiencia monetaria argentina entre los años 1935–1943.* 2 vols. Buenos Aires, 1972.

Banco de la Nación Argentina. *Economic Review* 1, no. 1 (Aug. 1928); series 2: 1, no. 1 (1937).

Baran, Paul A. *The Political Economy of Growth* [tr. by S. Ferreira da Cunha as *Economia política de desenvolvimento econômico.* Rio de Janeiro, 1960]. New York, 1957.

Bartra, Roger, et al. *Modos de producción en América Latina.* Lima, 1976.

Baumol, William J., and Ellen Viner Seller. "Jacob Viner." *International Encyclopedia of the Social Sciences.* Vol. 18, pp. 784–85. New York, 1979.

Belaúnde, César H. "Corporatismo." Licenciado thesis, Facultad de Ciencias Económicas, Universidad de Buenos Aires, 1939.

Benenati, Antonio. *Le développement inégale en Italie.* Paris, 1982.

Berend, Ivan T., and Gyorgy Ranki. *East Central Europe in the Nineteenth and Twentieth Centuries.* Budapest, 1977.

——. *Economic Development in East-Central Europe in the Nineteenth and Twentieth Centuries.* New York, 1974.

——. *The European Periphery and Industrialization, 1780–1914.* Cambridge, Eng., 1982.

Berle, Adolf A., Jr., and Gardiner C. Means. *The Modern Corporation and Private Property.* New York, 1934.

Bernstein, Eduard. *Evolutionary Socialism: A Criticism and Affirmation.* New York, 1909 [Ger. orig. 1899].

Beveraggi-Allende, Walter. "Argentine Foreign Trade Under Exchange Control." Ph.D. diss., Harvard University, 1952.

Bhaduri, Amit. "Disguised Unemployment." In John Eatwell et al., eds., *The New Palgrave: Economic Development*, pp. 109–13. New York, 1989 [1987].

Bhagwati, Jagdish N. "Comment on Raúl Prebisch, 'Five Stages in My Thinking on Development.'" In Gerald M. Meier and Dudley Seers, eds., *Pioneers in Development*, pp. 197–204. New York, 1984.

Bielschowsky, Ricardo. "Brazilian Economic Thought in the Ideological Cycle of Developmentalism (1930–64)." Ph.D. diss., Leicester University, 1985.

Biersteker, Thomas J. "Reducing the Role of the State in the Economy: A Conceptual Exploration of IMF and World Bank Prescriptions." *International Studies Quarterly* 34 (1990): 477–92.

Blaug, Mark. *The Methodology of Economics: Or How Economists Explain.* Cambridge, Eng., 1980.

Bloch, Marc. *Feudal Society.* 2 vols. London, 1961 [Fr. orig. 1939].

Boeke, J[ulius] H. "Dualistic Economics." In Koninklijk Instituut voor de Tropen, ed., *Indonesian Economics*, q.v., pp. 165–92.

——. *Economics and Economic Policy of Dual Societies as Exemplified by Indonesia.* Haarlem, 1953.

——. *Tropisch-koloniale staathuishoudkunde: Het probleem.* Amsterdam, 1910.

Böker, Hugo. "Agriculture's Share in the National Income and the Agricultural Situation." *International Review of Agriculture* 32, no. 1 (Jan. 1941): 1E–30E.

Bottomore, Tom, et al. *A Dictionary of Marxist Thought.* Oxford, 1983.

Brandão, Octavio [pseud. Fritz Mayer]. "Fundamentos da estratégia do PCB." In Paulo Sérgio Pinheiro and Michael M. Hall, eds., *Classe operária no Brasil.* Vol. 1, pp. 270–74. São Paulo, 1979 [1924].

Brandão de Brito, José M. "O condicionamento industrial e o processo português de industrialização após a Segunda Grande Guerra." 2 vols. Ph.D. diss., Universidade Técnica de Lisboa, 1987.

——. "Os engenheiros e o pensamento econômico do Estado Novo." In José Luís Cardoso, ed., *Contribuições para a história do pensamento econômico em Portugal*, pp. 209–34. Lisbon, 1988.

Braudel, Fernand. *Civilization and Capitalism: 15th–18th Century* [*sic*]. Vol. 2. New York, 1982 [Fr. orig. 1979].

Brazil: Conselho de Desenvolvimento. Grupo de Trabalho para o Desenvolvimento do Nordeste [Celso Furtado, principal author.] *Uma política de desenvolvimento econômico para o Nordeste.* Rio de Janeiro, 1959.

Brazil: Directoria Geral de Estatistica. *Recenseamento do Brasil, 1920.* Vol. 5, part 1. Industria. Rio de Janeiro, 1922–29.

Brazil: Instituto Brasileiro de Geografia e Estatística. *Estatísticas históricas do Brasil.* Rio de Janeiro, 1990.

——. *Recenseamento geral do Brasil (1⁰ de setembro de 1940).* Vol. 3. Censos econômicos. Rio de Janeiro, 1950.

Brazil: Presidência da República. *Plano trienal de desenvolvimento econômico e social (1963– 1965): Síntese.* [Rio de Janeiro], 1963.

Bresser Pereira, Luiz Carlos. "Economic Reform and Cycles of State Intervention." *World Development*, 21, 8 (Aug., 1993): 1337–53.

Brewer, Anthony. *Marxist Theories of Imperialism: A Critical Survey.* London, 1980.

Brinkmann, Carl. "Mihail Manoilesco [*sic*] und die klassische Aussenhandelstheorie." *Weltwirtschaftliches Archiv* 48, part 2 (1938): 273–87.

Brown, William A., Jr. *The International Gold Standard Reinterpreted, 1917–1934.* 2 vols. New York, 1940.

Buesa Blanco, Miguel. "El estado en el proceso de industrialización: Contribución al estudio de la política industrial español en el período 1939–1963." Ph.D. diss., Universidad Complutense de Madrid, 1983.

Bukerow, Nicholas. "The Dynamic Role of Trade in Development: Romania's Strategy." Ph.D. diss., University of Notre Dame, 1980.

Buletinul Uniuniei Generale a Industriaşilor din România. Vols. 1–18. Bucharest, 1921–38.

Bussot, A. "Le bloc des états agricoles de l'Europe centrale et orientale et son programme." *Revue d'Economie Politique* 47 (1933): 1544–58.

Byé, M[aurice]. "Le congrès des économistes de langue française (1936)." *Revue d'Economie Politique* 1 (1937): 141–46.

Caballero, Manuel. *Latin America and the Comintern, 1919–1943.* Cambridge, Eng., 1986.

Caetano, Marcelo. *O sistema corporativo.* Lisbon, 1938.

Campos, Roberto [de Oliveira]. *A lanterna na popa: Memorias.* Rio de Janeiro, 1994.

Cardoso, Ciro Flamarion Santana. *Escravo ou camponês? O protocampesinato negro nas Américas.* São Paulo, 1987.

———. "The Peasant Breach in the Slave System: New Developments in Brazil." *Luso-Brazilian Review* 25, no. 1 (Summer 1988): 49–58.

Cardoso, Ciro F. S., and Hector Pérez Brignoli. *Historia económica de América Latina.* Vol. 2. *Economías de exportación y desarrollo capitalista.* Barcelona, 1979.

Cardoso, Eliana, and Albert Fishlow. "Latin American Economic Development, 1950–1980." *Journal of Latin American Studies* 24, Quincentenary Supplement (1992): 197–218.

Cardoso, Fernando Henrique. "Althusserianismo ou Marxismo? A próposito do conceito de classes em Poulantzas." In *O modelo político brasileiro,* q.v., pp. 104–22.

———. "Associated-Dependent Development: Theoretical and Practical Implications." In Alfred Stepan, ed., *Authoritarian Brazil: Origins, Policies and Future,* pp. 142–78. New Haven, 1973.

———. "The Consumption of Dependency Theory in the United States." *Latin American Research Review* 12, no. 3 (1977): 7–24.

———. "Desenvolvimento e dependência: Perspectivas teóricas na análise sociológica." In *Mundanças sociais na América Latina,* pp. 7–22. São Paulo, 1969.

———. *Empresário industrial e desenvolvimento econômico no Brasil.* São Paulo, 1964.

———. "The Entrepreneurial Elites of Latin America." *Studies in Comparative International Development* 2, no. 10 (1966): 145–62.

———. *Ideologías de la burguesía industrial en sociedades dependientes (Argentina y Brasil).* Mexico City, 1971.

———. *O modelo político brasileiro e outros ensaios.* São Paulo, 1972.

———. "Novas teses equivocadas." In *Autoritarismo e democratização.* Rio de Janeiro, 1974.

———. "Participação e marginalidade: Notas para uma discussão teórica." In *O modelo político brasileiro,* q.v., pp. 166–85.

———. "Teoria da dependência ou análises concretas de situações de dependência?" *CEBRAP. Estudos* 1 (1971): 25–45.

Cardoso, Fernando Henrique, and Enzo Faletto. *Dependencia y desarrollo en América Latina: Ensayo de interpretación sociológica.* Mexico City, 1969.

———. *Dependency and Development in Latin America* [tr. by Marjorie Urquidi from *Dependencia y desarrollo en América Latina,* q.v.]. Berkeley, 1979.

Cardoso, Fernando Henrique, and José Luis Reyna. "Industrialization, Occupational

Structure, and Social Stratification in Latin America." In Cole Blasier, ed., *Constructive Change in Latin America*, pp. 19–55. Pittsburgh, 1968.

Cardoso de Mello, João Manoel. *Capitalismo tardio: Contribuição a revisão crítica da formação e do desenvolvimento da economia brasileira*. São Paulo, 1982.

Carone, Edgard, ed. *O marxismo no Brasil (Das origens a 1964)*. Rio de Janeiro, 1986.

——. *O pensamento industrial no Brasil (1880–1945)*. São Paulo, 1971.

Cassel, Gustav. *Recent Monopolistic Tendencies in Industry and Trade: Being an Analysis of the Nature and Causes of the Poverty of Nations*. Geneva, 1927.

Castro, Antônio Barros de, and Carlos F. Lessa. *Introducción a la economía: Un enfoque estructuralista*, 11th ed. Mexico City, 1973 [Port. orig. 1967].

Castro, Armando. "O ensino da ciência econômica na segunda metade dos anos trinta e a acção pedagógica do Professor Doutor Teixeira Ribeiro." *Boletim da Faculdade de Direito de Coimbra*, número especial (1978): 1–11.

Castro, Josué de. *O livro negro da fome*. 3d ed. São Paulo, 1968 [1960].

Centre d'Etudes et de Recherches Marxistes. *Sur le "mode de production asiatique."* Paris, 1969.

[Centro das Indústrias do Estado de São Paulo]. "Préfacio." In Mihail Manoilesco [sic], *Theoria do proteccionismo e de permuta internacional*. São Paulo, 1931.

Chamberlin, Edward. *The Theory of Monopolistic Competition*. Cambridge, Mass., 1933.

Chaudhry, Kiren Aziz. "The Myths of the Market and the Common History of Late Developers." *Politics & Society* 21, 3 (Sept., 1993): 245–74.

Chayanov, A[lexander] V[asilievich]. *Die Lehre von der bäuerlichen Wirtschaft: Versuch einer Theorie der Familienwirtschaft im Landbau*. Berlin, 1923.

——. "On the Theory of Non-Capitalist Economic Systems." In *The Theory of Peasant Economy*, q.v., pp. 1–28 [Ger. orig., "Zur Frage," q.v., 1924].

——. "Peasant Farm Organization." In *The Theory of Peasant Economy*, q.v, pp. 29–271 [Russ. orig. 1925].

——. *The Theory of Peasant Economy* [ed. Daniel Thorner, Basile Kerblay, and R. E. F. Smith]. Homewood, Ill., 1966.

——. "Zur Frage einer Theorie der nichtkapitalistischen Wirtschaftssysteme." *Archiv für Sozialwissenschaft und Sozialpolitik* 51 (1924): 577–613.

Chenery, Hollis B. "The Structuralist Approach to Development Policy." *American Economic Review* 65, no. 2 (May 1975): 310–16.

Cherciu, A. "Comerţul, circulaţia bănească, finanţele şi creditul din deceniul al 7-lea al secolului al XIX-lea şi pînă la primul război mondial." In Nicolae Marcu, ed., *Istorie economică*, pp. 179–201. Bucharest, 1979.

Chiaramonte, José Carlos. *Formas de sociedad y economía en Hispanoamérica*. Mexico City, 1984.

Chirot, Daniel. "Neoliberal and Social Democratic Theories of Development: The Zeletin-Voinea Debate Concerning Romania's Prospects in the 1920's and Its Contemporary Importance." In Kenneth Jowitt, ed., *Social Change in Romania, 1860–1940: A Debate on Development in a European Nation*, pp. 31–52. Berkeley, 1978.

——. *Social Change in a Peripheral Society: The Creation of a Balkan Colony*. New York, 1976.

Chirot, Daniel, and Thomas D. Hall. "World-System Theory." *Annual Review of Sociology* 8 (1982): 81–106.

Christodorescu, Gheorghe. *O operă profesională: Colaborarea Uniunii Camerelor de Comerţ şi de Industrie cu puterile publice 1926–1936.* Vol. 1: *Criza economică.* Bucharest, [1935].

——. *Problema dezechilibriului dintre preţurile agricole şi cele industriale.* Bucharest, 1933.

Ciano, Galeazzo. *The Ciano Diaries, 1939–1943* [ed. Hugh Gibson]. New York, 1946.

Clark, Colin. *The Conditions of Economic Progress.* 2d ed. London, 1951 [1940].

——. *The Economics of 1960.* London, 1942.

Concha, Malaquías. "Balanza de comercio." *Revista Económica* 3, no. 23 (1 Mar. 1889): 305–33.

——. *La lucha económica: Estudio de economía social presentado al 4° congreso científico americano reunido en Santiago de Chile en 1908.* Santiago, 1910.

Condliffe, J. B. "Die Industrialisierung des wirtschaftlich rückstandigen Länder." *Weltwirtschaftliches Archiv* 37 (1933): 335–59.

Confederação Industrial do Brasil. "Relatório da Diretoria apresentado a Assembléia Geral Ordinária de 19 de maio de 1937." In Edgard Carone, ed., *O pensamento industrial no Brasil,* pp. 332–40. São Paulo, 1977.

[Confederação Nacional das Indústrias]. "Interpretação do processo de desenvolvimento econômico da América Latina." *Estudos Econômicos* 1, nos. 3–4 (Sept.–Dec. 1950): 271–306.

Conferência Nacional dos Bispos do Brasil. *Igreja e problemas da terra: Documento apurado pela 18ª. assembléia da CNBB.* São Paulo, 1980.

——. *Pastoral da terra: Posse e conflitos.* São Paulo, 1976.

Congrès International des Sciences Economiques. *Travaux du Congrès.* Vol. 1. Paris, 1937.

Congresso Brasileiro da Indústria. *Anais.* Vol. 1. São Paulo, 1945.

Constantinescu, Olga. *Critica teoriei "România—ţara eminamente agricolă."* Bucharest, 1973.

Contador, Cláudio R., and Cláudio L. Haddad. "Produto real, moeda e preços: A experiência brasileira no período 1861–1970." *Revista Brasileira de Estatística* 36, no. 143 (July–Sept. 1975): 407–40.

Corden, W. M. *Recent Developments in the Theory of International Trade.* Special Papers in International Economics, no. 7. Princeton, 1965.

Cornăţeanu, Nicolae D. *Cercetării asupra rentabilităţii agriculturii ţărăneşti.* Bucharest, 1935.

Corradini, Enrico. "Principles of Nationalism." In Adrian Lyttelton, ed., *Italian Fascism from Pareto to Gentile,* pp. 146–47. London, 1973 [Ital. orig. 1910].

Correia, Serzedelo I. "As indústrias nacionais." In Edgard Carone, ed., *O pensamento industrial no Brasil (1880–1945),* pp. 42–46. São Paulo, 1977 [1903].

Coutinho, Carlos Nelson. *O estruturalismo e a miséria da razão.* Rio de Janeiro, 1972.

Cresin, Roman. *Agricultura din judeţul Argeş: Rezultate ale recensământului agricol din 1941.* Bucharest, 1945.

——. "Puterea de cumpărare a agricultorilor." *Viaţa Agricolă* 25, no. 6 (June 1934): 228–33.

Cueva, Agustín. "El uso del concepto de modo de producción en América Latina: Algunos problemas teóricos." In Roger Bartra, ed., *Modos de producción en América Latina,* q.v., pp. 20–36.

Cuneo, Dardo. *Comportimiento y crisis de la clase empresarial*. Buenos Aires, 1967.

Dean, Warren. "The Brazilian Economy, 1870–1930." In Leslie Bethell, ed., *The Cambridge History of Latin America*. Vol. 5, pp. 685–724. Cambridge, Eng., 1986.

———. *The Struggle for Rubber: A Study in Environmental History*. Cambridge, Eng., 1987.

Decca, Edgar de. *O silêncio dos vencidos*. São Paulo, 1981.

Degener, Herrmann A. L. *Degeners Wer ist's?* Berlin, 1935.

Delaisi, Francis. *Les deux Europes*. Paris, 1929.

Del Canto Schramm, Jorge. "El concepto del 'costo comparativo' en el comercio internacional." *Economía* 4, nos. 8–9 (Sept. 1943): 3–39.

Demetrescu, Eugen. "Liberalismul economic în dezvoltarea României moderne." In *Enciclopedia României*. Vol. 3, pp. 261–74. Bucharest, [1940].

Desenvolvimento e Conjuntura 1, no. 1 (July 1957): 5–15.

De Soto, Hernando. *The Other Path: The Invisible Revolution in the Third World*. New York, 1989 [Sp. orig. 1986].

Diakosavvas, Dimitris, and Pasquale L. Scandizzo. "Trends in the Terms of Trade of Primary Commodities, 1900–1982: The Controversy and Its Origins." *Economic Development and Cultural Change* 39, no. 2 (Jan. 1991): 231–64.

Diamandi, Sterie. *Galeria oamenilor politici*. Bucharest, [1936?].

Díaz-Alejandro, Carlos F. *Essays on the Economic History of the Argentine Republic*. New Haven, 1970.

———. "Latin America in the 1930s." In Rosemary Thorp, ed., *Latin America in the 1930s: The Role of the Periphery in World Crisis*, pp. 17–49. New York, 1982.

———. "The 1940s in Latin America." Manuscript, Oct. 1982.

———. "Trade Policies and Economic Development." In Peter B. Kenen, ed., *International Trade and Finance: Frontier for Research*, pp. 93–150. New York, 1975.

Diccionario biográfico de Chile, 1948–1949. 7th ed. Santiago, n.d.

D'Incao e Mello, Maria Conceição. *A bóia fria: Acumulação e miséria*. Rio de Janeiro, 1975.

Diniz, Eli. "Empresário, estado e nacionalismo." In Diniz and Renato R. Boschi, *Empresariado nacional e estado no Brasil*, pp. 45–107. Rio de Janeiro, 1978.

Dobb, Maurice. *Studies in the Development of Capitalism*. New York, 1963 [1947].

"Dobrogeanu-Gherea, Constantin." In Gogoneață et al., eds., *Istoria filozofiei românești*, q.v. Vol. 1, pp. 588–604.

Dobrogeanu-Gherea, Constantin. "Ce vor socialiştii români: Expunerea socialismului ştiinţific şi programul socialist." In *Opere complete*. Vol. 2, pp. 7–126. Bucharest, 1976 [1886].

———. "Din ideile fundamentale ale socialismului ştiinţific." In *Opere complete*. Vol. 3, pp. 408–38. Bucharest, 1977 [1906].

———. "Din urmările regimului oligarhic." *Viaţa Socialistă* 1, no. 2 (Dec. 1920): 13–22.

———. "Geneza oligarhiei române." *Viaţa Socialistă* 1, no. 1 (Nov. 1920): 3–9.

———. "Karl Marx şi economiştii noştri." In *Opere complete*. Vol. 1, pp. 40–164. Bucharest, 1976 [1884].

———. "Un mic răspuns la o mică recenzie." In *Opere complete*. Vol. 3, pp. 456–66. Bucharest, 1977 [1908].

———. *Neoiobăgia*. In *Opere complete*. Vol. 4. Bucharest, 1977 [1910].

———. "Post-scriptum sau cuvinte uitate." In *Opere complete*. Vol. 3, pp. 476–504. Bucharest, 1977 [1908].

——. "Rolul păturii culte în transformările sociale." In *Opere complete*. Vol. 2, pp. 426–46. Bucharest, 1976 [1892].

——. *Socialismul în țările înapoiate*. Bucharest, 1945 [1912].

Dore, Elizabeth. "Peasantry." In Bottomore et al., eds., *A Dictionary of Marxist Thought*, q.v., pp. 363–65.

Dorfman, Adolfo. *Evolución industrial argentina*. Buenos Aires, 1942.

Dulles, John F. *Anarchists and Communists in Brazil, 1900–1935*. Austin, 1973.

Duncan, Kenneth, and Ian Rutledge. "Introduction." In Duncan and Rutledge, eds., *Land and Labour in Latin America: Essays on the Development of Agrarian Capitalism in the Nineteenth and Twentieth Centuries*, pp. 1–22. Cambridge, Eng., 1977.

Economist Intelligence Unit. *Country Profile: Brazil: 1994–95*. London, 1995.

——. *Country Profile: Romania 1994–95*. London, 1994.

Egoroff, Pawel P. "Die Arbeit in der Landwirtschaft." In Ianki Stefanov Molloff, ed., *Die sozialökonomische Struktur der bulgarischen Landwirtschaft*, pp. 131–59. Berlin, 1936.

Eidelberg, Philip Gabriel. *The Great Rumanian Peasant Revolt of 1907: Origins of a Modern Jacquerie*. Leiden, 1974.

Emmanuel, Arghiri. *Unequal Exchange: A Study of the Imperialism of Trade*. New York, 1972 [Fr. orig. 1969].

Ene, Ernest. *Spre statul țărănesc*. Bucharest, 1932.

Engels, Friedrich. "On Historical Materialism." In Lewis S. Feuer, ed., *Karl Marx and Friedrich Engels: Basic Writings on Politics and Philosophy*, pp. 47–67. Garden City, N.Y., 1959 [1892].

Equipe PIMES. *Desigualdades regionais no desenvolvimento brasileiro*. 4 vols. Recife, 1984.

Ercuță, Petre. *Die Genesis des modernen Kapitalismus in Rumänien*. Leipzig, 1941.

Escobar, Arturo. *Encountering Development: The Making and Unmaking of the Third World*. Princeton, 1995.

Esfahani, Hadi Salehi. "Exports, Imports, and Economic Growth in Semi-Industrialized Countries." *Journal of Development Economics* 35 (1991): 93–116.

Evans, Peter. *Dependent Development: The Alliance of Multinational, State, and Local Capital in Brazil*. Princeton, 1979.

El exilio español en México, 1939–1982. Mexico City, 1982.

Fajnzylber, Fernando. *Unavoidable Industrial Restructuring in Latin America*. Durham, N.C., 1990.

Fanganiello, Helena. *Roberto Simonsen e o desenvolvimento econômico*. São Paulo, 1970.

[Federação das Indústrias do Estado de São Paulo et al.] *Constituição de 10 de novembro de 1937 e a organização corporativa e sindical*. N.p., [1940].

Feinstein, Charles. "The Rise and Fall of the Williamson Curve." *Journal of Economic History* 48, no. 3 (1988): 699–729.

Ferreira Lima, Heitor. "Evolução industrial de São Paulo." *Revista Industrial de S. Paulo* 1, no. 7 (June 1945): 12–13.

——. *História do pensamento econômico no Brasil*. São Paulo, 1976.

Ferrer, Aldo. *La economía argentina: Las etapas de su desarollo y problemas actuales* [tr. by Marjorie Urquidi as *The Argentine Economy*. Berkeley, 1967]. Mexico City, [1963].

Ffrench-Davis, Ricardo, and Oscar Muñoz. "Latin American Economic Development and the International Environment." In Patricio Meller, ed., *The Latin American Development Debate*, pp. 9–26. Boulder, Colo., 1991.

Ffrench-Davis, Ricardo, Oscar Muñoz, and José Gabriel Palma. "The Latin American Economies, 1950–1990." In Leslie Bethell, ed., *Cambridge History of Latin America*. Vol. 6, pp. 159–249. Cambridge, Eng., 1994.

Figueroa, Adolfo. *Capitalist Development and Peasant Economy in Peru*. Cambridge, Eng., 1984.

Findlay, Ronald. "On W. Arthur Lewis' Contributions to Economics." *Scandinavian Journal of Economics* 82 (1980): 62–79.

Fishlow, Albert. "Comment on Raúl Prebisch, 'Five Stages in My Thinking on Development.'" In Gerald M. Meier and Dudley Seers, eds., *Pioneers in Development*, pp. 192–96. New York, 1984.

Fitzgerald, E. V. K. "ECLA and the Formation of Latin American Economic Doctrine." In David Rock, ed., *Latin America in the 1940s: War and Postwar Transitions*, pp. 89–108. Berkeley, 1994.

Fodor, Jorge C., and Arturo A. O'Connell. "Argentina y la economía atlántica en la primera mitad del siglo XX." *Desarrollo Económico* 13, no. 49 (Apr.–June 1973): 3–65.

"Forced Labor in Brazil Re-visited: On-site Investigations Document That Practice Continues." *Americas Watch: A Division of Human Rights Watch* 5, no. 12 (30 Nov. 1993), 8 pp.

Foster-Carter, Aiden. "From Rostow to Gunder Frank: Conflicting Paradigms in the Analysis of Underdevelopment." *World Development* 4, no. 3 (Mar. 1976): 167–80.

Foweraker, Joe. *The Struggle for Land: A Political Economy of the Pioneer Frontier in Brazil from 1930 to the Present Day*. Cambridge, Eng., 1980.

Francheschi, Gustavo. "Totalitarianismo, liberalismo, y catolicismo." *Criterio*, no. 662 (7 Nov. 1940): 221–27.

Frangeš, Otto. "Die Donaustaaten Südosteuropas und der deutsche Grosswirtschaftsraum." *Weltwirtschaftliches Archiv* 53, part 1 (1941): 284–320.

———. "L'industrialisation des pays agricoles du sud-est de l'Europe." *Revue Economique Internationale* 30, no. 3 (July–Sept. 1938): 27–77.

———. "Die treibenden Kräfte der wirtschaftlichen Strukturwandlungen in Jugoslawien." *Weltwirtschaftliches Archiv* 48, part 2 (1938): 309–40.

———. "Die wirtschaftlichen Beziehungen Jugoslawiens und die Eingliederung in die Weltwirtschaft." *Weltwirtschaftliches Archiv* 37, part 1 (1933): 113–45.

Frank, Andre Gunder. "Agricultura brasileira: Capitalismo e o mito do feudalismo." *Revista Brasiliense*, no. 51 (Jan.–Feb. 1964): 45–70 [publ. in Eng. as "Capitalism and the Myth of Feudalism in Brazilian Agriculture," q.v.].

———. "Capitalism and the Myth of Feudalism in Brazilian Agriculture." In *Capitalism and Underdevelopment in Latin America*, q.v., pp. 219–333.

———. *Capitalism and Underdevelopment in Latin America: Historical Studies of Chile and Brazil*. New York, 1969 [1967].

———. "¿Con qué modo de producción convierte la gallina maíz en huevos de oro?" *El Gallo Ilustrado: Suplemento Dominical de 'El Día'*, no. 173 (17 Oct. 1965): 2.

———. *Lumpenbourgeoisie, Lumpendevelopment*. New York, 1972 [Sp. orig. 1970].

———. *On Capitalist Underdevelopment*. Bombay, 1975.

———. "The Underdevelopment of Development." *Scandinavian Journal of Development Alternatives* 10, no. 3 (Sept. 1991): 5–72 [reprint].

Fritsch, Winston. "El nuevo marco internacional: Desafíos y oportunidades." In Osvaldo Sunkel, ed., *El desarrollo desde dentro*, q.v., pp. 397–416.

Fröhlich, Otto. "Wirtschaftliche Rechtfertigung des Zollschutzes?" *Weltwirtschaftliches Archiv* 48, part 2 (1938): 288–308.

Frunzănescu, A[urel]. *Munca omenească în actuala conjunctură agricolă*. Bucharest, 1935.

Fuentes Irurozqui, Manuel. "Prólogo." In Mihail Manoilesco [*sic*], *Teoría del protectionismo y del comercio internacional* [tr. by Manuel Fuentes Irurozqui from *Théorie du protectionnisme*, q.v.], pp. vii–xv. Madrid, 1943.

Furnivall, J. S. *Netherlands India: A Study of Plural Economy*. New York, 1944 [1939].

Furtado, Celso. *Accumulation and Development: The Logic of Industrial Civilization* [tr. by Suzette Macedo]. Oxford, 1983 [Port. orig. 1978].

——. "Adventures of a Brazilian Economist." *International Social Science Journal* [UNESCO] 25, nos. 1–2 (1973): 28–38.

——. *Os ares do mundo*. Rio de Janeiro, 1991.

——. "Capital Formation and Economic Development." In *International Economic Papers* no. 4 (1954): 124–44 [Port. orig. 1952].

——. "Características gerais da economia brasileira." *Revista Brasileira de Economia* 4, no. 1 (Mar. 1950): 1–37.

——. *Desenvolvimento e subdesenvolvimento*. Rio de Janeiro, 1961.

——. *Development and Underdevelopment*. Berkeley, 1964 [tr. of previous item].

——. *Diagnosis of the Brazilian Crisis*. Berkeley, 1965 [Port. orig. 1964].

——. *Uma economia dependente*. Rio de Janeiro, 1956.

——. *A economia brasileira. (Contribuçao á análise do seu desenvolvimento)*. Rio de Janeiro, 1954.

——. *Economic Development of Latin America: Historical Background and Contemporary Problems* [tr. by Suzette Macedo of *Formação económica da América Latina*, q.v.]. Cambridge, Eng., 1970.

——. *The Economic Growth of Brazil: A Survey from Colonial to Modern Times* [Eng. tr. by Ricardo W. de Aguiar and Eric Charles Drysdale of *Formação económica do Brasil*]. Berkeley, 1963 [Port. orig. 1959].

——. "L'économie coloniale brésilienne (XVIe et XVIIe siècles): Eléments d'histoire économique appliqués." Ph.D. diss., Faculté de Droit, Université de Paris, 1948.

——. "Elements of a Theory of Underdevelopment." In *Development and Underdevelopment*, q.v., pp. 115–40.

——. "External Disequilibrium in the Underdeveloped Economies." *Indian Journal of Economics* (Apr. 1958): 403–10.

——. "External Disequilibrium in the Underdeveloped Structures." In *Development and Underdevelopment*, q.v., pp. 141–71.

——. *A fantasia desfeita*. São Paulo, 1989.

——. *A fantasia organizada*. Rio de Janeiro, 1985.

——. *Formação económica da América Latina*. Rio de Janeiro, 1969.

——. *Formação económica do Brasil*. Rio de Janeiro, 1959.

——. "Fundamentos da programação económica." *Económica Brasileira* 4, nos. 1–2 (Jan.–June 1958): 39–44.

——. "The Historic Process of Development." In *Development and Underdevelopment*, q.v., pp. 77–114 [Port. orig. 1955].

———. *A operação nordeste.* Rio de Janeiro, 1959.

———. *Perspectivas da economia brasileira.* Rio de Janeiro, 1958.

———. Review of Albert Hirschman, "The Strategy of Economic Development." *Econômica Brasileira* 5, nos. 1–2 (Jan.–June 1959): 64–65.

———. *Subdesenvolvimento e estagnação na América Latina.* Rio de Janeiro, 1966.

———. *Underdevelopment and Dependence: The Fundamental Connections.* Center of Latin American Studies, Cambridge University, 22 Nov. 1973 [offset].

———. "Underdevelopment: To Conform or Reform." In Gerald M. Meier, ed., *Pioneers in Development.* 2d series, pp. 205–27. New York, 1987.

Gabeira, Fernando. *O que é isso, companheiro?* 2d ed. Rio de Janeiro, 1980 [1979].

Galbraith, John Kenneth. *American Capitalism: The Concept of Countervailing Powers.* New York, rev. ed., 1956 [1952].

Garavaglia, Juan Carlos. *Mercado interno y economía colonial.* Mexico City, 1983.

Garcia, Afrânio Raúl, Jr. *O Sul: Caminho do roçado: Estratégias de reprodução camponesa e transformação social.* São Paulo, 1990.

———. *Terra de trabalho.* Rio de Janeiro, 1983.

Geertz, Clifford. *Agricultural Involution: The Process of Ecological Change in Indonesia.* Berkeley, 1963.

Georgescu-Roegen, Nicholas. "Economic Theory and Agrarian Economics." In *Energy and Economic Myths: Institutional and Analytical Economic Essays,* pp. 103–45. New York, 1976 [1960].

———. "Manoilescu, Mihail." In John Eatwell et al., *The New Palgrave: A Dictionary of Economics.* Vol. 3, pp. 299–300. London, 1987.

Gerschenkron, Alexander. *Economic Backwardness in Historical Perspective.* Cambridge, Mass., 1962.

———. "Economic Development in Russian Intellectual History of the Nineteenth Century." In *Economic Backwardness,* q.v., pp. 152–87.

Gheorghiu, Mihnea. *Social and Political Sciences in Romania: An Outline History.* [Bucharest], n.d.

"Gherea (Dobrogeanu-Gherea), Constantin." In *Dicţionar Enciclopedic Romín.* Vol. 2, pp. 548–49. Bucharest, 1964.

Giannotti, José Arthur. *Origens da dialética do trabalho.* São Paulo, 1965.

Gogoneaţă, Nicolae, et al., eds., *Istoria filozofiei româneşti.* Vol. 1. Bucharest, 1972.

Golopenţia, Anton, and D. C. Georgescu, eds. *60 sate româneşti cercetate de echipele studenţeşti în vara 1938.* Vol. 2. *Situaţia economică.* Bucharest, 1941.

Gondra, Luis Roque. "Teorema ricardiano de los costos comparados." *Revista de Ciencias Económicas* 25, no. 195 (Oct. 1937): 863–71.

Gondra, Luis Roque, et al. *Pensamiento económico latino-americano: Argentina, Bolivia, Brasil, Cuba, Chile, Haití, Paraguay, Perú.* Mexico City, 1945.

González, Norberto, and David Pollock. "Del ortodoxo al conservador ilustrado: Raúl Prebisch en la Argentina, 1923–1943." *Desarrollo Económico* 30, no. 120 (Jan.–Mar. 1991): 455–86.

González Casanova, Pablo. "Internal Colonialism and National Development." *Studies in Comparative International Development* 1, no. 4 (1965): 27–37.

Gorman, Robert A., ed. *Biographical Dictionary of Neo-Marxism.* Westport, Conn., 1985.

Graf, Oscar P. *Die Industriepolitik Alt-Rumäniens und die Grundlagen der Industrialisierung Gross-Rumäniens*. Bucharest, n.d. [1927?].

Gramsci, Antonio. "The Southern Question." In *The Modern Prince and Other Writings*, pp. 28–54. New York, 1957 [Ital. orig. 1926].

Grilli, Enzo R., and Maw Cheng Yang. "Primary Commodity Prices, Manufactured Goods Prices, and the Terms of Trade of Developing Countries: What the Long Run Shows." *World Bank Economic Review* 2, no. 1 (Jan. 1988): 1–47.

Grindea, Dan. *Venitul național în Republica Socialistă România*. Bucharest, 1967.

Gual Villalbi, Pedro. *Teoría de la política comercial exterior*. Madrid, 1940.

Gudin, Eugênio. "A formação do economista." *Revista Brasileira de Economia* 10, no. 1 (Mar. 1956): 63–70.

——. "Notas sobre a economia brasileira desde a proclamação da República até os nossos dias." *Revista Brasileira de Economia* 26, no. 3 (July–Sept. 1972): 85–108.

——. "Rumos da política econômica." In Roberto Simonsen and Eugênio Gudin, *A controvérsia do planejamento na economia brasileira*, pp. 41–141. Rio de Janeiro, 1977 [Manuscript written Mar. 1945].

Guevara, Ernesto [Che]. *Guerrilla Warfare*. New York, 1961 [Sp. orig. 1960].

Gusti, Dimitrie. "Sociologie românească." *Sociologie Românească* 1, no. 1 (Jan. 1936): 1–9.

Haddad, Claudio L. S. "Growth of Brazilian Real Output, 1900–1947." Ph.D. diss., University of Chicago, 1974.

Hagen, Everett E. "An Economic Justification of Protectionism." *Quarterly Journal of Economics* 72, no. 4 (Nov. 1958): 496–514.

Hale, Charles A. "Political and Social Ideas in Latin America, 1870–1930." In Leslie Bethell, ed., *Cambridge History of Latin America*. Vol. 4, pp. 367–441. Cambridge, Eng., 1986.

Harnecker, Marta. *Los conceptos elementales del materialismo histórico*. 35th ed. Mexico City, 1976 [1969].

Harris, Richard. "Structuralism in Latin America." *Insurgent Sociologist* 9, no. 1 (Summer 1979): 62–73.

Hartz, Louis, ed. *The Founding of New Societies: Studies in the History of the United States, Latin America, South Africa, Canada, and Australia*. New York, 1964.

Hașdeu, Bogdan Petriceicu. "Agricultura și manufactura (1869–1870)." In Academia Republicii Populare Romîne: Institutul de Cercetări Economice, *Texte din literatura economică în România, secolul XIX*. Vol. 1, pp. 271–75. Bucharest, 1960.

Hauner, M. "Human Resources." In M[ichael] C. Kaser and E. A. Radice, eds., *The Economic History of Eastern Europe 1919–1975*. Vol. 1, pp. 66–147. Oxford, 1985.

Hechter, Michael. *Internal Colonialism: The Celtic Fringe in British National Development, 1536–1966*. Berkeley, 1975.

Hennebicq, Léon. Review of Mihail Manoilescu, "Théorie du protectionnisme et de l'échange international." *Revue Economique Internationale* 22 (Apr. 1930): 194–97.

Heynig, Klaus. "The Principal Schools of Thought on the Peasant Economy." *CEPAL Review*, no. 16 (Apr. 1982): 113–40.

Hilferding, Rudolf. *Finanzkapital: Eine Studie über die jungste Entwicklung des Kapitalismus*. Vienna, 1910.

Hilton, Rodney, ed. *The Transition from Feudalism to Capitalism*. London, 1976.

Hind, Robert J. "The Concept of Internal Colonialism." *Comparative Studies in Society and History* 26 (1984): 543–68.

Hirschman, Albert O. "A Generalized Linkage Approach to Development, with Special Reference to Staples." *Economic Development and Cultural Change* 25, supplement (1977): 67–98.

———. "Ideologies of Economic Development in Latin America." In Hirschman, ed., *Latin American Issues: Essays and Comments*, pp. 3–42. New York, 1961.

———. *National Power and the Structure of Foreign Trade.* Berkeley, 1945.

———. *The Strategy of Economic Development.* New Haven, 1958.

———. "The Turn to Authoritarianism in Latin America and the Search for Its Economic Determinants." In David Collier, ed., *The New Authoritarianism in Latin America*, pp. 69–98. Princeton, 1979.

Hitchins, Keith. *Rumania, 1866–1947.* Oxford, 1994.

Hodara, Joseph. *Prebisch y la Cepal: Sustancia, trayectoria y contexto institucional.* Mexico City, 1987.

Horovitz, M. "Despre unele particularități și limite ale acțiunii legii valorii în comerțul exterior socialist." *Probleme Economice* 11, no. 4 (Apr. 1958): 10–20.

Hugon, Paul. "A economia política no Brasil." In Fernando Azevedo, ed., *As ciências no Brasil.* Vol. 2, pp. 299–352. São Paulo, [1958?].

Hurezeanu, Damian. *Constantin Dobrogeanu-Gherea: Studiu social-istoric.* Bucharest, 1973.

———. "La revue 'Viața Românească' et les traditions radicales-démocratiques de Roumanie." *Revue Roumaine d'Histoire* 25, no. 4 (Oct.–Dec. 1986): 331–41.

Iacoș, Ion. "Studiu introductiv." In Cristian Racovski, *Scrieri social politice (1900–1916)*, q.v., pp. 5–35.

Ianculescu, C[onstantin]. *Problemele agrare și dezvoltarea industrială a României.* Bucharest, 1934.

Ibrăileanu, Garabet. Review of Constantin Dobrogeanu-Gherea, "Din ideile fundamentale ale socialismului științific." *Viața Românească* 1, no. 7 (1906): 137–39.

Iglésias, Francisco. "Introdução." In Caio Prado Júnior, *Caio Prado Júnior*, pp. 7–44. São Paulo, 1982.

"Industrialización [an editorial]." *Revista de Economía* [Mexico] 8, no. 10 (Oct. 1945): 5–6.

Institutul de Cercetări Agronomice al României, ed. *Studii privitoare la prețuri și rentabilitate în agricultura României.* Bucharest, 1936.

Institutul Românesc de Conjunctură. *Buletin* 1, nos. 3–4 [1933?], supplement.

Internacional Comunista. *VI Congreso.* Vol. 2: *Informes y Discusiones.* Mexico City, 1978 [The congress took place in 1928].

International Reference Library, ed. *Politics and Political Parties of Roumania.* London, 1936.

Ionescu, Ghiță. "Eastern Europe." In Ionescu and E. Gellner, eds., *Populism: Its Meaning and National Characteristics*, pp. 97–121. London, 1969.

Ionescu-Șișești, Gheorghe. "Pentru ce nu progresează agricultura." *Buletinul Informativ al Ministerului Agriculturii și Domeniilor* 11, no. 6 (June 1940): 617–19.

Ioța, Vasile. "Doctrina economică a lui A. Xenopol." Ph.D. diss., Academia de Studii Economice, Bucharest, 1968.

J. B. F. [unidentified]. "De vorbă cu domnul profesor W. Sombart." *Adevărul* (4 Jan. 1929): 3.

Jackson, Marvin. "Industrial Output in Rumania and Its Historical Regions, 1880 to 1930: Part I—1880 to 1915." *Journal of European Economic History* 15, no. 1 (Spring 1986): 59–111.

Jaguaribe, Hélio. "The Dynamics of Brazilian Nationalism." In Claudio Véliz, ed., *Obstacles to Change in Latin America*, pp. 102–87. London, 1965.

Jameson, Kenneth. "Latin American Structuralism: A Methodological Perspective." *World Development* 14, no. 2 (Feb. 1986): 223–32.

Janos, Andrew C. "Modernization and Decay in Historical Perspective: The Case of Romania." In Kenneth Jowitt, ed., *Social Change in Romania, 1860–1940: A Debate on Development in a European Nation*, pp. 72–116. Berkeley, 1978.

———. *The Politics of Backwardness in Hungary, 1825–1945.* Princeton, 1982.

Jelavich, Barbara B. *A History of the Balkans.* Vol. 1. Cambridge, Eng., 1983.

Johnson, Harry G. *Economic Nationalism in Old and New States.* Chicago, 1967.

———. "The Ideology of Economic Policy in the New States." In Johnson, *Economic Nationalism,* q.v., pp. 124–41.

———. "Keynes and Development." In Elizabeth S. Johnson and Harry G. Johnson, *The Shadow of Keynes,* pp. 227–33. Oxford, 1978.

"Junimea." In *Dicţionar Enciclopedic Romín.* Vol. 2, pp. 935–36. Bucharest, 1964.

Kahl, Joseph. "Fernando Henrique Cardoso." In *Modernization, Exploitation and Dependency in Latin America: Germani, González Casanova and Cardoso,* pp. 129–94. New Brunswick, N.J., 1976.

Kalecki, Michal. "The Problem of Financing Economic Development." In *Essays on Developing Economies,* pp. 41–63. Atlantic Highlands, N.J., 1976 [Sp. orig. 1954].

———. Review of Mihail Manoilescu, "Die Nationalen Produktivkräfte und der Aussenhandel." *Economic Journal* 48 (1938): 708–11.

———. "Unemployment in Underdeveloped Countries." In *Essays on Developing Economies,* q.v., pp. 17–19 [1960].

Katzman, Martin T. *Cities and Frontiers in Brazil: Regional Dimensions of Economic Development.* Cambridge, Mass., 1977.

Kautsky, Karl. *La cuestión agraria: Análisis de las tendencias de la agricultura moderna y de la política agraria de la social democracia.* Mexico City, 1974 [Ger. orig. 1899].

———. *The Social Revolution.* Chicago, 1903 [Ger. orig. 1902].

Kay, Cristóbal. *Latin American Theories of Development and Underdevelopment.* London, 1989.

Kindleberger, Charles P. "Flexibility of Demand in International Trade Theory." *Quarterly Journal of Economics* 1, no. 2 (Feb. 1937): 352–61.

———. "International Monetary Stabilization." In Seymour E. Harris, ed., *Postwar Economic Problems,* pp. 375–95. New York, 1943.

———. "Planning for Foreign Investment." *American Economic Review* 33, no. 1, supplement (Mar. 1943): 347–453.

———. *The World in Depression, 1929–1939.* London, 1973.

Kitching, Galvin. *Development and Underdevelopment in Historical Perspective: Populism, Nationalism, and Industrialization.* London, 1982.

Knight, Melvin M. "Backward Countries." In *Encyclopedia of the Social Sciences*. Vol. 2, pp. 379–81. New York, 1930.

Kochanowicz, Jacek. "Chayanov's Theory and Polish Views on Peasant Economy." Manuscript, 1988.

Kofman, Jan. "Economic Nationalism in East Central Europe in the Interwar Period." In Henryk Szlajfer, ed., *Economic Nationalism in East-Central Europe and South America, 1918–1939*, pp. 191–249. Geneva, 1990.

———. "How to Define Economic Nationalism? A Critical Review of Some Old and New Standpoints." In Henryk Szlajfer, ed., *Economic Nationalism in East-Central Europe and South America*, q.v., pp. 17–54.

Konder, Leandro. *A derrota da dialéctica*. Rio de Janeiro, 1988.

Kondratieff, N[ikolai] D. "Long Waves in Economic Life." *Review of Economic Statistics* 17, no. 6 (Nov. 1935): 105–15 [Russ. orig. 1925].

———. "Die Preisdynamik der industriellen und landwirtschaften Waren (Zum Problem der relativen Dynamik und Konjunktur)." *Archiv für Sozialwissenschaft und Sozialpolitik* 60 (1928): 1–85.

[Koninklijk Institut voor de Tropen, ed.] "Editorial Introduction." In *Indonesian Economics: The Concept of Dualism in Theory and Policy*, pp. 1–64. The Hague, 1961.

Kowarick, Lúcio. "Capitalismo, dependência e marginalidade urbana na América Latina: Uma contribuição teórica." *Estudos CEBRAP* 8 (Apr.–June 1974): 79–96.

Kubitschek, Juscelino de Oliveira [President of Brazil]. *Mensagem ao Congresso Nacional: . . . 1956*. Rio de Janeiro, 1956.

Kuhn, Thomas S. *The Structure of Scientific Revolutions*. 2d ed., enlarged [*International Encyclopedia of Unified Science*: Vol. 2, no. 2]. Chicago, 1970 [1962].

Laclau, Ernesto. "Feudalismo y capitalismo en América Latina." In Carlos Sempat Assadourian et al., *Modos de producción en América Latina*. 4th ed., pp. 23–46. Mexico City, 1977 [1973].

———. "Modos de producción, sistemas económicos y población excedente: Aproximación histórica a los casos argentino y chileno." *Revista Latinoamericana de Sociología* 5, no. 2 (1969): 276–316.

Lal, Deepak. *The Poverty of "Development Economics."* Cambridge, Mass., 1985 [1983].

Lampe, John, and Marvin Jackson. *Balkan Economic History, 1550–1950: From Imperial Borderlands to Developing Nations*. Bloomington, Ind., 1982.

Landes, David. *The Unbound Prometheus*. Cambridge, Eng., 1969.

League of Nations: Committee for the Study of the Problems of Raw Materials. *Report*. Geneva, 1937.

League of Nations [Societé des Nations]: Comité Economique. *Considerations relatives a l'évolution actuelle du protectionnisme agricole: 20 mai 1935*. Geneva, 1935.

League of Nations: Economic, Financial and Transit Department. *Commercial Policy in the Interwar Period*. Geneva, 1942.

———. *Industrialization and Foreign Trade*. Geneva, 1945.

Lebovics, Herman. *Social Conservatism and the German Middle Classes*. Princeton, 1969.

Ledesma Ramos, Ramiro. "El capitalismo español." In Ledesma Ramos, *Ramiro Ledesma Ramos (Antología)* [ed. by Antonio Macipe López], pp. 185–275. Barcelona, 1940.

Lenin, V[ladimir] I. *The Development of Capitalism in Russia: The Process of the Formation of a Home Market for Large-Scale Industry*. 2d ed. Moscow, 1956 [Russ. orig. 1899].

———. "Imperialism and the Split in Socialism." In *Collected Works*. Vol. 23, pp. 105–20. Moscow, 1960 [Russ. orig. 1916].

Leopoldi, M[aria] Antonieta P. "Industrial Associations and Politics in Contemporary Brazil: The Associations of Industrialists, Economic Policy-Making and the State with Special Reference to the Period 1930–1961." Ph.D. diss., St. Antony's College, Oxford University, 1984.

Lethbridge, E. "National Income and Product." In M[ichael] C. Kaser and E. A. Radice, eds., *The Economic History of Eastern Europe, 1919–1975*. Vol. 1, pp. 532–97. Oxford, 1985.

Levine, Ross, and David Renelt. "A Sensitivity Analysis of Cross-Country Growth Regressions." *American Economic Review* 82, no. 4 (Sept. 1992): 942–63.

Lewis, W. Arthur. "Economic Development with Unlimited Supplies of Labour." *Manchester School of Economic and Social Studies* 22, no. 2 (May 1954): 139–91.

———. *Economic Survey, 1919–1939*. London, 1949.

———. *The Evolution of the International Economic Order*. Princeton, 1978.

Liss, Sheldon B. *Marxist Thought in Latin America*. Berkeley, 1984.

List, Friedrich. *Sistemul național de economie politică*. Bucharest, 1973 [Ger. orig. 1841].

Love, Joseph L. "Economic Ideas and Ideologies in Latin America since 1930." In Leslie Bethell, ed., *Cambridge History of Latin America*. Vol. 6, pp. 393–460. Cambridge, Eng., 1994.

———. "Manoilescu, Prebisch, and the Thesis of Unequal Exchange." *Rumanian Studies* 5 (1980–86): 125–33.

———. "Modeling Internal Colonialism: History and Prospect." *World Development* 17, no. 6 (1989): 905–22.

———. "The Origins of Dependency Analysis." *Journal of Latin American Studies* 22 (1990): 143–68.

———. *São Paulo in the Brazilian Federation, 1889–1937*. Stanford, 1980.

———. " 'Third World': A Response to Professor Worsley." In Leslie Wolf-Philips et al., *Why 'Third World'?*, pp. 33–35. Third World Foundation Monograph 7. London, 1980.

Lowy, Michael, ed. *Le marxisme en Amérique latine de 1909 á nos jours: Anthologie*. Paris, 1980.

Lucena, Manuel de. "The Evolution of Corporatism Under Salazar and Caetano." In Lawrence S. Graham and Harry M. Makler, eds., *Contemporary Portugal*, pp. 47–88. Austin, Tex., 1979.

Ludwig, Armin K. *Brazil: A Handbook of Historical Statistics*. Boston, 1985.

Lupu, N. Z. "Experții financieri străini din România și legile de conversiune a datoriilor din anii 1932–1933." *Analele Institutului de Studii Istorice și Social-Politice de pe lîngă C.C. al P.C.R.* 13, no. 4 (1967): 98–110.

Luz: Revista Rumeno-Sul Americana 2, nos. 1–6 (1937).

Macario, Santiago. "Protectionism and Industrialization in Latin America." *Economic Bulletin for Latin America* 9, no. 1 (1964): 61–101.

Madgearu, Virgil. *Evoluția economiei românești după războiul mondial*. Bucharest, 1940.

———. *Imperialismul economic și Liga Națiunilor*. Bucharest, [1924?].

———. *Teoria economiei țărănești*. Bucharest, 1936 [1925].

———. *Zur industriellen Entwicklung Rumäniens: Die Vorstufen des Fabriksystems in der Walachei*. [Leipzig], 1911.

"Madgearu, Virgil." In *Dicţionar Enciclopedic Romîn*. Vol. 3, p. 194. Bucharest, 1962.

Magariños, Mateo. *Diálógos con Raúl Prebisch*. Mexico City, 1991.

Mahn Hecker, Edgar. "Sobre los argumentos proteccionistas de List y Manoilesco [*sic*]." *Economía* [U. de Chile], no. 17 (Dec. 1945): 59–70.

Maier, Charles. *Recasting Bourgeois Europe: Stabilization in France, Germany, and Italy in the Decade After World War I*. Princeton, 1975.

"Maiorescu, Titu." In Gogoneaţă et al., eds., *Istoria filozofiei româneşti*, q.v. Vol. 1, pp. 353–96.

Malinschi, Vasile. "The Development of Economic Sciences in Romania." *Revue Roumaine des Sciences Sociales: Série Sciences Economiques* 11, no. 1 (1967): 17–31.

——. *Profesorul Virgil Madgearu (1887–1940): Contribuţii la dezvoltarea gîndirii economice*. Bucharest, 1975.

Mandel, Ernest. *Late Capitalism* [tr. by Joris De Bres]. London, 1975 [Ger. orig. 1972].

Mandelbaum, Kurt. *The Industrialisation of Backward Areas*. Oxford, 1945.

——. "A Portrait of the Economist Kurt Mandelbaum Based on an Interview with Matthias Greffrath." *Development and Change* 10, no. 4 (Oct. 1979): 503–13.

Manoilesco, Mihail. See Manoilescu, Mihail.

Manoilescu, Grigore. "Şomuri şi şomaj." *Lumea Nouă* 2, no. 2 (Feb. 1933): 104–10.

Manoilescu, Mihail. "Anticipare." *Lumea Nouă* 1, no. 1 (Apr. 1932): 1–9.

——. "Autarhia economică." *Analele Economice şi Statistice* 17, nos. 7–9 (July–Sept. 1934): 11–26.

——. "Autour de la définition de la valeur." *Revue d'Economie Politique* 56–57, première partie (1946): 457–77; seconde partie (1947): 147–69.

——. "Cartelurile şi raţionalizarea." In Institutul Românesc de Organizare Ştiinţifică a Muncii, ed., *Raţionalizarea sub diferite aspecte*, pp. 35–55. Bucharest, 1930.

——. *Criterii sociale în finanţele publice*. Bucharest, 1926. [Reprint from *Arhiva pentru Ştiinţa şi Reforma Socială*, 1926].

——. "Criza agricolă în cadrul internaţional." *Viaţa Agricolă* 24, no. 3 (Mar. 1933): 113–27.

——. "Curiosităţi psihologice." *Lumea Nouă* 11, nos. 7–12 (July–Dec. 1942): 114–17.

——. "Doctrinele şi teoriile noastre în lumina criticei. (Răspuns Domnului Profesor Gheorghe Taşcă)." *Analele Economice şi Statistice* 20, nos. 3–5 (Mar.–May 1937): 26–92.

——. "Economia României în Europa unită." *Lumea Nouă* 11, nos. 1–6 (Jan.–June 1942): 47–54.

——. "Der Europäische Nationalismus am Scheidewege." *Politische Wissenschaft* 1 (1943): 16–26.

——. "European Economic Equilibrium." Royaume de Roumanie: Ministère de l'Industrie et du Commerce. *Correspondance Economique Roumaine* 13, no. 2 (Mar.–Apr. 1931): 1–15.

——. *Forţele naţionale productive şi comerţul exterior: Teoria protecţionismului şi a schimbului internaţional*. Bucharest, 1986 [Romanian ed. of Manoilescu, *Théorie du protectionnisme*, 1929, revised in 1940].

——. "Le génie latin dans le nouveau régime portuguais." In Comissão Executiva dos Centenários, Congresso do Mundo Português, comp., *Publicações*. Vol. 8, pp. 623–39. Lisbon, 1940.

——. *Ideia de plan economic naţional*. Bucharest, 1938.

——. *L'imperatif de la crise*. Bucharest, 1933.

——. "În ce constă inferioritatea industriei româneşti?" *Lumea Nouă* 9, nos. 3–4 (Mar.–Apr. 1940): 84–90.

——. *Încercări în filosofia ştiinţelor economice: Prelegeri anuale de deschidere a cursului de economie politică la Şcoala Politehnică din Bucureşti*. Bucharest, 1938.

——. *O lege economică reacţionară: Cuvântare rostită în şedinţa senatului din 16 septembrie 1932 la discuţia legii concordatului preventiv*. Bucharest, 1932.

——. "Lupta între două veacuri. Ultim răspuns Domnului George Taşcă." *Analele Economice şi Statistice* 21, nos. 4–6 (Apr.–June 1938): 11–101.

——. "Mehr Industrie in die Agrarländer?" *Internationale Agrarrundschau* (Sept. 1938): 259–61.

——. *Neoliberalismul*. Bucharest, [1923].

——. "A New Conception of Industrial Protectionism." Royaume de Roumanie: Ministère de l'Industrie et du Commerce. *Correspondance Economique Roumaine* 13, no. 1 (Jan.–Feb. 1931): 1–20.

——. "Nouii fanarioţi: Experţii." *Lumea Nouă* 2, no. 4 (Apr. 1933): 203–5.

——. "Până când nu vom avea o elită." *Lumea Nouă* 8, nos. 5–6 (May–June 1939): 121–24.

——. *Le parti unique: Institution politique des régimes nouveaux*. Paris, 1937.

——. *El partido único: Institución política de los nuevos regímenes* [tr. by Luis Jordana de Pozas of *Le parti unique*, q.v.]. Zaragoza, 1938.

——. "Partidul unic." *Lumea Nouă* 5, no. 7 (July 1936): 319–23.

——. "Politica muncii naţionale." In *Enciclopedia României*. Vol. 3, pp. 226–30. Bucharest, [1940].

——. "Prefaţă." In Lorenzo Baracchi-Tua, *Garda de fier*, pp. 7–9. Bucharest, [1940].

——. "Problematica războiului." *Lumea Nouă* 11, nos. 7–12 (July–Dec. 1942): 57–65.

——. "Probleme des Industrialisierungsprozesses in Südosteuropa." *Weltwirtschaftliches Archiv* 61, part 1 (Jan. 1945): 1–12.

——. "Productividad del trabajo y comercio exterior." *Economía* 8, nos. 22–23 (Sept. 1947): 50–77. [Tr. by Edgar Mahn from "Arbeitsproduktivität und Aussenhandel: Ein neuer Beitrag zur Theorie des internationalen Handels." *Weltwirtschaftliches Archiv* 42, part 1 (July 1925): 13–43.]

——. "Productivitatea şi rentabilitatea în economia românească." *Buletinul Institutului Economic Românesc* 20, nos. 1–6 (Jan.–June 1941): 1–31.

——. "Le régime préférentiel. Discourse á la deuxième conférence pour l'action économique concertée, convoquée par la Societé des Nations en Novembre 1930." *Independenţa Economică*, no. 4 (1930), 10 pp. [reprint].

——. *Rostul şi destinul burgheziei româneşti*. Bucharest, 1942.

——. *O século do corporativismo: Doutrina do corporativismo integral e puro* [tr. by Azevedo Amaral from *Le siècle du corporatisme*, q.v.]. Rio de Janeiro, 1938.

——. *Le siècle du corporatisme: Doctrine du corporatisme intégral et pur*. Paris, 1934.

——. *El siglo del corporatismo: Doctrina del corporatismo integral y puro* [tr. by Hernán G. Huidobro of *Le siècle du corporatisme*, q.v.]. Santiago, 1941.

——. "Solidaritatea economică a estului european." *Revista Cursurilor şi Conferinţelor Universitare*, nos. 3–4 (May–June 1939) [reprint].

——. "Die sozialökonomische Struktur Südosteuropas." *Weltwirtschaftliches Archiv* 60, nos. 1–2 (July–Sept. 1944): 1–22.

——. *Teoría del proteccionismo y del comercio internacional* [tr. by Manuel Fuentes Irurozqui of *Théorie du protectionnisme*, q.v.]. Madrid, 1943.

——. *Theoria do proteccionismo e de permuta internacional* [Port. tr. of *Théorie du protectionnisme*, q.v.]. São Paulo, 1931.

——. *Théorie du protectionnisme et de l'échange international.* Paris, 1929.

——. "Le triangle économique et social des pays agricoles: La ville, le village, l'étranger." *Internationale Agrarrundschau*, no. 6 (Jan. 1940): 16–26.

Manoliu, Florin E. *Bibliographie des travaux du Professeur Mihail Manoilesco [sic] précédée d'une biographie et suivie de la nomenclature des études critiques suscitées par ces travaux.* Bucharest, 1936.

——. "Comercio exterior y desarrollo de los países de economía tradicional." *Revista de Economía y Estadística de la Facultad de Ciencias Económicas de la Universidad Nacional de Córdoba* 12, nos. 3–4 (1968): 141–99.

——. *Politica prețurilor în economia românească.* Bucharest, 1939.

——. "Reflexiones acerca de algunas resistencias al desarrollo de la economía latinoamericana." *Rev. de Ciencias Económicas* 50, ser. 4, no. 18 (July–Dec. 1962): 3–23.

Mantega, Guido. *A economia política brasileira.* São Paulo, 1984.

Manuilă, Sabin. *Structure et évolution de la population rurale.* Bucharest, 1940.

Marc, Alfred. *Le Brésil: Excursion á travers ses 20 provinces.* Vol. 1. Paris, 1890.

Marcu, Nicolae. "Dezvoltarea capitalismului în agricultura României după reformele agrare de la mijlocul secolului al XIX-lea și pînă la primul război mondial." In Marcu, ed., *Istorie economică*, pp. 142–78. Bucharest, 1979.

Marcu, Nicolae, and I. Puia. "Evoluția economiei mondiale interbelice (1919–1939)." In Marcu, ed., *Istorie economică*, q.v., pp. 262–78.

Mariátegui, José Carlos. "Point de vue anti-imperialiste." In Michael Lowy, ed., *Le marxisme en Amérique latine*, q.v., pp. 112–16 [Sp. orig. 1929].

——. *Siete ensayos de interpretación de la realidad peruana.* Lima, 1959 [1928].

Marighela, Carlos. "On the Organizational Function of Revolutionary Violence." In Marighela, *For the Liberation of Brazil*, pp. 30–44. Harmondsworth, Eng., 1971 [Port. orig. 1969].

Marini, Ruy Mauro. "Brazilian Sub-Imperialism." *Monthly Review* 23, no. 9 (Feb. 1972): 14–24.

——. *Dialéctica de la dependencia.* 6th ed. Mexico City, 1982 [1973].

——. "Las razones del neodesarrollismo (respuesta a F.H. Cardoso y J. Serra)." *Revista Mexicana de Sociología*, número extraordinario (1978): 37–106.

——. *Subdesarrollo y revolución.* Mexico City, 1969.

Márquez, Gustavo. "Los informales urbanos en Venezuela: ¿Pobres o eficientes?" In Márquez and Carmen Portela, eds., *La economía informal*, pp. 1–41. Caracas, 1991.

Marson, Adalberto. *A ideologia nacionalista em Alberto Torres.* São Paulo, 1979.

Martínez Lamas, Julio. *Riqueza y pobreza del Uruguay: Estudio de las causas que retardan el progreso nacional.* Montevideo, 1930.

Marx, Karl. *Capital.* Vol. 1. Moscow, 1961 [Ger. orig. 1867].

——. "The Eighteenth Brumaire of Louis Napoleon." In Lewis S. Feuer, ed., *Karl*

Marx and Friedrich Engels: Basic Writings on Politics and Philosophy, pp. 318–48. Garden City, N.Y., 1959 [1852].

Marx, C. [Karl], and F[riedrich] Engels. *La revolución española, 1854–1873*. Moscow, n.d.

Masón, Diego. [Preface] to Mariano Abarca, *La industrialización de la Argentina*, pp. 5–6. Buenos Aires, 1944.

Maybury-Lewis, Alan Biorn. "The Politics of the Possible: The Growth and Political Development of the Brazilian Rural Workers' Trade Union Movement, 1964–1985." Ph.D. diss., Columbia University, 1991.

Meek, Ronald L. *Economics and Ideology and Other Essays: Studies in the Development of Economic Thought*. London, 1967.

Meier, Gerald. *The International Economics of Development: Theory and Policy*. New York, 1968.

Meisner, Maurice. *Li Ta-chao and the Origins of Chinese Marxism*. Cambridge, Mass., 1967.

Merrick, Thomas W., and Douglas H. Graham. *Population and Economic Development in Brazil, 1800 to the Present*. Baltimore, 1979.

———. "Population Redistribution, Migration, and Regional Economic Growth." In *Population and Economic Development in Brazil*, q.v., pp. 118–45.

Merton, Robert K. "Singletons and Multiples in Scientific Discovery: A Chapter in the Sociology of Science." In American Philosophical Society, *Proceedings* 105 (1961): 470–86.

Michelson, Paul. "Procesul dezvoltării naționale române: Contribuția lui Ştefan Zeletin." *Anuarul Institutului de Istorie şi Arheologie "A.D. Xenopol"* 24, no. 1 (1987): 365–74.

Millar, James R. "A Reformulation of A. V. Chayanov's Theory of the Peasant Economy." *Economic Development and Cultural Change* 18, no. 2 (Jan. 1970): 219–29.

Minerva: Enciclopedie Română. Cluj, 1930.

Miroshevski, V. M. "El 'populismo' en el Perú: Papel de Mariátegui en la historia del pensamiento social latinoamericano." In José Aricó, ed., *Mariátegui y los orígenes del marxismo latinoamericano*. 2d ed., pp. 55–70. Mexico City, 1980 [Russ. orig. 1941].

Mitchell, B[rian] R. *European Historical Statistics, 1750–1970*. New York, 1975.

Mitrany, David. *The Land and the Peasant in Rumania: The War and Agrarian Reform (1917–21)*. London, 1930.

Mitzman, Arthur. *Sociology and Estrangement: Three Sociologists of Imperial Germany*. New York, 1973.

Mladenatz, Gr[omoslav]. "Nouile fundamente ale ştiinţei economice. Partea 1." *Independenţa Economică* 25, no. 6 (Nov.–Dec. 1942): 1–44.

"Monetary Developments in Latin America." *Federal Reserve Bulletin* 31, no. 6 (June, 1945): 519–31.

Montias, John. "Notes on the Romanian Debate on Sheltered Industrialization, 1860–1906." In Kenneth Jowitt, ed., *Social Change in Romania, 1860–1940: A Debate on Development in a European Nation*, pp. 53–71. Berkeley, 1978.

Moore, Wilbert E. *Economic Demography of Eastern and Southern Europe*. New York, 1972 [1945].

Morais Filho, Evaristo de. "Jorge Street, o bom patrão." In Jorge Street, *Idéias sociais de Jorge Street*, pp. 15–118. Brasília, 1980.

Morgenstern, Oskar. *The Limits of Economics*. London, 1937.

Morris, Morris D. *Measuring the Condition of the World's Poor: The Physical Quality of Life Index*. New York, 1979.

Morse, Richard M. "Manchester Economics and Paulista Sociology." In John D. Wirth and Robert L. Jones, eds., *Manchester and São Paulo: Problems of Rapid Urban Growth*, pp. 7–34. Stanford, 1978.

Moura, Aristóteles. *Capitais estrangeiros no Brasil*. São Paulo, 1959.

Mouzelis, Nicos P. *Politics in the Semi-Periphery: Early Parliamentarism and Late Industrialization in the Balkans and Latin America*. New York, 1986.

Muñoz, Heraldo. "Cambio y continuidad en el debate sobre la dependencia y el imperialismo." *Estudios Internacionales* 2, no. 44 (Oct.–Dec. 1978): 88–138.

Murgescu, Costin. "Demisia lui Prebisch." *Viața Economică*, 6 Dec. 1968, p. 15.

———. *Mersul ideilor economice la români: Epoca modernă*. Vol. 1. Bucharest, 1987.

Murtinho, Joaquim. *Relatorio [do Ministro da Fazenda] apresentado ao Presidente da Republica dos Estados Unidos do Brasil no anno de 1899*. Rio de Janeiro, n.d.

Myrdal, Gunnar. "Diplomacy by Terminology." In Myrdal, *Approach to the Asian Drama: Methodological and Theoretical*, pp. 33–36. New York, 1970.

Navarrete, Alfredo R. "Exchange Stability, Business Cycles, and Economic Development: An Inquiry into Mexico's Balance of Payments Problems, 1929–1946." Ph.D. diss., Harvard University, 1950 [publ. in Sp. in 1951].

Nechita, Vasile C. "Doctrina economică şi corporatistă a lui Mihail Manoilescu." Ph.D. diss., Academia de Studii Economice, Bucharest, 1971.

———, ed. *Mihail Manoilescu: Creator de teorie economică*. Iaşi, 1993.

Neumark, Fritz. *Neue Ideologien der Wirtschaftspolitik*. Vienna, 1936.

Nicolae-Văleanu, Ivanciu. "Istoria gîndirii economice pînă la 1 decembrie 1918." In N. N. Constantinescu et al., eds., *Istoria ştiinţelor în România: Ştiinţe economice*, pp. 9–98. Bucharest, 1982.

———. "Raúl Prebisch şi doctrina economiei periferice." In Ivanciu Nicolae-Văleanu, ed., *Aspecte ale gîndirii social-economice din ţările în curs de dezvoltare*, pp. 27–47. Bucharest, 1980.

Nicolas-On [pseud. for Nikolai Danielson]. *Histoire du développement économique de la Russie depuis l'affranchissement des serfs*. Paris, 1902.

Niţescu, Constantin. *Monografia regiunii sud-estice a judeţului Vlaşca: Contribuţiuni la cunoaşterea caracterului agricol-tehnic şi social-economic al regiunii*. Bucharest, 1928.

Normano, J[ohn] F. *Brazil: A Study of Economic Types*. Chapel Hill, N.C., 1935.

North, Douglass. *Structure and Change in Economic History*. New York, 1981.

Novais, Fernando A. *Portugal e Brasil na crise do antigo sistema colonial (1777–1808)*. São Paulo, 1979.

Noyola Vázquez, Juan F. "El desarrollo económico y la inflación en México y otros países latinoamericanos." *Investigaciones Económicas* 16, no. 4 (1956): 602–48.

———. *Desequilibrio fundamental y fomento económico en México*. Mexico City, 1949. [Licenciado thesis, Universidad Nacional Autónoma de México.]

———. "La evolución del pensamiento económico del último cuarto de siglo y su influencia en la América Latina." *Trimestre Económico* 23, no. 3 (July–Sept. 1956): 269–83.

Nun, José. "Superpoblación relativa, ejército industrial de reserva y masa marginal." *Revista Latinoamericana de Sociología* 5, no. 2 (1969): 178–236.

Nurkse, Ragnar. *Problems of Capital Formation in Under-Developed Countries*. New York, 1953.

Nye, Joseph S. "UNCTAD: Poor Nations' Pressure Group." In Robert W. Cox et al., *The Anatomy of Influence: Decision Making in International Organizations*, pp. 334–70. New Haven, 1973.

Ohlin, Bertil. "Protectionism and Non-Competing Groups." *Weltwirtschaftliches Archiv* 33, part 1 (Jan. 1931): 30–45.

Olariaga, Luis. "La nueva teoría proteccionista: El Profesor Manoilesco [*sic*]." *Economía Española* 4, no. 39 (Mar. 1936): 221–31.

Olarra Jiménez, Rafael. *Evolución monetaria argentina*. Buenos Aires, 1968.

Oliveira, Francisco de. "A economia brasileira: Crítica a razão dualista." *Estudos CEBRAP* 2 (Oct. 1972): 3–82.

———. "Introdução." In Celso Furtado, *Celso Furtado: Economia* [ed. by F. de Oliveira], pp. 7–27. São Paulo, 1983.

O'Neil, Charles F. "Educational Innovation and Politics in São Paulo, 1933–34." *Luso-Brazilian Review* 8, no. 1 (June 1971): 56–68.

Ornea, Z[igu]. *Poporanismul*. Bucharest, 1972.

———. "Sociologia lui Gherea în ultimul deceniu de viaţă." In *Comentarii*, pp. 39–56. Bucharest, 1981.

———. *Ţărănismul: Studiu sociologic*. Bucharest, 1969.

Oulès, Firmin. "Nature des produits échangés et opportunité du commerce international." *Revue Economique Internationale* 2, no. 3 (June 1936): 469–87.

Packenham, Robert A. *The Dependency Movement: Scholarship and Politics in Development Studies*. Cambridge, Mass., 1992.

Paim, Antônio. *História das idéias filosóficas no Brasil*. 3rd rev. ed. São Paulo, 1984.

Păiuşan, Robert, and Daniela Buşă. "Manoilescu et Taşcă. Leur Polemique." *Revue Roumaine d'Histoire* 29, nos. 3–4 (July–Dec. 1990): 291–320.

Palma, José Gabriel. "Dependency: A Formal Theory of Underdevelopment or a Methodology for the Analysis of Concrete Situations of Underdevelopment?" *World Development* 6, nos. 7–8 (July–Aug. 1978): 881–924.

———. "Growth and Structure of Chilean Manufacturing Industry from 1830 to 1935. Origins and Development of Industrialization in an Export Economy." Ph.D. diss., Magdalen College, Oxford University, 1979.

———. "Structuralism." In John Eatwell et al., *The New Palgrave: A Dictionary of Economics*. Vol. 4, pp. 528–31. London, 1987.

Paredes, Ricardo. "Informe de la delegación latinoamericana [tr. by María Teresa Poyrazian and Nora Rosenfeld de Pasternac]." In Internacional Comunista, *VI Congreso*. Vol. 2: *Informes y Discusiones*, pp. 353–61. Mexico City, 1978 [1928].

París Eguilaz, Higinio. *La teoría de la economía nacional*. Madrid, 1945.

Partido Comunista Brasileiro. "Resolução política do V Congresso do PCB, 1960." In *Partido Comunista Brasileiro: Vinte anos de política, 1958–1979: Documentos*, pp. 39–69. São Paulo, 1980.

Passos Guimarães, Alberto. *Quatro séculos de latifúndio*. São Paulo, 1964.

Pasvolsky, Leo. Review of Mihail Manoilesco [*sic*], "The Theory of Protection and International Trade." *American Economic Review* 22, no. 3 (Sept. 1932): 477–78.

Pătrăşcanu, Lucreţiu. "Băncile şi beneficiile lor." In Pătrăşcanu, *Texte social-politice (1921–1938)*, pp. 103–55. Bucharest, 1975 [1928].

——. *Problemele de bază ale României.* Bucharest, 1947 [1944].

——. "Reforma agrară în România Mare și urmările ei." In *Studii economice și social-politice, 1925–1945,* pp. 9–129. Bucharest, 1978 [1925].

——. "Statul țărănesc." In *Texte social-politice (1921–1938),* pp. 238–53. Bucharest, 1975 [1936].

——. *Sub trei dictaturi.* 3d ed. Bucharest, 1970 [1944].

——. *Un veac de frămîntări sociale, 1821–1907.* 2d ed. Bucharest, 1969 [1945].

"El pensamiento de Oliveira Salazar." *Criterio,* no. 722 (1 Jan. 1942): 13–16.

Perroux, François. *Capitalisme et communauté de travail.* Paris, 1938.

——. "Capitalismo e corporativismo: Economia de mercado organizado, corporativismo social." *Revista de Trabalho* 4, no. 7 (July 1937): 293–95.

——. "Capitalismo e corporativismo: Funcionamento comparado do sistema capitalista e sistema coletivista." *Revista de Trabalho* 5, no. 8 (Aug. 1938): 333–35.

——. "Capitalismo e corporativismo: Socialização do produto—corporativismo e salário." *Revista Forense* 77, year 36 (Jan. 1939): 402–5.

——. *La coexistence pacifique.* Vol. 2. *Poles de développment ou nations?* Paris, 1958.

——. "Contra as trapaças do Marxismo." *O Estado de S. Paulo* (13 June 1937).

——. "The Domination Effect and Modern Economic Theory." *Social Research* 17, no. 2 (June 1950): 188–206.

——. "Economie corporative et système capitaliste: Idéologie et réalité." *Revue d'Economie Politique* 47 (1933): 1409–78.

——. "Esquisse d'une théorie de l'économie dominante." *Economie Appliquée,* nos. 2–3 (Apr.–Sept. 1948): 243–300.

——. *Lições de economia política.* Coimbra, 1936.

——. *A New Concept of Development: Basic Tenets.* London, 1983.

——. "Nobrezas e misérias de uma grande heresia." *O Estado de S. Paulo* (7 June 1936).

——. "Note on the Concept of Growth Poles." In David L. McKee et al., eds., *Regional Economics: Theory and Practice,* pp. 93–103. New York, 1970.

——. "An Outline of a Theory of the Dominant Economy." In George Modelski, ed., *Transnational Corporations and World Order: Readings in International Political Economy,* pp. 135–54. Seattle, 1979.

——. "Peregrinations of an Economist and the Choice of His Route." Banca Nazionale del Lavoro. *Quarterly Review,* no. 139 (June 1980): 147–62.

——. "A pessoa operária e o direito de trabalho." *Revista dos Tribunais* [São Paulo] 120 (July 1939): 703–28.

——. "Socialismo e cristianismo." *Revista do Trabalho* 4, no. 2 (Feb. 1937): 55–56; and 4, no. 5 (May 1937): 197–98.

——. "Uma trapaça marxista." *O Estado de S. Paulo* (16 May 1937).

Perroux, François, and Jacques Madaule. *Communauté et économie.* Paris, [1942?].

Phelps, D. M. "Industrial Expansion in Temperate South America." *American Economic Review* 25 (1935): 273–81.

Pinheiro, Paulo Sérgio, ed. *Trabalho escravo, economia, e sociedade: Conferência sobre história e ciências sociais, UNICAMP.* Rio de Janeiro, 1983.

Pinto Santa Cruz, Aníbal. *Chile, un caso de desarrollo frustrado.* Santiago, 1959.

Pinto Santa Cruz, Aníbal, and Carlos Fredes. *Curso de economia: Elementos de teoria económica.* 3d ed. [tr. by Edilson Alkmim Cunha]. Rio de Janeiro, 1970 [Sp. orig. 1962].

Plaza, V[ictorino] de la. *Estudio sobre la situación política, económica, y constitucional de la República Argentina.* Buenos Aires, 1903.

Polanyi, Karl. *The Great Transformation.* Boston, 1957 [1944].

Politi, Angel N. "El régimen corporativo." Licenciado thesis, Facultad de Ciencias Económicas, Universidad de Buenos Aires, 1955.

[Political and Economic Planning]. *Economic Development in S. E. Europe.* London, 1945.

Popa-Vereş, M[ihai]. "Geneza şi morfologia vieţii economice romaneşti." *Independenţa Economică* 21, nos. 4–6 (July–Dec. 1938): 44–103.

Popişteanu, Cristian, Dumitru Preda, and Mihai Retegan. "22 octombrie 1931–o joie neagră." *Magazin Istoric* 16, no. 1 (Jan. 1982): 38–44.

"Poporanism." *Dicţionar Enciclopedic Romîn.* Vol. 3, pp. 823–24. Bucharest, 1962.

Popper, Karl. *The Logic of Scientific Discovery.* New York, 1959.

Poulantzas, Nicos. *Political Power and Social Classes* [tr. by Timothy O'Hagen]. London, 1973.

Prado, Caio, Jr. *The Colonial Background of Modern Brazil* [Port. orig. *A formação do Brasil contemporâneo: Colônia*]. New York, 1969 [1942].

——. "Uma contribuição para a análise da questão agrária no Brasil." *Revista Brasiliense,* no. 28 (Mar.–Apr. 1960): 165–238.

——. *Esboço dos fundamentos de teoria econômica.* São Paulo, 1957.

——. *Evolução política do Brasil e outros estudos.* São Paulo, 1969 [1933].

——. "O programa da Aliança Nacional Libertadora [1935]." *Nova Escrita/Ensaio* 4, no. 10 [1983?]: 121–36.

——. *A questão agrária no Brasil.* São Paulo, 1979.

——. *A revolução brasileira.* São Paulo, 1966.

[Prado Jr., Caio.]. "Três etapas do comunismo brasileiro." *Cadernos do Nosso Tempo,* no. 2 (Jan.–June 1954): 123–38.

Prates da Fonseca, Tito. "Tendências corporativas." *Revista de Ciências Econômicas* 2, no. 4 (July–Aug. 1940): 219–24.

Prebisch, Raúl. "Análisis de la experiencia monetaria argentina (1935–1943)." In [Banco Central de la República Argentina], ed., *La creación del Banco Central,* q.v. Vol. 1, pp. 249–586.

——. *Anotaciones demográficas a propósito de los movimientos de la población.* Buenos Aires, 1926.

——. " 'La Argentina posible.' Entrevista de Emilio Zimerman." *Búsqueda,* no. 9 (Feb. 1982): 14–23.

——. *Capitalismo periférico: Crisis y transformación.* Mexico City, 1981.

——. "Commercial Policy in Underdeveloped Countries." *American Economic Review* 49, no. 2 (May 1959): 251–73.

——. "La conferencia económica y la crisis mundial." Banco de la Nación Argentina. *Revista Económica* 6, no. 1 (Jan. 1933): 1–10.

——. "A Critique of Peripheral Capitalism." *CEPAL Review,* first semester (1976): 9–76.

——. "Economic Development or Monetary Stability: A False Dilemma." *Economic Bulletin for Latin America* 6, no. 1 (Mar. 1961): 1–25.

——. "Historias para pensar y hacer: Conversación con el doctor R.P." [Interview by Agustín R. Maniglia] *La Prensa,* Buenos Aires (29 Sept. 1985), 2ª sección.

———. "La inflación escolástica y la moneda argentina." *Revista de Economía Argentina* 32, no. 193 (July 1934): 8–13; and no. 194 (Aug. 1934): 39–63.

———. *Introducción a Keynes.* Mexico City, 1947.

———. *Obras: 1919–1948.* 4 vols. Buenos Aires, 1991–1993.

———. "Observaciones sobre los planes monetarios internacionales." *Trimestre Económico* 11, no. 2 (July–Sept. 1974): 185–208.

———. "Panorama general de los problemas de regulación monetaria y crediticia en el continente americano: A. América Latina." In Banco de México, *Memoria: Primera reunión de técnicos sobre problemas de banca central del continente americano,* pp. 25–35. Mexico City, 1946.

———. "El patrón oro y la vulnerabilidad económica de nuestros países." *Revista de Ciencias Económicas* (Mar. 1944): 211–35.

———. "Planes para estabilizar el poder adquisitivo de la moneda." In Universidad Nacional de Buenos Aires: Facultad de Ciencias Económicas, ed., *Investigaciones de Seminario.* Vol. 2, pp. 459–513. Buenos Aires, 1921.

———. "El régimen de pool en el comercio de carnes." *Revista de Ciencias Económicas* 15 (Dec. 1927): 1302–21.

———. *Towards a Dynamic Development Policy for Latin America* [Eng. tr. of *Hacia una dinámica del desarrollo latinoamericano*]. New York, 1963.

Predescu, Lucian. "Madgearu, Virgil N." In *Enciclopedia Cugetarea,* p. 506. Bucharest, [1940].

Prestes, Luís Carlos. "Manifesto de agosto de 1950." In Moisés Vinhas, ed., *O Partidão: A luta por um partido de massas, 1922–1974,* pp. 140–58. São Paulo, 1982.

I [i.e., Primeiro] Congresso Brasileiro de Economia. *Anais.* 3 vols. Rio de Janeiro, 1943–46.

Prokopovicz, Sergei N. *L'industrialisation des pays agricoles et la structure de l'économie mondiale après la guerre* [tr. by N. Nicolsky]. Neuchatel, 1946.

Pugliese, Mario. "Nacionalismo económico, comercio internacional bilateral, e industrialización de los países agrícolas, desde el punto de vista de la economía argentina." *Revista de Ciencias Económicas,* series 2, year 27, no. 219 (Oct. 1939): 917–50.

Puiggrós, Rodolfo. "Los modos de producción en Iberoamérica." *El Gallo Ilustrado: Suplemento Dominical de 'El Día,'* no. 173 (17 Oct. 1965): 1–3.

Pupo Nogueira, O[ctavio]. "A propósito de modernização de uma grande indústria." *Revista Industrial de S. Paulo* 1, no. 6 (May 1945): 16–19.

———. *Em torno da tarifa aduaneira.* São Paulo, 1931.

Quijano, Aníbal. "Notas sobre el concepto de 'marginalidad social'." In *Imperialismo y 'Marginalidad' en América Latina,* pp. 31–100. Lima, 1977 [essay written in 1966].

Racovski, Cristian. "Autobiography." In Georges Haupt and Jean-Jacques Marie, eds., *Makers of the Russian Revolution: Biographies of Bolshevik Leaders,* pp. 385–403. Ithaca, N.Y., 1974.

———. "Chestia agrară. Probleme și soluții." *Viitorul Social* 1 (Aug. 1907): 27–43.

———. "Poporanism, socialism și realitate." *Viitorul Social* 1 (June–July 1908): 329–67.

———. *La Roumanie des boyards. (Contribution à l'histoire d'une oligarchie).* Bucharest, 1909.

———. *Scrieri social-politice (1900–1916).* Bucharest, 1977.

Rădăceanu, Lothar. "Oligarhia română." *Arhiva pentru Știința și Reforma Socială* 5, nos. 3–4 (1924): 497–532; 6, nos. 1–2 (1926): 160–84; 6, nos. 3–4 (1927): 435–59.

Rae, John. *Statement of Some New Principles on the Subject of Political Economy.* Boston, 1834.

Randall, Laura. *An Economic History of Argentina in the Twentieth Century.* New York, 1978.

Rangel, Ignácio. "A dinámica da dualidade brasileira." *Revista Brasileira de Ciências Sociais* 2, no. 2 (July 1962): 215–35.

Ratzer, José. *Los marxistas del 90.* Córdoba, Arg., 1969.

Răzmiritza, N. *Essai d'économie roumaine moderne, 1831–1931.* Paris, 1932.

Reale, Miguel. *Memórias.* Vol. 1: *Destinos cruzados.* São Paulo, 1986.

Reis, João José, and Eduardo Silva. *Negociação e conflito: A resistência negra no Brasil escravista.* Rio de Janeiro, 1989.

Reithinger, Anton. *Le visage économique de l'Europe.* Paris, 1937.

Review [anonymous] of Mihail Manoilescu, "The Theory of Protection in International Trade." *Times Literary Supplement* 31 (11 Feb. 1932): 83.

Revista Hispánica de Bucarest (1929), no. 6.

Rey, Pierre-Philippe. *Les alliances des classes.* Paris, 1973.

———. *Colonialisme, neo-colonialisme et transition au capitalisme.* Paris, 1971.

Reyes Gómez, Vicente. "Si la depreciación del papel moneda en Chile debe considerarse como una causa o un efecto de la baja del cambio." *Revista Económica* [Chile] 4, no. 14 (1 June 1888): 83–90.

Rist, Charles. *Rapport sur les finances publiques de la Roumanie.* Vol. 1: *Rapport général.* Mai 1932. N.p., [1932?].

Robert, Antonio. *Un problema nacional: La industrialización necesaria.* Madrid, 1943.

Roberts, Henry L. *Rumania: Political Problems of an Agrarian State.* Hamden, Conn., 1969 [1951].

Robinson, A[ustin]. "Pigou, Arthur Cecil." In John Eatwell et al., eds., *The New Palgrave: A Dictionary of Economics.* Vol. 3, pp. 876–79. London, 1987.

Robinson, Joan. "Disguised Unemployment." *Economic Journal* 46, no. 182 (June 1936): 225–37.

———. *The Economics of Imperfect Competition.* London, 1933.

Robles, Gonzalo. "Sudamérica y el fomento industrial." *Trimestre Económico* 14, no. 1 (Apr.–June 1947): 1–33.

Rocha, Antônio P. "O nascimento da economia política no Brasil." Ph.D. diss., Universidade de São Paulo, 1989.

Rodríguez, Octavio. *La teoría del subdesarrollo de la CEPAL.* Mexico City, 1980.

Romano, Roberto. *Brasil: Igreja contra estado (Crítica ao populismo católico).* São Paulo, 1979.

Romero, José Luis. *El desarrollo de las ideas en la sociedad argentina del siglo xx.* 2d ed. Buenos Aires, 1983 [1963].

Ros Jimeno, José. "La teoría de Manoilescu sobre el comercio exterior: Exposición y crítica." *Anales de Economía* 1, no. 2 (Apr.–June 1941): 261–76.

Rosas, Fernando. "As idéias sobre desenvolvimento econômico nos anos 30." In José Luís Cardoso, ed., *Contribuições para a história do pensamento econômico em Portugal,* pp. 185–208. Lisbon, 1988.

———. *O Estado Nôvo nos anos trinta (1928–1938).* Lisbon, 1986.

Rosenberg, Nathan. *Perspectives on Technology.* New York, 1976.

Rosenstein-Rodan, Paul. "The International Development of Economically Backward Areas." *International Affairs* 20, no. 2 (Apr. 1944): 157–62.

———. "Natura Facit Saltum: Analysis of the Disequilibrium Growth Process." In Gerald M. Meier and Dudley Seers, eds., *Pioneers in Development*, pp. 207–21. New York, 1984.

———. "Problems of Industrialization of Eastern and South-Eastern Europe." In A. N. Agarwala and S. P. Singh, eds., *The Economics of Underdevelopment*. London, 1958 [1943].

Rostow, W[alt] W[hitman]. *The Stages of Economic Growth: A Non-Communist Manifesto*. Cambridge, Eng., 1960.

Roumanian Institute of Social Science, 1921–1926. Bucharest, 1926.

Rozorea, Mircea. "Curentul poporanist în gîndirea social-economică din România." Ph.D. diss., Academia de Științe Economice, Bucharest, 1970.

Rumania: Consiliul Superior Economic: Oficiul de Studii, Cercetări și Îndrumări. *Aspecte ale economiei românești: Material documentar pentru cunoașterea unor probleme în cadrul planului economic*. Bucharest, 1939.

Rumania: Ministerul Agriculturei. *Ancheta industrială din 1901–1902*. Vol. 1. Bucharest, 1904.

Rumania: Ministerul de Industrie și Comerț. *Ancheta industrială din 1920*. Bucharest, 1921.

Rumania: Zentralinstitut für Statistik. *Statistisches Taschenbuch von Rumänien, 1941*. Bucharest, 1942.

Sachs, Ignacy. *La découverte du Tiers Monde*. Paris, 1971.

Sáenz Leme, Marisa. *A ideologia dos industriais brasileiros, 1919–1945*. Petrópolis, 1978.

Samuelson, Paul. "International Factor-Price Equalisation Once Again." *Economic Journal* 59 (June 1949): 181–97.

———. "International Trade and the Equalisation of Factor Prices." *Economic Journal* 58 (June 1948): 163–84.

Șandru, D. *Populația rurală a României între cele două războaie mondiale*. Iași, 1980.

Santos, Theotônio dos. *Socialismo o fascismo: Dilema latinoamericano*. Santiago, 1969.

———. "The Structure of Dependence." *American Economic Review* 60, no. 2 (May 1970): 231–36.

Saramago, José. *The Year of the Death of Ricardo Reis* [tr. by Giovanni Pontiero]. New York, 1991 [Port. orig. 1984].

Sauvy, Alfred. "Trois mondes, une planète." *L'Observateur*, no. 118 (14 Aug. 1952): 5.

Savu, Alexandru Gh. *Dictatura regală (1938–1940)*. Bucharest, 1970.

Schmitter, Philippe. "Reflections on Mihail Manoilescu and the Political Consequences of Delayed-Dependent Development on the Periphery of Western Europe." In Kenneth Jowitt, ed., *Social Change in Romania, 1860–1940: A Debate on Development in a European Nation*, pp. 117–39. Berkeley, 1978.

———. "Still the Century of Corporatism?" *Review of Politics* 36, no. 1 (Jan. 1974): 85–131.

Schultz, Theodore. "Tensions Between Economics and Politics in Dealing with Agriculture." In Gerald M. Meier, ed., *Pioneers in Development*, 2d series, pp. 17–48. New York, 1987.

———. *Transforming Traditional Agriculture*. New Haven, 1964.

Schumpeter, Joseph A. *Capitalism, Socialism, and Democracy.* 3d ed. New York, 1950.

——. *The Theory of Economic Development: An Inquiry into Profits, Capital, Credit, Interest, and the Business Cycle.* Cambridge, Mass., 1934 [Ger. orig. 1912].

Schwartz, Hugh. "Raúl Prebisch and Argentine Economic Policy-Making, 1950–1962: A Comment." *Latin American Research Review* 23, no. 2 (1988): 124–27.

Schwartz, Pedro, and Manuel-Jesús González. *Una historia del Instituto Nacional de Industria (1941–1976).* Madrid, 1978.

Scutaru, Ion. *Statul țărănesc din punct de vedere economic și politic.* Bucharest, [1935].

Sempat Assadourian, Carlos. *El sistema de la economía colonial: El mercado interior, regiones y espacio económico.* Mexico City, 1983.

Sen, Amartya. *Resources, Values and Development.* Oxford, 1984.

Sérgio, António. "A conquista de Ceuta." In *Ensaios,* 2d ed. Vol. 1, pp. 309–32. Coimbra, 1949 [1928].

Serra, José. "Three Mistaken Theses Regarding the Connection Between Industrialization and Authoritarian Regimes." In David Collier, ed., *The New Authoritarianism in Latin America,* pp. 99–163. Princeton, 1979.

Serra, José, and Fernando Henrique Cardoso. "Las desventuras de la dialéctica de dependencia." *Revista Mexicana de Sociología* 40, no. extraordinario (1978): 9–55.

Shanin, Teodor. *The Awkward Class: Political Sociology of Peasantry in a Developing Society, Russia, 1910–1925.* Oxford, 1972.

Siciliano, Alexandre, Jr. *Agricultura, comércio e indústria no Brasil (em face do regime aduaneiro).* São Paulo, 1931.

Sikkink, Kathryn A. "Developmentalism and Democracy: Ideas, Institutions, and Economic Policy Making in Brazil and Argentina (1955–1962)." Ph.D. diss., Columbia University, 1988.

——. *Ideas and Institutions: Developmentalism in Brazil and Argentina.* Ithaca, N.Y., 1991.

Silva, José Graziano da. *Modernização dolorosa: Estrutura agrária, fronteira agrícola e trabalhadores rurais no Brasil.* Rio de Janeiro, 1981.

Simonsen, Roberto. *Crises, Finances and Industry.* São Paulo, [1931?].

——. *História econômica do Brasil (1500–1820).* 4th ed. São Paulo, 1962 [1937].

——. *À margem da profissão: Discursos, conferências, publicações.* São Paulo, [1932?].

Singer, H[ans] W. "The Distribution of Gains Between Investing and Borrowing Countries." *American Economic Review: Papers and Proceedings* 40, no. 2 (May 1950): 473–85.

——. "Dualism Revisited: A New Approach to the Problems of the Dual Societies in Developing Countries." *Journal of Development Studies* 7 (Oct. 1970): 60–76.

——. "Economic Progress in Underdeveloped Countries." *Social Research* 16, no. 1 (Mar. 1949): 1–11.

——. *Estudo sobre o desenvolvimento econômico do Nordeste.* Recife, 1962.

——. "The Terms of Trade and Economic Development." In John Eatwell et al., eds., *The New Palgrave: A Dictionary of Economics.* Vol. 4, pp. 626–28. London, 1987.

——. "The Terms of Trade Controversy and the Evolution of Soft Financing: Early Years in the U.N." In Gerald M. Meier and Dudley Seers, eds., *Pioneers in Development,* pp. 77–128. New York, 1984.

——. "Trade and Fiscal Problems of the Brazilian Northeast." In *International Development: Growth and Change,* pp. 262–67. New York, 1964.

Singer, Paul. *Economia política da urbanização.* São Paulo, 1973.

Skidmore, Thomas E. *Politics in Brazil, 1930–1964: An Experiment in Democracy.* New York, 1967.

Soares, Henrique. *Corporativismo: Antecedentes e princípios.* Lisbon, 1946.

Societé des Nations: See League of Nations.

Sodré, Nelson W. *A formação histórica do Brasil.* 4th ed. Rio de Janeiro, 1967 [1962].

——. *A verdade sobre o ISEB.* Rio de Janeiro, 1978.

Sofri, Gianni. *O modo de produção asiático: História de uma controvérsia marxista* [tr. by Nice Rissone]. Rio de Janeiro, 1977 [Ital. orig. 1969].

Sollohub, W. A. "The Conversion of Agricultural Debts in Roumania." *Economic Journal* 42, no. 168 (Jan. 1932): 588–94.

Sombart, Werner. *L'apogée du capitalisme* [Fr. tr. of the final part of *Der moderne Kapitalismus,* q.v.]. Vol. 1. Paris, 1932.

——. "Capitalism." *Encyclopedia of the Social Sciences.* Vol. 3, pp. 195–208. New York, 1931.

——. "Critica profeţiilor Marxiste." *Analele Economice şi Statistice* 14, nos. 3–5 (Mar.–May 1931): 1–21.

——. *Deutscher Sozialismus.* Charlottenburg, 1934.

——. *Der moderne Kapitalismus: Historisch-systematische Darstellung des gesamteuropäischen Wirtschaftslebens von seinem Anfangen bis zür Gegenwart.* Munich, 1928.

——. *A New Social Philosophy* [tr. by Karl F. Geiser from *Deutscher Sozialismus,* q.v.]. Princeton, 1937.

——. "Procesul de desvoltare al capitalismului." *Excelsior* (17 Sept. 1938): 1–2.

——. *Die Rationalisierung in der Wirtschaft.* Leipzig, 1927.

——. *Zukunft des Kapitalismus.* Berlin, 1932.

Sommer, Louise. *Neugestaltung der Handelspolitik: Wege zu einem intereuropäischen Präferenzsystem.* Berlin, 1935.

——. "Pays agricoles—pays industriels: Une antithèse périmée." *Revue Internationale Economique* 30 (July 1938): 79–112.

Soutzo [Suţu], [Prince] Nicolas. *Notions statistiques sur la Moldavie.* Iaşi, 1840.

Souza Martins, José de. *Os camponeses e a política no Brasil: As lutas sociais no campo e seu lugar no processo político.* Petrópolis, 1981.

——. *O cativeiro da terra.* São Paulo, 1979.

——. *Expropriação e violência: A questão política no campo.* São Paulo, 1980.

Spraos, John. *Inequalising Trade? A Study of Traditional North / South Specialization in the Context of Terms of Trade Concepts.* Oxford, 1983.

——. "The Statistical Debate on the Net Barter Terms of Trade Between Primary Commodities and Manufactures." *Economic Journal* 90 (Mar. 1980): 107–28.

Srour, Robert Henry. *Modos de produção: Elementos da problemática.* Rio de Janeiro, 1978.

Stahl, Henri H. *Amintiri şi gînduri din vechea şcoală a monografiilor sociologice.* Bucharest, 1981.

——. "Şcoala monografică sociologică." In Mircea Vulcănescu et al., *D[imitrie] Gusti şi şcoala sociologică dela Bucureşti,* pp. 171–206. Bucharest, 1937.

——. "Théories de C. D. Gherea sur les lois de la pénétration du capitalisme dans les pays retardataires." *Review* [of the Fernand Braudel Center] 2, no. 1 (Summer 1978): 101–14.

——. *Traditional Romanian Village Communities: The Transition from the Communal to the Capitalist Mode of Production.* Cambridge, Eng., 1980 [Fr. orig. 1969].

Stănculescu, P., and C. Ştefănescu. "Analiza economică a gospodăriilor." In Golopenţia and Georgescu, *60 sate româneşti,* q.v., pp. 205–92.

Stepniak [pseud. for S. Kravchinsky]. *The Russian Peasantry: Their Agrarian Condition, Social Life and Religion.* New York, 1888.

"Stere, Constantin." In *Dicţionar Enciclopedic Romín.* Vol. 4, p. 508. Bucharest, 1962.

Stere, Constantin. "Cauzele mişcărilor agrare." In *Scrieri,* q.v., pp. 434–37 [1907].

——. "Fischerland." In *Scrieri,* q.v., pp. 365–72 [1909].

——. "Mizeria ţărănimii şi repartizarea proprietăţii." In *Scrieri,* q.v., pp. 454–68 [1908].

——. *Scrieri* [ed. by Zigu Ornea]. Bucharest, 1979.

——. "Socialdemocratism sau poporanism?" *Viaţa Românească* 2, nos. 8–11 (Aug.–Nov. 1907): 170–93, 313–41, 15–48 [*sic*], 173–208; 3, nos. 1 and 4 (Jan. and Apr. 1908): 49–75, 59–80.

——. "Ţară de latifundii." In *Scrieri,* q.v., pp. 373–90 [1906].

Stoica, Nicolae. "Problema agrar-ţărănească în gîndirea economică a socialiştilor români (1900–1916)." Ph.D. diss., Academia Ştefan Gheorghiu, Bucharest, 1972.

Stolcke, Verena. *Cafeicultura: Homens, mulheres e capital (1850–1980)* [tr. by Denise Bottmann and João R. Martins Filho]. São Paulo, 1986. Published in English as *Coffee Planters, Workers, and Wives.*

Stolcke, Verena, and Michael M. Hall. "The Introduction of Free Labour on São Paulo Coffee Plantations." *Journal of Peasant Studies* 10, nos. 2–3 (Jan.–Apr. 1983): 170–200.

Sunkel, Osvaldo. "Inflation in Chile: An Unorthodox Approach." *International Economic Papers,* no. 10 (1960): 107–31 [Sp. orig. 1958].

——. "The Pattern of Latin American Dependence." In Victor L. Urquidi and Rosemary Thorp, eds., *Latin America in the International Economy,* pp. 3–34. London, 1973.

——, ed. *El desarrollo desde dentro: Un enfoque neoestructuralista para la América Latina.* Mexico City, 1991. Published in English as *Development from Within: Toward a Neostructuralist Approach for Latin America.*

Sunkel, Osvaldo, and Pedro Paz. *El subdesarrollo latinoamericano y la teoría del desarrollo.* Madrid, 1970.

Sută-Selejan, Sultana, and Nicolae Sută. *Concepţia lui Mihail Manoilescu despre comerţul internaţional capitalist.* Bucharest, 1972.

Suzigan, Wilson. *Industria brasileira: Origem e Desenvolvimento.* São Paulo, 1986.

Szlajfer, Henryk, ed. "Editor's Introduction [tr. by Maria Chmielewska-Szlajfer and Piotr Goc]." In *Economic Nationalism in East-Central Europe and South America, 1918–1939,* pp. 1–13. Geneva, 1990.

Tandater, Enrique. *Coacción y mercado: La minería de la plata en el Potosí colonial: 1692–1826.* Cuzco, Peru, 1992.

——. "Sobre el análisis de la dominación colonial." *Desarrollo Económico* 16, no. 61 (Apr.–June 1976): 151–60.

Taşcă, Gheorghe. "Liberalism şi corporatism." *Analele Economice şi Statistice* 20, nos. 1–2 (Jan.–Feb. 1937): 1–69.

Tavares, Maria da Conceição. "The Growth and Decline of Import Substitution in Brazil." *Economic Bulletin for Latin America* 9, no. 1 (Mar. 1964): 1–59.

Tax, Sol. *Penny Capitalism: A Guatemalan Indian Economy.* Smithsonian Institution: Institute of Social Anthropology. Publication no. 16. Washington, D.C., 1953.

Teixeira Vieira, Dorival. "História da ciência económica no Brasil." In Mário Guimarães Ferri and Shozo Motoyama, eds., *História das ciências no Brasil.* Vol. 3, pp. 347–72. São Paulo, 1981.

Thorner, Daniel. "Chayanov's Concept of Peasant Economy." In A[lexander] V[asilievich] Chayanov, *The Theory of Peasant Economy,* q.v., pp. xi–xxiii.

Thorp, Rosemary, ed. *Latin America in the 1930s: The Role of the Periphery in World Crisis.* London, 1984.

Thorp, Rosemary, and Geoffrey Bertram. *Peru (1890–1977): Growth and Policy in an Open Economy.* London, 1978.

Thurow, Lester. *Head to Head: The Coming Economic Battle Among Japan, Europe, and America.* New York, 1992.

Todaro, Michael P. *Economic Development in the Third World: An Introduction to Problems and Policies in a Global Perspective.* 3d ed. London, 1985.

Tokman, Víctor. "Unequal Development and the Absorption of Labour: Latin America 1950–1980." *CEPAL Review* 17 (Aug. 1982): 121–34.

Toledo, Caio Navarro de. *ISEB: Fábrica de ideologias.* São Paulo, 1982.

Topalov, Christian. *Estruturas agrárias brasileiras* [tr. by Waltensir Dutra]. Rio de Janeiro, 1978.

Topik, Steven. "The Economic Role of the State in Liberal Regimes: Brazil and Mexico Compared, 1888–1910." In Joseph L. Love and Nils Jacobsen, eds., *Guiding the Invisible Hand,* pp. 117–44. New York, 1988.

Torres, Alberto. *A organisacão nacional.* São Paulo, 1914.

———. *O problema nacional brasileiro.* São Paulo, 1914.

Trebat, Thomas J. *Brazil's State-Owned Enterprises: A Case Study of the State as Entrepreneur.* Cambridge, 1983.

Trebici, Vladimir. *Romania's Population and Demographic Trends.* Bucharest, 1976.

Unión Industrial Argentina. *Anales;* subsequently *Argentina Fabril,* 1930–46.

United Nations: Department of Economic Affairs. *Measures for the Economic Development of Under-Developed Countries.* New York, 1951.

———. *Relative Prices of Exports and Imports of Under-Developed Countries: A Study of Postwar Terms of Trade Between Under-developed and Industrialized Nations.* Lake Success, N.Y., 1949.

United Nations: Economic Commission for Latin America. *The Economic Development of Latin America and Its Principal Problems.* New York, 1950 [Sp. orig. 1949].

———. *The Economic Development of Latin America in the Postwar Period.* New York, 1964.

———. *Economic Survey of Latin America, 1949.* New York, 1951 [Sp. orig. 1950].

———. *Economic Survey of Latin America, 1956.* New York, 1957.

———. "Preliminary Study of the Effects of Postwar Industrialization on Import Structures and External Vulnerability in Latin America." In *Economic Survey of Latin America, 1956,* q.v., pp. 115–63.

———. *The Process of Industrial Development in Latin America.* New York, 1966 [Sp. orig. 1965].

———. "The Situation in Argentina and the New Economic Policy." *Economic Bulletin for Latin America* 1, no. 1 (Jan. 1956): 26–45.

U[nited] S[tates] Bureau of the Census. *The Historical Statistics of the United States, Colonial Times to 1970*, part 1. Washington, D.C., 1975.

Uricoechea, Fernando. *The Patrimonial Foundations of the Brazilian Bureaucratic State.* Berkeley, 1980.

Van den Berghe, Pierre. *Race and Racism: A Comparative Perspective.* 2d ed. New York, 1978.

Vargas, Getúlio. *Mensagem apresentada ao Poder Legislativo em 3 de maio de 1937.* Rio de Janeiro, 1937.

——. *A nova política do Brasil.* 8 vols. Rio de Janeiro, 1938–41.

Vasile, R. "Economia României în timpul celui de-al doilea război mondial." In Nicolae Marcu, ed., *Istorie economică*, pp. 368–91. Bucharest, 1979.

Vásquez-Presedo, Vicente. *Crisis y retraso: Argentina y la economía internacional entre las dos guerras.* Buenos Aires, 1978.

Velasco Murviedro, Carlos. "El pensamiento autárquico español como diretriz de la política económica (1936–1951)." 2 vols. Ph.D. diss., Universidad Complutense, 1982.

Velho, Otávio Guilherme. "Antropologia para sueco ver." *Dados* 23, no. 1 (1980): 79–91.

——. *Capitalismo autoritário e campesinato.* 2d ed. São Paulo, 1979 [1976].

——. *Sociedade e agricultura.* Rio de Janeiro, 1982.

Véliz, Cláudio. "Introduction." In Cláudio Véliz, ed., *Obstacles to Change in Latin America*, pp. 1–8. London, 1965.

Venturi, Franco. *Roots of Revolution* [tr. by Francis Haskell]. New York, 1960 [Ital. orig. 1952].

Veverca, Ion. "Alexandru D. Xenopol și problemele dezvoltării economice a României." In A. D. Xenopol, *Opere economice*, q.v., pp. 7–71.

Vieira, Evaldo. *Autoritarismo e corporativismo no Brasil (Oliveira Vianna & Companhia).* 2d ed. São Paulo, 1981.

Vieira Souto, Luís. "Apresentação ao *Boletim do Centro Industrial do Brasil*." In Edgard Carone, ed., *O pensamento industrial no Brasil (1880–1945)*, pp. 47–57. Rio de Janeiro, 1977.

Villanueva, Javier. "Economic Development." In Mark Falcoff and Ronald H. Dolkart, eds., *Prologue to Perón: Argentina in Depression and War, 1930–1943*, pp. 57–82. Berkeley, 1975.

Villareal, René. *El desequilibrio externo en la industrialización de México (1929–75): Un enfoque estructuralista.* Mexico City, 1976.

Villela, Annibal Villanova, and Wilson Suzigan. *Política do governo e crescimento da economia brasileira, 1889–1945.* Rio de Janeiro, 1973.

Viner, Jacob. *International Trade and Economic Development.* Glencoe, Ill., 1952.

——. Review of Mihail Manoilesco [*sic*], "The Theory of Protection and International Trade." *Journal of Political Economy* 40, no. 1 (Feb. 1932): 121–25.

——. *Studies in the Theory of International Trade.* New York, 1937.

Vinhas, M[oisés]. *Problemas agrário-camponeses do Brasil.* Rio de Janeiro, 1968.

Voinea, Șerban. *Marxism oligarhic.* Bucharest, 1926.

——. "Der Sozialismus in den rückstandigen Ländern." *Der Kampf* 17 (Dec. 1924): 501–8.

Von Pohle, Ludwig. *Deutschland am Scheideweg.* Leipzig, 1902.

Von Thünen, Johann Heinrich. *Von Thünen's Isolated State* [tr. by Carla Wartenberg, ed. by Peter Hall]. Oxford, 1966 [Ger. orig. 1826; 1st complete ed. 1863].

Vulcănescu, Mircea. "D. Gusti, profesorul." In Mircea Vulcănescu et al., *D[imitrie] Gusti şi şcoala sociologică dela Bucureşti*, pp. 5–94. Bucharest, 1937.

Wagemann, Ernst. *Der neue Balkan: Altes Land—Junge Wirtschaft.* Hamburg, 1939.

——. *La población en el destino de los pueblos.* Santiago, 1949 [Sp. version of *Menschenzahl und Volkerschicksal* (1948)] tr. by Carlos Keller R.

——. *Struktur und Rhythmus der Weltwirtschaft: Grundlagen einer weltwirtschaftliches Konjunkturlehre* [Tr. in Sp. as *Evolución y ritmo de la economía mundial*, 1933]. Berlin, 1931.

Wagner, Adolf. *Die Problem des Agrar und Industriestaat.* Jena, 1902.

Walicki, Andrzej. *The Controversy over Capitalism: Studies in the Social Philosophy of the Russian Populists.* Oxford, 1969.

Wallerstein, Immanuel M. *The Modern World System.* New York, 1974, 1980, 1989.

——. "Periphery." In John Eatwell et al., eds., *The New Palgrave: A Dictionary of Economics.* Vol. 3, pp. 846–48. London, 1987.

Walther, Léon. "O que somos." *IDORT* 1, no. 1 (1931): 1–2.

Warriner, Doreen. *The Economics of Peasant Farming.* 2d ed. London, 1964 [1939].

Weber, Max. *General Economic History.* New York, 1927 [Ger. orig. 1923].

——. "Politics as a Vocation." In *From Max Weber: Essays in Sociology* [tr. and ed. by H. H. Gerth and C. Wright Mills], pp. 77–128. New York, 1958 [Ger. orig. 1919].

Whipple, Clayton E., and A. U. Toteff. "Comment on 'The Problem of Surplus Agricultural Population.'" *International Journal of Agrarian Affairs* 1, no. 1 (Oct. 1939): 73–75.

Williamson, J[effrey] G. "Regional Inequality and the Process of National Development: A Description of the Patterns." In L. Needleman, ed., *Regional Analysis: Selected Readings*, pp. 99–158. Baltimore, 1968 [1965].

Who's Who in the United Nations and Related Agencies. New York, 1975.

World Bank. *The East Asian Miracle: Economic Growth and Public Policy.* New York, 1993.

——. *The World Bank Atlas: 1995.* Washington, D.C., 1994.

Xenopol, A. D. "Studii economice." In *Opere economice.* Bucharest, 1967 [2d rev. ed., 1882].

Young, Allyn. "Increasing Returns and Economic Progress." *Economic Journal* 28 (Sept. 1928): 527–42.

Zañartu Prieto, Enrique. *Tratado de economía política.* 2d ed. Santiago, 1946.

Zane, Gh[eorghe]. "Burghezia română şi Marxismul." *Viaţa Românească* 19, no. 2 (Feb. 1927): 244–60; and 19, no. 3 (Mar. 1927): 323–34.

——. *Economia politică la Academia Mihăileană: La centenarul învăţământului economic în România.* Iaşi, 1943.

Zeletin, Ştefan. "Acumularea primitivă în România." In *Neoliberalismul*, q.v., pp. 157–67.

——. *Burghezia română: Originea şi rolul ei istoric.* Bucharest, 1925.

——. "Dezvoltarea capitalului naţional." In *Neoliberalismul*, q.v., pp. 33–56.

——. "Naţionalismul." In *Neoliberalismul*, q.v., pp. 199–211.

——. "Neoliberalismul." In *Neoliberalismul*, q.v., pp. 71–100.

———. *Neoliberalismul: Studii asupra istoriei și politicei burgheziei române.* Bucharest, 1927.

———. "Originea și formația burgheziei române." In *Neoliberalismul*, q.v., pp. 3–31.

———. "Plutocrația." In *Neoliberalismul*, q.v., pp. 139–56.

———. "Pseudo-burghezia." In *Neoliberalismul*, q.v., pp. 113–26.

———. "Socialism reacționar și socialism revoluționar." In *Neoliberalismul*, q.v., pp. 249–68.

Index

In this index an "f" after a number indicates a separate reference on the next page, and an "ff" indicates separate references on the next two pages. A continuous discussion over two or more pages is indicated by a span of page numbers, e.g., "57–59." *Passim* is used for a cluster of references in close but not consecutive sequence.

Library of Congress Cataloging-in-Publication Data

Love, Joseph L.
Crafting the third world : theorizing underdevelopment / Joseph L. Love.
p. cm.
Includes bibliographical references and index.
ISBN 0-8047-2546-2 (cloth) : ISBN 0-8047-2705-8 (pbk.)
1. Rumania—Dependency on foreign countries.   2. Rumania— Economic policy.   3. Socialism—
Rumania.   4. Brazil— Dependency on foreign countries.   5. Brazil—Economic policy.
6. Socialism—Rumania.   I. Title.
HC405.L68 1996
338.9498—dc20
95-22991   CIP

⊛ This book is printed on acid-free, recycled paper.

Original printing 1996
Last figure below indicates year of this printing:
05   04   03   02   01   00   99   98   97   96